Addictive Behaviors Across the Life Span

Prevention, Treatment, and Policy Issues

editors

John S. Baer, G. Alan Marlatt, and Robert J. McMahon

SAGE Publications
International Educational and Professional Publisher
Newbury Park   London   New Delhi

For information address:

SAGE Publications, Inc.
2455 Teller Road
Newbury Park, California 91320
E-mail: order@sagepub.com

SAGE Publications Ltd.
6 Bonhill Street
London EC2A 4PU
United Kingdom

SAGE Publications India Pvt. Ltd.
M-32 Market
Greater Kailash I
New Delhi 110 048 India

Printed in the United States of America

Library of Congress Cataloging-in-Publication Data

Main entry under title:
Addictive behaviors across the life span / edited by John S. Baer, G. Alan Marlatt, Robert J. McMahon.
    p. cm.
    Includes bibliographical references and index.
    ISBN 0-8039-5078-0 (cl.).—ISBN 0-8039-5079-9 (pbk.)
    1. Substance abuse—Congresses. I. Baer, John Samuel, 1958- .
II. Marlatt, G. Alan. III. McMahon, Robert J. (Robert Joseph), 1953- .
    (DNLM: 1. Behavior, Addictive—therapy—congresses, WM 176 A2245]
RC563.2.A315 1993
616.86—dc20
DNLM/DLC   92-49110

99 00 01 02 03 8 7 6 5 4 3

Sage Production Editor: Diane S. Foster

Contents

Preface

This volume is one in a continuing series of publications sponsored by the Banff International Conferences on Behavioural Science. These unique conferences have been held each spring since 1969 in Banff, Alberta, Canada. They serve the purpose of bringing together outstanding behavioral scientists and professionals in a forum where they can present and discuss data related to emergent issues and topics. Thus the International Conferences, as a continuing event, have served as an expressive "early indicator" of the developing nature and composition of behavioral science and scientific application.

Because distance, schedules, and restricted audience preclude wide attendance at the conferences, the resulting publications have equal status with the conferences proper. They are not, however, simply publications of the papers presented at the conferences. Presenters at the Banff Conference are required to write chapters specifically for the forthcoming book, separate from their presentations and discussions at the conference itself. Consequently, volumes from the conferences are not conference proceedings. Rather, they are integrated collections of chapters by leading researchers and practitioners who have had the unique opportunity of presenting and discussing ideas prior to preparing their chapters.

The topic for Banff XXIII, held in 1991, was "Addictive Behaviours Across the Lifespan: Prevention, Treatment, and Policy Issues." In organizing the conference and preparing this volume, we sought to bring together leaders in the addictive behaviors field to discuss how prevention, treatment, and policy for addictive problems must be conceptualized with considerable flexibility. Traditionally, a rather unidimensional model of addiction has been applied to a variety of problem behaviors such as drinking, gambling, eating, and relationships. From our perspective, however, theory and therapeutic applications should vary based on the type of problem presented and the specific characteristics of the client or population. In particular, we felt that the nature of problems as well as solutions vary with clients' ages and life positions.

The chapters in this volume describe theory and programming applied to assessment, prevention, and treatment of specific populations with specific addictive problems. In addition, broad policy considerations are discussed. Topics are arranged under four subheadings. Part I, Etiology and Course, includes reviews of alcoholism etiology and the epidemiology of alcohol problems later in life. Both of the chapters in this section emphasize the multivariate and interactive nature of the development and course of addictive problems. Part II, Models of Prevention and Early Intervention, includes chapters that detail new and integrative approaches to the prevention of addictive problems. These chapters describe community-based drug abuse prevention programs, computer-based early identification of addictive problems, prevention of alcohol problems with young adults, and the tremendous public health need for treatment of persons with lower-level alcohol problems (so-called problem drinkers). Part III, Integrative Treatment of Addictive Problems, organizes chapters devoted to services for specific addictive problem areas, such as adolescent relapse and recovery, treatment in prison systems, marijuana dependence, and models of integrated community services. Finally, Part IV, Policy Issues, includes chapters that address broad assumptions within addictive treatment and research. These chapters both review and critique policy that has an impact upon treatment and research pertaining to women, codependency, and harm minimization.

Taken collectively, these chapters convey an approach to addictions inconsistent with a unidimensional model. Addictive problems can occur at different points in the life course, manifest differently within different people, and remit under different conditions. From this broad and complex array of problems, professionals must adopt strategies that promote early identification, allow for heterogeneity of course, and respect differences based on gender, ethnicity, and age. Although such complexity creates more difficulty in designing treatment programs, it should lead to better treatment outcomes for clients.

This book is directed toward students, practitioners, and researchers who are interested in the study and treatment of addictive problems. It presumes a basic understanding of statistics and experimental design typical of advanced undergraduate training in the social sciences. We would like to express our appreciation to Ms. Catherine Hardie-Wigram and to Jeri Dellow in the Conferences Division at the Banff Centre. In addition to the editors of this volume, other members of the Conference Planning Committee who contributed substantial help and guidance to Banff XXIII were Kenneth D. Craig and Ray Peters. We also thank Susan Tapert at Addictive Behaviors Research Center at the University of Washington for her assistance in preparing the manuscript. Last, but certainly not least, we thank Terry Hendrix, Marquita Flemming, and Diane Foster at Sage Publications for their support and interest in the production of this volume.

J.S.B.
G.A.M.
R.J.McM.

PART I

Etiology and Course

1

Children of Alcoholics
and the Intergenerational
Transmission of Alcoholism:
A Biopsychosocial Perspective

KENNETH J. SHER

There is currently a great deal of interest in the study of children of alcoholics (COAs) as a group at risk for a number of negative outcomes, especially alcoholism. As a group, children of male alcoholics are approximately five times more likely than children of nonalcoholics (non-COAs) to become alcoholics themselves at some point in their lives. Behavior-genetic studies suggest an important role for both *genetic* and *environmental* factors in the intergenerational transmission of alcoholism. During recent years, numerous research efforts have attempted to identify variables at varying levels of biopsychosocial organization that might mediate both genetic and environmental effects. This chapter provides an

AUTHOR'S NOTE: Preparation of this chapter was supported in part by Grant 1R01 AA7231 from the National Institute on Alcohol Abuse and Alcoholism. John Baer and Eric Martin provided valuable comments on an earlier draft. Portions of this chapter were adapted from my recent book, *Children of Alcoholics: A Critical Appraisal of Theory and Research,* published by the University of Chicago Press.

3

overview of various models that hold potential for integrating the numerous and diverse findings that have been reported to date.

Evidence for Genetic Transmission

There are many recent reviews of studies suggesting genetic determinants of alcohol use and alcohol abuse/dependence (e.g., Goodwin, 1988; Searles, 1988). While most experts conclude that the weight of current evidence suggests that genetic factors play an important role in some forms of alcoholism, the nature and extent of genetic mediation, and how these might interact with various environmental influences, have yet to be specified. Although some reviewers (e.g., Peele, 1986; Searles, 1988) have argued that the importance of genetic factors has been overstated and that clear inconsistencies exist across studies, these critics do not contest the idea that genetic factors play an etiologic role. Because the data supporting a genetic etiology for some forms of alcoholism have been reviewed so often recently, only a brief overview will be presented here.

Family studies consistently find a high prevalence of alcoholism in the first-degree relatives of alcoholics (Cotton, 1979). A recent meta-analysis of the relation between sex of parent and sex of offspring on the transmission of alcoholism indicates that across family studies, paternal alcoholism is associated with increased rates of alcoholism in both sons and daughters, and maternal alcoholism is associated only with increased rates of alcoholism among daughters (Pollock, Schneider, Gabrielli, & Goodwin, 1987). Although consistent with a genetic etiology, the results of family studies are equally consistent with environmental transmission.

Twin studies provide a much stronger test of the hypothesis of genetic transmission because (under certain assumptions) they permit a quantitative assessment of genetic heritability. Although heritability estimates derived from various twin studies differ considerably, monozygotic twins are generally found to have higher concordance rates (or intraclass correlations) than dizygotic twins for alcoholism, selected aspects of drinking behavior, and attitudes about alcohol (see Sher, 1991). Clear inconsistencies exist across these studies (Murray, Clifford, & Gurling, 1983; Peele, 1986), and presumably these inconsistencies reflect methodological differences. At least one study failed to find any evidence of genetic predisposition for the diagnosis of alcoholism (Gurling, Murray, & Clifford, 1981), and in some studies heritability was found only for certain aspects of drinking behavior (see Sher, 1991). Perhaps the most accurate summary of the twin study data is that a number of dimensions of alcohol-related behavior appear to be under genetic control, but that the extent of this influence appears modest. That is, environmental factors and gene × environment interactions play an important role.

Adoption studies appear to provide the strongest data supportive of a genetic etiology of alcoholism. In the past 20 years, studies conducted in Denmark, Sweden, and the United States have yielded compelling data indicating the critical importance of an alcoholic biological background in predicting offspring liability to alcoholism (see Goodwin, 1988; Searles, 1988; Sher, 1991). The adoption studies clearly demonstrate the significant contribution of biological relatives' alcoholism (or alcohol-related problems) to alcoholism in male adoptees.

Although the adoption studies implicate genetic factors, the studies differ in the extent to which environmental variables are implicated, female adoptees are affected, and gene × environment interactions are present. Although some of these inconsistencies may be attributable to methodological differences among studies and to population differences, the work of Cloninger, Bohman, and their colleagues suggests that etiologic heterogeneity might represent an important but previously neglected issue (see, e.g., Cloninger, 1987; Cloninger, Bohman, & Sigvardsson, 1981). This research group delineated two types of alcoholism among adoptees. The more common, Type 1, found both in male and female adoptees, was associated with mild alcohol abuse and minimal criminality in the biological parents and a usually mild but possibly severe course (depending largely on postnatal factors). Type 2 alcoholism, on the other hand, was associated with severe alcohol abuse, criminality, and extensive treatment histories in the biological fathers of male adoptees, a moderate to severe course, and relatively little environmental moderation. Females in the families of Type 2 alcoholics were not found to have an excess of alcoholism, but were found to have an excess of somatizing complaints characterized by relatively low frequency of diverse physical complaints and rare psychiatric complaints. The work of the Swedish group, although in need of replication, strongly suggests that even at the grossest level it is hazardous to consider COAs to be a homogeneous group and that there might be multiple pathways linking parental and offspring alcoholism.

The Case for Environmental Causation

The family, twin, and adoption studies implicate an important role
for environmental factors in the development of alcoholism and psychiatric morbidity associated with a family history of alcoholism. For
example, family studies document that many alcoholics do not have
alcoholic near relatives. In twin studies, MZ concordance rates for
alcoholism do not approach unity. Adoption studies indicate gene ×
environment interactions for at least one form of alcoholism, and some
alcoholics do not have alcoholic biological parents. Moving away from
genetically focused studies, the large cultural, occupational, and religious group variations in alcohol use and abuse strongly suggest important determinants influencing the development of alcoholism (e.g.,
Goodwin, 1988). However, specific environmental variables that may
contribute to the development of alcoholism and other forms of dysfunctional behavior among COAs have not been delineated. This section provides an overview of factors posited to characterize the alcoholic
home and to have pathogenic effects on the child.

Before going ahead with this review, I should note two important
issues. First, although certain environmental conditions may characterize alcoholic homes, this does not imply that such conditions are
necessarily related to the development of alcoholism or other disorders.
In order to show a relationship with later alcoholism, variation in the
environment should be related to children's outcomes. Second, even
when environmental factors are correlated with the development of
alcoholism in offspring, causal connections cannot be assumed. The
appearance of environmental causation can be created by third variables
(e.g., gene/environment covariation; Plomin, Defries, & Loehlin, 1977).
Even if third variables can be excluded, correlations between family
variables (e.g., parenting behavior) and child outcomes still leave open
the direction of causality; children can influence the nature and amount
of their interactions with their parents and other family members. For
example, a recent analog study demonstrated that interactions with
oppositional children can lead to increased alcohol consumption in
adult caretakers (Lang, Pelham, Johnston, & Gelertner, 1989).

Many clinicians and writers assume a strong relation between family
violence and parental alcoholism. However, recent reviews of the empirical literature paint a less clear-cut picture (e.g., Hamilton & Collins,
1985; West & Prinz, 1987). The reason for the muddled picture lies, in

large part, with the methodological problems characterizing most of the research in this area (e.g., weak ascertainment of family violence and parental alcoholism, sampling from populations likely to have high rates of both familial alcoholism and violence, lack of appropriate controls). Consequently, it is not surprising that few consistent findings emerge or that some reviewers (e.g., Orme & Rimmer, 1981) state that no firm conclusions can be made. Given available prevalence estimates, the majority of studies appear to suggest increased prevalence of alcoholism among child-abusing parents (Hamilton & Collins, 1985). Although the relation between spouse abuse and alcoholism appears stronger, similar cautions must be made concerning research in this area.

A potentially important, but little researched, area concerns the relation between paternal alcoholism and sexual abuse (incest). Although several studies report very high rates of alcoholism among the parents of incest victims, much additional research in this area is needed (Russell, Henderson, & Blume, 1985).

A number of reviews summarizing the empirical research on family interaction and family environment have appeared in recent years (e.g., Jacob & Seilhamer, 1987; Seilhamer & Jacob, 1990; Sher, 1991). The following tentative conclusions seem warranted based on available data.

Studies of alcoholic families using the self-report Family Environment Scale (FES) indicate that alcoholic families report lower levels of family cohesion, expressiveness, independence, intellectual-cultural orientation, and active-recreational orientation and higher levels of conflict compared with nonalcoholic control families (Sher, 1991). Much of the family disruption appears related to ongoing drinking problems in the alcoholic, given that the family environments of recovered alcoholics did not differ significantly from those of nonalcoholic control families in one study (Moos & Billings, 1982). These studies utilizing the FES demonstrate that the milieus of alcoholic and nonalcoholic families differ, but that many of these differences appear to be related to the current drinking status of the alcoholic parent. Recent studies using other self-report measures of family functioning support this conclusion (Benson & Heller, 1987; Callan & Jackson, 1986).

A small number of studies have examined the interactions of alcoholic families using a variety of direct observational methods. Virtually all of these studies have been limited by small and possibly unrepresentative samples, but they demonstrate the feasibility of directly studying alcoholic families in the laboratory and in their home environments, and they provide intriguing preliminary data.

Perhaps the best-known work in this area is the research program of Steinglass and his associates (see Jacob & Seilhamer, 1987; Steinglass, Bennett, Wolin, & Reiss, 1987). Major findings from this programmatic research effort support the notions that (a) alcohol serves a variety of adaptive functions in different families (e.g., permitting the expression of certain behaviors and the inhibition of others); (b) behavioral observations of alcoholic families both at home and in the laboratory can differentiate families characterized by continued abstinence, continued drinking, and a mixed transitional pattern (i.e., phases of alcoholism); and (c) there is great heterogeneity in the interaction patterns among alcoholic families. Although a number of more specific findings have emerged from these studies, the ideas that drinking can serve adaptive functions and that there is heterogeneity among alcoholic families appear to be the most important generalizations that can be drawn from this research.

Studies comparing the family interactions of alcoholic and nonalcoholic families in the laboratory demonstrate that alcoholic families show impaired problem solving and more negative and hostile communications relative to nonalcoholic families (see, e.g., Jacob & Seilhamer, 1987; Sher, 1991). An important finding to emerge from those studies that included control groups of nonalcoholic distressed couples was that *disturbed family interaction was not specific to alcoholic families and tended to characterize other problem families as well.*

In addition to Steinglass's early work, a number of other investigators have examined the effect of alcohol on family interaction in the laboratory among alcoholic and nonalcoholic families (see Jacob & Seilhamer, 1987; Sher, 1991). Only one of these studies provides support for the hypothesis that alcohol consumption serves an adaptive or reinforcing role in the family. A recent longitudinal study of drinking in a small sample of male alcoholics characterized by either in-home drinking or out-of-home drinking demonstrated that the effects of drinking on marital functioning appear to differ as a function of the locale of typical alcohol consumption (Dunn, Jacob, Hummon, & Seilhamer, 1987). For in-home drinkers, drinking was associated with increased marital satisfaction. For out-of-home drinkers, both drinking and the anticipation of further drinking were associated with decreased marital satisfaction. These findings suggest that the adaptive point of view might apply only to a subset of alcoholic families.

Typically, the research on family environment and family interaction does not address the relation between family variables and offspring adjustment, and few studies have examined the relation between family variables and outcome. Wolin, Bennett, and Noonan (1979), using semistructured interviews, assessed the extent to which "family rituals" (e.g., celebrating holidays, taking vacations) were disrupted by the drinking of the alcoholic parent. On the basis of these interviews, families were classified as "distinctive" (little or no disruption of family rituals), "subsumptive" (family rituals subsumed by alcoholism), or "intermediate" (some family rituals subsumed by drinking while others spared). Wolin et al. found that subsumptive families and, to a lesser extent, intermediate families tended to produce alcoholic offspring, while distinctive families did not. There is some evidence, based on prospective and retrospective studies, that family disruption is related to difficulties in adult adjustment among COAs (see Sher, 1991), and additional research is needed to determine the parameters governing this relation and to rule out third-variable explanations.

One of the most straightforward hypotheses concerning the transmission of alcoholism from parent to child is that children's consumption patterns are acquired through imitative social learning, or *modeling*. Although the data from the half-sibling and adoption studies would appear to discount the importance of this type of social learning (and suggest that apparent modeling represents gene/environment covariation), modeling of parents' drinking could in principle represent an important causal pathway for at least some alcoholics.

Although the adoption studies appear to rule out the hypothesis that observed parent-offspring correlations in alcohol consumption are caused by simple imitative learning, parental modeling might exert its effects through interaction with other variables related to the family. The importance of such moderator variables has recently been demonstrated by McCord (1988), who showed that father-son transmission of alcoholism was more likely when the alcoholic father was held in high esteem by the mother. In addition, parental values concerning the use of alcohol and other alcohol-related social influence variables might exert important and somewhat independent effects (Glynn, 1981).

Mediation of Risk

Although it is clear that both genetic and environmental factors are important in the intergenerational transmission of alcoholism, detailed analysis of possible causal linkages requires us to think in terms of specific mediational mechanisms. By definition, a mediating variable is one that accounts for the relation between a predictor and a criterion variable. Extending this definition to research on COAs, we can view a *mediator* as a variable that accounts for the relation between alcoholism in a parent and the eventual development of alcoholism in offspring. By *accounts for,* I mean describes the mechanism of how alcoholism in a parent leads to problems in the offspring. In order for a variable to be a candidate for a mediator, three zero-order, bivariate conditions must be met: (a) Family history must be correlated with the outcome variable (e.g., alcoholism), (b) family history must be correlated with the presumed mediator, and (c) the presumed mediator must be correlated with the outcome variable. (More detailed discussions of the concept of mediation in behavioral research and, more specifically, in research on COAs, can be found in two recent papers: Baron & Kenny, 1986; Rogosch, Chassin, & Sher, 1990.)

In the case of complete or "perfect mediation," the *entire* relation between family history and the outcome variable can be statistically explained by the mediator. However, for a number of reasons (the heterogeneity of alcoholism, measurement error, and so on), it is unlikely that perfect mediation will ever be found. Partial mediation, however, can be identified when the three bivariate conditions are met, but a significant direct path between family history of alcoholism and offspring alcoholism remains after the indirect path involving the mediator is statistically accounted for. That is, the mediator accounts for *part of* the relation between family history and the outcome measure.

Multiple Mediators

Up until this point, only the case of single mediators has been considered. However, we can easily consider multiple mediators of risk. For example, it has been suggested that COAs possess vulnerability on multiple independent dimensions of temperament (e.g., Cloninger, 1987; Tarter, 1988) and on multiple independent measures of ethanol sensitivity (Schuckit & Gold, 1988). Consequently, we must consider the possibility that multiple mediators must be identified if we wish to explain completely the link between parental and offspring alcoholism. The notion of polygenic (or, more generally, multifactorial) transmission suggests (but does not dictate) that multiple mechanisms may be responsible for intergenerational transmission of risk in alcoholism. Multiple mechanisms are also implicated by theories positing that different alcoholism subtypes are associated with unique underlying mechanisms.

Mediational Chains

The research on differences between COAs and non-COAs has identified a range of possible differences at varying levels of biopsychosocial organization. For example, studies have reported differences related to neurotransmitter functioning, behavioral effects of alcohol, and self-reported expectancies of reinforcement from alcohol (see Sher, 1991). Rather than identifying independent deficits and implying multiple mediational mechanisms, it is plausible that research on these seemingly disparate variables is identifying a set of causally related phenomena. For example, it is possible that individual differences in neurotransmitter functioning mediate the magnitude of reinforcement from alcohol, which, in turn, mediates formation of favorable expectancies of alcohol consumption (by providing the direct experience critical to the development of expectancies), which mediate alcohol-seeking behavior. Presumably, as interdisciplinary research on COAs progresses, researchers will be able to conceptualize complex causal chains across levels of biopsychosocial organization. However, at present, the data base for attempting such modeling is extremely limited.

The Moderation of Risk:
Protective and Exacerbating Factors

In addition to considering variables that appear to mediate risk, we can also think of variables that *moderate* risk. According to Baron and Kenny (1986), "a moderator is a . . . variable that affects the direction and/or strength of the relation between a . . . predictor variable and a . . . criterion variable" (p. 1174). In terms of COA research, we can think of a moderator variable as one that attenuates or magnifies the relation between parental alcoholism and offspring alcoholism, that is, a variable that demonstrates a significant interaction with family history in predicting offspring adjustment.

Simple Moderation

The distinction between variables that mediate and variables that moderate risk has been clearly described by Rutter (1987): "The crucial difference between . . . protection processes and risk mechanisms is that the latter lead directly to disorder (either strongly or weakly), whereas the former operate indirectly with their effects apparent only by virtue of their interactions with the risk variable" (p. 319). Thus moderation (or protective mechanism) is indicated when the likelihood of parental alcoholism leading to offspring alcoholism is relatively high for individuals high on the moderator variable but not for those individuals who are low, *and* the moderator variable had no (or relatively little) effect on offspring alcoholism for individuals who lacked a family history of alcoholism.

Moderated Mediation

Although it is important to identify factors that moderate the relation between parental alcoholism and offspring outcomes, it needs to be emphasized that not all COAs can be assumed to be at risk for alcoholism and other negative outcomes; not all COAs are vulnerable (e.g., not all COAs would be expected to have genetic liability or to have been exposed to causal environmental factors). Ultimately, we wish to be able to identify variables that moderate the relation between *vulnerability* and outcome, that is, variables that moderate the effect of the mediator.

The idea of moderating the influence of true vulnerability as opposed to the more distal predictor variable (i.e., family history) has been termed *moderated mediation* (Baron & Kenny, 1986). A primary goal of research on COAs is to be able to specify mediational (i.e., risk) processes and how they might be moderated by any of a number of biopsychosocial variables.

Models of the
Intergenerational Transmission of Risk

Although mediators of risk have yet to be conclusively identified, existing research findings suggest several possible mechanisms of risk. The extent to which various simple mediational models are consistent with the empirical data will first be reviewed. By *simple,* I mean that these models are meant only to describe possible *basic* mechanisms; psychobiologically, these processes might be quite complex. After reviewing these simple models of risk, I will propose more complex models that attempt to subsume these simple models.

Simple Mediational Models

We can consider three broad categories of simple mediational models. The first category, *models related to individual differences in pharmacological effects of ethanol,* addresses the general hypothesis that COAs react to alcohol in an abnormal way (e.g., are overly sensitive or tolerant) and that these abnormal reactions place them at risk for the development of alcoholism. The second category, *models related to individual differences in drinking motivation,* addresses the general hypothesis that COAs have psychological or psychobiological disturbances that provide excessive motivation (e.g., self-medication) for alcohol consumption. The third category, *other models,* contains additional possible simple models not readily subsumed under the first two categories. In addition, the different proposed models are neither mutually exclusive nor exhaustive.

Models Related to Individual Differences in Pharmacological Effects of Alcohol

The notion that COAs have an inherited predisposition to react to alcohol in an aberrant way is inherently appealing. Given that alcohol consumption is a necessary condition for the development of alcohol abuse and dependence and that COAs are at high risk for becoming alcoholic, the idea that there is something in the psychobiological makeup of the COA that makes alcohol particularly addicting for him or her would appear to be a very plausible working hypothesis. There are numerous studies indicating fundamental differences in the ways COAs and non-COAs react to alcohol (see Newlin & Thomson, 1990; Pihl, Peterson, & Finn, 1990b; Sher, 1991), suggesting that this hypothesis holds great promise for helping us to understand the intergenerational transmission of alcoholism.

Before reviewing basic models relating individual differences in alcohol effects to risk for alcoholism, it should be emphasized that it does not appear that COAs and non-COAs differ in their rates of alcohol absorption and elimination, nor have there been any replicated findings demonstrating COA/non-COA differences in the rate or nature of alcohol metabolism (Sher, 1991). Thus the COA/non-COA differences in alcohol effects reported in the literature do not appear to be a simple function of differences in how alcohol is processed by the organism.

Sensitivity to reinforcing effects of alcohol. Studies demonstrating that COAs are more sensitive to the potentially reinforcing effects of alcohol (e.g., muscle-relaxing, stress-dampening, electroencephalographic, and mood effects) suggest that COAs may experience greater reinforcement from a given dose of alcohol (Finn & Pihl, 1987; Finn, Zeitouni, & Pihl, 1990; Levenson, Oyama, & Meek, 1987; Nagoshi & Wilson, 1987; Pollock et al., 1983; Savoie, Emery, & Moody-Thomas, 1988; Schuckit, Engstrom, Alpert, & Duby, 1981; Sher, Walitzer, Bylund, & Hartmann, 1989). Heightened reinforcement value might lead to drinking in increased frequency and/or increased quantity.

Initial insensitivity to reinforcing effects of alcohol. An alternative model concerning reinforcement from alcohol is that vulnerability may be mediated by a relative insensitivity to the reinforcing effects of alcohol. Such lack of self-awareness could lead to higher levels of alcohol consumption in order to achieve desired reinforcing effects. Over time, this increased consumption of alcohol could lead to a relatively rapid development of tolerance and other dependence phenomena. Research indicating that COAs appear to show less subjective intoxication following a challenge dose of ethanol is certainly consistent with this model (e.g., Moss, Yao, & Maddock, 1989; O'Malley & Maisto, 1985; Pollock, Teasdale, Gabrielli, & Knop, 1986; Schuckit, 1980, 1984). Also, if Vogel-Sprott and Chipperfield's (1987) finding that COAs show little subjective awareness of their greater behavioral impairment proves replicable, this suggests that COAs may be more likely to drink to levels likely to lead to negative consequences.

Insensitivity to adverse effects of alcohol. Goodwin (1988) has suggested that susceptibility to alcoholism might be mediated by a lack of sensitivity to the adverse effects of alcohol. Such a lack of sensitivity would permit COAs to consume relatively large amounts of alcohol without encountering acute, punishing consequences. Although an intriguing hypothesis, there is relatively little evidence directly supporting this notion. Newlin and Thomson's (1990) analysis of alcohol challenge studies with COAs points to two possible areas of support for this possibility. First, in their analysis of Schuckit's (1980, 1984) research on subjective intoxication, they found that the decreased sensitivity of COAs is relatively specific to adverse effects of alcohol. Second, their analysis concludes that COAs appear to be less affected by alcohol on the descending limb of the blood alcohol curve. Since the descending limb appears to be associated with more negative affective consequences of alcohol (e.g., Babor, Berglas, Mendelson, Ellingboe, & Miller, 1983), this is generally consistent with Goodwin's hypothesis.

Individual differences in alcohol expectancies. The three preceding models posit that individual differences in alcohol effects are somehow translated into differences in drinking behavior. Presumably, this translation involves personal beliefs or expectancies surrounding anticipated consequences of alcohol consumption. COAs appear to have stronger expectancies for reinforcement from alcohol than do non-COAs (Brown, Creamer, & Stetson, 1987; Mann, Chassin, & Sher, 1987; Sher, Walitzer, Wood, & Brent, 1991), and there appears to be a heritable basis for attitudes toward alcohol (Perry, 1973). However, available research has yet to show a clear relationship between individual differences in the pharmacological effects of alcohol and individually held alcohol expectancies (e.g., Sher, 1985; Sher & Walitzer, 1986). The work carried out to date has not yet assessed this issue systematically. Consequently, the extent to which COA/non-COA differences in alcohol expectancies are attributable to individual differences in ethanol sensitivity is an open question. The notion that alcohol expectancies serve as a "simple" mediational model is described in the next section as well, because the importance of this model does not necessarily rest on the reductionist assumption that such expectancies are based on pharmacological processes.

Proneness to tolerance development. Although the notion that COAs are prone to rapid development of tolerance seems quite plausible, few studies directly address this point. Newlin and Thomson's (1990) review concludes that COAs show greater acute (i.e., within-session) tolerance than do non-COAs. However, COAs have been found to show reverse tolerance (sensitization) to repeated administrations of ethanol over three sessions on autonomic measures (Newlin & Aldrich, 1986). Additional studies examining changes in ethanol sensitivity over time (both within and across sessions) are clearly needed to evaluate this model.

Proneness to develop medical consequences of alcoholism. There is strong evidence indicating that genetic factors are responsible for susceptibility to a number of alcohol-related medical illnesses, such as alcoholic liver disease (Saunders & Williams, 1983) and Wernicke-Korsakoff syndrome (Nixon, 1984). Although this is clearly an important avenue of research, this model concerns only the potential for physical morbidity given a personal history of excessive alcohol consumption. Thus, although the model might help explain, in part, COAs' excess of alcohol abuse and dependence (because medical consequences constitute a criterion for diagnosis), it does not necessarily address the issue of why COAs are more likely to drink in an excessive way, or to encounter social consequences.

Models Related to Individual Differences in Drinking Motivation

Irrespective of whether COAs respond to alcohol in ways different from non-COAs, it is conceivable that COAs might be more internally motivated to use alcohol for any of a number of reasons. For example, if COAs were found to be more prone to dysphoria than non-COAs, they might be expected to use alcohol more frequently for its mood-enhancing effects (i.e., self-medication). Alternatively, if COAs' coping abilities were limited and they were less effective at controlling their stress reactions (either by direct action or self-regulation), they might be more motivated to use alcohol as a coping device. The next broad class of models covers several simple models of drinking motivation that are not clearly tied to individual differences in the pharmacological effects of alcohol.

Predisposition to experience negative mood states. Another model posits that COAs may be more prone to experience negative mood states and consequently may consume more alcohol for symptomatic relief (i.e., self-medication). Existing data show mixed support for this model. Studies comparing COAs and non-COAs on Eysenck's Neuroticism Scale have yielded contradictory findings, with some studies showing that COAs are more neurotic (Finn & Pihl, 1987; Sher et al., 1991) and at least one study showing no difference (Schuckit, 1983). COAs have not been found to report high levels of trait anxiety; however, reports of high levels of depression in COAs are common, and one study found that COAs score high on a measure of "proneness to moderate depression" (see Sher, 1991).

The failure to consider heterogeneity of parental alcoholism may contribute to the mixed support for this model. If Cloninger's (1987) theory of alcoholism subtypes is correct, then only offspring of Type 1 alcoholics would be expected to show high levels of negative mood states. In addition, negative mood states might be more etiologically significant for alcoholism among women (Cloninger, 1987; Jones, 1971). Although available data do not paint a clear picture, the notion that high rates of negative mood states serve as an important motivation for alcohol consumption among COAs must be considered a viable hypothesis.

Predisposition to seek out altered states of consciousness (sensation seeking). The finding that COAs are at high risk for other forms of substance use (see Sher, 1991) suggests that drug-seeking behavior is not tied to the specific psychoactive effects of alcohol, but may be more related to the changes in consciousness brought about by different substances. Sensation seeking is one trait that has been related to the use of a number of different substances, including alcohol (Zuckerman, Neary, & Brustman, 1970). Studies by Alterman and his colleagues comparing COAs and non-COAs on Zuckerman's Sensation Seeking Scale do not demonstrate that COAs are significantly higher on sensation seeking (Alterman, Bridges, & Tarter, 1986; Alterman, Searles, & Hall, 1989). However, the magnitude of COA/non-COA differences on sensation seeking in the Alterman et al. (1989) study is approximately .5 standard deviations (a "medium" effect size). In addition, my colleagues and I have found that young adult COAs score higher on Cloninger's measure of novelty seeking, a construct similar, but not identical, to sensation seeking (Sher et al., 1991). Finally, findings suggesting that both sensation seeking and family history of alcoholism are related to low platelet MAO activity argue for continued evaluation of this model (see Sher, 1991).

Impulsivity. Although far from conclusive, existing data suggest that COAs tend to be impulsive (see Sher, 1991). Impulsivity can be viewed as a mediator of vulnerability in that impulsive individuals can be assumed to have difficulty in inhibiting responses likely to lead to immediate reward but later punishment. That is, if drinking begins to become problematic, highly impulsive individuals can be posited to be less likely to develop effective inhibitory control of drinking.

More generally, impulsivity can be viewed as leading to impaired coping, given that successful coping is thought to require a relatively high degree of reflection and consideration of available behavioral options. Although the impulsivity model is attractive, the empirical data base is still relatively weak. Even if COAs are conclusively shown to be more impulsive than non-COAs, the relation between impulsivity and the development of drinking problems will still need to be demonstrated.

Impaired coping. More generally, impaired coping can be seen as a potential model independent of impulsivity deficits. Demonstrated deficits in intellectual problem solving might be generalizable to personal and social problem solving as well. Individuals with impaired problem solving may prefer alcohol use as a coping strategy in comparison with others who have greater problem-solving resources. This general notion is supported by experimental studies of stress-induced drinking (Sher, 1987), survey studies (e.g., Cooper, Russell, & George, 1988), and clinical research (Marlatt & Gordon, 1985). Although COAs do appear to have cognitive deficits, the relations among these deficits, coping abilities (e.g., social problem solving), and the development of drinking remain largely unexplored.

Expectancies (once again). Alcohol expectancies have been demonstrated to be strong correlates of alcohol use and abuse, both cross-sectionally and prospectively. Furthermore, COAs have been shown to have stronger expectancies for reinforcement from alcohol, especially those expectancies concerning enhanced cognitive and motor functioning. As discussed above, it is possible that these expectancies are, in part, determined by genetic factors, possibly by individual differences in alcohol effects. However, it is also known that alcohol expectancies develop early, and prior to initiation of alcohol use. Although it is likely that these expectancies are altered by direct pharmacological experience with alcohol, important (nonbiological) social learning influences are presumed to have a major influence on expectancy development. Whatever the cause, enhanced expectancies for reinforcement from alcohol seem likely to play a significant role in mediating alcoholism risk (Sher et al., 1991). In addition to a possible simple mediating role, recent evidence suggests that expectancies might serve an important moderating function. For example, it appears that positive expectancies for alcohol use potentiate the correlations between alcohol involvement and presumed vulnerability factors such as undercontrolled personality traits (Mann et al., 1987), coping styles (Cooper et al., 1988), and anxiety (Kushner, 1990). Future research that integrates expectancies with other presumed vulnerability factors should help us better understand the role alcohol expectancies play in the transmission of alcoholism.

.

Other Models

At least two additional simple models can be posited that do not neatly fit into either of the two classes of models described above.

Proneness to school failure and its psychosocial sequelae. COAs have a variety of childhood behavior problems and intellectual deficits, and are at high risk for school problems (see Sher, 1991). One plausible model is that behavioral and cognitive deficits lead to school problems, social rejection, and consequent decreased self-esteem and/or the adoption of a deviant role. Although the sequencing of school failure, decreased self-esteem, and social deviance is open to debate, developmental models of adolescent problem behavior point to similar causal chains (Loeber, 1990). Either low self-esteem or deviant behavior may be seen as predisposing individuals to heavier alcohol consumption. Evaluation of this model requires detailed prospective studies of COAs that are currently lacking.

Exposure to alcohol. As mentioned earlier, exposure to parental drinking models can be viewed as a pathway toward the development of drinking problems. The greatest difficulty facing this model is evidence from adoption studies that shows a lack of influence of being raised in an alcoholic home in the absence of an alcoholic biological background. Nevertheless, under certain circumstances, modeling of an alcoholic parent's drinking behavior might prove to represent an important pathway to alcoholism (e.g., McCord, 1988).

Presumably, certain personality traits (e.g., sociability) might lead to greater involvement in social activities and exposure to drinking situations. One advantage of this type of "exposure" model is that it is potentially consistent with genetic etiology mediated by personality traits (a type of gene-environment correlation). However, I am not aware of any data directly supporting this model and, as noted before, COAs have not been found to be characterized by extroversion (a construct closely associated with sociability).

Summary

At present, none of the simple models described above can be ruled out. Although there are varying degrees of support for each of these

models, the etiologic significance of each has yet to be firmly established. Nevertheless, these models have utility for evaluating the significance of accumulating data from diverse areas of inquiry and for
generating research ideas.

It is likely that different models will have relevance for COAs
characterized by different parental subtypes of alcoholism. Consequently, future research will need to incorporate controls for several
possible sources of etiologic heterogeneity. This will require more
extensive evaluation of parental and other familial psychopathology. It
bears repeating that each of these models is undoubtedly overly simplistic, and needs to be elaborated to encompass a broader array of
psychosocial and physical influences over the life span.

Finally, assuming that the transmission of alcoholism is multifactorial and encompasses a relatively large number of genetic and environmental factors, it is possible that a number of these simple mediational
mechanisms operate in conjunction with each other to confer risk to the
individual. Consequently, more complex mediational models need to be
considered.

Etiologic Pathways

Considering the simple models described above and some of the
proposed linkages described by a variety of theorists, several more
complex etiologic pathways, each implicating individual-level variables, can be proposed. At present, the evidence for various components
of each pathway range from very strong to nonexistent. However, where
empirical support is weak or nonexistent, only theoretically plausible
mechanisms and linkages are proposed.

The purpose of the proposed pathways outlined below is to describe
several basic mechanisms that might mediate the intergenerational
transmission of risk for alcoholism. Although a family history of alcoholism is included in each pathway, the various pathways are thought
to represent general processes and to be broadly applicable to the
etiology of alcoholism. Note, however, that a number of important
variables (e.g., social class, ethnicity, alcohol regulatory policies) are
not included in the models. Thus the various pathways do not represent
a comprehensive theory of alcoholism etiology. It is anticipated that
important variables and/or pathways are omitted, and that some of the

hypothesized linkages might not hold up to empirical test. Nevertheless, the pathways proposed are seen as providing an integrative framework for understanding the mechanisms of intergenerational transmission of alcoholism. Implicit in this approach is that there are multiple, interrelated pathways with important genetic and environmental influences. However, determining the extent to which given variables reflect genetic versus environmental influences cannot be assumed on the basis of how ostensibly "environmental" the variable appears to be. That is, variables such as parenting behavior, life stress, and peer influence all appear to reflect environmental sources of variance, but each might have important genetic determination.

It should be stressed at the outset that most of the variables in each pathway are complex and multidimensional. For example, family history of alcoholism is clearly heterogeneous in terms of course, subtype, comorbid psychopathology, and spousal psychopathology. There are also multiple dimensions of variables such as parenting (e.g., control, nurturance), temperament/personality (e.g., emotionality, activity, sociability), cognitive dysfunction (e.g., attention, problem solving), coping ability (e.g., emotion-focused, problem-focused), and emotional distress (e.g., anxiety, depression). Nevertheless, for the sake of simplicity, it is of value to consider these broad, heterogeneous factors as conceptual entities. It should also be emphasized that all variables endogenous to the model probably have important influences beyond those specified; variables as diverse as temperament, life stress, and alcohol expectancies are presumably affected by systematic influences not considered here. Finally, a number of possible moderating variables are also considered, and some variables serve as both mediators and moderators within the model.

Family history of alcoholism is conceptualized as reflecting the clinical phenomenon of alcoholism in the individual's biological relatives and subsumes heritable influences, the influence of parental alcohol consumption on germ cells and on the fetus, and the psychosocial consequences of having an alcoholic parent (e.g., alcohol-related stressors, exposure to heavily drinking models).

I will describe three prototypical pathways for conceptualizing the intergenerational transmission of risk: (a) the enhanced reinforcement pathway, (b) the deviance proneness pathway, and (c) the negative affect pathway. However, none of these pathways can be viewed as entirely independent, and the boundaries between one pathway and another are ultimately arbitrary. Consequently, each of the pathways

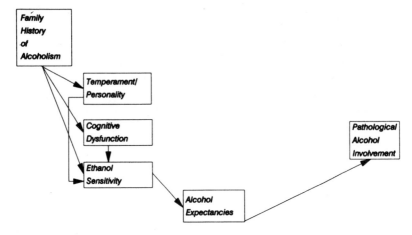

Figure 1.1. Schematic diagram of the enhanced reinforcement submodel. Note that most of the variables in the model are assumed to be heterogeneous (i.e., factorially complex).

SOURCE: From Kenneth J. Sher, *Children of Alcoholics: A Critical Appraisal of Theory and Research.* Copyright 1991 by The University of Chicago Press. Reprinted by permission.

will be delimited to several salient constructs for the purposes of illustration.

The Enhanced Reinforcement Pathway

In its most basic form, the enhanced reinforcement model (see Figure 1.1) posits that family history of alcoholism is causally related to increased reinforcement value from alcohol, which in turn is causally related to the likelihood of developing alcohol problems and dependence. (Although this model is focused on reinforcement, decreased sensitivity on the descending limb of the BAC [e.g., Newlin & Thomson, 1990] can be easily accommodated to the model.) The model posits a direct path from family history to ethanol sensitivity (perhaps due to direct effects of alcohol on brain centers related to reward). In addition, ethanol sensitivity is also posited to be related to cognitive dysfunction (e.g., Pihl, Peterson, & Finn, 1990a) and temperament/personality (e.g., Levenson et al., 1987; Sher & Levenson, 1982). It is further proposed that pharmacologically mediated individual differences in ethanol sen-

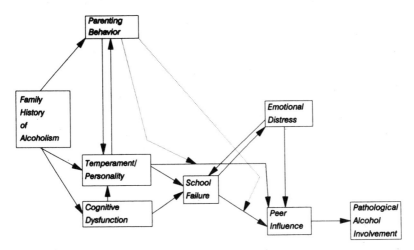

Figure 1.2. Schematic diagram of the deviance proneness submodel. Note that most of the variables in the model are assumed to be heterogeneous (i.e., factorially complex). Mediating paths are indicated by solid lines; moderating paths are indicated by dashed lines.

SOURCE: From Kenneth J. Sher, *Children of Alcoholics: A Critical Appraisal of Theory and Research.* Copyright 1991 by The University of Chicago Press. Reprinted by permission.

sitivity are translated into increased expectancies of reinforcement from alcohol with sufficient drinking experience. These expectancies are, in turn, thought to be the proximal mediator of drinking behavior.

The Deviance Proneness Pathway

In contrast to the enhanced reinforcement pathway, which focuses on individual differences in the pharmacological effects of alcohol, the key variables in the deviance proneness pathway (see Figure 1.2) are largely behavioral, and the major explanatory concept is deficient socialization. Although focusing on socialization processes, important individual difference variables figure prominently in this pathway. Family history of alcoholism is posited to have direct effects on parenting behavior (e.g., Dishion, Patterson, & Reid, 1988), temperament/personality (e.g., Tarter, Kabene, Escallier, Laird, & Jacob, 1990), and cognitive dysfunction (see Sher, 1991). A "difficult" temperament in transaction with ineffective parental control leads to unsocialized behavior, which results in poor academic adjustment and school failure. Associated cognitive deficits are also posited to contribute to school failure (see Hinshaw, 1992). School failure is posited to lead to association with deviant, substance-abusing peers both as a direct effect and as an indirect effect mediated by low self-esteem (e.g., Kaplan, 1975). (Increased emotional distress is assumed to be bidirectionally related to school failure.) In addition, a direct path from temperament/personality to peer influence is posited because it is assumed that more venturesome, sensation-seeking individuals are likely to seek out peers with similar traits. In this pathway, peer influence is viewed as the mediating mechanism most proximal to increased alcohol use.

In addition to the mediational pathways outlined above, moderating effects of parenting behavior on paths to peer influence are proposed. These moderating effects are viewed as representing the parents' success or failure at monitoring and controlling the child's relationships with deviant peers.

The Negative Affect Pathway

The negative affect pathway (see Figure 1.3) focuses on proneness to experiencing negative affective states, a high level of life stress, and the effectiveness of coping resources. (For reviews of stress and coping models of substance abuse, including alcoholism, see Shiffman & Wills, 1985.) Family history is posited to lead to temperamental characteristics such as "emotionality" and "neuroticism" that predispose the offspring to experience negative affective states such as anxiety and depression. Although it is clear that life stress is related to a family history of alcoholism (Brown, 1989; Roosa, Sandler, Gehring, Beales, & Cappo, 1988), the model is not limited to stressors directly related to a parent's drinking history. Also, the effects of stress related to parental behaviors are not necessarily restricted to acute effects, but could have delayed effects as well, as would be expected in survivors of sexual abuse (see Russell & Wilsnack, 1991). Life stress is posited to have direct effects on emotional distress, which, in turn, is moderated by temperament. Certain temperamental types are presumed to be especially vulnerable to certain forms of life stress (e.g., personal loss, threats to autonomy). Coping ability is thought to be influenced in part by inherited temperamental characteristics and cognitive abilities (see Sher, 1991). In this model, coping is thought to play a moderating role by buffering both the relationship between life stress and emotional distress (e.g., by actively reducing the impact of the stress) and the relationship between emotional distress and pathological drinking. Although less central in

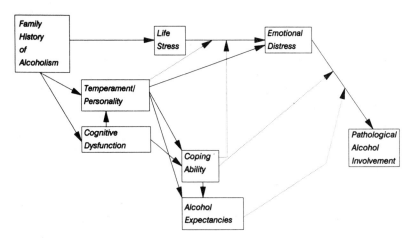

Figure 1.3. Schematic diagram of the negative affect submodel. Note that most of the variables in the model are assumed to be heterogeneous (i.e., factorially complex). Mediating paths are indicated by solid lines; moderating paths are indicated by dashed lines.

SOURCE: From Kenneth J. Sher, *Children of Alcoholics: A Critical Appraisal of Theory and Research.* Copyright 1991 by The University of Chicago Press. Reprinted by permission.

this pathway, alcohol-related expectancies for relief from psychological distress are posited to be related to impaired coping ability (Cooper et al., 1988; Cooper, Russell, Skinner, Frone, & Mudar, 1992). In addition, these expectancies are posited to moderate the path from emotional distress to pathological drinking (Kushner, 1990). Although the negative affect pathway emphasizes life stress and coping, a direct path from temperament/personality to emotional distress is also considered, because some individuals may experience considerable affective disturbance in the absence of precipitating stressors (e.g., individuals high on basic traits such as emotionality and neuroticism). This latter pathway might be more important for individuals with substantial family histories of affective and anxiety disorders.

Simultaneous Consideration of Multiple Pathways

As noted earlier, delimiting each of the three prototypical etiologic pathways to selected key constructs is ultimately arbitrary, and consequently there are no clear boundaries between pathways. Also, each of the three pathways can be thought to contribute "independently" to the

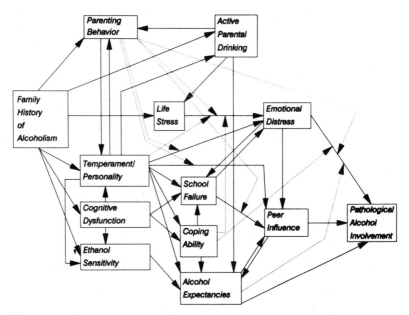

Figure 1.4. Comprehensive model of the relation between family history of alcoholism and pathological alcohol involvement in offspring. Note that most of the variables in the model are assumed to be heterogeneous (i.e., factorially complex). Mediating paths are indicated by solid lines; moderating paths are indicated by dashed lines.

SOURCE: From Kenneth J. Sher, *Children of Alcoholics: A Critical Appraisal of Theory and Research.* Copyright 1991 by The University of Chicago Press. Reprinted by permission.

likelihood that a given individual will develop alcohol problems. That is, although cases of alcoholism primarily "caused" by a single pathway can exist (and might be thought of as clear-cut exemplars of different alcoholism subtypes, e.g., Cloninger's Type 1 or Type 2), multiple pathways can additively contribute to risk. Figure 1.4 presents a more complex model that subsumes the three prototypical pathways and includes an additional construct (active parental drinking) and a number of additional paths supported by empirical data or theory. Most of these additional paths were omitted from consideration in the presentation of the prototypical pathways in order to focus attention on the key constructs relevant to each.

The overarching model summarized in Figure 1.4 should be viewed only as a starting point; again, it is likely that key constructs and pathways have been overlooked and have yet to be identified. Even more probable, the model is overinclusive, and some constructs and pathways may not be necessary for a complete understanding of the intergenerational transmission of alcoholism. Nevertheless, multifactorial models such as the one displayed in Figure 1.4 are useful in a number of ways if we wish to identify and understand the variables that mediate and moderate risk for alcoholism. These are briefly summarized below.

(1) There are numerous individual difference variables that are potential candidates for study in etiologic research on alcoholism. Theoretical models of etiology can guide our selection of variables and optimize our ability to identify those most fruitful for understanding risk processes.

(2) Mere knowledge that a variable predicts alcoholism tells little about *why* that variable might be important. For example, a specific cognitive deficit (e.g., inability to maintain a focus of attention) might correlate prospectively with incidence of alcoholism, but could do so for any number of diverse reasons: enhanced sensitivity to psychological effects of alcohol (suggested by Steele & Josephs's 1990 model of alcohol myopia), school difficulties and socialization problems, or impaired ability to use adaptive problem- or emotion-focused coping techniques for dealing with stressors or negative mood states. If we are to maximize prediction and develop optimal intervention strategies, a knowledge of how this deficit fits into causal etiologic chains is necessary.

(3) The lack of a simple correlation between a potential etiologically relevant variable and alcoholism does not necessarily indicate that the variable is not useful for understanding the causes of alcoholism. First, it could be that the variable is a moderator and takes on predictive significance only in the context of its interaction with other variables. Second, as discussed earlier, it is possible that the variable is positively correlated with one risk mechanism and negatively correlated with another, despite the fact that it is uncorrelated with the outcome.

(4) Identification of potential etiologic pathways and associated individual difference variables can help to identify other types of mediating and moderating variables (e.g., family and peer variables) that provide additional prediction and specificity.

Conclusion

Existing empirical research and theory have identified a number of plausible routes for the intergenerational transmission of alcoholism. Although a number of "simple" mediational pathways can be considered, it is likely that each of these pathways represents only a small part of the picture and that a comprehensive understanding of the effects of parental alcoholism must be considered in the context of a broad matrix of biopsychosocial influences. From this perspective, there is no simple cause of the increased risk of alcoholism for COAs. To some this might appear discouraging, but it should be borne in mind that alcoholism in humans is a complex, multifactorial problem, and an adequate explanation must consider a host of potentially important influences. It should be noted, however, that there might be a very limited number of final common pathways that could serve to make preventive efforts less complex. For example, expectancies of reinforcement from alcohol might prove to be a critical variable affecting most pathways, and interventions targeted at this variable might prove to have far-ranging preventive effects.

Several limitations of the models proposed deserve mention. First, a developmental perspective is generally lacking. Although it is likely that some submodels (e.g., deviance proneness) are more relevant to earlier onset problems while others (e.g., negative affect) are more relevant to later onset problems, a truly comprehensive model will incorporate different mediating mechanisms in the prospective context of developmentally specific life tasks and transitions. Also, although some moderating influences are considered in the models presented here, this aspect is relatively undeveloped.

More than a decade ago, Robins, West, Ratcliff, and Herjanic (1979) stated:

Studies of the transmission of alcoholism from parent to child that do not examine the chain of pathologies through which that transmission takes place can produce an illusion of simplicity. Further, they may seem to conflict with studies that emphasize family and personality structure as predictors of alcoholism when no real conflict exists. . . . Parental alcoholism, family structure, and pre-alcoholic behavior patterns form a complex of closely interrelated patterns that are passed on together from generation to generation. (p. 326)

It is my hope that the models described above may move us a step closer toward conceptualizing these patterns.

References

Alterman, A. I., Bridges, K. R., & Tarter, R. E. (1986). Drinking behavior of high-risk college men: Contradictory preliminary findings. *Alcoholism: Clinical and Experimental Research, 10,* 1-6.

Alterman, A. I., Searles, J. S., & Hall, J. G. (1989). Failure to find differences in drinking behavior as a function of familial risk for alcoholism: A replication. *Journal of Abnormal Psychology, 98,* 50-53.

Babor, T. F., Berglas, S., Mendelson, J. H., Ellingboe, J., & Miller, K. (1983). Alcohol, affect, and disinhibition of verbal behavior. *Psychopharmacology, 80,* 53-60.

Baron, R. M., & Kenny, D. A. (1986). The moderator-mediator variable distinction in social psychological research: Conceptual, strategic, and statistical considerations. *Journal of Personality and Social Psychology, 51,* 1173-1182.

Benson, C. S., & Heller, K. (1987). Factors in the current adjustment of young adult daughters of alcoholic and problem drinking fathers. *Journal of Abnormal Psychology, 90,* 305-312.

Brown, S. A. (1989). Life events of adolescents in relation to personal and parental substance abuse. *American Journal of Psychiatry, 146,* 484-489.

Brown, S. A., Creamer, V. A., & Stetson, B. A. (1987). Adolescent alcohol expectancies in relation to personal and parental drinking patterns. *Journal of Abnormal Psychology, 96,* 117-121.

Callan, V. J. & Jackson, D. (1986). Children of alcoholic fathers and recovered alcoholic fathers: Personal and family functioning. *Journal of Studies on Alcohol, 47,* 180-182.

Cloninger, C. R. (1987). Neurogenetic adaptive mechanisms in alcoholism. *Science, 236,* 410-416.

Cloninger, C. R., Bohman, M., & Sigvardsson, S. (1981). Inheritance of alcohol abuse: Cross fostering analysis of adopted men. *Archives of General Psychiatry, 38,* 861-868.

Cooper, L., Russell, M., & George, W. (1988). Coping, expectancies, and alcohol abuse: A test of social learning formulations. *Journal of Abnormal Psychology, 97,* 218-230.

Cooper, L., Russell, M., Skinner, J. B., Frone, M. R., & Mudar, P. (1992). Stress and alcohol use: The moderating effects of gender, coping and alcohol expectancies. *Journal of Abnormal Psychology, 101,* 139-154.

Cotton, N. (1979). The familial incidence of alcoholism: A review. *Journal of Studies on Alcohol, 40,* 89-116.

Dishion, T. J., Patterson, G. R., & Reid, J. R. (1988). Parent and peer factors associated with drug sampling in early adolescence: Implications for treatment. In E. R. Rahdert & J. Grabowski (Eds.), *Adolescent drug abuse: Analyses of treatment research* (NIDA Research Monograph 77) (pp. 69-93). Rockville, MD: National Institute on Drug Abuse.

Dunn, N. J., Jacob, T., Hummon, N., & Seilhamer, R. A. (1987). Marital stability in alcoholic-spouse relationships as a function of drinking pattern and location. *Journal of Abnormal Psychology, 96,* 99-107.

Finn, P. R., & Pihl, R. O. (1987). Men at high risk for alcoholism: The effect of alcohol on cardiovascular response to unavoidable shock. *Journal of Abnormal Psychology, 96,* 230-236.

Finn, P. R., Zeitouni, N. C., & Pihl, R. O. (1990). Effects of alcohol on psychophysiological hyperreactivity to nonaversive and aversive stimuli in men at high risk for alcoholism. *Journal of Abnormal Psychology, 99,* 79-85.

Glynn, T. J. (1981). From family to peer: Transitions of influence among drug-using youth. In D. J. Lettieri & J. P. Ludford (Eds.), *Drug abuse and the American adolescent* (NIDA Research Monograph 38) (pp. 57-81). Rockville, MD: National Institute on Drug Abuse.

Goodwin, D. W. (1988). *Is alcoholism hereditary?* (2nd ed.). New York: Ballantine.

Gurling, H. M. D., Murray, R. M., & Clifford, C. (1981). Genetic contributions to alcohol dependence and its effect on brain function. In G. L. Parisi & W. A. Nance (Eds.), *Twin research* (Vol. 3, pp. 77-87). New York: A. R. Liss.

Hamilton, C. J., & Collins, J. J., Jr. (1985). The role of alcohol in wife beating and child abuse: A review of the literature. In J. J. Collins, Jr. (Ed.), *Drinking and crime: Perspectives on the relationship between alcohol consumption and criminal behavior* (pp. 253-287). New York: Guilford.

Hinshaw, S. P. (1992). Externalizing behavior problems and academic underachievement in childhood and adolescence: Causal relationships and underlying mechanisms. *Psychological Bulletin, 111,* 127-155.

Jacob, T. & Seilhamer, R. A. (1987). Alcoholism and family interaction. In T. Jacob (Ed.), *Family interaction and psychopathology: Theories, methods, and findings* (pp. 535-580). New York: Plenum.

Jones, M. C. (1971). Personality antecedents and correlates of drinking patterns in women. *Journal of Consulting and Clinical Psychology, 36,* 61-69.

Kaplan, H. B. (1975). Increase in self-rejection as an antecedent of deviant responses. *Journal of Youth and Adolescence, 4,* 281-292.

Kushner, M. (1990). *Moderators of the alcohol-anxiety relation.* Unpublished doctoral dissertation, University of Missouri.

Lang, A. R., Pelham, W. E., Johnston, C., & Gelertner, S. (1989). Levels of adult alcohol consumption induced by interactions with child confederates exhibiting normal versus externalizing behaviors. *Journal of Abnormal Psychology, 98,* 294-299.

Levenson, R. W., Oyama, O. N., & Meek, P. S. (1987). Greater reinforcement from alcohol for those at risk: Parental risk, personality risk, and gender. *Journal of Abnormal Psychology, 96,* 242-253.

Loeber, R. (1990). Development and risk factors of juvenile antisocial behavior and delinquency. *Clinical Psychology Review, 10,* 1-41.

Mann, L. M., Chassin, L., & Sher, K. J. (1987). Alcohol expectancies and the risk for alcoholism. *Journal of Consulting and Clinical Psychology, 55,* 411-417.

Marlatt, G. A., & Gordon, J. (Eds.). (1985). *Relapse prevention: Maintenance strategies in the treatment of addictive behaviors.* New York: Guilford.

McCord, J. (1988). Identifying developmental paradigms leading to alcoholism. *Journal of Studies on Alcoholism, 49,* 357-362.

Moos, R. H., & Billings, A. G. (1982). Children of alcoholics during the recovery process: Alcoholic and matched control families. *Addictive Behaviors, 7,* 155-164.

Moss, H. B., Yao, J. K., & Maddock, J. M. (1989). Responses by sons of alcoholic fathers to alcoholic and placebo drinks: Perceived mood, intoxication, and plasma prolactin. *Alcoholism: Clinical and Experimental Research, 13,* 252-257.

Murray, R. M., Clifford, C. A., & Gurling, H. M. (1983). Twin and adoption studies: How good is the evidence for a genetic role? In M. Galanter (Ed.), *Recent developments in alcoholism* (Vol. 1, pp. 25-48). New York: Plenum.

Nagoshi, C. T., & Wilson, J. R. (1987). Influence of family alcoholism history on alcohol metabolism, sensitivity, and tolerance. *Alcoholism: Clinical and Experimental Research, 11,* 392-398.

Newlin, D. B., & Aldrich, K. (1986). Reverse tolerance to alcohol in sons of alcoholics. *Alcoholism: Clinical and Experimental Research, 10,* 98. (Abstract)

Newlin, D. B., & Thomson, J. B. (1990). Alcohol challenge with sons of alcoholics: A critical review and analysis. *Psychological Bulletin, 108,* 383-402.

Nixon, P. F. (1984). Is there a genetic component to the pathogenesis of the Wernicke-Korsakoff syndrome? *Alcohol & Alcoholism, 19,* 219-221.

O'Malley, S. S., & Maisto, S. S. (1985). Effects of family drinking history and expectancies on responses to alcohol in men. *Journal of Studies on Alcohol, 46,* 289-297.

Orme, T. & Rimmer, J. (1981). Alcoholism and child abuse: A review. *Journal of Studies on Alcohol, 42,* 273-287.

Peele, S. (1986). The implications and limitations of genetic models of alcoholism and other addictions. *Journal of Studies on Alcohol, 47,* 63-73.

Perry, A. (1973). The effect of heredity on attitudes toward alcohol, cigarettes and coffee. *Journal of Applied Psychology, 58,* 275-277.

Pihl, R. O., Peterson, J., & Finn, P. (1990a). An heuristic model for the inherited predisposition to alcoholism. *Psychology of Addictive Behavior, 4,* 12-25.

Pihl, R. O., Peterson, J., & Finn, P. (1990b). The inherited predisposition to alcoholism: Characteristics of sons of male alcoholics. *Journal of Abnormal Psychology, 99,* 291-301.

Plomin, R., Defries, J. C., & Loehlin, J. C. (1977). Genotype-environment interaction and correlation in the analysis of human behavior. *Psychology Bulletin, 84,* 309-322.

Pollock, V. E., Schneider, L. S., Gabrielli, W. F., & Goodwin, D. W. (1987). Sex of parent and offspring in the transmission of alcoholism: A meta-analysis. *Journal of Nervous and Mental Disease, 173,* 668-673.

Pollock, V. E., Teasdale, T. W., Gabrielli, W. F., & Knop, J. (1986). Subjective and objective measures of response to alcohol among young men at risk for alcoholism. *Journal of Studies on Alcohol, 47,* 297-304.

Pollock, V. E., Volavka, J., Goodwin, D. W., Mednick, S. A., Gabrielli, W. F., Knop, J., & Schulsinger, F. (1983). The EEG after alcohol administration in men at risk for alcoholism. *Archives of General Psychiatry, 40,* 857-861.

Robins, L. N., West, P. A., Ratcliff, K. S., & Herjanic, B. M. (1979). Father's alcoholism and children's outcomes. In F. A. Seixas (Ed.), *Currents in alcoholism: Vol. 4. Psychiatric, psychological, social, and epidemiological studies* (pp. 313-327). New York: Grune & Stratton.

Rogosch, F., Chassin, L., & Sher, K. J. (1990). Personality variables as mediators and moderators of family history risk for alcoholism: Conceptual and methodological issues. *Journal of Studies on Alcohol, 51,* 310-318.

Roosa, M., Sandler, I., Gehring, M., Beales, J., & Cappo, L. (1988). The Children of Alcoholics Life Events Schedule: A stress scale for children of alcohol-abusing parents. *Journal of Studies on Alcohol, 49,* 422-429.

Russell, M., Henderson, C., & Blume, S. (1985). *Children of alcoholics: A review of the literature.* New York: Children of Alcoholics Foundation.

Russell, S. A., & Wilsnack, S. C. (1991). Adult survivors of childhood sexual abuse: Substance abuse and other consequences. In P. Roth (Ed.), *Alcohol and drugs are women's issues: Vol. 1. A review of the issues* (pp. 61-70). New York: Women's Action Alliance.

Rutter, M. (1987). Psychosocial resilience and protective mechanisms. *American Journal of Orthopsychiatry, 57,* 316-331.

Saunders, L. B., & Williams, R. (1983). The genetics of alcoholism: Is there an inherited susceptibility to alcohol-related problems? *Alcohol & Alcoholism, 18,* 189-217.

Savoie, T. M., Emery, E. K., & Moody-Thomas, S. (1988). Acute alcohol intoxication in socially drinking female and male offspring of alcoholic fathers. *Journal of Studies on Alcohol, 49,* 430-435.

Schuckit, M. A. (1980). Self-ratings of alcohol intoxication by young men with and without family histories of alcoholism. *Journal of Studies on Alcohol, 41,* 242-249.

Schuckit, M. A. (1983). Extroversion and neuroticism in young men at higher or lower risk for alcoholism. *American Journal of Psychiatry, 140,* 1223-1224.

Schuckit, M. A. (1984). Subjective responses to alcohol in sons of alcoholics and control subjects. *Archives of General Psychiatry, 41,* 879-884.

Schuckit, M. A., Engstrom, D., Alpert, R., & Duby, J. (1981). Differences in muscle-tension response to ethanol in young men with and without family histories of alcoholism. *Journal of Studies on Alcohol, 42,* 918-924.

Schuckit, M. A., & Gold, E. O. (1988). A simultaneous evaluation of multiple markers of ethanol/placebo challenges in sons of alcoholics and controls. *Archives of General Psychiatry, 45,* 211-216.

Searles, J. S. (1988). The role of genetics in the pathogenesis of alcoholism. *Journal of Abnormal Psychology, 97,* 153-167.

Seilhamer, R. A., & Jacob, T. (1990). Family factors and adjustment of children of alcoholics. In M. Windle & J. S. Searles (Eds.), *Children of alcoholics: Critical perspectives* (pp. 168-186). New York: Guilford.

Sher, K. J. (1985). Subjective effects of alcohol: The influence of setting and individual differences in alcohol expectancies. *Journal of Studies on Alcohol, 46,* 137-146.

Sher, K. J. (1987). Stress response dampening. In H. T. Blane & K. E. Leonard (Eds.), *Psychological theories of drinking and alcoholism* (pp. 227-271). New York: Guilford.

Sher, K. J. (1991). *Children of alcoholics: A critical appraisal of theory and research.* Chicago: University of Chicago Press.

Sher, K. J., & Levenson, R. W. (1982). Risk for alcoholism and individual differences in the stress-response-dampening effect of alcohol. *Journal of Abnormal Psychology, 91,* 350-368.

Sher, K. J., & Walitzer, K. S. (1986). Individual differences in the stress-response-dampening effect of alcohol. *Journal of Abnormal Psychology, 95,* 159-167.

Sher, K. J., Walitzer, K. S., Bylund, D. B., & Hartmann, J. (1989). Alcohol, stress, and family history of alcoholism. *Alcoholism: Clinical and Experimental Research, 13,* 337. (Abstract)

Sher, K. J., Walitzer, K. S., Wood, P., & Brent, E. E. (1991). Characteristics of children of alcoholics: Putative risk factors, substance use and abuse, and psychopathology. *Journal of Abnormal Psychology, 100,* 427-448.

Shiffman, S., & Wills, T. A. (Eds.). (1985). *Coping and substance abuse.* New York: Academic Press.

Steele, C. M., & Josephs, R. A. (1990). Alcohol myopia: Its prized and dangerous effects. *American Psychologist, 45,* 921-933.

Steinglass, P., Bennett, L. A., Wolin, S. J., & Reiss, D. (1987). *The alcoholic family.* New York: Basic Books.

Tarter, R. E. (1988). Are there inherited behavioral traits that predispose to substance abuse? *Journal of Consulting and Clinical Psychology, 56,* 189-196.

Tarter, R. E., Kabene, M., Escallier, E. A., Laird, S. B., & Jacob, T. (1990). Temperament deviation and risk for alcoholism. *Alcoholism: Clinical and Experimental Research, 14,* 380-382.

Vogel-Sprott, M., & Chipperfield, B. (1987). Family history of problem drinking among male social drinkers: Behavioral effects of alcohol. *Journal of Studies on Alcohol, 48,* 430-436.

West, M. O., & Prinz, R. J. (1987). Parental alcoholism and childhood psychopathology. *Psychological Bulletin, 102,* 204-218.

Wolin, S. J., Bennett, L. A., & Noonan, D. L. (1979). Family rituals and the reoccurrence of alcoholism over generations. *American Journal of Psychiatry, 136,* 589-593.

Zuckerman, M., Neary, R. S., & Brustman, B. A. (1970). Sensation-seeking scale correlates in experience (smoking, drugs, alcohol, "hallucinations," and sex) and preference for complexity (designs). *Proceedings of the 78th Annual Meeting of the American Psychological Association, 5,* 317-318. (Summary)

2

A Life-Span Perspective on
Natural Recovery (Self-Change)
From Alcohol Problems

LINDA C. SOBELL
JOHN A. CUNNINGHAM
MARK B. SOBELL
TONY TONEATTO

There is a growing recognition that there are multiple paths to recovery from alcohol problems (e.g., treatment, self-help, natural recovery; Institute of Medicine, 1990; Sobell, Sobell, & Toneatto, 1992). One of these paths, natural recovery (self-change), involves individuals who have never received treatment. As has been noted

AUTHORS' NOTE: The views expressed in this chapter are those of the authors and do not necessarily reflect those of the Addiction Research Foundation. Portions of this chapter were presented at the Banff International Conference on Behavioural Science, Banff, Alberta, Canada, March 1991. The research presented here was supported, in part, by Grant AA08593-01A1 from the National Institute on Alcohol Abuse and Alcoholism. We wish to thank Ms. Joanne Jackson for her patience and diligence in typing repeated drafts of the manuscript and Ms. Sangeeta Agrawal for her statistical consultation.

elsewhere, there are several reasons for studying those who have made natural recoveries (Sobell et al., 1992):

(1) The alcohol field does not have enduring effective treatments; an understanding of the natural recovery process may lead to the development of more effective treatments.

(2) The field has failed to reach large numbers of individuals with alcohol problems—the ratio of *untreated to treated* alcohol abusers is estimated to range from a conservative 3:1 ratio to a liberal 13:1 ratio.

(3) Based on studies of natural recoveries, it may be possible to develop self-change strategies for those who are unwilling, unlikely, or not ready to enter traditional alcohol treatment programs, but who might otherwise want to change their drinking.

(4) Because individuals in treatment programs represent a small proportion of all those who have alcohol problems, our understanding of this disorder may be highly biased or circumscribed if based solely on treated individuals.

While there are few studies of natural recoveries from alcohol problems, it has been speculated that the prevalence of such recoveries is far greater than previously suspected (Fillmore, 1988; Sobell & Sobell, 1991; Sobell et al., 1992). Unfortunately, little is known about the phenomenon of natural recovery—about the patterns of behavior change, the severity of dependence of those who recover, or what triggers the recoveries. Also, the few published studies of natural recoveries all have had serious methodological weaknesses. The present study was designed to address several problems evident in past research:

(1) The resolution period in past studies typically has ranged from 6 to 12 months; in the present study, subjects had to have been recovered for at least three years.

(2) In the present study, collateral informants were required to confirm subjects' histories of alcohol problems and their recoveries, a feature lacking in most other studies.

(3) The present study had a large sample size compared with previous studies.

(4) This is the first study to present detailed drinking histories and alcohol-related consequences for subjects.

(5) In this study, unlike previous studies, data for abstinent and moderation outcomes are reported separately.

(6) Data are presented separately in this study for subjects who reported never having received treatment and for subjects who had formal help or treatment but said it was not related to their eventual recoveries (previous studies combined these types of recovery).

The most significant innovation in the present study was the use of a nonresolved, nontreated control group. A control group is critical because "if only recovered subjects are studied, then it is impossible to determine whether any observed relationships between life events and recovery are functionally related or merely coincidental" (Sobell et al., 1992, p. 201). Because alcohol abusers may experience certain types of life events frequently, a critical requirement of natural recovery studies is to obtain similar information about life events from individuals who have similarly severe problems, who have never been treated, and who have not recovered when interviewed. If such individuals experience the same constellation or types of events as reported by naturally recovered individuals, then it is unlikely that recovery can be attributed solely to the occurrence of these events. The present study addressed this problem by including a comparison group of persons with alcohol problems who had never sought formal help or treatment for their problems and had not recovered at the time of the interview. The nonresolved, nontreated control subjects were interviewed about life events they experienced during a randomly selected year several years earlier. Use of the random year controlled for memory differences between groups (i.e., recovered subjects had to recall a period at least 3 years back).

When studies are evaluated from a life-span perspective, the findings presented are age related. In the present study, natural recoveries were examined from the perspective of a person's age at the time of his or her recovery. A key question is whether natural recoveries occur at the same rate across all age cohorts or whether they involve a maturational process (i.e., associated with transition to adulthood; see, e.g., Cahalan, 1970; Cahalan, Cisin, & Crossley, 1969; Cahalan & Room, 1974; Zinberg & Jacobson, 1976). A major review of longitudinal studies examining alcohol use across the life span found considerable variability in natural remission across the life course by age and gender (Fillmore, 1988). Maturational curves for men suggest that recovery from alcohol problems is most frequent in youth and old age. Although there are considerably fewer studies with females, the age pattern for onset of drinking problems appears to differ for women and men. Women's problems appear to peak in their 40s and then drop considerably after their 50s. While data from these longitudinal studies are impressive, most suffer from significant methodological problems: (a) Most have surveyed general or nonrepresentative populations (e.g., antisocial young males), (b) none has included diagnosed or treated alcohol abusers, (c) definitions of *problem drinking* vary from study to study, and (d) none has explored the reasons people cease problem drinking (Fillmore, 1988).

Since the present study had a large sample of diagnosed alcohol abusers who had reported long-term natural recoveries, we decided that conducting life-span analyses of the data could serve as an important vehicle for hypothesis testing (e.g., Do most natural recoveries occur during young adulthood?) as well as for generating hypotheses (e.g., Are different factors associated with recoveries in different age groups?). The study has two phases: an initial interview and a follow-up interview with all subjects and their respective collaterals at least five years after the first interview. This chapter focuses on data from the first phase, specifically, data examining the recovery process from a life-span perspective. The first phase had two major objectives: to identify factors antecedent to and associated with (i.e., maintenance) the successful resolution of alcohol problems without treatment. As we have reported these results elsewhere (Sobell, Sobell, Toneatto, & Leo, in press), they will not be repeated here. Rather, in this chapter we will investigate the study's original objectives further by categorizing subjects by age at recovery (random target year for nonresolved control subjects) and examining patterns of resolution across the life span.

Experimental Design and Method

The conduct of this study was approved by a joint Addiction Research Foundation/University of Toronto Ethics Committee. We have described the subject selection process and recruitment strategies in considerable detail in two earlier reports (Sobell et al., 1992, in press), so only a few major points will be repeated here. All subjects were recruited through various media advertisements, a strategy that has been successful in other natural recovery studies with drug and alcohol abusers (Biernacki, 1990; Klingemann, 1991; Ludwig, 1985; Stall, 1983; Tuchfeld, 1981; Tucker, Vuchinich, Gladsjo, Hawkins, & Sherrill, 1989). The key wording of the advertisements for resolved subjects read: "Have you successfully overcome a drinking problem without formal treatment?" Interestingly, some individuals who responded to these advertisements reported that they had received treatment in the past, but that they attributed their recoveries to themselves and not to treatment. Similar responses were reported in a study examining the natural recoveries of alcohol and heroin abusers (Klingemann, 1991). Because we felt that unsuccessfully treated subjects who later resolved their problems on their own would provide an interesting comparison group, we included these subjects as a separate group in the design of the study (as resolved abstinent treatment, or RAT, subjects). The key wording of the advertisements for the control subjects (nontreated, nonresolved) asked for "anyone who presently feels that they have a drinking problem, but who has never received any formal treatment." The advertisement also stated that participation in a treatment program was not required, but that participation in the study "could provide valuable information which may help to plan treatment for people who have similar problems and desire treatment."

Subjects were screened by phone and, if eligible, sent a short questionnaire containing demographic and alcohol-related history questions, the Michigan Alcoholism Screening Test (MAST; Selzer, Vinokur, & van Rooijen, 1975), an introductory letter explaining the study, an initial consent form giving the interviewers permission to schedule an interview with the subject, and a stamped self-addressed envelope. More than 75% of all questionnaires mailed out were returned, a very respectable rate for mailed questionnaires. Of the respondents returning questionnaires, about half were eligible to be interviewed. Finally, of the subjects initially interviewed, about 20% were ineligible (e.g., unwilling to provide a collateral who could be interviewed).

Inclusion criteria for all subjects were as follows: (a) signing an informed consent; (b) providing at least one collateral who was willing to be interviewed and who could corroborate the subject's drinking history and resolution; (c) no history of formal treatment or help for alcohol problems, except for resolved abstinent treatment subjects (for a complete description of how "formal treatment or help" was defined, see Sobell et al., 1992); (d) alcohol free when interviewed (Sobell & Sobell, 1975); and (e) a MAST score of ≥ 5, which is suggestive of having had an alcohol problem at some time (Selzer, 1971).

Study Design

A detailed description of the study design and interview format have been reported elsewhere (Sobell et al., 1992). Although in this chapter we present data by age cohorts rather than by the original four subject groups, it is important to understand the criteria by which the 182 subjects were originally assigned to their respective groups:

(1) The 71 *resolved abstinent* (RA) subjects had resolved their drinking problems on their own through abstinence and had to have been recovered for 3 or more years.

(2) The 21 *resolved nonabstinent* (RNA) subjects had resolved their drinking problems on their own, and any drinking after their resolutions had to meet explicit criteria as nonhazardous and without evidence of alcohol-related problems (for detailed criteria, see Sobell et al., 1992). These subjects also had to have been recovered for a minimum of 3 years.

(3) The 28 *resolved abstinent treatment* (RAT) subjects responded to the same media solicitations as the first two groups and reported that although they had received formal help or treatment, they found it not to be helpful and later resolved their drinking problems on their own through abstinence. The minimum resolution length for this group was one year.

(4) The 62 *nonresolved, nontreated* (NR) subjects had to have had drinking problems for a minimum of 5 years when interviewed and could not have received previous help or treatment for their drinking problems.

The life-span analyses involved three age cohorts: 20 to 35, 36 to 50, and 51 to 65+ (only one subject's resolution occurred after age 65). These intervals were chosen because they represent fairly typical life-course distinctions (i.e., young adult, middle age, late life; e.g., see Fillmore, 1988). For resolved subjects, the age category reflects *age at the time of resolution*; for nonresolved control subjects, it represents *age during the random target year*.

There were sufficient numbers of resolved and nonresolved subjects in each age cohort to allow meaningful statistical comparisons. Data for the three resolved groups (RA, RNA, RAT) are combined in the present chapter for two reasons. First, the percentage of subjects in the original three resolved groups did not differ significantly across the three age cohorts ($\chi^2 = 1.5$, df = 4, $p > .05$). Second, the three resolved groups were similar in terms of demographic variables (Sobell et al., 1992) and reports of life events preceding and factors in maintaining their recoveries (Sobell et al., in press). The percentages of resolved and non-resolved subjects did not differ significantly across the three age groups ($\chi^2 = 2.3$, df = 2, $p > .05$).

Data Analysis

Although log-linear models provide several advantages over chi-square tests of independence, the application of this method has been more common in fields other than psychology (e.g., sociology, biostatistics). One major advantage of log-linear models is their ability to analyze data from multiway cross-classification tables, particularly three-way and higher interactions. Used in this way, log-linear modeling "becomes much like the flexible model-testing approaches of analysis of variance and multiple regression. The contribution of each variable to the estimated expected frequencies, and the contributions of the association among variables, can be assessed precisely" (Green, 1988, p. 5).

Multiway cross-classification tables were analyzed using the SPSSX hierarchical log-linear technique with backwards elimination. There is no dependent variable in this type of analysis. The overall models were assessed using the chi-square likelihood ratio goodness-of-fit test (G^2). Chi-square (G^2) values that are high ($p < .05$) indicate that the model does not fit the data adequately (i.e., the expected frequencies are significantly different from the observed frequencies). For log-linear models that fit the observed data adequately, the chi-square value is low ($p > .05$). (For an introductory explanation to log-linear analysis of cross-classification tables, including tables with nominal and ordinal variables, see Green, 1988.)

The interactions (two-way and higher) selected within each log-linear model can be interpreted in a manner analogous to chi-square tests of independence. As with the chi-square test of independence, a significant interaction means that the null hypothesis (i.e., two variables are independent) can be rejected. In log-linear models, the significance level reported along with each interaction is the observed significance level for the change that would occur in the overall likelihood ratio chi-square (for the log-linear model) if that interaction were removed. Higher (more significant) chi-square values indicate that the interactions are more necessary in the model in order to describe the observed data adequately.

Interviews

Several trained interviewers conducted the interviews. All subject interviews were conducted in person and tape-recorded. With few exceptions, collateral interviews were conducted by telephone (96.2%, 175/182). The subjects were not reimbursed for their interviews, but collaterals were offered $10 for their participation.

Subject and collateral interviews were intensive, employed several data-gathering techniques, and covered multiple topics related to alcohol problems and recovery. We have described all questionnaires and interview formats in detail in two other reports (Sobell et al., 1992, in press), so only questionnaires relevant to this chapter are described below:

(1) *Drinking data* were collected using a modified version of the Lifetime Drinking History questionnaire (LDH; Skinner & Sheu, 1982; Sobell et al., 1988).

(2) *Life events* were obtained for the 12 months prior to the subjects' resolutions (12 months prior to the target year for NR subjects) using the Recent Life Change Questionnaire (RLCQ; Rahe, 1975). All reported events were probed along several dimensions (e.g., effect on life, importance). Subjects were also provided an opportunity to report events not on the RLCQ.

(3) *Alcohol-related consequences* (5 dependence-related consequences, e.g., hallucinations, delirium tremens; 11 psychosocial consequences, e.g., legal, marital) were assessed using a consequence list previously used in a major alcoholism treatment study (Polich, Armor, & Braiker, 1981).

(4) *Postresolution drinking and consequence data* were obtained for RNA subjects from the date of recovery to the date of the interview.

(5) *An open-ended interview* probed factors reported as helping subjects maintain their resolutions within the first 12 months after recovery as well as factors that hindered subjects from seeking treatment.

Owing to the study's design, interviews with resolved subjects and with their collaterals were significantly longer than interviews with their nonresolved counterparts ($F[1, 176] = 40.8$, $p < .001$; $F[1, 176] = 21.8$, $p < .001$, respectively). Interviews with resolved subjects averaged slightly more than 2 hours; those with their respective collaterals, about one hour. Respective interviews with nonresolved subjects and their collaterals were slightly shorter because questions about a resolution phase were not applicable. Based on the observed data, more nonresolved (66.1%) than resolved (50.0%) subjects chose to be interviewed at the Addiction Research Foundation. Across all subjects, 77.5% responded to newspaper advertisements, with the remainder coming from other media solicitations (i.e., cable TV, radio). For both resolved and nonresolved subjects, the majority of collaterals were spouses.

Comparison of Subject and Collateral Reports

In the present study, a collateral was asked to confirm each subject's drinking problem and recovery. Subjects' and collaterals' reports of the subjects' resolution dates as well as the reason(s) for the resolutions were found to be in close agreement; 80.8% (97/120) reported the same resolution date (month and year), and 96.7% (116/120) of collaterals confirmed their subjects' resolution dates within one year (mean [*SD*] months different = 8.5 [10.4]). The vast majority (85.8%) of collaterals reported being "fairly sure" of the dates they reported for the subjects' resolutions. Further, 80.0% (96/120) of subject-collateral pairs gave similar reasons for the subjects' resolutions, 14.2% gave different reasons, and 5.8% of the collaterals had no idea why the subjects resolved their drinking problems. These data suggest that the subjects' reports of the dates and reasons for their resolutions can be given considerable credibility.

Subjects' and collaterals' reports of various aspects of the subjects' drinking were compared for resolved and nonresolved subject-collateral pairs for which there were complete data. Paired (two-tailed) *t* tests indicated that nonresolved subjects' and collaterals' reports (*n* = 56) for mean years problem drinking did not differ significantly (*t*[55] = .09, *p* = .93). Although the difference between the resolved subjects' and their respective collaterals' reports (*n* = 108) was significant (*t*[107] = 2.60, *p* = .01), both reported substantially long drinking problem histories (13.4 years and 11.3 years, respectively). Correlations for this variable for nonresolved (*r* = .45, *p* < .001) and resolved (*r* = .47, *p* < .001) subject-collateral pairs were significant.

There was also good agreement between subjects' and collaterals' reports of the subjects' drinking for percentage of days drinking and mean drinks per drinking day during the 6 years preresolution. For both drinking variables, paired (two-tailed) *t* tests indicated that nonresolved subjects' and collaterals' reports did not differ significantly (*t*[55] = −.92, *p* = .36, and *t*[51] = 1.10, *p* = .28, respectively). For resolved subject-collateral pairs, only their reports of mean drinks per drinking day were significantly different (mean drinks per drinking day, *t*[101] = 2.87, *p* < .01; percentage of days drinking, *t*[110] = 1.12, *p* = .27). Despite a significant difference between subject and collateral reports of mean drinks per drinking day preresolution, both reports were high (subjects = 14.1; collaterals = 11.7). All correlations for nonresolved and resolved subject-collateral pairs for percentage of days drinking preresolution (*r* = .57, *p* < .001, and *r* = .63, *p* < .001, respectively) and mean drinks per drinking day preresolution (*r* = .43, *p* < .01, and *r* = .51, *p* < .001, respectively) were significant.

For the RNA group there was also good agreement between subjects' and collaterals' reports ($n = 18$) of the subjects' *postresolution* drinking for percentage of drinking days and mean drinks per drinking day. Paired (two-tailed) t tests indicated that for number of days drinking in the postresolution period, subjects' and collaterals' reports did not differ significantly ($t[17] = .16$, $p = .88$). Although the correlation for this variable was not significant ($r = .10$, $p = .63$), the scatter plot suggests that the lack of a significant correlation might be related to four very discrepant outliers (e.g., subject reported 2,400 days and collateral reported 176 days; subject reported 10 days and collateral reported 968 days). For mean drinks per drinking day in the postresolution period, there was a significant difference between subjects' reports and their respective collaterals' reports ($t[17] = -2.43$, $p = .03$), with subjects reporting an average of one fewer drink per drinking day than their collaterals (2.1 and 3.0, respectively). Although subjects' and collaterals' reports of postresolution mean drinks per drinking day differed significantly, their reports were significantly correlated ($r = .72$ $p < .001$).

Results and Discussion

For parametrically scaled variables, 3×2 (age cohort $\times$ resolution type) analyses of variance (ANOVAs) were performed, and for nonparametric variables log-linear models were used to determine likelihood ratio chi-square (G^2) changes. Because of the large number of analyses, only significant findings will be discussed.

Demographic and Alcohol-Related History Variables

Table 2.1 displays demographic and alcohol-related history variables for resolved and nonresolved subjects across the three age cohorts. The majority of subjects in all three age groups were males, had high school education, and at the time of resolution were married and employed.

The log-linear model that best fits the data for the cross-classification table of sex by age cohort by resolution type had a likelihood ratio chi-square (G^2) of 4.3 (df = 5, $p = .50$). This model had one significant interaction (age by sex: G^2 change = 6.4 [df = 2, $p = .04$]). From the observed data it appears that a higher percentage of males are in the

TABLE 2.1 Percentages, Means, and Standard Deviations for Demographic and Drinking History Variables by Age Cohort for Resolved and Nonresolved Subjects

| | Age Cohort (years) | | | | | | Likelihood Ratio |
| | 20-35 | | 36-50 | | 51-65+ | | Chi-Square (G^2) |
Variable	Resolved (n = 37)	Nonresolved (n = 26)	Resolved (n = 55)	Nonresolved (n = 23)	Resolved (n = 28)	Nonresolved (n = 13)	Statistic or Main Effect
% male	73.0	61.5	87.3	82.6	71.4	84.6	Sex × A[a]
% employed at resolve[b,c]	77.8[d]	96.2	75.0[d]	100.0	68.0[d]	92.3	A***R**
% married at resolve[b]	60.0	61.5	79.2	63.6	72.0	84.6	
Mean (SD) age at resolve[b]	30.4 (3.3)	27.6 (3.9)	43.3 (4.3)	42.0 (4.3)	57.1 (5.2)	55.7 (4.1)	A***R**
Mean (SD) years of education	12.7 (2.3)	12.8 (2.5)	11.5 (2.8)	12.1 (2.3)	11.8 (2.7)	12.8 (3.4)	
Mean (SD) weighted MAST score	24.9 (8.3)	20.8 (8.6)	25.9[e] (11.1)	18.0 (6.3)	20.8[f] (11.5)	15.8 (6.4)	R**
Mean (SD) years problem drinking	8.2 (3.6)	11.1 (4.4)	15.2 (6.9)	14.8 (7.3)	15.7 (10.4)	19.7 (12.8)	A**
Mean (SD) age problem drinking began	22.2 (4.2)	16.5 (4.4)	28.1 (7.6)	27.2 (9.0)	41.5 (10.5)	36.0 (12.6)	R**A***

NOTE: Symbols in chi-square or main effect column indicate main effects or interactions that reached statistical significance in 3 × 2 (age cohort × resolution type) analysis of variance or log-linear analysis of cross-classification tables. A = age cohort; R = resolution type.
a. Sex × age: G^2 change, $p = .04$.
b. Nonresolved subjects = 6 years prior to their random target date.
c. Log-linear models not determinable as more than 20% of the cells have expected frequencies of < 5.
d. 20-35: n = 36; 36-50: n = 52; 51-65+: n = 25.
e. n = 54.
f. n = 27.
*$p < .05$; **$p < .01$; ***$p < .001$.

44

middle age (36 to 50 years) cohort. For age at resolution, there were significant main effects for age cohort ($F[2, 176] = 488.1, p < .001$) and resolution type ($F[1, 176] = 7.4, p < .01$). For both variables, Scheffé post hoc paired comparisons showed that all three groups differed significantly ($p < .05$) from one another. This, however, is an artifact of the age cohort classification criteria. Resolved subjects were slightly older than nonresolved subjects.

MAST scores provide one indication of the severity of subjects' alcohol problems. A score of ≥ 5 is suggestive of an alcohol problem. Across the groups the mean weighted MAST scores ranged from 16 to 26. Although a 3 (age cohort) × 2 (resolution type) ANOVA found no significant differences across the three age cohorts, there was a significant main effect for resolution type ($F[1, 174] = 13.1, p < .001$); resolved subjects had higher MAST scores than did nonresolved subjects. As the MAST is a lifetime measure of alcohol impairment, and given that the nonresolved subjects still had a drinking problem at the time of the interview, their MAST scores could increase over time.

The mean length of time subjects in the six groups reported having alcohol problems ranged from 8 to 20 years. A 3 (age cohort) × 2 (resolution type) ANOVA revealed a significant main effect for age ($F[2, 176] = 15.4, p < .001$). Scheffé post hoc comparisons revealed that subjects in the younger age group reported significantly ($p < .05$) shorter drinking problem histories than did subjects in the other two groups. This was expected; however, what was unexpected was that the two oldest age groups reported similar-length problem drinking histories. If the onset of most drinking problems occurs during the late teens or early 20s, then subjects in the oldest age group should have had longer problem drinking histories. Fortunately, the reported mean ages when drinking problems began shed some light on this finding. For this variable there were two significant main effects. For resolution type ($F[1, 176] = 9.9, p < .01$), subjects in the resolved groups reported that their drinking problems developed at significantly older ages compared with subjects in the nonresolved groups. For each age cohort ($F[2, 176] = 69.0, p < .001$), drinking problems developed about a decade apart. Scheffé post hoc comparisons revealed that for age of problem onset, all three groups differed significantly ($p < .05$) from each other. For resolved and nonresolved subjects by age cohort, respectively, the mean age when drinking problems began was (a) youngest age cohort, 22 and 17; (b) middle age cohort, 28 and 27; and (c) oldest age cohort, 42 and 36. These data suggest that not all alcohol abusers develop alcohol problems in their early 20s. For those subjects who resolved their problems after age 50, the drinking problem had a very late onset—on average it developed almost two decades after the average onset age for the youngest age group. These data are consistent with several other reports showing that onset of drinking problems in middle age is not an isolated phenomenon (Atkinson, Tolson, & Turner, 1990; Atkinson, Turner, Kofoed, & Tolson, 1985; Brennan & Moos, 1991; Fillmore, 1974; Stall, 1987; see also Sobell & Sobell, Chapter 6, this volume).

Drinking Problem Severity

The severity of a person's drinking can be assessed in several ways (Davidson, 1987; Polich & Kaelber, 1985). In the present study, the severity of subjects' preresolution drinking was examined in three ways: (a) alcohol-related consequences (i.e., problems associated with a person's drinking), (b) severity of dependence (i.e., percentage diagnosed by DSM-III-R criteria as alcohol dependent and percentage classified as having high, low, or no dependence symptoms), and (c) extent of preresolution drinking in the six years prior to the resolution (i.e., quantity, frequency, drinks per drinking day, longest number of consecutive abstinent days).

Alcohol-related consequences. Table 2.2 displays means and standard deviations for preresolution consequences and dependence symptoms by age cohort for resolved and nonresolved subjects. Consequences were examined in three ways: (a) all consequences ($n = 16$), (b) dependence-related consequences only ($n = 5$), and (c) nondependence consequences only ($n = 11$). Across the six groups, subjects reported experiencing an average of seven to nine consequences. Across all three consequence categories, only one significant main effect occurred (resolution type × dependence consequences: $F[1, 176] = 8.4$, $p < .01$). Subjects in the resolved groups reported significantly more dependence-related consequences than did their nonresolved counterparts. Given that the nonresolved subjects had active drinking problems when interviewed, it is likely that as their drinking continues some subjects will experience more dependence consequences. This will be examined in the second phase of the study, when subjects are followed up five years after their first interviews.

Dependence symptoms. The severity of subjects' drinking problems was evaluated using the criteria found in the *Diagnostic and Statistical Manual of Mental Disorders* (DSM-III-R; American Psychiatric Association, 1987).

TABLE 2.2 Percentages, Means, and Standard Deviations for Preresolution Dependence Consequences and Symptoms by Age Cohort for Resolved and Nonresolved Subjects

| | Age Cohort (years) | | | | | | Main Effect |
| | 20-35 | | 36-50 | | 51-65+ | | |
Variable	Resolved (n = 37)	Nonresolved (n = 26)	Resolved (n = 55)	Nonresolved (n = 23)	Resolved (n = 28)	Nonresolved (n = 13)	
Mean (SD) all consequences (n = 16)	9.1 (2.1)	7.9 (2.4)	8.5 (2.9)	7.9 (2.8)	7.5 (2.7)	7.2 (2.2)	
Mean (SD) dependence consequences (n = 5)	1.8 (1.0)	1.3 (0.8)	1.8 (1.0)	1.3 (1.2)	1.5 (0.8)	1.2 (0.7)	R**
Mean (SD) nondependence consequences (n = 11)	7.4 (1.7)	6.6 (1.9)	6.6 (2.2)	6.5 (1.8)	6.0 (2.3)	6.1 (1.8)	
% high dependence symptoms[a,b]	27.0	15.4	29.1	17.4	14.3	0.0	
% low dependence symptoms[a,b]	67.6	69.2	63.6	56.5	78.6	84.6	
% no dependence symptoms[a,b]	5.4	15.4	7.3	26.1	7.1	15.4	
% DSM-III-R alcohol dependence diagnosis[b]	100.0	92.3	100.0	95.7	92.9	84.6	

NOTE: Symbols in main effect column indicate main effects or interactions that reached statistical significance in the 3 × 2 (age cohort × resolution type) analysis of variance. R = resolution type.
a. High dependence = seizures, delirium tremens, and/or auditory/visual hallucinations; low dependence = none of the above, but relief drinking and/or psychomotor agitation (shakes); not dependent = none of the high or low dependence symptoms.
b. Log-linear models not determinable as more than 20% of cells have expected frequencies of < 5.
**p < .01.

47

As shown in Table 2.2, almost all subjects (96.2%, 175/182) met the DSM-III-R criteria for alcohol dependence. Subjects were further grouped by dependence symptoms: (a) *high dependence* (i.e., seizures, delirium tremens, and/or hallucinations), (b) *low dependence* (i.e., no high dependence symptoms, but relief drinking and/or psychomotor agitation upon stopping drinking), and (c) *no dependence symptoms*. Log-linear models for cross-classification tables for dependence symptoms and the DSM-III-R diagnosis were not determinable (more than 20% of cells had expected frequencies of < 5). Only one fifth (21%) of all subjects reported experiencing serious dependence symptoms, with about two thirds (68%) reporting low dependence symptoms only. The percentage of subjects with high dependence symptoms was lower than would normally be expected of individuals seeking treatment for alcohol problems.

Preresolution drinking. Drinking data for the resolved groups were examined for the 6 years prior to the subjects' resolution dates (6 years prior to the randomly target year for NR subjects). Table 2.3 displays mean drinks per drinking day, mean longest number of consecutive abstinent days, and mean percentage of days drinking for the 6 years prior to the resolution or target date by age cohort for resolved and nonresolved subjects. Prior to their resolutions, subjects reported drinking very frequently, on average at least 70% of all days (with one exception), and quite heavily, an average of 7 to 16 standard drinks per drinking day (1 standard drink = 13.6 g of absolute ethanol). Given the high frequency of drinking days, subjects' mean longest abstinent period in the 6 years prior to resolution was quite short (means ranged from 2 to 8 weeks).

A significant main effect for age cohort was found for number of drinking days ($F[2, 176] = 3.8, p = .03$). Scheffé post hoc comparisons revealed that the youngest group had significantly ($p < .05$) fewer drinking days in the 6-year period compared with the middle age group. For drinks per drinking day, there was a significant main effect for resolution type ($F[1, 176] = 22.0, p < .001$) and a significant age cohort by resolution type interaction ($F[2, 176] = 3.0, p = .05$). The resolved subjects reported drinking more drinks per drinking day than their nonresolved counterparts. Scheffé post hoc tests probing the significant interaction found three significant pairwise comparisons. The resolved subjects in the middle and older age cohorts reported consuming significantly more drinks per drinking day than did their nonresolved counterparts ($p < .001$ and $p = .02$, respectively). The third significant pairwise comparison revealed that resolved subjects in the youngest age

TABLE 2.3 Means and Standard Deviations for Drinking Six Years Prior to the Resolution by Age Cohort for Resolved and Nonresolved Subjects

| | Age Cohort (years) | | | | | | |
| | 20-35 | | 36-50 | | 51-65+ | | |
Variable	Resolved (n = 37)	Nonresolved[a] (n = 26)	Resolved (n = 55)	Nonresolved[a] (n = 23)	Resolved (n = 28)	Nonresolved[a] (n = 13)	Main Effect
Mean (SD) drinks/drinking day	11.8 (6.1)	9.4 (5.2)	15.8 (9.9)	6.6 (3.0)	13.2 (10.0)	7.0 (4.5)	R***I*
Mean (SD) longest consecutive abstinent days	55.9 (155.2)	12.1 (47.6)	28.1 (82.3)	41.7 (151.8)	27.3 (55.1)	16.2 (49.9)	
Mean (SD) % days drinking[b]	75.6	62.0	81.7	79.6	77.3	71.0	A*

NOTE: Symbols in main effect column indicate main effects or interactions that reached statistical significance in the 3 × 2 (age cohort × resolution type) analysis of variance. A = age cohort; R = resolution type; I = interaction.
a. For nonresolved subjects data are for the six years prior to their target date.
b. Out of 2,160 days in the six-year interval.
*p < .05; ***p < .001.

cohort drank significantly ($p = .02$) less than resolved subjects in the middle age cohort.

Postresolution Drinking

While subjects in two (RA, RAT) of the three groups resolved their drinking problems through abstinence, those in one group (RNA) resolved their drinking problems by drinking moderately without negative consequences. The postresolution drinking of the RNA subjects has been presented in detail in an earlier report (Sobell et al., 1992), and so only major features of that group's postresolution drinking will be discussed here.

All RNA subjects had to have minimum 3-year resolutions, but their mean (SD) resolution length of 6.7 (3.6) years far exceeded this requirement. Their monthly average drinking had to be ≤ 5 standard drinks ($\le$ 68 g of absolute ethanol) per drinking day, and they could not have reported any adverse consequences related to their postresolution drinking. A collateral confirmed each subject's postresolution drinking and the absence of consequences. Some subjects reported isolated instances of drinking that slightly exceeded the criteria, but warranted classification as resolved. A complete description of these exceptions is available in Sobell et al. (1992).

Somewhat surprisingly, 57% (12/21) of RNA subjects began their resolutions with an extended abstinence period (mean = 22.6 months; range = 3-68 months; median = 12 months). There was a dramatic pre-postresolution change in the type of beverage consumed, primarily involving reduced use of hard liquor and increased use of wine postresolution.

When subjects' postresolution drinking patterns were examined, with one exception (one subject had a holiday drinking pattern that did not meet the criteria) two drinking patterns emerged. The first, labeled *functionally abstinent,* was defined as drinking less than once a month, experiencing no adverse consequences, and consuming no more than 2 drinks per occasion. It characterized 42.9% (9/21) of the RNA subjects. The second pattern, displayed by about half of the subjects (52.4%, 11/21), was labeled *low ethanol consumption* and involved consumption of ≤ 5 drinks per occasion with no adverse consequences.

Because it has been shown that as people grow older their drinking decreases (e.g., Fillmore, 1988), we decided to examine RNA subjects' postresolution drinking as a function of age at resolution. The same age cohorts as those used throughout this study were used in these analyses.

There were no significant differences for drinks per drinking day at either time interval (age at resolution, $F[2, 18] = 1.9$, $p > .05$; age at interview, $F[2, 18] = 1.0$, $p > .05$). One reason for the lack of significant findings might relate to most subjects' drinking at very low levels—more than 40% limited their consumption to the occasional celebratory drink.

While safe limits of consumption are not known, several studies suggest that protracted average daily consumption of between 60 and 80 g or more of absolute ethanol is associated with health risks (Babor, Kranzler, & Lauerman, 1987; Hilton, 1987; Klatsky, Friedman, Siegelaub, & Gerard, 1977; Kranzler, Dolinsky, & Kaplan, 1990; Rimm et al., 1991). All of the RNA subjects' postresolution drinking was well below levels conventionally considered to be hazardous. After these subjects' resolutions, their reports indicated that 76.2% (16/21) never drank more than 2 drinks per drinking day, 85.7% (18/21) never drank more than 3 drinks per drinking day, and 76.2% (16/21) never drank more than 6 days per month.

Life Events and Reasons for Resolutions

One of the major objectives of this study was to explore why people cease problem drinking without treatment. A standard life events checklist, the Recent Life Change Questionnaire (Rahe, 1975), was used to examine the relationship between life events and recovery. The RLCQ contains an overall life event scale that includes six subscales. For details relating to the administration of the RLCQ, readers are referred Sobell et al. (in press); we provide only a brief overview here.

Subjects were asked to use the RLCQ to report life events that occurred in the year before their resolutions (for NR subjects, in the year prior to the random target year). Each subject was asked to provide an in-depth explanation of each event, and to rate each event on four dimensions: (a) how the event *affected the subject's life* when it occurred, (b) how the event *affected the subject's drinking* when it occurred, (c) the *importance* of the event, and (d) whether the event was a *surprise* or had been *expected*. The life event interview was designed to be both "searching and structured," as several investigators have found that structured probes elicit more information about the nature of the events than do simple checklists (Brown & Harris, 1978, 1986; Dohrenwend, Link, Kern, Shrout, & Markowitz, 1987; Paykel, 1980, 1983).

The checklist was used initially to avoid asking subjects what triggered or contributed to their recoveries. Presumably, the reason(s) for the recoveries would emerge when subjects were queried about events that occurred in the year prior to recovery. After all life events that were originally checked on the RLCQ were probed, subjects were asked to report other events that had occurred in the year prior to their resolutions (target year for NR subjects) that were not on the checklist, but that might be related to the resolutions.

Because one of the goals of this chapter is to examine the hypothesis that resolution-related events would differ by age cohort, life events occurring in the year prior to the resolution were examined along several dimensions for resolved and nonresolved subjects across the three age cohorts. When the 79 life events on the RLCQ were examined for the original subject groups (RA, RNA, RAT, NR), no significant differences ($p > .05$) were observed between the groups for the overall RLCQ scale or its six subscales. However, when life events were examined across the life span (i.e., classifying subjects by their resolution dates into different age cohorts), differences among the three age groups emerged. Table 2.4 displays the means and standard deviations for life event scales and life event ratings by age cohort for resolved and nonresolved subjects. A main effect for age cohort was observed for the full RLCQ ($F[2, 176] = 19.7, p < .001$) as well as for four of the six subscales (Health, $F[2, 176] = 4.7, p = .01$; Work, $F[2, 176] = 10.4$, $p < .001$; Home, $F[2, 176] = 7.5, p < .001$; Personal/Social, $F[2, 176] = 16.7, p < .001$). Scheffé post hoc comparisons for each significant main effect revealed the same pattern: Subjects in the youngest group had significantly ($p < .05$) more life events compared with subjects in the older two groups. For the full scale score, subjects in the younger group reported an average of four to six more life events than did subjects in the two older groups.

These findings suggest that younger alcohol abusers, independent of resolving a drinking problem, experience more life events annually than do older alcohol abusers. More significantly, these results underscore the importance of a control group. Without this group, we might have erroneously concluded that younger alcohol abusers who resolve drinking problems experience more events than their older counterparts, when life events are simply a more frequent occurrence in the lives of younger alcohol abusers or perhaps younger people generally.

Only one of the four life event rating dimensions demonstrated any significant main effect. For the rating of whether the life event was a surprise or expected, two main effects were noted (age cohort, $F[2, 176] = 7.0, p < .001$; resolution type, $F[1, 176] = 9.4, p < .01$). Scheffé post

TABLE 2.4 Means and Standard Deviations for Life Events by Age Cohort for Resolved and Nonresolved Subjects

| | 20-35 | | | | 36-50 | | | | 51-65+ | | | | |
| | Resolved (n = 37) | | Nonresolved (n = 26) | | Resolved (n = 55) | | Nonresolved (n = 23) | | Resolved (n = 28) | | Nonresolved (n = 13) | | Main Effect |
Variable	M	SD	M	SD	M	SD	M	SD	M	SD	M	SD	
Life Events Scale (n)[a]													
Health (6)	1.9	1.5	1.4	1.5	1.1	1.3	1.0	1.3	1.2	1.1	0.6	0.9	A**
Work (18)	3.4	3.0	4.7	2.7	2.4	2.5	2.7	2.5	1.9	1.9	1.6	1.9	A***
Home (13)	1.7	1.5	1.8	1.6	1.1	1.4	1.1	1.3	0.9	1.0	0.5	0.7	A***
Marriage (17)	1.3	1.4	1.8	1.7	1.1	1.5	0.9	1.2	1.1	1.6	1.3	1.5	
Personal/Social (18)	4.2	2.3	5.2	3.1	3.1	2.4	2.5	1.8	2.4	1.7	2.2	1.1	A***
Financial (7)	1.4	1.1	1.6	1.5	1.3	1.2	1.2	1.0	0.7	0.8	1.5	1.0	
RLCQ (79)	13.9	7.0	16.5	7.5	10.0	6.4	9.5	4.9	8.2	4.5	7.7	3.4	A***
Additional Life Events													
(N = variable)	1.4	0.8	0.0	0.2	1.4	0.9	0.1	0.3	1.5	1.0	0.0	0.0	R***
Life Event Ratings													
drink impact effect	2.2	0.4	2.2	0.5	2.3	0.4	2.3	0.5	2.3	0.3	2.5	0.4	
life impact effect	2.0	0.5	1.9	0.4	1.9	0.5	1.8	0.4	1.8	0.5	1.7	0.4	
event importance rating	3.9	0.4	3.8	0.5	3.9	0.7	3.8	0.7	4.0	0.6	4.1	0.8	
surprise/expected evaluation	1.5	0.2	1.5	0.2	1.5	0.3	1.2	0.2	1.4	0.2	1.3	0.2	A***R**

NOTE: Symbols in main effect column indicate main effects or interactions that reached statistical significance in the 3 × 2 (age cohort × resolution type) analysis of variance. A = age cohort; R = resolution type.
a. Subscale and total scale scores on the Recent Life Change Questionnaire (RLCQ); n = number of subscale or scale items.
**$p < .01$; ***$p < .001$.

hoc comparisons indicated that the youngest subjects reported that they were significantly more surprised by the life events than did subjects in the oldest group. Also, resolved subjects described the life events they experienced as more of a surprise to them than did the nonresolved subjects.

As noted earlier, at the end of the RLCQ checklist, all subjects were asked to report other events or happenings that had occurred in the target year that were not on the checklist. While significant main effects for age were found for several life event subscales, reports of life events not on the checklist revealed a significant ($F[1, 176] = 134.7, p < .001$) main effect for resolution type. Resolved subjects, regardless of age cohort, reported significantly ($p < .001$) more additional life events than nonresolved subjects. As a group, nonresolved subjects reported virtually no extra life events (mean [SD] = 0.05 [0.22]), compared with a mean (SD) of 1.43 (0.88) additional life events reported by all resolved subjects. The question of what triggers subjects' recoveries from alcohol problems is currently being probed by content analyses of subjects' open-ended reports of the reasons for their resolutions.

Maintenance Factors

Besides the questions about variables antecedent to their resolutions, all resolved subjects were asked about factors that might have specifically helped them maintain their recoveries during the first 12 months postresolution. Table 2.5 displays, by age cohort, the percentages of subjects endorsing factors that were helpful for maintaining recovery during the first postresolution year. Of these 21 factors, 17 were adopted from Tuchfeld's (1976, 1981) study. The last 4 variables in Table 2.5 were idiosyncratically nominated by subjects, and thus were not asked of all subjects. Subjects were asked to rate the helpfulness of each endorsed factor on a 5-point scale (1 = no help, 3 = helped somewhat, 5 = helped very much) in terms of how it aided the maintenance of their recoveries.

For 7 of the 16 variables for which chi-square tests could be performed (chi-square tests were not determinable for five variables because more than 20% of the cells had expected frequencies of < 5), there were significant ($p < .05$) differences across the three age cohorts for the percentage of subjects endorsing each factor. For 5 of the 7 significant variables, the observed relationship revealed a greater percentage of younger subjects endorsing the factor as being helpful in maintaining recovery compared with subjects in the two older age groups. This trend occurred for almost three quarters (71.4%, 15/21) of all maintenance

TABLE 2.5 Percentage of Resolved Subjects by Age Cohort Endorsing Factors Helpful to Maintaining Their Recovery 1 to 12 Months Postresolution

Maintenance Factor	Age Cohort (years)			Helpfulness Rating of Endorsed Factors Across All Resolved Groups[a]	
	20-35 (n = 37)	36-50 (n = 55)	51-65+ (n = 28)	M	SD
Spouse support[b]	75.0	66.0	57.1	4.4	0.9
Family support	37.8	50.9	46.4	4.4	0.9
Friends support	62.2	50.9	35.7	3.9	1.1
Employer support	21.6	12.7	7.1	3.8	1.1
Change in friends[c]	54.1	38.2	10.7	4.3	0.8
Change in jobs	21.6	20.0	3.6	4.4	0.9
Religious influence	16.2	23.6	17.9	4.6	0.8
Social life activities change[c]	59.5	54.5	17.9	4.2	0.9
Recreational/leisure activities change[c]	64.9	40.0	28.6	4.1	1.0
Residence change[d]	18.9	10.9	7.1	4.2	1.1
Financial status change	24.3	25.5	17.9	4.0	1.2
Drug use change[d]	13.5	7.3	17.9	4.0	0.9
Change in diet[c]	51.4	30.9	14.3	3.9	0.9
Physical health change[c]	64.9	38.2	42.9	4.1	1.1
Smoking habits change[d]	24.3	7.3	7.1	3.9	1.1
Self-control/willpower change[c]	78.4	63.6	46.4	4.6	0.7
Major life-style change	45.9	36.4	21.4	4.4	1.0
Past drinking problems recalled[e]	24.3	18.2	14.3	4.4	0.9
Sense of accomplishment/ pride[c,e]	18.9	29.1	3.6	4.8	0.5
Gain respect/goal commitment[d,e]	10.8	9.1	3.6	4.8	0.6
AA/self-help[d,e]	13.5	5.5	0.0	2.9	1.5

a. Helpfulness ratings ranged from 1 to 5: 1 = no help, 3 = helped somewhat, 5 = helped very much.
b. Married subjects only: 20-35, $n = 28$; 36-50, $n = 50$; 51-65+, $n = 21$.
c. Significant ($p < .05$) chi-square tests.
d. Chi-square tests were not determinable as more than 20% of cells had expected frequencies of < 5.
e. These were additional factors nominated by subjects, and thus were not asked of all subjects.

factors. Prominent among factors reported by subjects in the younger group as helping them maintain their recoveries during the first 12 months were changes in social activities as well as receiving more support from friends and from their spouses. The younger group also reported experiencing more physical health and willpower changes that helped maintain their recoveries. In contrast, very few subjects in the older cohort reported these same factors as being helpful in maintaining recovery during their first postresolution year.

With one exception (i.e., AA/self-help), all endorsed maintenance factors were rated very highly. Finally, across all three age groups, spousal support was mentioned most frequently as helping subjects maintain recovery. This finding is consistent with the literature showing that social support or a positive family milieu is one of the strongest predictors of beneficial outcomes for alcohol abusers in treatment (Bromet & Moos, 1977; Ward, Bendel, & Lange, 1982) as well as for those who recover on their own (Stall, 1983; Tuchfeld, 1976, 1981).

Smoking and Drinking

Although the focus of the first phase of this study was on subjects' recovery from drinking problems, all subjects were asked a few questions about their smoking. Consistent with the findings of other studies, almost all (resolved = 91.7%; nonresolved = 91.9%) subjects had formerly smoked or were currently smoking cigarettes (Bobo, 1989; Kozlowski, Jelinek, & Pope, 1986; Sobell, Sobell, Kozlowski, & Toneatto, 1990; U.S. Department of Health and Human Services, 1988). By the first interview, however, more than half had stopped smoking (resolved = 55.5%; nonresolved = 35.1%). Table 2.6 displays the percentages, means, and standard deviations for smoking history variables for resolved and nonresolved subjects in each age cohort. For the percentage of subjects who had ever smoked, log-linear models were not determinable because more than 20% of cells had expected frequencies of < 5.

The log-linear model that best fits the data for the cross-classification table of smoking status at the interview by age cohort by resolution status had a G^2 of 3.6 (df = 4, p = .46). This model contains two, two-way interactions (age cohort $\times$ smoking status, G^2 change = 6.2 [df = 2, p < .05]; resolution type $\times$ smoking status, G^2 change = 6.3 [df = 1, p < .01]). Based on the observed data, it appears that a lower percentage of smokers in the youngest age cohort had quit prior to the first interview, and that a higher percentage of resolved than nonresolved subjects had quit smoking before the interview.

The smoking history of alcohol abusers in each age cohort who had quit smoking prior to the interview was examined for the number of years they reported smoking cigarettes, the number of cigarettes smoked

TABLE 2.6 Percentages, Means, and Standard Deviations for Smoking History Variables by Age Cohort for Resolved and Nonresolved Subjects

| | Age Cohort (years) | | | | | | Likelihood Ratio Chi-Square (G^2) Statistic or Main Effect |
| | 20-35 | | 36-50 | | 51-65+ | | |
Variable	Resolved ($n = 37$)	Nonresolved ($n = 26$)	Resolved ($n = 55$)	Nonresolved ($n = 23$)	Resolved ($n = 28$)	Nonresolved ($n = 13$)	
% (n) ever smoked cigarettes[a]	86.5 (32)	92.3 (24)	94.5 (52)	91.3 (21)	92.9 (26)	92.3 (12)	Smoking × A[b]
% (n) smokers who quit before the interview	43.8 (14)	25.0 (6)	59.6 (31)	52.4 (11)	61.5 (16)	25.0 (3)	Smoking × R[c]
Mean (SD) years smoked cigarettes[d]	14.1 (4.7)	9.0 (5.9)	24.5 (12.3)	27.5 (9.2)	29.7 (14.7)	24.5 (19.9)	A***
Mean (SD) number cigarettes smoked per day[d]	37.6 (14.6)	21.8 (13.9)	38.9 (21.4)	32.3 (14.2)	32.4 (18.7)	39.2 (10.1)	A*
Mean (SD) years quit smoking[d]	5.9 (4.3)	8.0 (5.4)	11.9 (10.5)	8.1 (6.2)	14.2 (11.6)	18.3 (11.1)	
Mean (SD) age began smoking[d]	16.6 (3.5)	17.8 (3.1)	16.6 (5.5)	16.3 (3.9)	19.9 (8.9)	20.8 (8.0)	

NOTE: Symbols in chi-square or main effect column indicate main effects or interactions that reached statistical significance in the 3 × 2 (age cohort × resolution type) analysis of variance or log-linear analysis of cross-classification tables. A = age cohort; R = resolution type.
a. Log-linear models not determinable as more than 20% of cells have expected frequencies of < 5.
b. Age × smoking status: G^2 change, $p < .05$.
c. Resolution × smoking status: G^2 change, $p < .01$.
d. Sample size (n): resolved, 20-35 = 14, 36-50 = 31, 51-65+ = 16; nonresolved, 20-35 = 6, 36-50 = 11, 51-65+ = 3.
*$p < .05$;   ***$p < .001$.

per day prior to quitting, the number of years since they had quit smoking cigarettes, and age when they first started smoking cigarettes. The amount of smoking reported by these subjects was considerable, averaging between one and two packs (i.e., 20 cigarettes per pack) per day prior to quitting. Across the three age cohorts, the average length of smoking resolution ranged from 6 to 14 years. For two of these variables there was a significant main effect for age cohort (years smoked cigarettes, $F[2, 75] = 9.8$, $p < .001$; years quit smoking, $F[2, 75] = 3.2$, $p = .05$). Scheffé post hoc comparisons indicated that subjects in the oldest age cohort had smoked for significantly ($p < .001$) more years than subjects in the youngest age group. This is not surprising, of course; the difference can be explained by the subjects' ages. For years quit smoking, the youngest group had stopped smoking significantly ($p < .05$) fewer years before than had the other two groups. Again, this was not unexpected, as the younger group had considerably less time to have been ex-smokers. However, despite shorter smoking histories, the number of cigarettes smoked per day by the younger subjects prior to quitting was not significantly ($p > .05$) different from the number smoked by their older counterparts. In contrast to the variable "age when drinking problem began," there were no significant main effects or interactions for the variable age when smoking began. Across the six groups, mean age when smoking began ranged from 16 to 21 years.

Reasons for Not Seeking Treatment

One major objective of this study was to determine why subjects never sought formal help or treatment for their alcohol problems. In the open-ended interview, three of the four subject groups ($n = 154$; RAT subjects were excluded) were asked why they had never sought formal help or treatment. Besides responding to 5 of 10 questions (see Table 2.7), subjects could offer additional reasons. For each reason, subjects were asked to indicate on a 5-point scale (1 = not at all, 3 = somewhat, 5 = very much affected or influenced) how much the reason affected or influenced the decision not to seek treatment. All additional reasons were coded by two raters into one of the 10 categories shown in Table 2.7. Discrepancies were resolved through discussion. Because multiple responses were coded, the percentages do not always sum to 100. Two of the five idiosyncratic reasons given, although not anticipated, were reported by sizable proportions of subjects (no problem perceived/no help needed/no need to seek help, 45.5%; wanted to handle problem on own, 37.7%).

Separate three-way cross-classification tables (reason endorsed [yes; no] × age cohort [20 to 35; 36 to 50; 51 to 65+] × resolution type [resolved; RA and RNA; nonresolved]) were conducted for each of the 10 reasons in Table 2.7. As only one chi-square (G^2) change was significant (stigma), the data in Table 2.7 were collapsed across age cohorts. Log-linear models for the last four variables in Table 2.7 were not determinable (because more than 20% of the cells had expected frequencies of < 5). The log-linear model that best fits the data for the cross-classification table for percentage of subjects that endorsed "stigma" by age cohort and resolution type had a G^2 of 8.4 (df = 5, p = .14). A significant interaction occurred for only one variable (stigma × age cohort, G^2 change = 7.7, df = 2, p = .02). From the observed data, it appears that stigma was more of a treatment barrier for the younger age cohort than for the two older age groups (20 to 35, 54.7% [29/53]; 36 to 50, 34.8% [23/66]; 51 to 65+, 40.0% [14/35]).

All 10 reasons for not seeking treatment had a mean influence rating of ≥ 4 (i.e., considerably to very much influenced or affected), suggesting that all endorsed reasons were quite influential in keeping subjects from seeking help or treatment for their drinking problems. When all reasons for not seeking treatment were summed for each subject, a significant main effect for age was found (F[2, 148] = 3.3, p = .04; age 20 to 35, resolved = 3.0 [1.2], nonresolved = 3.2 [1.3]; age 36 to 50, resolved = 2.1 [1.4], nonresolved = 3.0 [1.7]; age 51 to 65+, resolved = 2.5 [1.5], nonresolved = 2.2 [1.1]). Scheffé post hoc comparisons revealed that the youngest age cohort reported significantly more barriers to treatment than did the middle (p = .03) and oldest age cohorts (p = .01)

Summary and Conclusions

The present study was designed to address several major problems evident in previous studies of natural recovery from alcohol problems. It compared four groups of subjects—three different resolved groups and one nonresolved group. The first two reports of this study have presented the data in terms of group differences (Sobell et al., 1992, in press), but in this chapter the data were examined from a life-span perspective. The critical variable was the subject's age at the time of recovery.

Considering the number and types of variables examined, there were few age-related findings. Those findings that did emerge, however,

TABLE 2.7   Reasons for Not Seeking Treatment Across the Three Age Cohorts[a]

Reason	% Endorsing Reason (n)	Mean (SD) Rating of How Much the Reason Affected or Influenced Decision Not to Seek Treatment[b]
Embarrassment/pride[c]	47.4 (73)	4.1 (1.1)
No problem perceived/no help needed/no need to seek help	45.5 (70)	4.4 (1.0)[d]
Unable to share problems[c]	43.5 (67)	4.0 (0.9)
Stigma[c]	39.6 (61)	4.2 (1.0)
Wanted to handle problem on own	37.7 (58)	4.5 (1.0)[e]
Negative attitude toward treatment[c]	26.0 (40)	4.3 (0.9)[f]
Costs involved[c,g]	10.4 (16)	4.2 (0.8)
Ignorance of treatment or availability[g]	8.4 (13)	4.3 (1.0)
Barriers to treatment[g]	3.9 (6)	4.0 (1.1)
Other[g]	1.9 (3)	4.0 (1.0)

a. For 154 subjects for whom these questions were applicable (resolved abstinent, $n = 71$; resolved nonabstinent, $n = 21$; nonresolved, nontreated, $n = 62$). Because only one of the chi-square (G^2) changes was significant, the data for all reasons were collapsed across all subjects.
b. Rating scale values for how much the reason influenced or affected the subject's decision not to seek formal help or treatment: 1 = not at all, 2 = slightly, 3 = somewhat, 4 = considerably, 5 = very much. The ratings were collapsed across all subjects because, with one exception, there were no differences found by age category or resolution type (resolved, nonresolved) and a previous report (Sobell et al., in press) found no differences among the three different resolution groups (RA, RNA, NR).
c. These questions were asked of all subjects.
d. $n = 58$.
e. $n = 54$.
f. $n = 39$.
g. Log-linear models not determinable as more than 20% of cells had expected frequencies of < 5.

were quite striking. One interesting and surprising finding did not involve the resolution process. Rather, it related to the fact that many subjects in the older age cohort had middle-age problem onset and, consequently, shorter drinking problem histories. While this finding is consistent with several other reports showing that problem onset in middle age is not unusual, it contradicts clinical folklore that most alcohol abusers develop their problems in their teens or early 20s. In addressing this issue, Atkinson et al. (1990) recently asserted that despite the evidence, "for many years geriatricians and alcoholism specialists have been skeptical about the existence of late onset alcoholism" (p. 575). An excellent example of how the evidence has been ignored can be found in the DSM-III-R, which states, "In males, symptoms of Alcohol Dependence or Abuse rarely occur for the first time after age 45" (American Psychiatric Association, 1987, p. 174). In contrast, middle-age onset of smoking was not evident; almost all subjects reported starting smoking cigarettes in their late teens. Older subjects who quit smoking also had longer histories of smoking compared with their younger counterparts. Thus late problem onset appears to be substance specific, occurring for alcohol but not for nicotine.

Another significant age cohort finding was that younger subjects reported more factors as helping them maintain recovery during the first postresolution year than did subjects in the other two age groups. Overall, subjects in the oldest age cohort reported few factors as helping them maintain their recoveries. As expected, for all three age cohorts spousal support was the most frequently nominated maintenance factor.

Subjects in the youngest age cohort also differed significantly from the two older age cohorts in terms of reasons for not seeking treatment. Compared with the two older age cohorts, younger subjects not only reported more reasons for not seeking treatment, they also more often reported that the stigma of being labeled an alcoholic was a barrier to their seeking treatment. From an early intervention perspective, where the goal is to get alcohol abusers to seek treatment as early as possible, this finding is significant. It suggests that existing treatment services should consider offering alternatives to traditional services, because the latter are often perceived as being for chronic alcoholics (see Sobell & Sobell, Chapter 6, this volume).

Another important finding relates to the control group (nonresolved subjects). Specifically, while younger subjects reported experiencing more life events in the preresolution (or target) year, compared with their older counterparts, this applied to nonresolved as well as to resolved subjects. Thus the greater frequency of life events was simply related to younger subjects and not to resolution type. Further, there was no evidence relating life event type to age cohort. The use of the control group in studies of this nature cannot be overlooked—without this group erroneous conclusions about the importance and number of life events could have been drawn.

Finally, while it is possible that younger subjects endorsed more life events on the RLCQ because it contains a greater proportion of events that occur predominantly among younger people (e.g., marriage), this group also endorsed more reasons for not seeking treatment as well as more maintenance strategies than their older counterparts. In combination, these findings argue against a bias in the RLCQ and suggest that there are some real differences between younger and older people in terms of life-style. Younger alcohol abusers—or, more likely, younger people in general—probably experience more active (or less stable) life-styles than do older people (Finney & Moos, 1992). It is not that life events are less significant for older subjects; the importance ratings for life events did not differ across the age cohorts. Rather, younger people's lives appear to be characterized by more transitional events and turmoil.

Phase II: An Eye Toward the Future

The second phase of this study, in which subjects and their collaterals will be interviewed at least five years after their initial interviews, has the following objectives for resolved subjects: (a) to evaluate whether the subjects' natural recoveries have been maintained; (b) to evaluate whether subjects who had stopped smoking at the first interview have maintained their smoking resolution; (c) to examine the temporal ordering of and factors related to dual (alcohol and tobacco) resolutions, given that preliminary data from the first interviews suggest a possible relationship between stopping problem drinking and stopping smoking; and (d) to explore the interrelationships of multiple substance use and health-related changes, because the effects of stopping drinking on the use of other substances is unknown. For all subjects (resolved and nonresolved) there are two additional objectives: (a) to gather data on family history of alcohol problems and (b) to gather reports on how many people the subjects know who have recovered from alcohol problems on their own. Finally, the recovery rate of all subjects in the NR control group will be examined from the date of the first interview, and reasons for recoveries will be probed. Heather (1986) has suggested that simply responding to advertisements (i.e., to be interviewed, although not for a treatment project) is symbolic of a shift from contemplation to action in a stages of change model of recovery (DiClemente et al., 1991). Consistent with this hypothesis is the finding that in the present study 67.8% (42/62) of NR subjects inquired about treatment during the first interview, and of all the nonresolved subjects, 40.3% (25/62) requested and received some type of therapeutic intervention after their interviews (i.e., they received treatment at an addictions facility or were given self-help manuals; Sanchez-Craig, 1987).

Implications of This Research

Research on natural recovery or self-change from alcohol problems is a fertile area of investigation that is likely to yield considerable benefits for those in treatment as well as for those who will not seek services at existing alcohol treatment facilities. Findings from the present study are expected (a) to increase our understanding of the nature and stability of recoveries from alcohol problems; (b) to suggest reasons that health care services are underutilized by persons with alcohol problems; (c) to elucidate possible relationships between the successful resolution of drinking problems and the resolution of tobacco problems; (d) to provide direction for developing and testing new self-change interventions; and, specific to the life-span analyses, (e) to reduce barriers to treatment, particularly for younger alcohol abusers; and (f) to explore further how individuals who develop alcohol problems in middle life differ from those who develop such problems early in life and whether these populations require different interventions. A final, very important, long-term goal is to promote and accelerate natural recovery processes for individuals who are unwilling, unlikely, or not ready to enter formal treatment programs, but who wish to modify their drinking. Although research on natural recoveries from alcohol problems is in its infancy, it is clear that the addictions field has much to learn from the study of individuals who recover from drinking or other drug problems on their own.

References

American Psychiatric Association. (1987). *Diagnostic and statistical manual of mental disorders* (3rd ed., rev.). Washington, DC: Author.

Atkinson, R. M., Tolson, R. L., & Turner, J. A. (1990). Late versus early onset problem drinking in older men. *Alcoholism: Clinical and Experimental Research, 14,* 574-579.

Atkinson, R. M., Turner, J. A., Kofoed, L. L., & Tolson, R. L. (1985). Early versus late onset alcoholism in older persons: Preliminary findings. *Alcoholism: Clinical and Experimental Research, 9,* 513-515.

Babor, T. F., Kranzler, H. R., & Lauerman, R. J. (1987). Social drinking as a health and psychosocial risk factor: Anstie's limit revisited. In M. Galanter (Ed.), *Recent developments in alcoholism* (Vol. 5, pp. 373-402). New York: Plenum.

Biernacki, P. (1990). Recovery from opiate addiction without treatment: A summary. In E. Y. Lambert (Ed.), *The collection and interpretation of data from hidden popula-*

tions (NIDA Research Monograph 98) (pp. 113-119). Rockville, MD: National Institute on Drug Abuse.

Bobo, J. K. (1989). Nicotine dependence and alcoholism epidemiology and treatment. *Journal of Psychoactive Drugs, 21,* 323-329.

Brennan, P. L., & Moos, R. F. (1991). Functioning, life context, and help-seeking among late-onset problem drinkers: Comparison with nonproblem and early-onset problem drinkers. *British Journal of Addiction, 86,* 1139-1150.

Bromet, E., & Moos, R. H. (1977). Environmental resources and the posttreatment functioning of alcoholic patients. *Journal of Health and Social Behavior, 18,* 326-338.

Brown, G. W., & Harris, T. (1978). *Social origins of depression: A study of psychiatric disorder in women.* London: Tavistock.

Brown, G. W., & Harris, T. (1986). Establishing causal links: The Bedford College studies of depression. In H. Katschnig (Ed.), *Life events and psychiatric disorders: Controversial issues* (pp. 107-200). New York: Cambridge University Press.

Cahalan, D. (1970). *Problem drinkers: A national survey.* San Francisco: Jossey-Bass.

Cahalan, D., Cisin, I. H., & Crossley, H. M. (1969). *American drinking practices.* New Brunswick, NJ: Rutgers Center of Alcohol Studies.

Cahalan, D., & Room, R. (1974). *Problem drinking among American men.* New Brunswick, NJ: Rutgers Center of Alcohol Studies.

Davidson, R. (1987). Assessment of the alcohol dependence syndrome: A review of self-report screening questionnaires. *British Psychological Society, 26,* 243-255.

DiClemente, C. C., Prochaska, J. O., Fairhurst, S. K., Velicer, W. K., Velasquez, M. M., & Rossi, J. S. (1991). The process of smoking cessation: An analysis of precontemplation, contemplation, and preparation stages of change. *Journal of Consulting and Clinical Psychology, 59,* 295-304.

Dohrenwend, B. P., Link, B. G., Kern, R., Shrout, P. E., & Markowitz, J. (1987). Measuring life events: The problem of variability within event categories. In B. Cooper (Ed.), *Psychiatric epidemiology: Progress and prospects* (pp. 103-119). London: Croom Helm.

Fillmore, K. (1974). Drinking and problem drinking in early adulthood and middle age. *Quarterly Journal of Studies on Alcohol, 35,* 819-840.

Fillmore, K. M. (1988). *Alcohol use across the life course: A critical review of 70 years of international longitudinal research.* Toronto: Addiction Research Foundation.

Finney, J. W., & Moos, R. H. (1992). The long-term course of treated alcoholism: 2. Predictors and correlates of 10-year functioning and mortality. *Journal of Studies on Alcohol, 53,* 142-153.

Green, J. A. (1988). Loglinear analysis of cross-classified ordinal data: Applications in developmental research. *Child Development, 59,* 1-25.

Heather, N. (1986). Change without therapists: The use of self-help manuals by problem drinkers. In W. R. Miller & N. Heather (Eds.), *Treating addictive behaviors: Processes of change* (pp. 121-174). New York: Pergamon.

Hilton, M. (1987). Drinking patterns and drinking problems in 1984: Results from a general population survey. *Alcoholism: Clinical and Experimental Research, 11,* 167-175.

Institute of Medicine. (1990). *Broadening the base of treatment for alcohol problems.* Washington, DC: National Academy Press.

Klatsky, A. L., Friedman, G. D., Siegelaub, A. B., & Gerard, M. J. (1977). Alcohol consumption and blood pressure. *New England Journal of Medicine, 296,* 1194-1200.

Klingemann, H. K.-H. (1991). The motivation for change from problem alcohol and heroin use. *British Journal of Addiction, 86,* 727-744.

Kozlowski, L. T., Jelinek, L. C., & Pope, M. A. (1986). Cigarette smoking among alcohol abusers: A continuing and neglected problem. *Canadian Journal of Public Health, 77,* 205-207.

Kranzler, H. R., Dolinsky, Z., & Kaplan, R. F. (1990). Giving ethanol to alcoholics in a research setting: Its effect on compliance with disulfiram treatment. *British Journal of Addiction, 85,* 119-123.

Ludwig, A. M. (1985). Cognitive processes associated with "spontaneous" recovery from alcoholism. *Journal of Studies on Alcohol, 46,* 53-58.

Paykel, E. S. (1980). Recall and reporting of life events. *Archives of General Psychiatry, 37,* 485.

Paykel, E. S. (1983). Methodological aspects of life events research. *Journal of Psychosomatic Research, 27,* 341-352.

Polich, J. M., Armor, D. J., & Braiker, H. B. (1981). *The course of alcoholism: Four years after treatment.* New York: John Wiley.

Polich, J. M., & Kaelber, C. T. (1985). Sample surveys and the epidemiology of alcoholism. In M. A. Schuckit (Ed.), *Alcohol patterns and problems* (pp. 43-77). New Brunswick, NJ: Rutgers Center of Alcohol Studies.

Rahe, R. H. (1975). Epidemiological studies of life change and illness. *International Journal of Psychiatry in Medicine, 6,* 133-146.

Rimm, R. B., Giovannucci, E. L., Willett, W. C., Colditz, G. A., Ascherio, W. C., Rosner, B., & Stampfer, M. J. (1991). Prospective study of alcohol consumption and risk of coronary disease in men. *Lancet, 338,* 464-468.

Sanchez-Craig, M. (1987). *Dealing with drinking: Steps to abstinence or moderate drinking.* Toronto: Addiction Research Foundation.

Selzer, M. L. (1971). The Michigan Alcoholism Screening Test: The quest for a new diagnostics instrument. *American Journal of Psychiatry, 127,* 89-94.

Selzer, M. L., Vinokur, A., & van Rooijen, L. (1975). A self-administered Short Michigan Alcoholism Screening Test (SMAST). *Journal of Studies on Alcohol, 36,* 117-126.

Skinner, H. A., & Sheu, W. J. (1982). Reliability of alcohol use indices: The lifetime drinking history and the MAST. *Journal of Studies on Alcohol, 43,* 1157-1170.

Sobell, L. C., & Sobell, M. B. (1991, November). *Cognitive mediators of natural recoveries from alcohol problems: Implications for treatment.* Paper presented as part of a symposium, Therapies of Substance Abuse: A View Towards the Future, at the annual meeting of the Association for Advancement of Behavior Therapy, New York.

Sobell, L. C., Sobell, M. B., Kozlowski, L. T., & Toneatto, T. (1990). Alcohol or tobacco research versus alcohol and tobacco research. *British Journal of Addiction, 85,* 263-269.

Sobell, L. C., Sobell, M. B., Riley, D. M., Schuller, R., Pavan, D. S., Cancilla, A., Klajner, F., & Leo, G. I. (1988). The reliability of alcohol abusers' self-reports of drinking and life events that occurred in the distant past. *Journal of Studies on Alcohol, 49,* 225-232.

Sobell, L. C., Sobell, M. B., & Toneatto, T. (1992). Recovery from alcohol problems without treatment. In N. Heather, W. R. Miller, & J. Greeley (Eds.), *Self-control and the addictive behaviours* (pp. 198-242). Botany Bay, NSW, Australia: Maxwell Macmillan.

Sobell, L. C., Sobell, M. B., Toneatto, T., & Leo, G. I. (in press). What triggers the resolution of alcohol problems without treatment? *Alcoholism: Clinical and Experimental Research.*

Sobell, M. B., & Sobell, L. C. (1975). A brief technical report on the Mobat: An inexpensive portable test for determining blood alcohol concentration. *Journal of Applied Behavior Analysis, 8,* 117-120.

Stall, R. (1983). An examination of spontaneous remission from problem drinking in the bluegrass region of Kentucky. *Journal of Drug Issues, 13,* 191-206.

Stall, R. (1987). Research issues concerning alcohol consumption among aging populations. *Drug and Alcohol Dependence, 19,* 195-213.

Tuchfeld, B. S. (1976). *Changes in patterns of alcohol use without the aid of formal treatment: An exploratory study of former problem drinkers* (Final Report, Contract No. ADM 281-75-0023; RTI Project 24U-1158). Research Triangle Park, NC: Research Triangle Institute.

Tuchfeld, B. S. (1981). Spontaneous remission in alcoholics: Empirical observations and theoretical implications. *Journal of Studies on Alcohol, 42,* 626-641.

Tucker, J. A., Vuchinich, R. E., Gladsjo, J. A., Hawkins, J. L., & Sherrill, J. T. (1989, November). *Environmental influences on the natural resolution of alcohol problems without treatment.* Paper presented at a poster session at the annual meeting of the Association for the Advancement of Behavior Therapy, Washington, DC.

U.S. Department of Health and Human Services. (1988). *The health consequences of smoking: Nicotine addiction. A report of the Surgeon General* (DHHS Publication No. 88-8406). Washington, DC: Government Printing Office.

Ward, D. A., Bendel, R. B., & Lange, D. (1982). A reconsideration of environmental resources and the posttreatment functioning of alcoholic patients. *Journal of Health and Social Behavior, 23,* 310-317.

Zinberg, N. E., & Jacobson, R. C. (1976). The natural history of "chipping." *American Journal of Psychiatry, 133,* 37-40.

PART II

Models of Prevention and Early Intervention

3

Comparative Effects of Community-Based Drug Abuse Prevention

MARY ANN PENTZ

The face and substance of drug abuse prevention have changed dramatically in the past decade. Drug prevention programs, particularly those implemented in schools, are no longer considered isolated experiments confined to settings with drug problems (Johnson, 1986). Prevention programs are an acknowledged part of most schools' curricula, rather than a brief topic buried in a health education course (Connell, Turner, & Mason, 1985; Johnson, 1986). Programming is initiated before or during the years associated with gateway drug use onset, usually middle or junior high school, rather than after drug use is prevalent, in high school (Connell et al., 1985; Tobler, 1986). Coincidentally, an

AUTHOR'S NOTE: Preparation of this chapter was supported by Public Health Service Grant DA03976.

69

increasing number of programs are designed for continuous or at least periodic K-8 or K-12 implementation, rather than "one-shot" implementation in a single grade or class (Connell et al., 1985). Program content has changed from teaching what drugs look like and how they are used to training skills in how to avoid drug use and drug use situations (Battjes & Bell, 1985; Tobler, 1986). Methods of program delivery involve active social learning techniques of modeling, role playing, and discussion, often with student peer leaders assisting teachers or health educators, rather than teacher-delivered didactic instruction (Flay, 1986). Standardized training in prevention program theory, delivery methods, and drug use epidemiology has replaced the simple distribution of printed or audiovisual materials in most schools (Connell et al., 1985).

With these innovations, most of which have evolved from results of social psychological research on behavior change, drug prevention research, and epidemiological research on drug use development, it is no surprise that recent prevention programs show more promise for changing youthful drug use behavior than previously had been thought possible (Botvin, 1986). Among the most widely evaluated drug prevention programs are school programs taught in middle or junior high schools. Results of research are consistent in showing 20% or larger net reductions in rates of drug use onset from school programs that focus on counteracting social influences to use drugs and include standardized teacher or staff training, multiple class sessions, boosters, student peer leaders, and active social learning methods (Botvin, 1986; Tobler, 1986). Unfortunately, few of these studies have evaluated program effects beyond 2 years or effects on prevalence rates rather than delay of onset of use. The exceptions are in the area of smoking prevention: two studies have shown maintenance of effects from seventh through twelfth grade, but not after high school (Flay et al., 1989; Murray, Pirie, Luepker, & Pallonen, 1989); one study has shown variable effects from fourth through tenth grade (Walter, Vaughan, & Wynder, 1989).

Prevention program effects are qualified in other respects as well. First, prevention programs are by and large demand reduction strategies; that is, if one teaches youth to avoid drugs, the demand for drugs will be reduced. However, little is known about the relative effectiveness of demand and supply reduction strategies, because they have not been compared in the same studies. Second, most prevention programs are aimed at available (i.e., school-attending) youth. Little is known about program effects on school dropouts and students in identified high-risk groups. Third, school programs are limited in their capacity to reach youth only during school hours. Strategies that include other prospective program channels (e.g., mass media) have been evaluated as single-component programs, but relatively little is known about their capacity to enhance the effects of school-based programs. These qualifications, although not inclusive of all of the limitations of drug prevention research, have given rise to the development of new perspectives on the field of drug prevention. These perspectives are described below.

Contemporary Perspectives

Integrated Demand and Supply Reduction

Historically, demand and supply reduction strategies have been treated as independent approaches to drug abuse control, with separate budgets, personnel, and targets for intervention. The former have focused primarily on youth; the latter, on adults and criminal populations (Bennett, 1990). Supply reduction strategies aimed at interdiction have been heavily criticized in recent years for their cost and lack of success in deterring drug sales and related crimes. Failures of interdiction strategies often have been generalized to all supply reduction strategies. However, research on supply reduction policies aimed at raising the drinking age, limiting access to alcohol (in public bars, restaurants, and stores), and DUI monitoring on highways has shown significant reductions in alcohol consumption and sales, DUI behavior, and alcohol- and other drug-related accidents for short-term periods of up to 2 years (e.g., Moskowitz, 1989). Recent research suggests that policies aimed jointly at supply *and* demand reduction—for example, cigarette smoking and drug use policies in schools that limit supply by establishing drug-free zones *and* reduce demand by providing educational drug prevention programs—show promise for decreasing drug use among youth (e.g., Pentz, Brannon, et al., 1989). More extreme policy approaches have been recommended that would attempt to limit supply and demand jointly by legalizing the sale of drugs; these approaches have not been evaluated in the United States and have received little support thus far (Nadelmann, 1989).

Demand reduction strategies have focused primarily on teaching youth how to recognize drug use risk situations and influences and how to avoid them (Battjes & Bell, 1985). Demand reduction appeals to educators, lends itself easily to educational instruction, and meets federal and state educational mandates for drug abuse prevention (Anti-Drug Abuse Acts of 1986 and 1988). It may be an insufficient focus, however, for programs aimed at parents and community groups. For example, the nationally recognized grass-roots group Mothers Against Drunk Driving focuses primarily on supply reduction by lobbying for limited public access to alcohol and increased penalties for drunk driving.

Increasingly, schools and communities are including both demand and supply reduction in their drug abuse prevention programs. One of the most visible attempts to include both foci in schools is Project DARE (Drug Abuse Resistance Education). DARE utilizes trained police in uniform to deliver resistance skills training to youth in school classroom settings. The uniformed officers serve as representatives of community supply reduction strategies as well as implementors of a demand reduction program. DARE is generally recognized as the most rapidly diffused school drug prevention program in the United States; it has been implemented in more than 4,000 schools since 1983, and has been received positively by most communities (Clayton & Cattarello, 1991).

Other integrated strategies are emerging at school, community, state, and national levels. Schools are attempting to integrate demand and supply reduction strategies by including school drug policy change as a component of drug prevention programs. One study has shown that schools with prevention-oriented smoking and drug policies that mandate drug-free zones, support for students with drug use problems, and prevention programming as a regular part of the school educational curriculum have lower smoking prevalence rates among students than do schools with more punishment- or supply reduction-oriented policies (Pentz, Brannon, et al., 1989). One ongoing community-based trial, described in a later section of this chapter, follows school-based demand reduction programs with revision of school and community drug policies to include both demand and supply reduction components; policy change is then implemented by parents, school administrators, and community leaders as part of parent and community organization programs that complement the school program (Pentz, Dwyer, et al., 1989). On a larger scale, statewide policies, such as the Minnesota plan for smoking prevention, have been designed to guide the development of integrated demand and supply reduction strategies at the community level (Schultz et al., 1986).

At the national level, grass-roots parent groups such as Mothers Against Drunk Driving, the National Federation of Parents for Drug Free Youth, and Parents Who Care are increasingly offering or referring parents to demand reduction educational programs as a means to complement their lobbying efforts for supply reduction. Finally, federal research agencies, especially the Alcohol, Drug Abuse, and Mental Health Administration, have initiated grants programs that require community and youth agency "partnerships" for drug prevention programming. The guidelines for these grant programs require the cooperation of demand and supply reduction-oriented agencies in a community.

Strategic Versus Primary Prevention

Primary prevention programs were originally developed from public health models of low-cost educational strategies aimed at a whole population, assuming that most of the population is disease free at the point of intervention (Green, 1985; Wallack, 1984). The rationale for primary prevention programs is shifting toward a model based as much on social norms as on public health. Since the mid-1980s, primary prevention programs have increasingly incorporated strategies for correcting misperceived social norms about drug use and social normative expectations about the consequences of drug use. Results of recent studies suggest that social norms and other related social influences (for example, peer and parent acceptance of drug use) are significant predictors of drug use in adolescents and significant mediators of primary prevention program effects (e.g., MacKinnon et al., 1991). Based on these results, some researchers contend that social influence-based primary prevention programs show potential for affecting high-risk would-be drug users as well as other youth. Decreases in social norms and acceptance of drug use that are achieved through prevention programs may result in positive pressure on *all* youth not to use drugs, regardless of whether individual youth participate directly in these programs. In the broadest sense, a primary prevention program that includes a focus on changing social norms for drug use in a community may represent a systems-level intervention rather than an individual-level intervention as skills training and social influence programs are usually conceived.

Despite their effectiveness with school-attending adolescents, primary prevention programs may have limited utility for effecting significant changes in the drug use behavior of school dropouts or of populations with special needs for which a standardized program is not culturally relevant or meaningful. An alternative worth considering is "strategic" prevention. Yet to be evaluated systematically in research, strategic prevention would include at least four components introduced sequentially during childhood or early adolescence, and maintained through late adolescence.

The first component consists of primary prevention programs with whole populations of youth in available normative settings. Because schools remain the single most available normative setting for youth, the primary prevention program would logically be implemented with all youth in a school. Some qualitative results of process evaluations suggest that, if implemented before the high school years, primary prevention programs promote increases in student requests for additional, special-topic programs, such as avoidance and coping with drug use and pregnancy, depression, and family drug use problems; student self- and sibling referrals for early intervention; and parent requests for parent-child communications training related to drug prevention (Pentz, Johnson, et al., 1989). Thus, as a first component of strategic prevention, primary prevention programs may create a stigma-free environment for treating high-risk youth as well as provide drug prevention education for whole populations of youth and their families.

The second proposed component consists of high-interest, special-topic activities and brief group counseling-oriented programs that are scheduled such that they complement the delivery of primary prevention programs and are elective or voluntary. This component provides a forum for student and parent requests for detailed information and assistance about drug abuse-related problems that may be too complex or embarrassing to address within the context of a primary prevention program.

The third proposed component of strategic prevention involves standardized student assistance programs (SAPs) for schools. In general, SAPs are intended to provide supplementary support to students who exhibit academic, social, or behavioral difficulties that affect their performance in school. Thus SAPs are designed for students who have been identified by the school as at high risk for problems, including drug abuse. Results of studies using student peers as leaders in primary prevention programs and as peer counselors in SAPs are generally positive; in some studies, peer leaders have been shown to be as effective as or more effective than teachers (e.g., Perry, Klepp, Halper, Hawkins, & Murray, 1986).

The fourth component is prevention-treatment linkage. Treatment identification and referral procedures should be a logical outgrowth of SAPs. Currently, however, the prevention-treatment linkage is hampered by at least three factors. First, school staff may be reluctant to refer students to treatment for fear of liability for treatment outcome and breach of family confidentiality about drug use problems. Second, specialized treatment services and inpatient beds for youth drug abusers are scarce. Third, if outcomes of previous educational programs are an indication, the tracking, preparation, and final mainstreaming of youth from outside treatment programs back into school constitute a labor-intensive process beyond the budgetary capabilities of most schools (e.g., Goodstadt, 1986). Recent community organization efforts may reduce these problems. For example, the Kansas City Drug Abuse Task Force, the community organization evaluated as part of the Midwestern Prevention Project (see below), has initiated changes in state liability laws to protect teachers who refer students to drug abuse treatment programs, passed a beer tax to raise revenues for funding an increased number of adolescent inpatient beds in drug abuse treatment units, and pooled the financial resources of local private foundations to increase funding for drug abuse prevention, including staff.

Comprehensiveness

Since the 1970s, drug abuse prevention programs and strategies have been developed that are increasingly more comprehensive in terms of theoretical basis, polymorphic relationships with other health and disease prevention programs, developmental appropriateness, and use of multiple program modalities within a community.

Theory-Based Programming. Comparisons of prevention studies conducted in the 1960s and early 1970s with later studies have been instrumental in demonstrating that certain theoretical underpinnings of prevention programs are associated with greater effects on adolescent drug use behavior. By and large, programs that are atheoretical, or that are based on knowledge-attitude-behavior theoretical models that overemphasize knowledge transmission, and/or that depend on traditional didactic instruction techniques have no effect on changing adolescent drug use behavior (see Battjes & Bell, 1985; Botvin, 1986; Flay, 1986; Tobler, 1986). In contrast, programs that utilize active teaching methods from social learning theory (e.g., modeling, role playing, Socratic discussion with feedback) and focus on changing social influences on drug use, based on attribution and expectancy-value theories (e.g., peer pressure, perceived social norms for drug use), show significant effects on delaying the onset of use of gateway drugs—cigarettes, alcohol, and marijuana.

Recently, some programs have expanded to include theories that may explain protection or resilience of adolescents against drug use (see Hawkins, Lishner, & Catalano, 1985). Prominent among this movement are programs that focus on promoting "bonding" of adolescents. With roots in social support, coping, social learning, and developmental research, bonding currently refers to promoting positive, nondrug use support relationships of adolescents to their parents, peers, and perhaps teachers.

In addition to bonding, the theoretical frameworks of some prevention programs have expanded to include theories that explain environmental as well as individual-level social influences. Adapted from community-based heart disease prevention research, these frameworks incorporate theories of communication, diffusion, organizational development, and person × situation × environment transactions (Perry & Murray, 1985). Such frameworks have enabled drug prevention programmers and researchers to mount and explain the effects of community-level interventions that include behavior change skills programs aimed at individuals as well as communications and policy interventions aimed at community agencies and systems (e.g., Pentz, 1986).

Integration With Other Health and Prevention Programs. Researchers have debated for almost a decade over the question of whether drug prevention programs need to be behavior specific (i.e., focused entirely and specifically on drug use) or should be more socially generalizable (i.e., focused on a broad range of life skills that include but are not limited to drug use prevention) in order to be most effective (Botvin, 1986). Collectively, reviews of specific and general skills programs suggest that both are effective if they include pressure resistance and assertiveness skills (Battjes & Bell, 1985; Botvin, 1986; Flay, 1986; Murray et al., 1989; Tobler, 1986). Related to the general life skills question is whether drug prevention messages can be effective if delivered within the context of broader health programs. A national evaluation of school-based health education programs conducted in the early 1980s, the School Health Education Evaluation Project (SHEE), showed that smoking, alcohol, and other drug prevention content could be incorporated into a broad-based health education curriculum and show significant effects on student-reported cigarette smoking (Johnson, 1986). More recent evaluation of a popular K-12 health education curriculum, Know Your Body, has also shown some effects on reducing cigarette smoking among youth (Walter et al., 1989). Results of these studies are promising for educators, because they suggest that drug prevention can be incorporated into existing programs without sacrificing educational objectives.

Regular Programming Across the Life Span. Developmental and epidemiological studies have been consistent in showing that the first risk period for onset of drug use is the early adolescent years, particularly the year associated with transition to middle or junior high school (Hawkins et al., 1985; Perry & Murray, 1985). Early generations of drug prevention programs, focused almost exclusively on high school-age youth, were too late to delay onset or prevent drug use (Flay et al., 1985; Tobler, 1986). Drug prevention programs aimed at early adolescents have shown more promising results, yielding short-term reductions of 20%-67% in the rate of increase of gateway drug use in intervention compared with control groups of sixth-, seventh-, and eighth-grade students (e.g., Botvin, 1986; Tobler, 1986). Despite the effectiveness of these narrow-band grade programs, support is growing nationally for comprehensive drug prevention programs that are aimed at grades K-12. The most long-term evaluation of a multiple-grade program to date, the 6-year results of the Know Your Body program implemented in grades 4 through 10, has shown some effects on reducing cigarette smoking in one school district (Walter et al., 1989).

Multiple Program Modalities Within a Community. The final reflection of movement toward more comprehensive drug prevention programming is the use of multiple channels for program delivery. The general rationale for multichannel programs is an exposure or dose-response argument: The more a youth is exposed to consistent drug prevention messages, the less likely he or she is to use drugs. With few exceptions, such as national campaigns delivered through major television and radio networks (e.g., the National Institute on Drug Abuse "Just Say No" campaigns and National Partnership for Drug Free America's celebrity advertising), most drug prevention program channels operate within the boundaries of cities and communities.

The first and still foremost channel employed for drug prevention programming is the school (Battjes & Bell, 1985; Tobler, 1986). Some school programs have included other program channels on a limited basis, usually in the context of research studies. For example, school programs have been evaluated with and without parent involvement through homework, parent communications training, mass media programming, and prevention policy change; with some exceptions, the addition of other program channels has been shown to increase the effectiveness of school programs (Murray et al., 1988; Pentz, Brannon, et al., 1989; Pentz, Dwyer, et al., 1989). A few community programs have included schools, parents, mass media, community agencies, and local law enforcement and/or policy groups as program channels (Pentz, Dwyer et al., 1989; Vartiainen, Fallonen, McAlister, & Puska, 1990). In general, the effects obtained from these interventions tend to last longer than school programs alone or other single-channel programs and, for some substances, they produce larger effects (Pentz, Dwyer, et al., 1989; Vartiainen et al., 1990).

Comprehensive Community-Based
Drug Abuse Prevention:
The Midwestern Prevention Project

Background

The Midwestern Prevention Project (MPP) is a comprehensive, multicomponent community trial for prevention of adolescent drug abuse. The project integrates demand and supply reduction strategies by combining programs aimed at teaching youth drug resistance skills with local school and community policy change aimed at institutionalizing prevention programming and limiting youth access to drugs. The MPP emphasizes primary prevention of drug abuse; however, collectively, the program components and community activities represent a *strategic prevention* approach to drug abuse prevention: Primary prevention programs are complemented by special-topic activities and campaigns, augmentation of existing student assistance programs, and improvement (through the activities of the community organization) of prevention-treatment linkages. The approach is also *comprehensive,* relying on integrated social learning, communications, and systems-level theories; integrating drug prevention into existing school schedules and curricula; requiring active participation from the early through late adolescent years; and employing five program modalities (school, mass media, parent, community organization, and health policy channels).

Methods

Design. The Midwestern Prevention Project is a comprehensive population-based drug abuse intervention program aimed at decreasing the rates of onset and prevalence of drug use in early adolescents and, secondarily, their parents and other residents of all communities in two major metropolitan areas in the Midwest/North Central region of the United States (Kansas City, $n = 1.3$ million population, 15 communities with distinct town and school district boundaries; Indianapolis, $n = 1.2$ million population, 11 communities with distinct town and school district boundaries, plus one large private school district, encompassing the metropolitan area). The overall intervention effect of the MPP is evaluated with a 2×2 research design within each site (intervention or delayed intervention control by program initiation in grade 6 or 7, with school as the unit of assignment and analysis). The design and intervention effects on drug use have been described elsewhere (Pentz, Dwyer, et al., 1989).

Intervention. The intervention consists of five program components introduced in sequence to communities: mass media, school, parent, community organization, and health policy. Collectively, the components focus on promoting drug use resistance and counteraction skills by adolescents (direct skills training); prevention practices and support of adolescent prevention practices by parents and other adults, including teachers, expected to serve as role models for adolescents (indirect skills training); and dissemination and support of nondrug use social norms and expectations in the community (environmental support). Components are introduced at the rate of 6 months to 1 year apart, with the exception of mass media programming, which is initiated with the school program. The programs are continuously implemented in both sites.

Mass Media. The mass media component consists of approximately 31 television, radio, and print broadcasts per year about the intervention. The broadcasts range from hour-long talk shows and press conferences to 15-second commercials and public service announcements. News coverage and commercials each year are designed to introduce new program components to the community, and to illustrate through simple messages the underlying theoretical premise of the components.

School Program. The school program component is delivered by trained teachers and includes 10-13 classroom sessions in grade 6 or 7 (the transition year to middle or junior high school), a 5-session booster in the following year, and peer counseling and support activities in high school. The school program focuses on increasing skills to resist and counteract pressures to use drugs, and to change the social climate of the school to accept a nondrug use norm. The school program component is designed to address specific educational and training issues in drug prevention. Research staff monitor and provide feedback to teachers about quality of program implementation; comprehensive, standardized teacher training in the first year is complemented with brief, reinforcing "refresher" training sessions in subsequent years in order to maintain interest and quality of program implementation.

Parent Program. The parent program component is delivered by a trained core group consisting of the principal, four to six parents, and two student peer leaders from each school. The parent program includes regular meetings throughout each school year to plan and implement an annual parent skills night for all parents, focusing on parent-child communication and prevention support skills; to conduct monitoring activities to keep the school grounds and surrounding neighborhood drug free; and to refine school policy to institutionalize prevention programming in the school. The focus is to develop family support for drug abuse prevention and a nondrug use norm in school neighborhoods.

Community Organization. The community organization component involves the identification, commitment, and training of existing city leaders to plan and implement drug abuse prevention services, funds and other resources, and activities that complement the other program components. The focus is on networking agencies and facilitating referrals for services across agencies. The community organization component matches natural leadership capabilities and expectations to different types of organizations.

Health Policy. The health policy change component is implemented by a government subcommittee of the community organization and other local government leaders. This component focuses on changing local ordinances restricting cigarette smoking in public settings, increasing alcohol pricing and limiting availability, and including prevention and support provisions in drug policies aimed at deterrence.

Subjects. The primary subjects of the MPP are school-attending adolescents who are first assessed in the transition grade to middle school (sixth grade, average age = 10 years). All 50 public middle/junior high schools are included in Kansas City, and all 57 public ($n = 29$) and private/parochial schools ($n = 28$) are included in Indianapolis. The majority of the private/parochial schools in Indianapolis are Roman Catholic.

In Kansas City, three sampling plans are used to collect data on students: a panel sample, whereby individuals are tracked over time ($n = 1,600$); a cross-sectional grade cohort sample, whereby 25% of students are randomly sampled by classroom from the target grade cohort each year ($n = 3,900$); and a time-sequential sample, whereby 6-8 classrooms from each of grades 8 and 10 are randomly sampled from across the pool of schools each week during the school year ($n = 14,000$). An additional sample is provided by Kauffman Foundation funding for late high school comparisons: a 25% sample of twelfth-grade students randomly sampled by classroom ($n = 2,500$). The total student sample in Kansas City is approximately 22,500 per year.

In Indianapolis, two sampling plans are used: three successive panels ($n = 2,500$ from each of the entering sixth/seventh grade cohorts for 1987, 1988, and 1989); and a time-sequential sample of grades 10 and 12 ($n = 6,700$). The total is about 14,200 students per year.

Measurement. Outcome data are collected annually from self-report surveys and a biochemical measure of cigarette smoking. Self-report surveys and biochemical measurements of expired air (CO) from cigarette smoking are administered annually to approximately 29,000 adolescents who are sampled repeatedly as part of a longitudinal panel or randomly from the grade cohort, and an additional 3,000-6,000 students who are not part of the study cohort but who are randomly sampled from the entering sixth or seventh grade each year. The survey includes items about gateway drug use (tobacco, alcohol, marijuana) and hard drug use (cocaine, amphetamines, barbiturates, heroin), hypothesized mediators of program effect (resistance skills, communication skills, social support seeking, environmental support, perceived social norms), and program participation.

Data Analysis. Data are analyzed with linear and logistic regression analyses, with stepwise inclusion of demographic covariates (Dwyer et al., 1989). The major demographic covariates include socioeconomic status (indexed by father's occupation and a composite variable of occupation, family income, and percentage of school students receiving free lunch), urbanicity of school or community (inner-city urban, urban/ suburban, suburban, rural; r = more than .70 with population density), grade of transition of student (sixth or seventh), and race/ethnicity (white or nonwhite). Depending on the model of analysis—unconditional (repeated measures) or conditional—baseline drug use is also included as a covariate. School is used as the primary unit of analysis, although results are compared with individual as the unit of analysis. With the school as the unit of analysis, models are compared using school of origin, endpoint school at last wave of measurement, and schools pooled across waves of measurement. Logits and proportions of drug use are compared as outcomes.

Results

Effects of the MPP through the first 4 years in Kansas City, and at baseline in Indianapolis, have been published elsewhere (e.g., Dwyer et al., 1989; Pentz, Dwyer, et al., 1989; Pentz, Johnson, et al., 1989). Adolescents in schools assigned to the intervention condition show consistently lower prevalence rates of cigarette, alcohol, and marijuana use than do adolescents in schools assigned to the control condition; by the fourth year in Kansas City (ninth/tenth grade), adolescents in intervention schools also showed less cocaine and crack use compared with adolescents in control schools. Several analyses have also been conducted on adolescent data to address specific issues in drug abuse prevention, including mediational analyses to address the theoretical coherence of the intervention, whether analytic strategies affect program outcome (units of analysis, treatment of the dependent variable, conditional or unconditional models), and interactive program effects, particularly whether the program works only with certain population subgroups or with low- versus high-risk groups.

Mediational analyses of adolescent attitudes, perceived norms, and skills have shown (a) that the intervention has had a significant effect on changing levels of hypothesized mediators in directions consistent with its theoretical basis, with the largest changes in decreasing social acceptance of and perceived norms about drug use (MacKinnon et al., 1991); and (b) that the changes in these variables have a significant mediational effect on subsequent drug use. Other mediational analyses have addressed the gateway drug use theory developed from epidemiological research. The gateway drug use theory posits that adolescents who use tobacco, alcohol, and/or marijuana early relative to their peers are more likely than their peers to progress to harder drug use later on (Kandel, 1975). Mediational analyses of program effects on cocaine and crack use at ninth/tenth grade have shown that approximately 95% of the program effect was mediated by the earlier program effects on tobacco and marijuana use in grades 6 through 8, a finding that logically extends the gateway drug use theory to prevention effects.

Comparisons of analytic strategies have shown few differences in program effects using individual or school as the unit of analysis, logits or proportions as the dependent variable, or conditional or unconditional regression models (Dwyer et al., 1989). However, while school of origin and endpoint school as units of analysis yield comparable results, schools that represent mixed program and control groups over time (for example, program and control middle schools that consolidate into one high school) show weaker program effects than do schools that retain a program group over time (Pentz, MacKinnon, et al., 1989).

Finally, analyses conducted on different subgroups through three-year follow-up have shown the following (Johnson et al., 1990). Program effects on gateway drug use are significant, whether data are unadjusted or adjusted for race, grade, gender, urbanicity, and socioeconomic status. Analyses of stratified groups show similar results. Analyses of high- and low-risk groups, with risk defined first in terms of single variables (minority status, urban schools, low socioeconomic status, high levels of parent drug use, high levels of baseline use, high rebelliousness, perceived positive consequences of use) and then in terms of a composite score of these variables, have shown significant program effects on all risk groups.

Conclusions

Theoretical and research developments over the past decade suggest the use of drug prevention strategies that integrate demand and supply reduction, primary and secondary prevention, and multiple program channels to achieve significant reductions in adolescent drug use. The magnitude of the MPP effects suggests that comprehensive community-based drug abuse prevention programs may achieve the largest and most sustained results in preventing drug use. Whether MPP effects will maintain after adolescents leave high school and, perhaps, the supportive prevention climate afforded by the intervention cities is the focus of evaluation for the next 5 years. Several directions of inquiry will be pursued in the MPP and should be evaluated in other studies as they relate to the effectiveness of integrated, strategic, comprehensive programming for drug abuse prevention. These include evaluation of the contributions of novelty effects, quality of program implementation, consumer ownership, access to hard-to-reach groups, saturation effects, and local policy change to overall intervention effects through 10-year follow-up.

References

Battjes, R. J., & Bell, C. S. (1985). Future directions in drug abuse prevention research. *National Institute of Drug Abuse Research Monograph Series, 83,* 221-228.

Bennett, W. J. (1990). *National drug control strategy.* Washington DC: Government Printing Office.

Botvin, G. J. (1986). Substance abuse prevention research: Recent developments and future directions. *Journal of School Health, 56,* 369-374.

Clayton, R. R., & Cattarello, A. (1991). Prevention intervention research: The challenges and opportunities. In Z. Amsel, C. Leukefield, & W. Bukoski (Eds.), *Prevention intervention research.* Rockville, MD: National Institute on Drug Abuse.

Connell, D. B, Turner, R. R., & Mason, E. F. (1985). Summary of findings of the school health education evaluation: Health promotion effectiveness, implementation, and costs. *Journal of School Health, 55,* 316-321.

Dwyer, J. H., MacKinnon, D. M., Pentz, M. A., Flay, B. R., Hansen, W. B., Wang, E. Y. I., & Johnson, C. A. (1989). Estimating intervention effects in longitudinal studies. *American Journal of Epidemiology, 130,* 781-795.

Flay, B. R. (1986). Efficacy and effectiveness trials (and other phases of research) in the development of health promotion programs. *Preventive Medicine, 15,* 451-474.

Flay, B. R., Koepke, D., Thomson, S. J., Santi, S., Best, J. A., & Brown, K. S. (1989). Six year follow-up of the first Waterloo smoking prevention trial. *American Journal of Public Health, 19,* 1371-1376.

Flay, B. R., Pentz, M. A., Johnson, C. A., Sussman, S., Mestell, J., Scheier, L., Collins, L. M., & Hansen, W. B. (1985). Reaching children with mass media health promotion programs: The relative effectiveness of an advertising campaign, a community-based program, and a school-based program. In D. S. Leathar (Ed.), *Health education and the media* (Vol. 2). Oxford, UK: Pergamon.

Goodstadt, M. J. (1986). School based drug education in North America: What is wrong? What can be done? *Journal of School Health, 56,* 278-281.

Green, L. W. (1985). *Toward a healthy community: Organizing events for community health promotion* (DHHS Publication No. [PHS] 80-50113). Washington, DC: Government Printing Office.

Hawkins, J. D., Lishner, D. M., & Catalano, R. F. (1985). Childhood predictors and the prevention of adolescent substance abuse. In C. L. Jones & R. J. Battjes (Eds.), *Etiology of drug abuse: Implications for prevention* (NIDA Research Monograph 56). Washington, DC: National Institute on Drug Abuse.

Johnson, C. A. (1986). Prevention and control of drug abuse. In J. M. Last (Ed.), *Maxcy-Rosenau: Public health and preventive medicine* (pp. 1075-1087). Norwalk, CT: Appleton-Century-Crofts.

Johnson, C. A., Pentz, M. A., Weber, M. D., Dwyer, J. H., MacKinnon, D. P., Flay, B. R., Baer, N. A., & Hansen, W. B. (1990). The relative effectiveness of comprehensive community programming for drug abuse prevention with risk and low risk adolescents. *Journal of Consulting and Clinical Psychology, 58,* 447-456.

Kandel, D.B. (1975). Stages in adolescent involvement in drug use. *Science, 190,* 912-914.

MacKinnon, D. P., Johnson, C. A., Pentz, M. A., Dwyer, J. H., Hansen, W. B., Flay, B. R., & Wang, E. Y. I. (1991). Mediating mechanisms in a school-based drug prevention program: First year effects of the Midwestern Prevention Project. *Health Psychology, 10*(3), 164-172.

Moskowitz, J. M. (1989). The primary prevention of alcohol problems: A critical review of the research literature. *Journal of Studies on Alcohol, 50,* 54-88.

Murray, D. M., Jacobs, D. R., Perry, C. L., Pallonen, U., Harty, K. C., Griffin, G., Moen, M. E., & Hanson, G. (1988). A statewide approach to adolescent tobacco-use prevention: The Minnesota-Wisconsin Adolescent Tobacco-Use Research Project. *Preventive Medicine, 17,* 461-474.

Murray, D. M., Pirie, P., Luepker, R. V., & Pallonen, U. (1989). Five- and six-year results from four seventh-grade smoking prevention strategies. *Journal of Behavioral Medicine, 12,* 207-218.

Nadelmann, E. A. (1989). Drug prohibition in the United States: Costs, consequences, and alternatives. *Science, 243,* 939-947.

Pentz, M. A. (1986). Community organization and school liaisons: How to get programs started. *Journal of School Health, 56,* 382-388.

Pentz, M. A., Brannon, B. R., Charlin, V. L., Barrett, E. J., MacKinnon, D. P., & Flay, B. R. (1989). The power of policy: The relationship of smoking policy to adolescent smoking. *American Journal of Public Health, 79,* 857-862.

Pentz, M. A., Dwyer, J. H., MacKinnon, D. P., Flay, B. R., Hansen, W. B., Wang, E. Y. I., & Johnson, C. A. (1989). A multi-community trial for primary prevention of adolescent drug abuse: Effects on drug use prevalence. *Journal of the American Medical Association, 261,* 3259.

Pentz, M. A., Johnson, C. A., Dwyer, J. H., MacKinnon, D. P., Hansen, W. B., & Flay, B. R. (1989). A comprehensive community approach to adolescent drug abuse prevention: Effects on cardiovascular disease risk behaviors. *Annals of Medicine, 21,* 219-222

Pentz, M. A., MacKinnon, D. P., Dwyer, J. H., Wang, E. Y. I., Hansen, W. B., Flay, B. R., & Johnson, C. A. (1989). Longitudinal effects of the Midwestern Prevention Project (MPP) on regular and experimental smoking in adolescents. *Preventive Medicine, 18,* 304-321.

Perry, C. L., Klepp, K. I, Halper, A., Hawkins, K. G., & Murray, D. M. (1986). A process evaluation study of peer leaders in health education. *Journal of School Health, 56*(2), 62-67.

Perry, C. L., & Murray, D. M. (1985). Preventing adolescent drug abuse: Implications from etiological, developmental, behavioral, and environmental models. *Journal of Primary Prevention, 6,* 31-52.

Schultz, J. M., Moen, M. E., Pechacek, T. F., Harty, K. C., Skubic, M. A., Gust, S. W., & Dean, A. G. (1986). The Minnesota plan for nonsmoking and health: The legislative experience. *Journal of Public Health Policy, 7,* 300-313.

Tobler, N. S. (1986). Meta-analyses of 143 adolescent drug prevention programs: Quantitative outcome results of program participants compared to a control or comparison group. *Journal of Drug Issues, 17,* 537-567.

Vartiainen, E., Fallonen, U., McAlister, A. L., & Puska, P. (1990). Eight-year follow-up results of an adolescent smoking prevention program: The North Karelia Youth Project. *American Journal of Public Health, 80,* 78-79.

Wallack, L. (1984). Practical issues, ethical concerns and future directions in the prevention of alcohol-related problems. *Journal of Primary Prevention, 4,* 199-224.

Walter, H. J., Vaughan, R. D., & Wynder, E. L. (1989). Primary prevention of cancer among children: Changes in cigarette smoking and diet after six years of intervention. *Journal of the National Cancer Institute, 81,* 995-999.

4

Early Identification
of Addictive Behaviors
Using a Computerized
Life-Style Assessment

HARVEY A. SKINNER

In the past decade, there has been increasing emphasis on the early identification of addictive behaviors, especially alcohol and drug abuse, at various stages of the life span. For example, a major study conducted for the U.S. Congress by the Institute of Medicine (1990) argued for a broader definition of alcohol (and drug) problems, along with the responsibility of the community for early identification and brief intervention. Primary care physicians and nurses are often in an excellent position to identify potentially addictive behaviors, such as excessive drinking, cigarette smoking, and drug misuse, and to intervene with brief advice or counseling (Skinner, 1990; Skinner & Holt, 1983).

AUTHOR'S NOTE: The research presented in this chapter was supported, in part, by Grant 66-6-3002-43 from the National Health Research Development Program, Health and Welfare Canada. I would like to thank Barbara Allen, Douglas Gavin, Margo George, Robin Kay, Marion McIntosh, Wilfred Palmer, Martha Sanchez-Craig, and Wen-Jenn Sheu for their help on studies with the Computerized Lifestyle Assessment.

Recent studies have shown that brief intervention by physicians and nurses can be effective in motivating patients to reduce their excessive drinking and to quit cigarette smoking (Babor, 1990; Kottke, Battista, DeFriese, & Brakke, 1988; Wallace, Cutler, & Haines, 1988). Nevertheless, alcohol- and drug-related problems often go undetected, many times because screening and case identification techniques are not being used routinely.

This chapter describes a basic strategy for the early identification of health risks and addictive behaviors. Emphasis is placed on the use of the Computerized Lifestyle Assessment (CLA) in health care settings with individuals at different life stages, from adolescence to old age. Roemer (1984) argues that an ideal opportunity for health promotion and disease prevention arises when patients seek help in hospitals and family practices. Embedding potentially sensitive items about addictive behaviors within a broader life-style assessment greatly enhances the likelihood that individuals will be interested in completing such an assessment and that they will give accurate responses. Moreover, administering the assessment by microcomputer allows for instant feedback using computer graphics and detailed printed reports. This chapter (a) discusses the rationale for assessing life-styles as part of health promotion and disease prevention strategies; (b) provides a synopsis of research on the reliability, validity, and acceptability of the Computerized Lifestyle Assessment in health care settings; and (c) describes how life-style assessment and feedback can be used in behavioral change strategies for addictions.

Why Assess Life-Style?

In 1974, Mark Lalonde, the national minister of Health and Welfare Canada, published a now-classic report that identified four major determinants of health: life-style, human biology, environment, and the health care system. When experts analyzed the 10 leading causes of death in the United States, they found that "perhaps as much as half of U.S. mortality in 1976 was due to unhealthy behavior or lifestyle, 20% to environmental factors, 20% to human biological factors and 10% to inadequacies in health care" (U.S. Surgeon General, 1979). The heaviest burden of illness in North America today is related to individual life-style behavior (Hamburg, Elliott, & Parron, 1982). For example, it has been estimated that more than half (54%) of the decline in ischemic heart disease between 1968 and 1976 is attributable to life-style changes involving the reduction of serum cholesterol levels and cigarette smoking, whereas 39% is explained by advances in medical care, such as coronary care units (Goldman & Cook, 1984).

The relative merits of prevention (life-style change) versus medical care are underscored in a recent study of premature deaths in Canada. Wigle, Semenciw, McCann, and Davies (1990) found that of the almost 100,000 premature deaths (before age 75), an estimated 50,000, or more than 50%, are preventable through control of the following risk factors: cigarette smoking, hypertension (related to obesity/diet/exercise), cholesterol (related to obesity/diet/exercise), adult-onset diabetes (related to obesity/diet/exercise), and excessive alcohol consumption (see Figure 4.1). In contrast, only about 6,000 premature deaths (6%) are avoidable through improvements in medical care.

The importance of life-style factors was demonstrated in a prospective study of 6,928 adult residents of Alameda County, California (Berkman & Breslow, 1983). A 9-year follow-up found that not smoking cigarettes, moderate or no use of alcohol, getting regular physical exercise, maintaining desirable weight in relation to height, and getting 7 to 8 hours of sleep each night were positively and strongly associated with good health and lower risk of disease and mortality. The effect was cumulative; that is, the greater the number of personal health habits practiced, the greater the probability of leading a longer life. Berkman and Breslow (1983) also found a strong link between social networks and mortality.

In brief, there is compelling evidence that a few simple life-style habits are directly related to health and the risk of disease. Yet, preventive programs involving life-style assessment and intervention are not routinely incorporated in clinical practice. For example, Wechsler, Levine, Idelson, Rohman, and Taylor (1983) found in their survey of physicians that nearly three out of four felt it was definitely the responsibility of physicians to educate patients about life-style behaviors such as cigarette smoking, alcohol and other drug use, stress, exercise, and diet. However, only 27% reported that they routinely gathered information about these life-style behaviors from their patients.

On the other hand, patients are often willing to talk about sensitive life-style issues, such as drinking or sexual problems, but they are not likely to do so spontaneously (Murphy, 1980). In an investigation of patients' perspectives on life-style activities, Wallace and Haines (1984) found that most patients felt that their doctor should be interested in the

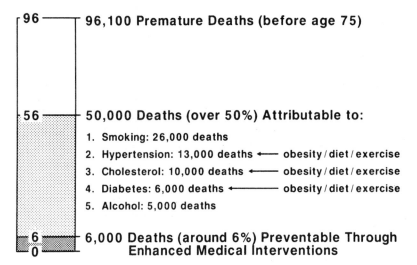

Figure 4.1. Comparison of life-style change and medical care in the prevention of premature death (before age 75) in Canada.

SOURCE: Data are from Wigle et al. (1990).

patients' weight control, cigarette smoking, alcohol use, and physical exercise. However, less than half of the patients reported that their physician had seemed concerned and inquired about these issues. Many patients are willing to discuss their life-style concerns with their doctors if they are given the opportunity to do so. The Computerized Lifestyle Assessment provides a practical and effective strategy for ensuring that a meaningful dialogue takes place between the health professional and patient regarding life-style strengths and concerns.

The CLA examines a broad range of life-style activities, provides graphic feedback at various points during the assessment, and generates a printed report on life-style strengths and weaknesses. This assessment takes approximately 20 to 30 minutes to complete. The content areas include *substance use* (alcohol, cigarettes, caffeine, nonmedical drugs), *health-maintaining practices* (nutrition, weight control, physical activity, sleep), *preventive activities* (medical/dental checkups, motor vehicle safety), *social issues* (social relationships, family functioning, leisure activities, sexual activities), and *emotional well-being* (stress, depression, life satisfaction). Figure 4.2 illustrates the final graph on

LIFESTYLE SUMMARY

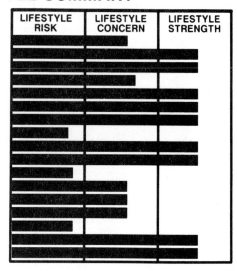

Nutrition (Food Groups)
Eating Habits
Caffeine Use
Physical Activity
Weight Control
Sleep
Social Relationships
Family Interactions
Use of Cigars or Pipes
Use of Cigarettes
Alcohol Use
Non-medical Drug Use
Medical/Dental Care
Motor Vehicle Safety
Sexual Activities
Work & Leisure
Emotional Health

Figure 4.2. Example of the summary graph of life-style strengths, concerns, and risks depicted on the computer screen and reproduced in the printed report.

the computer screen that summarizes the respondent's life-style strengths, concerns, and risks. This graph is also reproduced on the first page of the printed report. Information from the printed report can be used as a starting point for a more detailed assessment of identified risk behaviors, for facilitating a dialogue on life-style issues and related health concerns, and for stimulating the patient's self-examination regarding life-style choices.

Caveat

A very important caution must be raised regarding the potential for overselling the merits of individual life-style change. That is, a concentration on life-style may obscure a focus on broader factors such as culture and economic status, as well as on population and environmental interventions (Brownell, 1991; Bunton, Murphy, & Bennett, 1991; Evans & Stoddart, 1990; Stokols, 1992). At the First International Conference on Health Promotion, held in Ottawa, Canada, in 1986, a Charter for Action was adopted by the World Health Organization for the achievement of "health for all" by the year 2000 and beyond. The Ottawa Charter emphasizes five interdependent actions:

(1) Build healthy public policy.
(2) Create supportive environments.
(3) Strengthen community action.
(4) Develop personal skills.
(5) Reorient health services.

Individual life-style issues are subsumed under personal skills in this framework. Hence it should be clear that life-style assessment and change is only one component of a much broader framework for health (Epp, 1986).

Jeffery (1989) provides an excellent review of individual versus population perspectives on health risks. He identifies the conditions under which individual life-style strategies are likely to be most effective: Benefits to the individual are large, time interval before the individual will benefit is short, and effort required to change the behavior is low relative to the expected benefit. The use of fluoridated toothpaste for the prevention of dental caries is an example. In comparison, population approaches to health behavior change are most effective when the environmental context is well defined where the behavior occurs, it is in the public domain, and intervention is politically and economically feasible (e.g., water sanitation). However, in many cases individual and population strategies are mutually supportive. For instance, Jeffery describes how the decline in cigarette smoking over the past two decades has resulted from a complex interplay of individual, community, and population factors.

Research on the Computerized Lifestyle Assessment

The CLA has evolved from an ongoing program of research concentrating on the accuracy and acceptability of computerized assessments, as well as on how microcomputer technology can be used to facilitate health education and early intervention programs for life-style behaviors such as alcohol, tobacco, and drug use. This section reviews research on the acceptance of computerized assessments, and then describes studies on the reliability and validity of the CLA.

Acceptance of Computerized Assessments

When research began on the CLA in 1980, various concerns were expressed regarding the acceptability of computerized assessments to both patients and staff (Skinner & Pakula, 1986). Certainly, if patients have major concerns about answering questions on a microcomputer, or if staff are uncomfortable or resistant to using the software, then computerized life-style assessment would not be feasible. Previous studies have indicated, however, that a broad range of individuals feel positive about being tested or interviewed by computers. Indeed, many actually prefer computerized assessments over traditional approaches (Angle, Ellinwood, Hay, Johnsen, & Hay, 1977; Klinger, Miller, Johnson, & Williams, 1977). In contrast, staff acceptance of certain computer applications in health care has been a persistent problem (Byrnes & Johnson, 1981; Hedlund, Evenson, Sletten, & Cho, 1980; Leader & Klein, 1977).

Studies of the CLA have used an experimental paradigm in which subjects are randomly assigned to receive a life-style assessment in one of three formats: microcomputer, interview, or questionnaire. Afterwards, subjects are asked to rate the experience of the assessment. The first study focused on 150 clients who had come to the Addiction Research Foundation, Toronto, for help with alcohol- and/or drug-related problems (Skinner & Allen, 1983). Differential ratings of the assessment experience were observed. The computerized interview was rated as less friendly, but shorter, more relaxing, lighter, more interesting, and faster than the interview or questionnaire formats. Detailed analysis of client factors within each assessment format revealed that the computerized interview was most acceptable to persons with good visual-motor performance skills and least preferred by better-educated and defensive clients.

The next study examined 180 patients in a family practice setting (Skinner, Allen, McIntosh, & Palmer, 1985a, 1985b). Patients were asked to evaluate the assessment formats on a five-point semantic differential scale. Statistically significant differences were found. The computer assessment format was rated as more mechanical and impersonal, but it was also rated as more interesting than the personal interview and the paper-and-pencil questionnaire.

An important finding was that patients' acceptance of microcomputers can be favorably influenced through direct experience with computerized assessment (Skinner et al., 1985a). Prior to being asked any questions about their life-styles, patients ranked their preferences for the three assessment formats: computer, interview, and questionnaire. Initially, most selected the interview as their first choice, followed by the questionnaire and computer formats. However, when preferences were reranked after the patients had completed the life-style assessment, there was a significant increase (13% to 43%) in first-choice preference for the computer among those completing the computerized assessment. No change in preference was observed for patients who had been randomly assigned to either the interview or questionnaire formats. More detailed analyses revealed that the greatest increase in preference for the computer was among those who had had no previous computer experience. This suggests that direct, "hands-on" experience increases the acceptance of computerized assessments.

A survey of 516 patients at the Family Practice Service of Toronto General Hospital evaluated patients' attitudes toward having their doctors use microcomputers for taking life-style histories (see Table 4.1). Most patients stated that they would feel comfortable answering questions on a microcomputer, would give honest answers, and would want to read the printed report. While patients generally felt that computerized assessment would save their physicians time, they raised concerns that they would lose the personal touch of their doctors, and they worried about the confidentiality of their answers. However, these data were collected before patients had an opportunity to complete the CLA, and only a small proportion of patients had previous experience with computerized assessments. Our earlier study in this setting has shown that when patients are given direct experience in completing a life-style assessment using a computer, their attitudes toward the experience are positively increased (Skinner et al., 1985a).

When patients were asked how important it was for their family physicians to be up-to-date about their life-style habits, 44% said it was "very important," 47% said it was "important," 7% said it was "unimportant," and only 2% rated it "very unimportant." This survey indicates that most patients believe that their family doctors should be interested in their life-style behaviors. Moreover, patients expect their family doctor to intervene when appropriate. Patients were asked about the level of help they expected from their family doctors regarding potential life-style problems (see Table 4.2). The ratings ranged from no involvement for financial problems to an expectation of expert help from the physician for chronic pain and drug abuse. Brief advice and support

TABLE 4.1 Evaluation of Computerized Life-Style Assessment (in percentages; $n = 531$ family practice patients)

How would you feel if your doctor used a microcomputer for taking life-style histories?

	Strongly Agree	Agree	Don't Know	Disagree	Strongly Disagree
It would save doctor's time	24	52	17	5	2
I would answer honestly.	37	52	8	3	1
I would want to read report	46	41	8	5	4
Computer is a good way to ask life-style questions	13	45	29	9	4
I would feel comfortable answering questions on a computer	11	50	23	11	4
Computer will help doctor with routine life-style questions	10	63	19	6	2
Computers can be trusted	5	40	41	11	3
Doctor will make better assessment with computer	10	46	31	10	4
Worry about confidentiality	14	31	16	27	12
Doctors would spend less time with patient	6	19	23	41	12
I don't want certain information on the computer	11	19	20	41	9
I would find another doctor	4	9	21	45	20
Too many mistakes will be made with the computer	4	11	37	39	9
Lose personal touch of doctor	10	46	31	10	4

were seen as constituting an appropriate level of involvement by the family physician for life-style problems and potentially addictive behaviors regarding cigarette smoking, excessive drinking, and eating behaviors.

Concerning staff acceptance, we have witnessed a gradual increase in interest shown by staff. Before the computerized assessment studies began at the Family Practice Service of Toronto General Hospital, initial reactions of physicians, nurses, and receptionists ranged from enthusiastic acceptance to indifference, overt dislike, and mistrust. However, many of the staff who initially held negative opinions voiced interest and more favorable attitudes once they personally completed the

TABLE 4.2 Level of Involvement Patients Expect From Their Family Doctors

Level 1 None	Level 2 Refer to a Specialist	Level 3 Advice and Support	Level 4 Counseling/ Treatment
Financial problems	Parenting prob- lems Death in family Caffeine use Social isolation Marital separa- tion/divorce	Poor nutrition Nervousness Drinking problems Weight control Sleep problems Depression Family violence Cigarette smoking Exercise Sexual problems	Long-term pain Drug abuse

NOTE: Modal response from n = 516 family practice patients.

CLA. After patients were assessed and computer-generated reports of their life-style habits were made available to physicians, several doctors spontaneously approached the research team and pointed out that the CLA had elicited important new information about their patients.

Reliability

Reliability refers to the consistency that individuals show in responding to items both on a single occasion (internal consistency) and across two occasions (test-retest). Our first study found that the type of assessment format (computer, interview, questionnaire) did not influence patients' consistency in answering items (Skinner & Allen, 1983). For example, an internal consistency reliability estimate (alpha) of .90 was obtained on the Michigan Alcoholism Screening Test when this 25-item questionnaire was administered via the computer, interview, and questionnaire formats.

A recent study focused on the test-retest reliability of the CLA (Skinner, Palmer, Sanchez-Craig, & McIntosh, 1987). The assessment was administered to 117 family practice patients on two occasions separated by an average of 3.3 weeks (standard deviation = 2.3). The median test-retest correlation was .85 for 20 life-style factors. Reliability coefficients ranged from .99 (weight) to .66 (nutrition status).

Indeed, nutrition was the only index that had a reliability estimate below .70. Subsequently, this section of the CLA was modified, so that a separate question is now directed at each food group. Our expectation is that this modification will increase the reliability of the nutrition index.

The median test-retest reliability of .85 can be considered excellent. This reliability is somewhat higher than the median estimate of .75 for a similar, but briefer, life-style assessment (Wilson, Nielsen, & Ciliska, 1984) and is also higher than estimates for items on the Health Hazard Appraisal (Sacks, Krushat, & Newman, 1980; Wagner, Beery, Schoenbach, & Graham, 1982). The test-retest correlations reflect the stability over two occasions of the ranking by patients. Potential changes in mean levels of life-style factors were examined using t tests. No statistically significant differences were observed. In most cases, the Time 1 and Time 2 means were virtually identical (Skinner et al., 1987).

The CLA also contains items that address the patient's concerns regarding seven life-style factors. Table 4.3 compares patients' consistency in reporting life-style concerns to the microcomputer and to their doctors during consultation. In general, there is a high level of consistency, with a mean proportion of agreement of .92 and a kappa statistic of .74. Kappa corrects for chance and, in this context, reflects the level of agreement beyond chance between the computer and physician assessments. Fleiss (1981) suggests that kappa values greater than .75 represent excellent agreement, and values between .40 to .75 denote fair to good agreement beyond chance.

For comparison purposes, Table 4.3 gives patients' responses to the microcomputer on the two testing occasions (Time 1 and Time 2). The overall proportion of agreement and kappa statistics for the two testing occasions are very similar to the comparison between the computer and doctor assessments. Patients were most consistent in reporting life-style concerns regarding their cigarette use, weight control, and sleep habits. They were somewhat less consistent in reporting life-style concerns regarding physical exercise.

In summary, these studies indicate that life-style factors can be assessed reliably and efficiently using microcomputers.

Validity

An ongoing program of research has been aimed at establishing the validity properties of the CLA. Originally, interest in computerized assessment was sparked by the question, Does the computer make a

TABLE 4.3 Patient's Consistency in Reporting Life-Style Concerns to the Microcomputer and to the Doctor

Life-Style Concern	Computer (Time 1) Versus Doctor		Computer Time 1 Versus Time 2	
	Proportion	Kappa	Proportion	Kappa
Nutrition	0.96	0.65	0.85	0.67
Caffeine use	0.88	0.74	0.98	0.70
Physical exercise	0.77	0.54	0.82	0.64
Sleep	0.95	0.88	0.87	0.67
Weight control	0.92	0.84	0.86	0.72
Cigarette use	0.99	0.97	0.98	0.93
Alcohol use	0.88	0.64	0.90	0.71
Median	0.92	0.74	0.87	0.70

NOTE: Life-style concerns about nutrition, caffeine, exercise, cigarettes, and alcohol were coded 1 = no or not a consumer, 2 = yes or sometimes. Sleep was coded 1 = right amount, 2 = too much or too little. Weight was coded 1 = ideal range, 2 = underweight or overweight.

difference in comparison with traditional interview and questionnaire formats? One of the more compelling aspects of computerized assessment is the possibility that individuals may give more accurate information about sensitive areas to computers than they would in personal interviews or on questionnaires. For instance, Greist and Klein (1981) found that medical outpatients tended to prefer computerized assessment as topics became more sensitive. Female respondents were more likely to confide sexual problems to a computer than they were to a psychiatrist in an interview. Carr, Ghosh, and Ancill (1983) found that a computerized psychiatric history identified an average of 5.4 items unknown to the clinicians that were important for patient management. In the assessment of alcohol consumption, some studies using alcoholic patients (Lucas, Mullin, Luna, & McInrov, 1977) and general population surveys (Duffy & Waterton, 1984; Waterton & Duffy, 1984) have found that computer interviewing elicits reports of greater alcohol consumption (for a review, see Gavin, Skinner, & George, 1992).

Because of a tendency for individuals to underreport alcohol use (Midanik, 1982), we investigated whether greater and presumably more accurate substance use (alcohol, drugs, tobacco) would be reported to the computer than to a human interviewer or on a paper-and-pencil questionnaire. In the first study, 150 patients who voluntarily sought help for an alcohol and/or drug problem were randomly assigned to one of the three assessment formats: computer, interview, questionnaire (Skinner & Allen, 1983). Multivariate analyses revealed no significant differences in consumption patterns or level of problems reported across the three assessment formats.

Because the patients in this study were voluntarily seeking help for substance use problems, they might have been less likely to distort or minimize consumption patterns. Consequently, the study was replicated using 180 general medical patients at the Family Practice Service of Toronto General Hospital (Skinner et al., 1985a). Again, patients were randomly assigned to computer assessment, interview, or a self-administered questionnaire. Results from this study confirmed the earlier work. No significant differences in alcohol, drug, or tobacco consumption levels were reported across the three assessment formats. Finally, a replication of this study with 300 general practice patients at the University of Adelaide's Family Practice Unit, Australia, found that the method of assessment did not affect levels of reported consumption (Bungey, Pols, Mortimer, Frank, & Skinner, 1989).

Research with the CLA did not find any significant differences among methods of assessment in reporting levels of consumption of alcohol, cigarettes, or drugs, or related problems. Because each method of assessment yields the same quality of data, the decision about the method to use will depend on which is most efficient in a particular setting. As low-cost microcomputers are becoming widely available, assessment by computer is quite feasible. In addition, the computer offers certain advantages, such as rapid scoring, immediate feedback, and individualized reports.

Because the psychometric properties are preserved when an instrument is transferred from questionnaire or interview to the computerized format, one may rely on the validity findings underlying the various instruments incorporated in the CLA: the Health Practices Index (Berkman & Breslow, 1983), the Social Network Index (Berkman & Breslow, 1983), the Family Assessment Measure (Skinner, Steinhauer & Santa-Barbara, 1983), the CAGE Questionnaire (Beresford, Blow, Hill, Singer, & Lucey, 1990; Bush, Shaw, Delbanco, & Aronson, 1987; King, 1986), the Alcohol Dependence Scale (Ross, Gavin, & Skinner, 1990; Skinner & Horn, 1984), the Alcohol Problems Questionnaire (Polich & Orvis, 1979), the Drug Abuse Screening Test (Skinner, 1982; Skinner & Goldberg, 1986), and the Canada Health Survey (1981). Finally, there is substantial evidence linking individual life-style factors with health consequences (Berkman & Breslow, 1983; Fitzgerald, Litt, Ciliska, Delmore, &

Butson, 1984; Hamburg et al., 1982; Sherk, Thomas, Wilson, & Evans, 1985).

Another approach in validating the CLA is to compare results of this assessment with an independent assessment of the individual's status. Skinner et al. (1985b) had physicians rate whether a patient's problem was related to alcohol, tobacco, or drug use, and whether the patient had a history of problems of abuse. Overall, there was a high level of agreement between the patient (as shown by the CLA) and the doctor about the presence or absence of problems with alcohol (79%), cigarette smoking (79%), and nonmedical drug use (85%). In some instances, the doctor indicated a problem that the patient either disagreed with or denied. This disagreement was least evident for cigarette smoking and most prominent for nonmedical drugs. Patients who failed to acknowledge alcohol problems tended to be middle-aged (mean 41 years) men with low education (half had not completed secondary school), employed in unskilled occupations, who had seen the doctor before. By contrast, in less than half of the cases where the patient self-identified a problem, the doctor either did not rate a problem or was unaware of it. The doctors tended to miss alcohol problems among younger patients (mean 34 years) who were better educated and employed in professional occupations, and who were on the first visit to the doctor. Similarly, patients with smoking problems that the doctors failed to detect tended to be younger (mean 31 years), better educated, and female.

One of the most important findings of the research was the reaction that patients had to the life-style assessment. Each patient was asked if he or she had come to see the doctor with the intention of discussing a problem of substance use (see Figure 4.3). After completing the life-style assessment and receiving brief feedback on the results, the patient was again asked if he or she intended to discuss a problem with the doctor. A twofold to threefold ($p < .01$) increase was evident across all classes of substances in Figure 4.3. Hence the life-style assessment and feedback had a "priming effect" in encouraging patients to think about their patterns of consumption and encouraged them to raise concerns with the doctor. Presumably, this set the stage for a more meaningful discussion between patient and physician.

A final aspect of validity involves some preliminary studies on the use of "response latencies" for detecting inconsistent and inaccurate responses (Gavin et al., 1992). Response latency is the time delay an individual takes in responding to a potentially "sensitive" item. Within the field of personality assessment, response latencies have been found

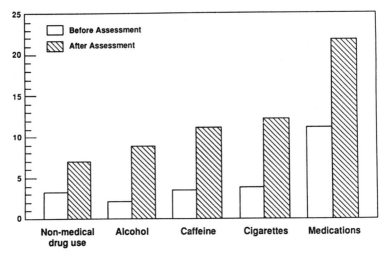

Figure 4.3. Impact of assessment feedback on increasing patients' intentions of discussing a substance use concern with their family physicians.

SOURCE: Adapted from Skinner et al. (1985b)

to be the best predictor of whether an individual will change his or her response to an item upon retesting. Since response latencies can easily be recorded unobtrusively while an individual responds to questions presented by a microcomputer, this approach could lead to significant advances for increasing the accuracy of life-style assessments. The basic strategy is to identify individuals with extreme response latencies who may be giving inaccurate information. Then, one can intervene with probes (e.g., rephrase a question or ask related questions) in order to enhance the accuracy of their self-reports. Preliminary studies with the CLA support the value of recording response latencies for detecting when subjects are faking responses (George & Skinner, 1989, 1990).

Use of the CLA in Behavioral Change

The comprehensive model of change proposed by Prochaska and DiClemente (1986) provides a useful framework for understanding how the Computerized Lifestyle Assessment can be used to facilitate change of life-style behaviors. This model emphasizes three components of change: stages, processes, and levels. From their studies of cigarette smokers, Prochaska and DiClemente identify four common stages of change:

(1) *precontemplation:* unaware of a problem
(2) *contemplation:* thinking about making a change
(3) *action:* initial attempts to change
(4) *maintenance:* long-term change

Most individuals do not progress in a linear fashion through these stages of change. Relapses are common, and an individual may recycle from relapse (maintenance) back through the contemplation and action stages. Prochaska and DiClemente (1986) found that cigarette smokers who are attempting self-change make at lease three revolutions through the stages of change before they achieve long-term abstinence. Another syndrome commonly seen in health care settings is the chronic "contemplator." This individual may think about changing a life-style behavior, such as losing weight or cutting down on drinking, for many years, but not take action to initiate the change. Other individuals may be largely unaware (precontemplation) or may be denying that a particular life-style behavior (e.g., a high-fat, fast-food diet) may have long-term implications for their health. A basic hypothesis is that change is most likely to occur if both the individual and the health professional are focusing on the same stage of change.

Weinstein (1988) proposes a similar model, the "precaution adoption process model," that may be more relevant with health hazards that are recently recognized, such as home radon testing (Weinstein & Sandman, 1992). In this model, Weinstein expands precontemplation to include stages of (a) being unaware of the issue and (b) being aware but not personally engaged. Also, contemplation is differentiated according to (a) deciding about acting and (b) deciding not to act.

The Computerized Lifestyle Assessment is a useful instrument for assessing where a client is with respect to stage of change for a given life-style concern, as well as for facilitating the movement of an individual through the stages toward long-term goal attainment. Figure 4.4 presents a "stages of change ladder" that summarizes barriers to change (Olson, 1992) and therapeutic processes of change (Prochaska & DiClemente, 1986). The ladder concept is adapted from the "contemplation ladder" that Biener and Abrams (1991) found to be a useful indicator of readiness to consider smoking cessation.

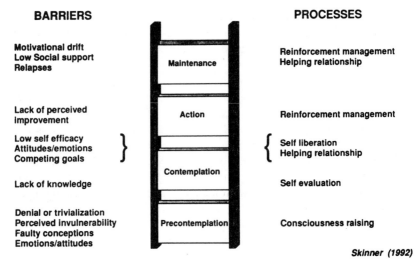

BARRIERS

Motivational drift
Low Social support
Relapses

Lack of perceived
improvement

Low self efficacy
Attitudes/emotions
Competing goals

Lack of knowledge

Denial or trivialization
Perceived invulnerability
Faulty conceptions
Emotions/attitudes

Maintenance

Action

Contemplation

Precontemplation

PROCESSES

Reinforcement management
Helping relationship

Reinforcement management

Self liberation
Helping relationship

Self evaluation

Consciousness raising

Skinner (1992)

Figure 4.4. The stages of change ladder: barriers to change and therapeutic processes that are relevant at each of the four stages of change.

At the *precontemplation stage,* the individual is (largely) unaware or denying that a particular life-style behavior is a health risk. Olson (1992) describes four psychological barriers, including trivialization or denial (e.g., that overexposure to sunlight has health risk), perceived invulnerability (e.g., individuals typically estimate that their own risk of a health problem such as lung cancer is lower than that of their peers), faulty conceptions (e.g., some individuals believe they can tell when their blood pressure is elevated based on symptoms such as headaches), and debilitating emotions and attitudes (e.g., an individual may avoid a medical checkup because of fear of a disease such as cancer).

The major process of change found to be useful at this stage is *consciousness-raising.* The aims are to educate individuals about their susceptibility to health problems, to describe early signs of problems, to frame health risks in ways that individuals can personally understand, to address faulty conceptualizations of health concerns, and to deal with fear-arousing misperceptions. Feedback from the Computerized Life-style Assessment can be helpful in educating an individual that a specific health behavior may be a risk or concern, and in motivating the individual to think further about this concern. Practical experience with the CLA has shown that individuals frequently report that the assessment stimulated concern over a health behavior they had previously not consciously considered. In addition, Skinner et al. (1985b) found that feedback from the CLA had a "priming effect" in raising the intentions of patients to talk about health concerns with their family doctors (see Figure 4.3).

At the *contemplation stage,* the individual admits to a health problem and is thinking about making a change. Barriers to initial action include lack of knowledge, low self-efficacy, and dysfunctional attitudes and emotions. Feedback from the Computerized Lifestyle Assessment can facilitate the self-evaluation process of change. That is, assessment feedback is valuable not only for establishing the extent of a health risk, but also for providing information on how to proceed with changing an undesirable life-style behavior. The printed report from the CLA provides detailed feedback on the individual's status for a given life-style domain, describes healthy standards of behavior, and makes specific recommendations for goal setting and behavior change. Because of the priming effect noted above, the CLA sets the stage for a more meaningful dialogue between the individual and his or her health professional in establishing a *helping relationship* process of change. The health professional can assist the patient in dealing with attitudes and emotional blocks with respect to a particular life-style issue. Results from the CLA can be helpful for engaging other individuals, especially family members, in helping with the health problem. Research has found that self-efficacy, or the belief that "I can do," is an important predictor of behavior change and is central to the *self-liberation* process of change (Bandura, 1977). Self-efficacy is important for both the initiation and maintenance of change, because expectations of personal efficacy strongly influence motivation in performing a new behavior and in using different coping strategies.

The next stage is *action,* where initial attempts are made to change life-style behavior. One important barrier is lack of perceived improvement. Thus it is important to set specific goals and identify improvements that can occur quickly. A key process of change is to define a *reinforcement management* procedure that includes realistic expectations about improvement, timely feedback, and specific schedules to follow. Readministration of the Computerized Lifestyle Assessment after an initial period (e.g., 3 months) could provide a useful mechanism for giving feedback on behavioral change in comparison with the initial assessment.

Maintenance of long-term change is the fourth stage. Key barriers include motivational drift, lack of social support, and relapses. Indeed, for many areas of behavioral change, relapse is common (Marlatt & Gordon, 1985). Important processes of change include continuation of the helping relationship and reinforcement management. The Computerized Lifestyle Assessment could be used as an important element of follow-up visits for maintaining motivation (e.g., at 3 months, 6 months, and 12 months following initial assessment). Research on brief interventions by health professionals for patients with cigarette smoking and alcohol problems has found that scheduled follow-up visits are vital for long-term maintenance of behavioral change (Babor, 1990; Kottke et al., 1988).

The CLA can also function as part of a strategy for improving an individual's sense of personal empowerment (Lord & Farlow, 1990). Health promotion has been defined as "the process of enabling people to increase control over, and to improve their health" (World Health Organization, 1986). The Computerized Lifestyle Assessment provides individuals with personalized feedback on their health strengths and areas of concern, describes standards for health maintenance, and gives specific recommendations on ways to improve health status. This assessment can be done in a private fashion, entirely without the assistance or intervention of a professional or agency. In this way, assessment information can help the individual take personal control over life-style choices and behaviors, without fostering dependence on health or social services. The key is to make the CLA conveniently available to individuals in the community.

Conclusion

Compelling evidence links life-style behaviors with emotional well-being, health status, and premature death, yet life-style-related problems such as addictive behaviors often go undetected in individuals at different life stages. Early intervention programs using brief counseling from health professionals and guided self-management techniques have proved their effectiveness for cigarette smoking cessation and reduction of harmful alcohol consumption. Nevertheless, these programs are not available routinely in health care and other community settings. Microcomputer technology offers part of the solution; fairly sophisticated assessment, immediate feedback of results, and guided self-management strategies can be administered by a microcomputer. The health professional can build upon this process by providing emotional support, personalized instruction, and follow-up. Finally, the Computerized Lifestyle Assessment is an intervention in its own right that can be used strategically for helping an individual deal with personal barriers and advance through the stages of change.

References

Angle, H. V., Ellinwood, E. H., Hay, W. M., Johnsen, T., & Hay, L. (1977). Computer-aided interviewing in comprehensive behavioral assessment. *Behavior Therapy, 8,* 747-754.

Babor, T. F. (1990). Brief intervention strategies for harmful drinkers: New directions for medical education. *Canadian Medical Association Journal, 143,* 1070-1074.

Bandura, A. (1977). Self-efficacy: Toward a unifying theory of behavioral change. *Psychological Review, 84,* 191-215.

Beresford, T. P., Blow, F. C., Hill, E., Singer, K., & Lucey, M. R. (1990). Comparison of CAGE questionnaire and computer assisted laboratory profiles in screening for covert alcoholism. *Lancet, 236,* 482-485.

Berkman, L. F., & Breslow, L. (1983). *Health and ways of living: The Alameda County study.* New York: Oxford University Press.

Biener, L., & Abrams, D. B. (1991). The contemplation ladder: Validation of a measure of readiness to consider smoking cessation. *Health Psychology, 10,* 360-365.

Brownell, K. D. (1991). Personal responsibility and control over our bodies: When expectation exceeds reality. *Health Psychology, 10,* 303-310.

Bungey, J. B., Pols, R. G., Mortimer, K. P., Frank, O. R., & Skinner, H. A. (1989). Screening alcohol and drug use in a general practice unit: Comparison of computerized and traditional methods. *Community Health Studies, 4,* 471-483.

Bunton, R., Murphy, S., & Bennett, P. (1991). Theories of behavioral change and their use in health promotion: Some neglected areas. *Health Education Research, 6,* 153-162.

Bush, B., Shaw, S., Delbanco, T. L., & Aronson, M. D. (1987). Screening for alcohol abuse using the CAGE questionnaire. *American Journal of Medicine, 82,* 231-235.

Byrnes, E., & Johnson, J. H. (1981). Changing technology and the implementation of automation in mental health care settings. *Behavior Research Methods and Instrumentation, 13,* 151-158.

Canada Health Survey. (1981). *The health of Canadians* (Cat. No. 82-538E). Ottawa: Health and Welfare Canada & Statistics Canada.

Carr, A. C., Ghosh, A., & Ancill, R. J. (1983). Can a computer take a psychiatric history? *Psychological Medicine, 13,* 151-158.

Duffy, J. C., & Waterton, J. J. (1984). Under-reporting of alcohol consumption in sample surveys: The effect of computer interviewing in field work. *British Journal of Addiction, 79,* 303-308.

Epp, J. (1986). *Achieving health for all: A framework for health promotion.* Ottawa: Government of Canada.

Evans, R. G., & Stoddart, G. L. (1990). Producing health, consuming health care. *Social Science and Medicine, 31,* 1347-1363.

Fitzgerald, D., Litt, J., Ciliska, D., Delmore, B., & Butson, T. (1984). Health consequences of selected lifestyle factors: A review of the evidence. *Canadian Family Physician, 30,* 2548-2554.

Fleiss, J. L. (1981). *Statistical methods for rates and proportions* (2nd ed.). New York: John Wiley.

Gavin, D. R., Skinner, H. A., & George, M. S. (1992). Computerized approaches to alcohol assessment. In R. Lytton & J. Allen (Eds.), *Measuring alcohol consumption* (pp. 21-39). Totowa, NJ: Humana.

George, M. S., & Skinner, H. A. (1989). Innovative uses of microcomputers for measuring the accuracy of assessment questionnaires. In R. West, M. Christie, & J. Weinman (Eds.), *Microcomputers, psychology and medicine.* London: John Wiley.

George, M. S., & Skinner, H. A. (1990). Using response latency to detect inaccurate responses in a computerized lifestyle assessment. *Computers in Human Behavior, 6,* 167-175.

Goldman, L., & Cook, F. (1984). Decline in ischemic heart disease mortality rates: An analysis of the comparative effects of medical interventions and changes in lifestyle. *Annals of Internal Medicine, 101,* 825-836.

Greist, J. H., & Klein, M. H. (1981). Computers in psychiatry. In S. Arieti & H. K. H. Brodie (Eds.), *American handbook of psychiatry* (2nd ed., Vol. 7, pp. 750-777). New York: Basic Books.

Hamburg, D. A., Elliot, G. R., & Parron, D. L. (1982). *Health and behavior frontiers of research in the biobehavioral sciences.* Washington, DC: National Academy Press.

Hedlund, J. L., Evenson, R. C., Sletten, I. W., & Cho, W. D. (1980). The computer and the clinical prediction. In J. B. Sidowski, J. H. Johnson, & T. A. Williams (Eds.), *Technology in mental health care delivery systems* (pp. 201-235). Norwood, NJ: Ablex.

Institute of Medicine. (1990). *Broadening the base of treatment for alcohol problems.* Washington, DC: National Academy of Sciences Press.

Jeffery, R. W. (1989). Risk behaviors and health: Contrasting individuals and population perspectives. *American Psychologist, 44,* 1194-1202.

King, M. (1986). At-risk drinking general practice attenders: Validation of the CAGE questionnaire. *Psychological Medicine, 16,* 213-217.

Klinger, D. E., Miller, D. A., Johnson, J. H., & Williams, T. A. (1977). Process evaluation of an on-line computer-assisted unit or intake assessment of mental health patients. *Behavior Research Methods and Instrumentation, 9,* 110-116.

Kottke, T. E., Battista, R. N., DeFriese, G. H., & Brakke, M. L. (1988). Attributes of successful smoking interventions in medical practice: A meta-analysis of 39 controlled trials. *Journal of the American Medical Association, 259,* 2883-2889.

Lalonde, M. (1974). *A new perspective on the health of Canadians: A working document.* Ottawa: Government of Canada.

Leader, M. A., & Klein, D. F. (1977). Reflections on instituting a computerized psychological history in a clinical facility. *Comprehensive Psychiatry, 18,* 489-496.

Lord, J., & Farlow, D. M. (1990, Fall). A study of personal empowerment: Implications for health promotion. *Health Promotion,* pp. 2-8.

Lucas, R. W., Mullin, P. J., Luna, C. B., & McInrov, D. C. (1977). Psychiatrists and a computer as interrogators of patients with alcohol-related illnesses: A comparison. *British Journal of Psychiatry, 131,* 160-167.

Marlatt, G. A., & Gordon, J. (1985). *Relapse prevention: Maintenance strategies in the treatment of addictive behaviors.* New York: Guilford.

Midanik, L. (1982). The validity of self-report alcohol consumption and alcohol problems: A literature review. *British Journal of Addiction, 77,* 357-382.

Murphy, H. B. M. (1980). Hidden barriers to the diagnosis and treatment of alcoholism and other alcohol misuses. *Journal of Studies in Alcohol, 41,* 417-428.

Olson, J. M. (1992). Psychological barriers to behaviour change. *Canadian Family Physician, 38,* 309-319.

Polich, J. M., & Orvis, B. R. (1979). *Alcohol problems: Patterns and prevalence in the U.S. Air Force* (No. R-2308-AF). Santa Monica, CA: RAND Corporation.

Prochaska, J. O., & DiClemente, C. C. (1986). Toward a comprehensive model of change. In W. R. Miller & N. Heather (Eds.), *Treating addictive behaviors: Processes of change* (pp. 3-27). New York: Plenum.

Roemer, M. I. (1984). The value of medical care for health promotion. *American Journal of Public Health, 74,* 243-248.

Ross, H. E., Gavin, D. R., & Skinner, H. A. (1990). Diagnostic validity of the MAST and Alcohol Dependence Scale in the assessment of DSM-III alcohol disorders. *Journal of Studies on Alcohol, 51,* 506-513.

Sacks, J., Krushat, W. M., & Newman, J. (1980). Reliability of the health hazard appraisal. *American Journal of Public Health, 70,* 730-732.

Sherk, C., Thomas, H., Wilson, D. M. C., & Evans, C. E. (1985). Health consequences of selected lifestyle factors: A review of the evidence, part 2. *Canadian Family Physician, 31,* 129-139.

Skinner, H. A. (1982). The drug abuse screening test. *Addictive Behaviors, 7,* 363-371.

Skinner, H. A. (1990). Spectrum of drinkers and intervention opportunities. *Canadian Medical Association Journal, 143,* 1054-1059.

Skinner, H. A., & Allen, B. A. (1983). Does the computer make a difference? Computerized versus face-to-face versus self-report assessment of alcohol, drug and tobacco use. *Journal of Consulting and Clinical Psychology, 51,* 267-275.

Skinner, H. A., Allen, B. A., McIntosh, M. C., & Palmer, W. H. (1985a). Lifestyle assessment: Applying microcomputers in family practice. *British Medical Journal, 290,* 212-214.

Skinner, H. A., Allen, B. A., McIntosh, M. C., & Palmer, W. H. (1985b). Lifestyle assessment: Just asking makes a difference. *British Medical Journal, 290,* 214-216.

Skinner, H. A., & Goldberg, A. E. (1986). Evidence for a drug dependence syndrome among narcotic users. *British Journal of Addiction, 81,* 479-484.

Skinner, H. A., & Holt, S. (1983). Early intervention for alcohol problems. *Journal of the Royal College of General Practitioners, 33,* 787-791.

Skinner, H. A., & Horn, J. L. (1984). *Alcohol dependence scale users guide.* Unpublished manuscript, Addiction Research Foundation, Toronto.

Skinner, H. A., & Pakula, A. (1986). Challenge of computers in psychological assessment. *Professional Psychology: Research and Practice, 17,* 44-50.

Skinner, H. A., Palmer, W., Sanchez-Craig, M., & McIntosh, M. (1987). Reliability of a lifestyle assessment using microcomputers. *Canadian Journal of Public Health, 78,* 329-334.

Skinner, H. A., Steinhauer, P. D., & Santa-Barbara, J. (1983). The family assessment measure. *Canadian Journal of Community Mental Health, 2,* 91-105.

Stokols, D. (1992). Establishing and maintaining healthy environments: Toward a social ecology of health promotion. *American Psychologist, 47,* 6-22.

U.S. Surgeon General. (1979). *Healthy people: The surgeon general's report on health promotion and disease prevention* (DHEW Publication No. [PHS] 79-55071). Washington, DC: Government Printing Office.

Wagner, E. H., Beery, W. L., Schoenbach, V. J., & Graham, R. M. (1982). An assessment of health hazard/health risk appraisal. *American Journal of Public Health, 72,* 347-352.

Wallace, P. G., Cutler, S., & Haines, A. P. (1988). Randomized controlled trial of general practitioner intervention in patients with excessive alcohol consumption. *British Medical Journal, 297,* 663-668.

Wallace, P. G., & Haines, A. P. (1984). General practitioner and health promotion: What patients think. *British Medical Journal, 289,* 534-536.

Waterton, J. J., & Duffy, J. C. (1984). A comparison of computer interviewing techniques and traditional methods in the collection of self-report alcohol consumption data in a field survey. *International Statistical Review, 52,* 173-182.

Wechsler, H., Levine, S., Idelson, R. K., Rohman, M., & Taylor, J. O. (1983). The physician's role in health promotion: A survey of primary-care practitioners. *New England Journal of Medicine, 308*(2), 97-100.

Weinstein, N. D. (1988). The precaution adoption process. *Health Psychology, 7,* 355-386.

Weinstein, N. D., & Sandman, P. M. (1992). A model of the precaution adoption process: Evidence from home radon testing. *Health Psychology, 11,* 170-180.

Wigle, D. T., Semenciw, M. R., McCann, C., & Davies, J. W. (1990). Premature deaths in Canada: Impact, trends and opportunities for prevention. *Canadian Journal of Public Health, 81,* 376-381.

Wilson, D. M. C., Nielsen, M., & Ciliska, D. (1984). Lifestyle assessment: Development and use of the FANTASTIC checklist. *Canadian Family Physician, 30,* 1527-1532.

World Health Organization. (1986). *Ottawa charter for health promotion.* Geneva: Author.

5

Etiology and Secondary Prevention of Alcohol Problems With Young Adults

JOHN S. BAER

The consumption of alcohol by young people constitutes an enormous social problem. A host of ongoing social problems are associated with alcohol use, including date rape, vandalism, relationship difficulties, academic failure, and driving while intoxicated (Institute of Medicine, 1990). Alcohol-related accidents are the leading cause of death in this age group (National Institute on Alcohol Abuse and Alcoholism, 1984). Because drinking and associated problems of young people are so common, costs to society are greater for this age group than for any other (Cahalan & Room, 1974; Institute of Medicine, 1990).

In this chapter a model of secondary prevention for alcohol use by young adults is presented. *Secondary prevention* is typically defined as

AUTHOR'S NOTE: This research was supported by National Institute on Alcohol Abuse and Alcoholism Grant 5 R37 AA05591 and Grant 1 RO1 AA08632. I would like to thank Dan Kivlahan for comments on an earlier draft of this chapter, Susan Tapert for diligent work in preparation of the manuscript, and Jewel Brien for graphics.

the provision of early programming for those most at risk or those showing early or prodromal signs of a disorder. I will argue that both primary prevention and tertiary care have limited impact with this age group, and that secondary prevention approaches provide a flexible and individualized approach to a complex and multidetermined problem. Secondary prevention can also serve to integrate services from primary to tertiary levels (see Pentz, Chapter 3, this volume). Before presenting a more detailed rationale for secondary prevention and a model program at the University of Washington, I will review briefly the nature and etiology of young peoples' alcohol use.

How Young People Drink

Young people, as a group, are the heaviest drinkers in American and other Western societies (Cahalan & Room, 1974; Institute of Medicine, 1990). For example, in a 2-year longitudinal study of young adults aged 17-25, Grant, Harford, and Grigson (1988) noted that 58% of men and 33% of women consumed 6 or more drinks on at least two occasions in the past month. These rates are considerably higher and more dangerous than those found in older age groups. Young people, on average, tend to drink in a style different from that of older individuals. A young person who consumes 10 drinks a week will likely do so within two drinking occasions, in comparison with an older person, who is more likely to drink 10 drinks over four or five occasions. Young people typically reach high blood alcohol levels (>.10%) and experience considerable intoxication. Alcohol is used as a "drug" for a specific purpose, "to get high." Older individuals are more likely to say that alcohol facilitates some other activity, particularly participation in social events.

Problems associated with alcohol are also more common among the young than they are among older age groups (Cahalan & Room, 1974; Fillmore, 1988). Problems cover the full range of adjustment domains, from academic and employment functioning to health risks and social relationships. Yet these problems also tend to be more isolated in younger age groups (Fillmore & Midanik, 1984). Individuals in their fourth or fifth decade of life are more likely to report multiple alcohol-related problems.

The course of youthful drinking over time is quite variable (see Baer, 1991; Donovan, Jessor, & Jessor, 1983; Fillmore, 1988; Fillmore &

Midanik, 1984; Sobell, Cunningham, Sobell, & Toneatto, Chapter 2, this volume). Most young people who drink heavily in their teens and early to mid-20s moderate their use in their later 20s and their 30s (Fillmore, 1988). The problems of young peoples' drinking seem relatively transitory compared with long-standing addictive patterns of alcohol use more typically noted in older populations. Nevertheless, a subpopulation of young people (approximately 30%) do show continuity of heavy drinking into mid-life (Fillmore, 1988; Zucker, in press). At the current level of understanding, however, it is quite difficult to identify young people most at risk for continued heavy drinking.

Developmental and Environmental Factors Associated With Youthful Drinking

Alcohol use and abuse by young people can be understood as a combination of developmental processes, environmental influences, and individual differences in responses to alcohol. Alcohol use is a common behavior of adults (80% of American adults drink at least monthly; National Institute on Alcohol Abuse and Alcoholism, 1990), thus most young people must learn to drink at some point in time. The process of learning to drink can occur with varying degrees of difficulty and risk. It is likely that factors associated with experimentation with alcohol are different from factors associated with abuse of alcohol (see Glantz & Pickens, 1992). Heavy drinking during adolescence is associated with a variety of adjustment problems, including truancy, other drug use, and early sexual activity (Jessor & Jessor, 1975). Young people who drink at earlier ages tend to have more risk of alcohol-related problems (Windle, 1990) and tend to assume other adult behaviors, such as parenting and live-in relationships, early as well (Newcomb, 1987).

A variety of risk factors, at both environmental and personal levels, are associated with this problem development. *Social influence* is typically defined as the impact of the environment, particularly the behavior of others. Social influence processes can take many forms, such as positive or negative reinforcement of behavior by family or peers, modeling of certain behaviors, direct instruction, and efforts to behave consistently with social norms. Peer influences, particularly peer drinking rates, are the single best predictor of alcohol use among young people (Jessor & Jessor, 1977; Kandel & Andrews, 1987). On college campuses, different living arrangements (such as Greek houses) are associated with different patterns of drinking (Johanson, Baer, Kivlahan, Collier, & Marlatt, 1988). In other words, students tend to drink at rates consistent with those of the people with whom they live.

The manner in which peers influence one another is not clear, however. Peers can model, imitate, reinforce, and persuade each other to use alcohol. They can also make alcohol more available to each other. Hence young people may "socialize" each other to use alcohol. Alternatively, young people can pick their friends from among other young people who also want to use alcohol (or other drugs). This "selection" process suggests that young people seek out others like themselves to befriend (see Jacob & Leonard, 1991). Kandel (1986) has provided data that suggest both processes are important. In a study using a prospective design, young people who shared attitudes toward drug use (positive or negative) were shown to associate with one another and to reinforce those attitudes.

Family relationships are also important. Rates of alcohol use and incidence of problems of children and adolescents are associated with alcohol use by parents (Cahalan, Cissin, & Crossley, 1969). Adolescents' perceptions of parental alcohol use are related to their own use (Kandel, Kessler, & Margulies, 1978). All studies are not consistent, however. When parental drinking becomes extreme, adolescents are less likely to imitate (Harburg, Davis, & Caplan, 1982). Parents who abstain are more likely to have children who abstain, but when children of abstaining parents do drink, there is some evidence that they tend to do so in a more deviant fashion (Barnes, Farrell, & Cairns, 1986).

More generally, the quality of the parent-child relationship and the skill of parents to socialize children are related to all kinds of childhood and adolescent adjustment difficulties, including alcohol use and abuse (for reviews, see Jacob & Leonard, 1991; Patterson, Reid, & Dishion, in press; Snyder & Huntley, 1990). Adequate parenting is typically described as providing high levels of parental support and moderate levels of control (Barnes, 1990). Parental failure to provide either clear rules, contingencies, and attention or warmth, support, and caring is likely to increase adolescents' risks of more antisocial and delinquent behaviors (Dishion, Patterson, Stoolmiller, & Skinner, 1991; Holmes & Robins, 1987).

Stressful life events and chronic conflict also have an impact on young peoples' use of alcohol. Young people report greater alcohol use coincident with greater difficulty in social relationships (Labouvie, 1986), stressful life events (Chassin, McLaughlin Mann, & Sher, 1988;

Wills, 1985), and family conflict (Baer, Garmezy, McLaughlin, Pokorny, & Wernick, 1987). For example, Chassin et al. (1988) assessed high school students at the beginning and again at the end of the school year, and found that alcohol use was associated with negative life events.

Despite a host of social influences, alcohol use can also be understood as a function of individual personality styles and more physiologically based responses to alcohol. As noted above, Jessor and Jessor (1977) have identified a "problem behavior syndrome," describing a pattern where young people who drink early and with greater frequency are also likely to have difficulties with truancy, other drug use, and precocious sexual activity. This pattern of problem-prone adolescent behavior has been described as part of a broader personality style variously described as sensation seeking, impulsive, unable to delay gratification, undercontrolled, or thrill seeking. This undercontrolled behavioral pattern is the only personality pattern prospectively linked to alcohol problems (Cox, 1987). It is thought to be linked in time to earlier problems with hyperactivity, and to later problems with adult sociopathy (Zucker, 1986, in press; Zucker & Gomberg, 1986). Zucker (1986), through a careful review of research literature, concludes that adolescents with antisocial behavior patterns are at high risk for later alcoholism. In addition, adolescents who later have problems with alcohol show difficulty with achievement in school and are more loosely connected to others (less dependent, less considerate, more indifferent).

A number of individual differences in temperament, physiology, learning, and motivation have been hypothesized to account for developmental and personality differences that are associated with alcohol problems. Some differences may be genetically based. Having parents with alcohol problems increases the likelihood of offspring developing alcohol problems, even when children are raised by adoptive parents (Cadoret, 1990). (Although some genetic influences no doubt exist, not all reviewers agree on the magnitude and reliability of the heritability of addiction problems; see Searles, 1990.) Children of alcoholics are somewhat more likely to manifest hyperactive behavior patterns at early ages and conduct disorders at later ages. An "undercontrolled" behavioral style was shown to mediate the relationship between family history of alcohol problems and individual drinking rates in a recent study of college students (Sher, Walitzer, Wood, & Brent, 1991).

Parental or familial history of alcoholism and impulsive personality styles have also been linked to individual differences in alcohol reinforcement. Reinforcement can be conceptualized as the amount of pleasure, stress reduction, social facilitation, or general change in hedonic tone accompanied by the consumption of alcohol. Recently, models of stress-response dampening (Sher, 1987, 1991; see also Chapter 1, this volume) have been used to describe differences in responses to alcohol. Children of alcoholic parents (Finn & Pihl, 1987) and those with impulsive personality patterns (Sher & Levenson, 1982) tend to show greater dampening of heart rate stress responses after the consumption of alcohol. Such dampening could relate to a greater experience of stress reduction for those most at risk for alcohol problems. Newlin and Thomson (1990) have recently suggested that children of alcoholics are at risk for problems due to several different responses to alcohol. Children of alcoholics, for example, may be more likely to develop sensitivity to the initial effects of alcohol, but also more likely to develop early tolerance to the more long-term and negative effects of the depressant drug in comparison to peers of nonalcoholic parents. Thus risk for alcoholism may be related to greater positive reinforcement from initial positive alcohol effects, and less punishment for later more negative alcohol effects.

Differences in young people's social environments, as well as individual responses to alcohol, lead to different expectations or beliefs about the effects of alcohol. Beliefs in alcohol's effects are affected by environment and are related to alcohol use in the home (Brown, Creamer, & Stetson, 1987; Mann, Chassin, & Sher, 1987). Beliefs about alcohol are evident in very young children, long before alcohol is personally experienced (Miller, Smith, & Goldman, 1990), and adolescents' beliefs are predictive of later experimentation with alcohol (Christiansen, Smith, Roehling, & Goldman, 1989). Beliefs in alcohol effects are also a product of personal experience. Adolescents who drink more report more positive effects from alcohol (Christiansen, Goldman, & Inn, 1982). In Sher et al.'s (1991) study of college student children of alcoholics, beliefs that alcohol acts to enhance performance were found to mediate the relationship between family history of alcoholism and behavioral undercontrol in the prediction of alcohol use. Thus beliefs about the effects of alcohol may be a central risk factor predictive of young people's alcohol use.

It is noteworthy that individual differences in risk for alcohol problems are most likely augmented or attenuated by the variety of environmental factors noted above. Zucker and Fitzgerald (in press) present a developmental scheme whereby "a preexisting structure of risky behavior (or risky biology) is likely to be enhanced by a contextual structure that elicits risky behavior; this, in turn, leads to increasing differentiation and crystallization of the behavioral repertoire." Essentially, these authors are describing a process of specialization that takes place when individual differences (personality or alcohol reinforcement) interact with environments (such as family structure and peer use) that increase risk or, at the least, do not temper or reduce risk. Zucker (in press) emphasizes the importance of continuity and discontinuity of risk factors over time affecting the probability of an alcoholic outcome.

In other words, it is unlikely that any single risk factor, such as impulsive personality style, alcohol availability, deviant peers, norms for heavy use, beliefs about alcohol effects, stress, or absent parents, will result in alcohol problems. Rather, it is the compilation and continuity of risk over time that leads to negative outcomes. This developmental complexity leads to considerable difficulty in predicting the course of alcohol problems for any individual. There is no single high-risk profile; rather, there are likely several developmental paths to alcohol abuse (see Glantz & Pickens, 1992). Numerous factors not only increase risk for alcohol abuse, but serve to protect individuals as well. In addition, developmental processes may be more active for young people than for older people. Thus behavior is more variable, and perhaps more subject to environmental changes. Recall that, among young people, dependency syndromes are less well developed and rigidified. The fact that many heavy drinkers at young ages moderate their use in adulthood would be consistent with changes in risk factors over time leading to more moderate use. This conceptualization suggests the need for a highly flexible, individualized approach to the treatment of alcohol problems in young people.

Limits of Treatment
and Prevention for Young People

Complex patterns and causes of youthful drinking present both theoretical and practical problems for professionals attempting to understand and minimize individual and societal harm. Although doing so is illegal, most adolescents consume alcohol, and a considerable proportion do so in a risky fashion. Learning to manage alcohol (as well as other drugs and sexuality) is a critical developmental process in becoming an adult. Primary prevention programs have difficulty being sensitive to these developmental issues. For example, instructing all young people to avoid alcohol (following state laws) may be inconsistent with common developmental processes of adopting behaviors that are legal (and advertised) for adults. Simple educational programs tend to change attitudes, but not drinking behavior (Kraft, 1984). (See Pentz, Chapter 3, this volume, for examples of broader, more integrated programs with more encouraging results.)

Furthermore, some young people need more help than others. The data reviewed above suggest that alcohol problems are not isolated, but associated with undercontrolled personality styles and other behavioral problems. Primary prevention messages, targeted to a general population, may not reach those individuals experiencing the greatest problems.

In addition, traditional models of addiction do not accurately describe the drinking habits of most young people or those who drink most heavily. As noted above, few young people display moderate or severe dependency syndromes more commonly noted in older populations. Although alcohol use can interfere with social and occupational functioning, it usually does so with lower levels of severity and inconsistently. Tolerance and withdrawal syndromes are usually minimal as well (Cahalan & Room, 1974; Fillmore & Midanik, 1984). Environmental factors, such as peer use or living setting in college, are powerfully related to drinking rates. Thus few young people are "addicted" in the traditional sense. From a clinical perspective, few young people volunteer for treatment, and few easily accept traditional treatment prescriptions. Most young people come into contact with treatment via coercion from family or the courts. Furthermore, most young people do not feel "powerless over alcohol"; most resist treatment goals of lifelong abstinence. It should not be surprising that tertiary treatment for young people based on traditional theories of addiction are limited in effectiveness (see Baer, 1991).

Based on this analysis, another approach for understanding and treating youthful drinking is needed. One must address the critical etiologic factors noted for young people, but also be flexible given the tremendous variability of drinking patterns noted in this age group. Below, I describe a model of secondary prevention for alcohol problems developed at the University of Washington Addictive Behaviors Research Center. This approach is meant to augment and integrate existing programming, provide messages in a style that young people accept, and provide considerable flexibility for tailoring materials to individual personal risk factors.

The High Risk Drinkers Project:
An Integrated Approach to
Early Intervention With College Students

The High Risk Drinkers Project at the University of Washington is designed to test the effectiveness of an integrated approach to early intervention with college students. College students are one group of young people at risk for alcohol-related problems and are noted as a special population in need of services in the recent report by the Institute of Medicine (1990). Because alcohol use is a problem associated with normal development, environmental influences, and certain adjustment difficulties, we have attempted to develop a program in which a variety of risk factors can be addressed, but labels of "problem drinking" and "alcoholism" can be avoided. Because few young people seek alcohol risk programming, we actively screen and encourage participation. We have chosen to target students "at risk" but not yet experiencing severe alcohol-related problems. The intervention is designed to challenge beliefs about alcohol effects, increase motivation to examine drinking habits, and encourage either self-change or utilization of services. We hope to demonstrate a reduction in the number of emerging alcohol problems and show that emerging problems can be treated earlier when service systems are readily available. The secondary prevention program can be described in terms of four stages: screening, assessment, initial intervention, and subsequent contact and programming.

Screening

Despite considerable harm due to alcohol use on college campuses, not all college students drink heavily. Our first task was to identify those most at risk for alcohol-related problems. Note that we did not attempt to find only those students already experiencing severe problems or who might be deemed alcohol dependent. Rather, we cast a wide net that encompassed factors known to relate to risk of future problems without those problems being clearly evident at that point in time.

We screened all entering freshman to the University of Washington via a questionnaire sent during the spring prior to enrollment. Assessment domains were selected based on the research literature reviewed above. Risk factors included drinking patterns, previous problems associated with alcohol, family history of drinking problems, and history of conduct-disordered behavior (a result of impulsive, undercontrolled behavioral styles).

By offering a small payment ($5) and entrance into a drawing for larger prizes ($100 gift certificates for the university bookstore), we obtained a 51% return rate (2,152 of more than 4,250 mailed) on the questionnaires. Our plan was to select approximately the top 25% of the sample based on risk of future alcohol-related problems. How to define such risk based on multiple factors proved challenging. After evaluating a number of schemes, we chose to select young people for the study based on two criteria: (a) self-reported drinking of at least five to six drinks on one occasion in the past month, or (b) self-reported history of three or more alcohol-related negative consequences occurring at least three times in the past three years (based on the Rutgers Alcohol Problem Index, RAPI; White & Labouvie, 1989). Drinking six or more drinks on one occasion increases the likelihood of accidents and other problems, and exceeds criteria typically considered to define "heavy drinking" (five or more on one occasion; see Johnston, O'Malley, & Bachman, 1989). Criteria for negative consequences (RAPI items) reflected not only the occurrence of low-level negative outcomes as a result of drinking, but also the repeated nature of this behavior pattern over an extended period of time.

Thus students in our "high-risk" sample were those who drank in a risky fashion in high school or who reported the beginnings of alcohol-related consequences. Although behavior may change considerably in college (toward reduced risk, one would hope), these high school behaviors represent the best initial predictors of college drinking. These selection criteria proved to include virtually all students who reported histories of conduct problems, thus selection on the basis of conduct problems was unnecessary. If we had been more restricted in the number of students we could study, the presence of conduct problems would have been a logical selection criterion for those at highest risk. Positive history of family alcohol problems, although associated with risk of addiction, is not clearly a risk factor for alcohol problems in all populations. More specifically, many children of alcoholics show excellent psychological adjustment, perhaps avoiding alcohol due to their parents' difficulties. College students, in general, may be one such example. Recent studies, in fact, show that college students who are children of alcoholic parents actually drink less than their similar-age counterparts (Alterman, 1987). In our screening sample, children of alcoholics did not drink more during high school, and were not specifically selected. We did, however, carefully evaluate this risk factor for those who met criteria for inclusion based on drinking rates and problems.

Characteristics of the high-risk sample while in high school are shown in Table 5.1. On average, the high-risk student, while in high school, drank three and a half times a month, with an average of more than four drinks per drinking occasion. The most alcohol consumed on one occasion in the past month averaged almost six drinks. The average number of problems related to alcohol use was more than eight. Parental history of alcohol problems, using the Short Michigan Alcoholism Screening Test (SMAST; Selzer, Vinokur, & van Rooijen, 1975), was noted by 13.6% of the sample. In Table 5.1, data describing these high-risk students are displayed next to data describing the entire screening sample to provide a "normal" comparison.

Assessment

Subjects selected were asked to enroll in a 4-year longitudinal study of college life-styles and drinking habits. As part of the research aspect of the study, students agreed to complete assessments on an annual basis and to be randomly assigned to receive secondary prevention programming (a feedback and advice interview—described below) during their freshman year.

The initial or baseline assessment was in some respects the most important. At this assessment we obtained information about risk factors in much more detail than in questionnaire assessment during the spring of the senior year in high school. Information from this assessment was then used to guide individual feedback sessions for those in the experimental group (see Miller's drinkers' checkup; Miller & Sovereign, 1989). The interview protocol was based on three standardized interviews: the Brief Drinker Profile (BDP; Miller & Marlatt, 1984), the Family Tree Questionnaire (Mann et al., 1987), and the Diagnostic Interview Schedule (DIS; Robins, Helzer, Croughan, & Ratcliff, 1981). From these protocols we assessed typical drinking quantity and frequency, alcohol-related life problems, history of conduct disorder, DSM-III-R (American Psychiatric Association, 1987) alcohol dependency criteria, and family history of drinking problems and other psychopathology. In addition, questionnaire assessment completed at baseline included indices of the type of living situation, alcohol expectancies, perceived risks, psychiatric symptomatology (Brief Symptom Inventory; Derogatis & Spencer, 1982), perceived norms for alcohol consumption, and sexual behavior.

TABLE 5.1 Sample Description

	Screening Sample		High-Risk Sample	
Percentage of female subjects	54		53	
Alcohol use				
frequency (occasions/month)	1.25 [2.40]	(2.13)	3.39	(2.79)
quantity (drinks/occasion)	1.50 [2.87]	(2.17)	4.23	(2.27)
peak (highest occasion in past 30 days)	2.20 [4.09]	(2.92)	5.94	(2.67)
Alcohol problems (RAPI)				
number of times occurring				
1-2	3.1	(4.3)	8.3	(4.6)
3-5	0.9	(2.2)	3.4	(3.3)
Family alcoholism				
F-SMAST ≥ 4	235	(10.8%)	69	(13.6%)
M-SMAST ≥ 4	58	(2.7%)	23	(4.5%)

NOTE: Standard deviations appear in parentheses; means (denoting only those who drink) appear in square brackets.

Motivational Intervention

The intervention was based on two research programs, our own and that of William Miller at the University of New Mexico. Both have demonstrated drinking reductions for those showing early signs of alcohol problems, but who may not be diagnosed as alcohol dependent (Baer et al., 1992; Kivlahan, Marlatt, Fromme, Coppel, & Williams, 1990; Miller & Rollnick, 1991).

Over the past several years we have developed a skills-based approach to intervention for high-risk college drinking. The program will be described briefly here; more detail is available elsewhere (Baer, Kivlahan, Fromme, & Marlatt, 1989, 1992; Baer et al., 1992; Kivlahan, Coppel,

Fromme, Miller, & Marlatt, 1990). College students who drink heavily have been recruited in two studies to participate in either a 6- or 8-week small group program to discuss alcohol use and related risks. The program is nonconfrontational in tone, but nevertheless seeks to challenge students' assumptions about the effects of alcohol, in particular, the assumption that if some alcohol is good, "more is better." We also challenge the presumed necessity of alcohol consumption for improved social relationships and parties. Information and class discussion of blood alcohol levels, biphasic effects of alcohol, homework assignments to experiment with drinking less, and placebo beverage consumption assist students in evaluating their beliefs (for more details, see Baer et al., 1989, 1992a, 1992b; Kivlahan, Coppel, et al., 1990). Results from this type of program have been encouraging, with students reporting drinking rate reductions of 40%-50% and maintaining such reductions for 1- and 2-year follow-up periods (Baer et al., in press; Kivlahan, Marlatt, et al., 1990).

In our more recent study, this type of group intervention was compared to a single feedback interview (Baer et al., 1989, 1992b). In this feedback interview, a staff member met individually with the student and gave him or her concrete, individualized feedback about his or her drinking patterns, risks, and beliefs about alcohol effects. The student's drinking rates were compared to college averages, and risks (grades, blackouts, accidents) were addressed as issues the student might consider. Issues pertaining to family history of alcohol problems were raised where appropriate. Beliefs about alcohol effects were more directly confronted through discussions of placebo effects and the nonspecifics of alcohol's effects on social behavior. Suggestions for risk reduction were outlined. To our surprise, the effects of this brief intervention were quite comparable to those achieved with a complete 6-week course (Baer et al., 1992b).

Our approach shares much with models of motivational interviewing developed by William Miller at the University of New Mexico (Miller & Rollnick, 1991). Motivational interviewing is a technique designed to minimize resistance of those experiencing alcohol- and drug-related problems. People with alcohol-related problems are assumed to be ambivalent about changing, and, at best, only contemplating change (see Prochaska & DiClemente, 1986, for a description of a model for stages of change). The therapist's goal is to assist the client to move from considering change to attempting change. Confrontational communications, such as, "You have a problem with alcohol and you are in denial," are thought to create a defense response in the client and thus to work against motivation to change. In contrast, simply placing the available evidence in front of the client and avoiding arguments about labels is thought to allow the client to evaluate his or her situation and become ready to change behavior. Miller and Rollnick (1991) have documented in considerable detail the many therapeutic strategies that can be used from a motivational interviewing framework. Research using this approach also has documented considerable success in promoting drinking reduction and treatment utilization.

We chose this form of intervention not only because of the encouraging data from previous studies, but also because of the conceptual match to the risk factors and style of our youthful college student population. Motivational interviewing is not confrontational, and thus avoids the trap of labeling young people as "alcoholic" or "having a problem" when they do not easily accept such labels. Furthermore, the technique is flexible in that each interview is tailored to the specific history and risk factors of each individual. Issues of setting (i.e., life in a fraternity), peer use, beliefs about alcohol effects, prior conduct difficulties, and family history can be addressed if applicable. Individual beliefs about alcohol effects and drinking norms can be questioned. Motivational techniques also assume that the client is in a state of ambivalence, and must come to his or her own conclusion regarding the need to change behavior and reduce risks. This style leaves responsibility with the client and hence treats all clients as thoughtful adults. Our work with young people suggests that this approach is much more acceptable to them than being told what to do. Finally, despite an apparently complex screening, assessment, and interviewing procedure, individual feedback can be completed with relatively little professional time (two hours per client).

The motivational intervention for the High Risk Drinkers Project was organized into two parts: feedback about (a) drinking rates and norms and (b) risk factors associated with drinking. The clinician's style throughout the interview was empathic and questioning. We used information from the baseline interview to generate individualized feedback. The student's drinking rates and patterns were reviewed first, and in each case the student's drinking was compared with norms for others his or her age. Typical blood alcohol concentrations (BAC) were calculated based on data from the Brief Drinker Profile, and students were encouraged to think about different levels of BAC and their effects. The biphasic effects of alcohol were reviewed as well. A personalized BAC card (specific for gender and weight) was also provided.

Individual risk factors, previously acknowledged by the student, were reviewed next. History of conduct problems and family history of alcohol problems were noted and the notion of increased risk as a function of these factors was described. Alcohol-related negative consequences, previously reported by the student, were raised for discussion and clarification. "Problems" were not labeled; an understanding of the role of alcohol in broader life-style issues was sought. In addition, students' beliefs about alcohol effects were challenged via discussion of typical placebo effects from alcohol. Finally, students were asked about what, if anything, they wished to change about their drinking, and how they might go about it. Only if the student expressed a desire to change would planning and goal setting take place. In many cases, goals were discussed without specific plans; in some cases, specific plans were developed and monitored through follow-up appointments.

Subsequent Contact and Programming

Motivational interviewing is based on the idea that personal change is a process of moving through several stages of readiness, and that treatments assist people first to make a commitment to change, next to get started changing, and subsequently to keep the changes they have successfully accomplished. Thus programming needs to be not only flexible in content, but available whenever the client is ready to move on. In the High Risk Drinkers Project, we end each contact, clinical or otherwise (e.g., data collection), with the statement, "We are always happy to meet with you to discuss issues about alcohol use or any other life-style concern." Students are encouraged to use us as a resource, and to make follow-up appointments as desired. In addition, one year after the motivational interviews, all subjects who received our secondary prevention treatment were sent graphic feedback depicting their patterns of alcohol use over time. Additional programming available to the students includes further individual evaluation and counseling, small group meetings, a safe life-style college course, and referral to area agencies. Through this variety of options, each student's programming can be adjusted or "stepped up" depending on need and preference. Thus secondary programming, as conceptualized in the High Risk Drinkers Project, is ongoing and provides many options for students to evaluate and change risky drinking practices.

Continued assessment also allows for determination of increasing risk and subsequent intervention if necessary.

Preliminary Results
of the High Risk Drinkers Project

Data from the High Risk Drinkers Project can be used to test both assumptions about the context of college students' drinking and the effectiveness of our motivational intervention. Initial analyses have evaluated drinking rates across the transition from high school to college. Recall that the top twenty-fifth percentile of drinkers ($n = 508$ of 2,041 usable questionnaire responders) were recruited for the longitudinal study based on responses in the spring prior to entry to the university. Of these, 454 were successfully enrolled and reassessed the following fall. Three key questions were initially asked: (a) Does alcohol use increase when students enter the university? (b) If changes in drinking occur, are they related to previous patterns of consumption from the high school years? (c) Do personal factors associated with risk of addiction affect the transition from high school to college? For this sample, family history of alcohol problems and history of conduct problems were the most likely factors to evaluate. The type of residence that students both planned and actually lived in was also assessed.

In addition to a sample of heavy-drinking students, a smaller group of students ($n = 151$) was selected randomly from the entire screening sample to represent a normative base for comparison. Of these students, 131 were successfully recruited the following fall.

Students were classified as *family history positive* if either natural parent was judged by the student as being an alcoholic or having significant drinking problems based on criteria in the Family Tree Questionnaire (Mann et al., 1987). Students were classified as *conduct disorder positive* if they acknowledged three or more conduct problems at or before age 15 (see DSM-III-R; American Psychiatric Association, 1987). In analyses presented below, three measures of drinking (typical quantity, frequency, peak consumption previous month) are evaluated using MANOVA methods. For purposes of illustration, however, only peak quantity is displayed.

Figure 5.1 displays changes in self-reported peak quantity of alcohol consumed on any single drinking occasion during the past month, first

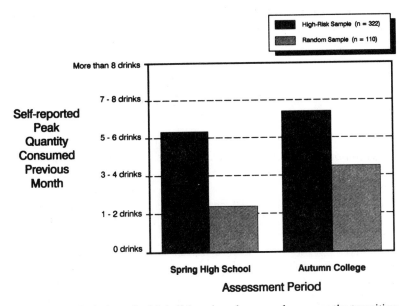

Figure 5.1. Alcohol use for high-risk and random samples across the transition from high school to college.

assessed during the last spring in high school and again during the first autumn in college. This figure displays a pattern of increased drinking noted in all measures of alcohol consumption (quantity, frequency, peak consumption) for the sample as a whole (MANOVA $F[3, 428] = 52.45$, $p < .0001$). For the random sample (representing students in general), average frequency of consumption increased from about once a month to 2-3 times a month, and the average quantity per drinking occasion increased from 1-2 to 2-3. Drinking in the high-risk sample increased as well, although the magnitude of increase was somewhat smaller than among the random sample ($F[3, 428] = 5.08, p < .002$). This significant interaction may be due to ceiling or regression-to-the-mean effects. In the first autumn in college, the high-risk students consumed an average of 4-5 drinks per occasion, 1-2 times a week.

Figure 5.2 displays self-reported peak quantity of drinking in the prior month assessed during high school and during college among those in the high-risk group, broken down by history of conduct problems and parental history of alcoholism. MANOVA for changes in quantity, frequency, and

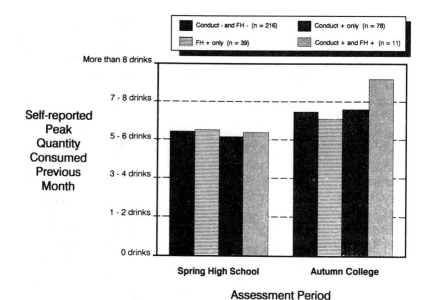

Figure 5.2. Alcohol use by high-risk students across the transition from high school to college by history of conduct disorder and familial alcoholism.

peak alcohol consumption revealed significant main effects for conduct problems ($F[3, 341] = 5.31$, $p < .001$) and family history ($F[3, 341] = 3.07$, $p < .028$). The interaction of family history and conduct problems was not significant in the MANOVA ($F[3, 341] = 1.81$, ns); however, two univariate interaction tests (quantity and peak consumption) approached significance ($F[1, 343] = 4.18$ and 3.36, both $ps < .06$). This pattern of results suggests that students with histories of conduct problems, and those with family histories of alcoholism, show greater increases in consumption when entering college. The combination of family history of alcoholism and prior conduct problems may be especially problematic. These differences were noted primarily in average quantity and peak quantity of drinks when consuming, but less so in frequency of consumption. It is noteworthy that those with both family history of alcoholism and history of conduct problems constitute less than 5% of the sample ($n = 11$).

Although subject gender was consistently related to amount of drinking (males drinking more than females), in no analysis did gender interact with the factors discussed above.

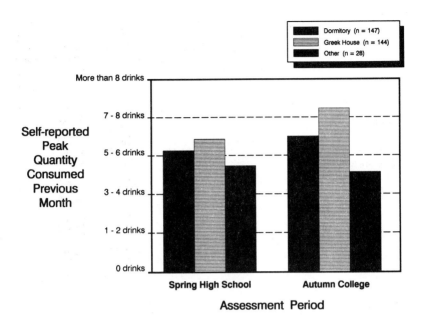

Figure 5.3. Alcohol use by high-risk students across the transition from high school to college by residence type.

The type of residence students lived in was also evaluated as a predictor of changes in drinking across the transition entering college. Figure 5.3 shows these relationships; again, only peak quantity is displayed. High school students who planned to live in the Greek system already reported drinking more frequently ($F[2, 317] = 3.88, p < .02$) and with higher peak quantity ($F[2, 317] = 3.34, p < .04$) than high school students planning to live in dormitories or in apartments. Nevertheless, those who ended up living in Greek residences increased drinking more (MANOVA repeated measure for quantity, frequency, and peak consumption, $F[2, 316] = 14.76, p < .000$).

Thus entering college appears to be a life transition typically associated with increased consumption of alcohol. Those who drank the most in high school continue to drink more in college. Among those who drink in the top quartile in high school (our high-risk group), drinking increases appear exacerbated by personal histories of conduct disorder and familial alcoholism. This effect is most striking in terms of drinking quantity per occasion. Living in the Greek system also is associated with drinking increases. The fact that those who plan to live in Greek houses already drink more in high school suggests that processes of peer selection and peer socialization noted above are both supported by our data.

Our motivational interventions were completed in the winter term of the freshman year for a random half of the high-risk group ($n = 157$). The other high-risk subjects received only assessment procedures (control group, $n = 164$). All subjects were reassessed with questionnaires in the spring. Results of multivariate tests of three indices of drinking (frequency, average quantity, peak quantity) indicated significantly greater drinking reductions by the treatment group (repeated measures MANOVA, $F[1, 319] = 7.19, p < .008$), despite a general trend among both groups to report less drinking in the spring compared with the previous autumn (MANOVA $F[1, 319] = 20.01, p < .000$). Univariate comparisons revealed significant treatment effects for each of the dependent variables: quantity, frequency, and peak quantity. Figure 5.4 displays this pattern for our measure of peak consumption during the previous month. A measure of alcohol-related problems (RAPI) showed a similar trend in favor of the treatment group, although not reaching statistical significance ($F[1, 319] = 1.97, p < .16$). Analyses suggested that family history of alcoholism was unrelated to drinking rates or changes. Prior conduct problems were associated with higher drinking rates at both assessments, but not with differential response to treatment.

The 4-year longitudinal study of these students allows us to ask quite a number of questions in the future. We will assess whether changes in drinking result in changes in alcohol-related problem scores and the development of alcohol dependency syndromes. We can assess whether changes in drinking are accompanied by changes in other risk factors, particularly alcohol expectancies and perceived risk. In addition, we will assess whether these encouraging changes persist over time, if normal samples "catch up" in terms of drinking rates, and if other life changes (changes in living situation, dropout from college, graduation) result in other marked changes in alcohol consumption and adjustment.

Bridging Primary and Tertiary Treatments

As described above, the High Risk Drinkers Project is designed as secondary prevention; that is, it is oriented toward those most at risk for alcohol-related problems. As a middle ground between primary

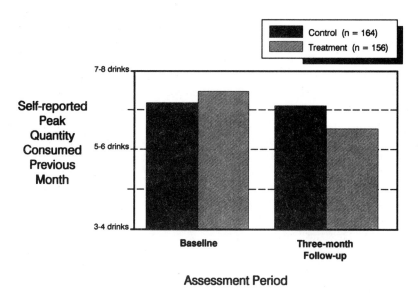

Figure 5.4. Alcohol use by high-risk students as a function of motivational intervention.

prevention and tertiary care, the program is quite flexible and contains several strategies that integrate other approaches to the treatment of alcohol problems.

Screening. Screening is necessary in order to target clients for secondary prevention. In addition to those at risk, clearly some individuals are found to have significant dependency syndromes. Thus an active screening process serves to identify cases in need of immediate care as well. In our study to date, 11 individuals have been removed from random assignment and provided feedback and referral information. As ongoing follow-ups continue with our sample, some individuals may develop dependency syndromes over time. These individuals can also be referred for treatment. Thus the longitudinal nature of the program also provides links to tertiary care, leading, we hope, to early detection and early referral for severe dependency problems.

Stepped Care. By utilizing a stepped approach to care, we minimize initial commitment and allow maximum use of personal resources.

Indeed, many individuals get better on their own, without formal treatment (Sobell, Sobell, & Toneatto, 1992). There is good evidence that graded motivational interventions actually create less resistance than do the confrontational tactics so commonly used in the addictions field (Miller & Rollnick, 1991). Those who do not respond to initial programming can receive more. This approach therefore minimizes unnecessary programming by allowing the least amount of intervention to work and minimizes reactance to the treatment system.

Influencing Norms. By addressing normative issues directly (asking what the individual perceives as normal), we begin to alter not only how the individual perceives his or her own risk, but how that person perceives the risk of those around them. A common question from our participants is, "What should I say to someone else I am worried about?" Thus the intervention provides a primary prevention function as well. The drinking norms of entire groups might be changed as individuals change what they are willing to do, as well as what they are willing to accept and/or criticize among their friends. Data on perceived norms in this sample will allow us to test if our motivational intervention changes these perceptions. Ongoing organizational interventions aimed at fraternities, sororities, and dormitories are designed to alter such social influence processes.

Future Directions
for Intervention and Research

There is much we do not know about youthful drinking and responses to different forms of intervention. Future research can be directed at further illuminating the natural history of heavy drinking in this population. Rates and contexts of natural moderation processes may contribute considerable information in the development of treatments. Knowledge of the relationship between individual differences and chronicity of heavy drinking should lead to better techniques of early identification. In the study of moderation processes, more complex models of the interaction between environments and personal differences are needed. Is living in a fraternity or sorority particularly dangerous in the long term for certain individuals? If so, in what way or by which processes do these environmental factors lead to increased problems? Relatedly, there is much we do not know about natural developmental processes in this age group. How does becoming legally capable of purchasing alcoholic beverages affect drinking rates and problems? Data from our own studies suggest that turning 21 leads to increased drinking, but only temporarily (Baer et al., 1992b). Is this transition more problematic for certain individuals?

In terms of evaluating intervention programs, much more research is needed. Data from our program are encouraging. With a brief feedback session of less than one hour, we have been able to reduce freshman drinking rates significantly. We await future follow-ups to assess the longevity of the impact of the intervention, as well as the assessment of "real-life" outcomes, such as college dropout, accidents, and grades. It is likely that informal interactions within families and peer groups are the single greatest limiting factor for risky behavior. Programming targeted specifically to social settings, such as athletic dorms, members of individual Greek houses, and those in military organizations should be attempted. These interventions can test if informal norms for drinking can be identified and altered within organizations. Although it seems that this is a clear area for future research, it also remains to be seen if programming can change these well-established, albeit informal, influence processes.

References

Alterman, A. I. (1987). Patterns of familial alcoholism, alcohol severity, and psychopathology. *Journal of Nervous and Mental Disease, 176,* 167-175.

American Psychiatric Association. (1987). *Diagnostic and statistical manual of mental disorders* (3rd ed., rev.). Washington, DC: Author.

Baer, J. S. (1991). Implications for early intervention from a biopsychosocial perspective on addiction. *Behavior Change, 8*(2), 51-59.

Baer, J. S., Kivlahan, D., Fromme, K., & Marlatt, G. A. (1989). A comparison of three methods of secondary prevention of alcohol abuse with college students: Preliminary results. In T. Loberg, W. R. Miller, P. E. Nathan, & G. A. Marlatt (Eds.), *Addictive behaviors: Prevention and early intervention* (pp. 157-171). Amsterdam: Swets & Zeitlinger.

Baer, J. S., Kivlahan, D., Fromme, K., & Marlatt, G. A. (1992a). Secondary prevention of alcohol abuse with college students: A skills training approach. In N. Heather, W. P. Miller, & J. Greeley (Eds.), *Self-control and the addictive behaviours* (pp. 339-356). Botany Bay, NSW, Australia: Maxwell Macmillan.

Baer, J. S., Marlatt, G. A., Kivlahan, D. R., Fromme, K., Larimer, M., & Williams, E. (1992b). An experimental test of three methods of alcohol risk-reduction with young adults. *Journal of Consulting and Clinical Psychology.*

Baer, P. E., Garmezy, L. B., McLaughlin, R. J., Pokorny, A. D., & Wernick, M. J. (1987). Stress, coping, family conflict, and adolescent alcohol use. *Journal of Behavioral Medicine, 10,* 449-466.

Barnes, G. M. (1990). Impact of the family on adolescent drinking patterns. In R. L. Collins, K. E. Leonard, & J. S. Searles (Eds.), *Alcohol and the family* (pp. 137-161). New York: Guilford.

Barnes, G. M., Farrell, M. P., & Cairns, A. L. (1986). Parental socialization factors and adolescent drinking behaviors. *Journal of Marriage and the Family, 48,* 27-36.

Brown, S. A., Creamer, V. A., & Stetson, B. A. (1987). Adolescent alcohol expectancies in relation to personal and parental drinking patterns. *Journal of Abnormal Psychology, 96,* 117-121.

Cadoret, R. J. (1990). Genetics of alcoholism. In R. L. Collins, K. E. Leonard, & J. S. Searles (Eds.), *Alcohol and the family* (pp. 39-78). New York: Guilford.

Cahalan, D., Cissin, I. H., & Crossley, H. M. (1969). *American drinking practices: A national study of drinking behavior and attitudes* (Monograph No. 6). New Brunswick, NJ: Rutgers Center of Alcohol Studies.

Cahalan, D., & Room, R. (1974). *Problem drinking among American men.* New Brunswick, NJ: Rutgers Center of Alcohol Studies.

Chassin, L., McLaughlin Mann, L., & Sher, K. J. (1988). Self-awareness theory, family history of alcoholism, and adolescent alcohol involvement. *Journal of Abnormal Psychology, 97,* 206-217.

Christiansen, B. A., Goldman, M. S., & Inn, A. (1982). Development of alcohol-related expectancies in adolescents: Separating pharmacological from social-learning influences. *Journal of Consulting and Clinical Psychology, 50,* 336-344.

Christiansen, B. A., Smith, G. T., Roehling, P. V., & Goldman, M. S. (1989). Using alcohol expectancies to predict adolescent drinking behavior after one year. *Journal of Consulting and Clinical Psychology, 19,* 337-361.

Cox, W. M. (1987). Personality theory and research. In H. T. Blane & K. E. Leonard (Eds.), *Psychological theories of drinking and alcoholism* (pp. 55-89). New York: Guilford.

Derogatis, L. R., & Spencer, P. M. (1982). *The Brief Symptom Inventory (BSI): Administration, scoring and procedures manual—I.* Baltimore: Johns Hopkins University of Medicine.

Dishion, T. J., Patterson, G. R., Stoolmiller, M., & Skinner, M. L. (1991). Family, school and behavioral antecedents to early adolescent involvement with antisocial peers. *Developmental Psychology, 27,* 172-180.

Donovan, J. E., Jessor, R., & Jessor, L. (1983). Problem drinking in adolescence and young adulthood. *Journal of Studies on Alcohol, 44,* 109-137.

Fillmore, K. M. (1988). *Alcohol use across the life course.* Toronto: Alcoholism and Drug Addiction Research Foundation.

Fillmore, K. M., & Midanik, L. (1984). Chronicity of drinking problems among men: A longitudinal study. *Journal of Studies on Alcohol, 45,* 228-236.

Finn, P. R., & Pihl, R. O. (1987). Men at high risk for alcoholism: The effect of alcohol on cardiovascular response to unavoidable shock. *Journal of Abnormal Psychology, 96,* 230-236.

Glantz, M., & Pickens, R. (1992). *Vulnerability to drug abuse.* Washington, DC: American Psychological Association.

Grant, B. F., Harford, T. C., & Grigson, M. B. (1988). Stability of alcohol consumption among youth: A national longitudinal study. *Journal of Studies on Alcohol, 49,* 253-260.

Harburg, E., Davis, D. R., & Caplan, R. (1982). Parent and offspring alcohol use: Imitative and aversive transmission. *Journal of Studies on Alcohol, 43,* 497-516.

Holmes, S. J., & Robins, L. N. (1987). The influence of childhood disciplinary experiences on the development of alcoholism and depression. *Journal of Child Psychology and Psychiatry, 28,* 399-415.

Institute of Medicine. (1990). *Broadening the base of treatment for alcohol problems.* Washington, DC: National Academy Press.

Jacob, T., & Leonard, K. (1991, November). *Family and peer influences in the development of adolescent alcohol abuse.* Paper presented at the NIAAA-supported conference, Working Group on the Development of Alcohol-Related Problems in High-Risk Youth: Establishing Linkages Across Biogenetic and Psychosocial Domains, Washington, DC.

Jessor, R., & Jessor, S. L. (1975). Adolescent development and the onset of drinking: A longitudinal study. *Journal of Studies on Alcohol, 36,* 27-51.

Jessor, R., & Jessor, S. L. (1977). *Problem behavior and psychosocial development: A longitudinal study of youth.* New York: Academic Press.

Johanson, M. E., Baer, J. S., Kivlahan, D. R., Collier, W., & Marlatt, G. A. (1988, June). *Drinking behavior in college fraternities.* Paper presented at the meeting of the Research Society on Alcoholism, Wild Dunes (Charleston), SC.

Johnston, L. D., O'Malley, D. M., & Bachman, J. G. (1989). *Drug use, drinking, and smoking: National survey results from high school, college, and young adult populations, 1975-1988* (DHHS Publication No. [ADM] 89-1638). Rockville, MD: Alcohol, Drug Abuse, and Mental Health Administration.

Kandel, D. B. (1986). Processes of peer influences in adolescence. In R. K. Silbereisen (Ed.), *Development as action in context.* Berlin: Springer-Verlag.

Kandel, D. B., & Andrews, K. (1987). Processes of adolescent socialization by parents and peers. *International Journal of the Addictions, 22,* 319-342.

Kandel, D. B., Kessler, R. C., & Margulies, R. Z. (1978). Antecedents of adolescent initiation into stages of drug use: A developmental analysis. In D. B. Kandel (Ed.), *Longitudinal research on drug use* (pp. 73-99). Washington, DC: Hemisphere.

Kivlahan, D. R., Coppel, D. B., Fromme, K., Miller, E., & Marlatt, G. A. (1990). Secondary prevention of alcohol-related problems in young adults at risk. In K. D. Craig & S. M. Weiss (Eds.), *Health enhancement, disease prevention, and early intervention* (pp. 287-300). New York: Springer.

Kivlahan, D. R., Marlatt, G. A., Fromme, K., Coppel, D. B., & Williams, E. (1990). Secondary prevention with college drinkers: Evaluation of an alcohol skills training program. *Journal of Consulting and Clinical Psychology, 58,* 805-810.

Kraft, D. P. (1984). A comprehensive prevention program for college students. In P. M. Miller & T. D. Nirenberg (Eds.), *Prevention of alcohol abuse* (pp. 327-370). New York: Plenum.

Labouvie, E. W. (1986). Alcohol and marijuana use in relation to adolescent stress. *International Journal of the Addictions, 21,* 333-345.

Mann, L. M., Chassin, L., & Sher K. J. (1987). Alcohol expectancies and the risk for alcoholism. *Journal of Consulting and Clinical Psychology, 55,* 411-417.

Miller, P. M., Smith, G. T., & Goldman, M. S. (1990). Emergence of alcohol expectancies in childhood: A possible critical period. *Journal of Studies on Alcohol, 51,* 343-349.

Miller, W. R., & Marlatt, G. A. (1984). *Brief drinker profile.* Odessa, FL: Psychological Assessment Resources.

Miller, W. R., & Rollnick, S. (1991). *Motivational interviewing: Preparing people for change.* New York: Guilford.

Miller, W. R., & Sovereign, R. G. (1989). The check-up: A model for early intervention in addictive behaviors. In T. Loberg, W. R. Miller, P. E. Nathan, & G. A. Marlatt (Eds.), *Addictive behaviors: Prevention and early intervention* (pp. 219-231). Amsterdam: Swets & Zeitlinger.

National Institute on Alcohol Abuse and Alcoholism. (1984). *Report of the 1983 Prevention Planning Panel.* Rockville, MD: Author.

National Institute on Alcohol Abuse and Alcoholism. (1990). *Seventh special report to the U.S. Congress on alcohol and health* (DHHS Publication No. [ADM] 90-1656). Washington, DC: Government Printing Office.

Newcomb, M. D. (1987). Consequences of teenage drug use: The transition from adolescence to young adulthood. *Drugs & Society, 1*(4), 25-60.

Newlin, D. B., & Thomson, J. B. (1990). Alcohol challenge with sons of alcoholics: A critical review and analysis. *Psychological Bulletin, 108,* 383-402.

Patterson, G. R., Reid, J., & Dishion, T. (in press). *Antisocial boys.* Eugene, OR: Castalia.

Prochaska, J. O., & DiClemente, C. C. (1986). Toward a comprehensive model of change. In W. R. Miller & N. Heather (Eds.), *Treating addictive behaviors: Processes of change* (pp. 3-27). New York: Plenum.

Robins, L., Helzer, J., Croughan, J., & Ratcliff, K. (1981). NIMH Diagnostic Interview Schedule. *Archives of General Psychiatry, 38,* 381-389.

Searles, J. S. (1990). The contribution of genetic factors to the development of alcoholism: A critical review. In R. L. Collins, K. E. Leonard, & J. S. Searles (Eds.), *Alcohol and the family* (pp. 3-38). New York: Guilford.

Selzer, M., Vinokur, A., & van Rooijen, L. (1975). A self-administered Short Michigan Alcoholism Screening Test (SMAST). *Journal of Studies on Alcohol, 36,* 117-126.

Sher, K. J. (1987). Stress response dampening. In H. T. Blane & K. E. Leonard (Eds.), *Psychological theories of drinking and alcoholism* (pp. 227-271). New York: Guilford.

Sher, K. J. (1991). *Children of alcoholics: A critical appraisal of theory and research.* Chicago: University of Chicago Press.

Sher, K. J., & Levenson, R. W. (1982). Risk for alcoholism and individual differences in the stress-response dampening effect of alcohol. *Journal of Abnormal Psychology, 91,* 350-367.

Sher, K. J., Walitzer, K. S., Wood, P. K., & Brent, E. E. (1991). Characteristics of children of alcoholics: Putative risk factors, substance use and abuse, and psychopathology. *Journal of Abnormal Psychology, 100,* 427-448.

Snyder, J., & Huntley, D. (1990). Troubled families and troubled youth: The development of antisocial behavior and depression in children. In P. E. Leone (Ed.), *Understanding troubled and troubling youth.* Newbury Park, CA: Sage.

Sobell, L. C., Sobell, M. B., & Toneatto, T. (1992). Recovery from alcohol problems without treatment. In N. Heather, W. R. Miller, & J. Greeley (Eds.), *Self-control and the addictive behaviours* (pp. 198-242). Botany Bay, NSW, Australia: Maxwell Macmillan.

White, H. R., & Labouvie, E. W. (1989). Towards the assessment of adolescent problem drinking. *Journal of Studies on Alcohol, 50,* 30-37.

Wills, T. A. (1985). Stress, coping, and tobacco and alcohol use in early adolescence. In S. Shiffman & T. A. Wills (Eds.), *Coping and substance abuse* (pp. 63-94). Orlando, FL: Academic Press.

Windle, M. (1990). Temperament and personality attributes of children of alcoholics. In M. Windle & J. S. Searles (Eds.), *Children of alcoholics* (pp. 129-167). New York: Guilford.

Zucker, R. A. (1986). The four alcoholisms: A developmental account of the etiologic process. In P. C. Rivers (Ed.), *Nebraska Symposium on Motivation: Vol. 34. Alcohol and addictive behaviors* (pp. 27-83). Lincoln: University of Nebraska Press.

Zucker, R. A. (in press). Alcohol involvement over the life span: A developmental perspective on theory and course. In L. S. Gaines & P. H. Brooks (Eds.), *Alcohol studies: A lifespan perspective.* New York: Springer.

Zucker, R. A., & Fitzgerald, H. E. (in press). Early developmental factors and risk for alcohol problems. *Alcohol Health and Research World.*

Zucker, R. A., & Gomberg, E. S. L. (1986). Etiology of alcoholism reconsidered: The case for a biopsychosocial process. *American Psychologist, 41,* 783-793.

6

Treatment for Problem Drinkers:
A Public Health Priority

MARK B. SOBELL
LINDA C. SOBELL

From a broad perspective, alcohol problems are public health problems, manifested in several ways and amenable to several types of interventions. In particular, there is a large population of persons who have identifiable alcohol problems but who have not experienced severe consequences or serious alcohol withdrawal symptoms. These individuals, called problem drinkers in this chapter, often respond well to nonintensive interventions aimed at helping them assert control over their behavior, whether through abstinence or through moderation. However, while considerable progress has been made in developing treatments for problem drinkers, most alcohol treatment programs continue to offer these individuals only traditional intensive treatments (Miller & Hester, 1986). This chapter focuses on where the treatment of problem drinkers fits into a public health approach to alcohol problems.

AUTHORS' NOTE: The views expressed in this chapter are those of the authors and do not necessarily reflect the views or policies of the Addiction Research Foundation. We are grateful to Gloria Leo for graphics assistance, and to Joanne Jackson and Lonya Miller for word-processing assistance with the manuscript.

Problem Drinkers

For years there has been an imbalance of services available for alcohol abusers compared with the prevalence of different types (i.e., severities) of alcohol problems (Sobell & Sobell, 1986-1987). Although approaches to the treatment of alcohol problems are gradually changing in North America, the need to provide services for problem drinkers constitutes a formidable challenge for the alcohol treatment field. In part this relates to the fact that serious concern for alcohol abusers of all types has developed only in the past few decades. In the United States, for example, a coordinated federal effort to provide services for alcohol problems began with the establishment of the National Institute on Alcohol Abuse and Alcoholism (NIAAA) in 1970 (NIAAA, 1971).

Prior to the establishment of widespread services for alcohol problems, the most severe cases were the ones that captured our attention. This occurred because such individuals were not only the most ill, but the most visible (see Pattison, Sobell, & Sobell, 1977). By the early 1970s, however, the alcohol field started to have greater visibility and government support and became an active area for researchers. As a result of this research, several epidemiological studies started to show that although chronic alcoholics had the public's eye, they represented just the tip, albeit a highly visible tip, of the iceberg (Cahalan, 1970; Cahalan & Room, 1974; Fillmore & Midanik, 1984; Hilton, 1987; Polich, 1981; Vaillant, 1983). As noted by Cahalan (1987b), whose early work was influential in this area, "Clinically defined alcoholics constitute only a relatively small proportion of those whose drinking creates significant problems for themselves and society" (p. 363). The remaining individuals with alcohol problems will be referred to here as *problem drinkers.*

A recent report by the Institute of Medicine of the U.S. National Academy of Sciences to the NIAAA suggests that the ratio of problem drinkers to those seriously dependent on alcohol is about 4:1 (Institute of Medicine, 1990). While the exact ratio varies as a function of the definitions invoked, the important point is that the population of problem drinkers is not only quite large, but considerably larger than the population of persons who are severely dependent on alcohol (Kristenson, 1987; Room, 1980; Skinner, 1990). This relationship is graphically illustrated in Figure 6.1.

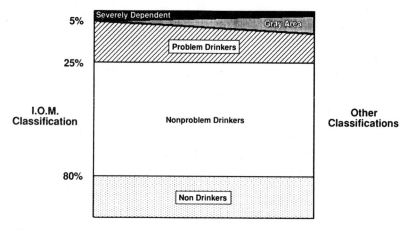

Figure 6.1. The distribution of nondrinkers and drinkers in the U.S. adult population, as classified by Institute of Medicine (1990) criteria (left) and other systems (right), indicating the greater prevalence of problem drinkers compared with severely dependent drinkers.

Characteristics of Problem Drinkers:
A Closer Look

Despite the tendency to consider alcohol problems as a unitary phenomenon, in practice such problems are quite diverse, having in common the manifestation of adverse consequences related to alcohol consumption. While domains or categories will overlap, meaningful distinctions can be made among three broad types of alcohol problem patterns (Polich & Kaelber, 1985). The first category involves regular excessive consumption of alcohol. Although the drinking of individuals in this category has not yet resulted in consequences, the amount and frequency of drinking puts them at risk for developing problems, especially health-related consequences. The second category includes social and health problems that are a consequence of excessive drinking. It is important to recognize that problems related to heavy drinking can occur in individuals who are seldom "drunk" (i.e., do not attain high blood alcohol levels) and who are not physically dependent on alcohol. Jellinek (1960b), for example, noted such cases among some Europeans who regularly consumed large amounts of wine, but seldom in a pattern that would produce a high blood alcohol level or dependence. The third category consists of problems related to *dependence*, including the manifestation of alcohol withdrawal symptoms upon the cessation of drinking, and consequences related to long periods of intoxication (e.g., job loss).

While there is overlap in these three domains, the population of concern in this chapter—problem drinkers—suffers largely from consequences related to excessive consumption. In part this is by definition, as problem drinkers have been defined by an absence of severe dependence on alcohol. However, while the drinking behavior of problem drinkers is typically not characterized by features such as compulsive alcohol seeking, daily drinking, or high blood alcohol levels sustained over lengthy periods of time (i.e., aspects of severe dependence), most current alcohol treatment programs are directed at these very features. Consequently, such programs are not appropriate for problem drinkers. The irony here is that when agencies seek funding, their budget requests are based largely on data stemming from the formidable costs incurred to society by problem drinkers. However, once the funding is received it is largely devoted to providing services for severely dependent individuals (Cahalan, 1987a; Institute of Medicine, 1990; Miller & Hester, 1986). This, of course, results in an imbalance in the provision of services compared with needs. While there are many possible explanations for this imbalance (Sobell & Sobell, 1986-1987), one of the most important reasons relates to the belief that alcohol problems represent a progressive disorder.

Are Alcohol Problems Inexorably Progressive?

The progressivity notion may be summarized as follows: Once someone develops an alcohol problem, if he or she continues to drink the problems will inevitably worsen, following a predictable course of symptoms. The foundation for this concept derives from the work of Jellinek (1946, 1952, 1960a). The approach used by Jellinek and others who have attempted to replicate his work (see Pattison et al., 1977) was to interview severe alcoholics retrospectively and have them reconstruct the symptoms they experienced and when they were experienced. Although studies disagree about the specific ordering of symptoms (see Mandell, 1983), severely dependent alcohol abusers report, typically having experienced less serious symptoms earlier in their drinking problem careers. Although this may be consistent with common sense, it does not demonstrate that the disorder is progressive. What it does tell us—and nothing more—is that persons with severe problems will report that they experienced less severe problems in the past.

The way to determine empirically whether or not alcohol problems are progressive is to study cases prospectively (e.g., longitudinal research). When this is done, the research shows that alcohol problems are progressive for only a minority of cases (i.e., reported problems at one point in time continue at the same or a more severe level at a later point; Fillmore, 1988; Hasin, Grant, & Endicott, 1990; Mandell, 1983). The more common pattern can be described as persons moving into and out of periods of alcohol problems of varying severity, with problem periods separated by periods of either abstinence or drinking without problems (Cahalan, 1970; Cahalan & Room, 1974; Pattison et al., 1977). Except in a few instances (i.e., well-advanced problem drinking histories; Fillmore & Midanik, 1984), it is impossible to predict with any confidence whether someone who has alcohol problems and does not get treatment will still have problems at a later point in time, or what the severity of problems will be if they persist (i.e., the problems might be less serious than at the earlier point in time; see Hasin et al., 1990). In fact, some have even hypothesized that problem drinkers may be a qualitatively different population from those individuals who become chronic alcoholics (e.g., Hill, 1985; Kissin, 1983). Alternatively, problem drinkers might be viewed as simply at the low-severity end of a continuum of alcohol dependence (Edwards, 1986).

Despite the lack of evidence for progressivity, the notion is very deeply ingrained in thinking about alcohol problems. Consider, for example, that a recently released report to the U.S. Congress by the NIAAA (1990) states that "7.2 million abuse alcohol, but do not yet show symptoms of dependence" (p. ix). The inference from the word "yet" is quite clear; there is an expectation that these individuals will become dependent unless they are somehow steered from that course.

A major problem for the alcohol field is that many existing treatment approaches are predicated on the assumption that anyone who is identified as having alcohol problems is in the midst of a progressive deterioration toward full-blown alcoholism unless he or she stops drinking. Based on this premise, all alcohol abusers are viewed as suitable for the same treatment. The argument is that some individuals simply will have deteriorated less than others at treatment entry. In this regard, a study conducted in the United States by Hansen and Emrick (1983) found that alcohol treatment programs did not distinguish between persons having minor problems and those having more serious problems—the same treatment was recommended for everyone.

The issue addressed in this chapter is whether alternative services should be available for problem drinkers. By now the answer should be obvious to readers. Before discussing the rationale for this position, however, we feel it is important to review what is known about problem drinkers.

Problem Drinkers: What We Know

In characterizing problem drinkers, two sources of evidence will be considered: a brief summary of the research literature and some recent assessment data from a group of problem drinkers in a research project at the Addiction Research Foundation. Based on the literature, we know several things about the population referred to as problem drinkers. First, they lack a history of physical dependence, especially major withdrawal symptoms. Correspondingly, problem drinkers will typically score low in the distribution of scores on scales measuring alcohol dependence (Heather, 1990). They also tend to report problem drinking histories shorter than 10 years and fewer health and social consequences related to their drinking, and often have not received prior treatment (Sanchez-Craig & Wilkinson, 1986-1987; Sobell, Sobell, & Toneatto; 1992). Consequently, problem drinkers tend to have greater personal, social, and economic resources and stability than do severely dependent drinkers. Also, frequent drinking and the need to ensure the availability of alcohol do not pervade the problem drinker's life as is often the case with severely dependent persons, who when drinking maintain a high blood alcohol level to avoid the onset of withdrawal symptoms. Further, problem drinkers tend not to view themselves as "alcoholics," or as basically different from persons who do not have alcohol problems (Miller, Sovereign, & Krege, 1988; Skinner & Allen, 1982; Sobell, et al., 1992).

Motivationally, two factors are important in working with problem drinkers. On the one hand, while problem drinkers often have not suffered multiple serious consequences related to their drinking, they are usually aware that they could suffer severely if their drinking problems continue. This can provide an incentive for them to change their behavior. On the other hand, their lives usually have not been so disrupted by their drinking problems that they are ready to make large sacrifices simply to comply with treatment. That is, the demands of treatment compete with other aspects of the individual's life (e.g., work, family, personal needs). If the demands of treatment are too great, then noncompliance can be expected (Miller, 1986-1987; Pomerleau, Pertschuk, Adkins, & Brady, 1978). As traditional treatments are intensive and demanding, alternative, less restrictive treatments are needed for problem drinkers.

Some data from our research with problem drinkers further illustrate the nature of this population (Sobell & Sobell, 1990). The 100 subjects in this study differ from those in many previous studies of problem drinkers (e.g., Miller, Taylor, & West, 1980; Sanchez-Craig, Annis, Bornet, & MacDonald, 1984) in that they voluntarily sought treatment, as opposed to being solicited by advertisements. In this regard, one study that compared clients who volunteered for treatment with those who were solicited by media advertisements found that although those in the solicited group reported heavier drinking and perceived themselves to be more dependent than the clients who sought treatment, they reported fewer drinking-related consequences (Zweben, Pearlman, & Li, 1988). This suggests that persons who enter treatment programs, compared with those solicited for studies, are more likely to have been affected by drinking-related consequences even though their alcohol consumption may not be as great as that of solicited clients.

The problem drinker clients in this study voluntarily participated in a treatment research program with a self-management orientation. Although the literature suggests that many problem drinkers have the capacity to assume the major responsibility for planning and implementing their own behavior change strategies, clients entering this treatment research project were given this explicit expectation. On average, the clients were slightly over 37 years of age (standard deviation = 8.82 years; range = 21-59 years) and had reported having alcohol problems for an average of slightly more than 6 years. While there is a tendency to expect that problem drinkers will be young (perhaps as a derivative of the progressivity notion), many subjects reported a "middle-age" problem onset, a phenomenon reported previously in the literature (Atkinson, Tolson, & Turner, 1990; Atkinson, Turner, Kofoed, & Tolson, 1985; Fillmore, 1974; Moorhead, 1958; Stall, 1987). Clients in their 40s and 50s often had experienced drinking problems for only a few years prior to entering treatment.

Almost all clients (88%) were employed, and 76% had white-collar occupations. The mean education level was nearly 15 years, 87% had at least a high school education, and 49% were married. Interestingly, 36% of all subjects were female, compared with approximately 20% of all admissions to the treatment agency from which the sample was drawn. Other studies have shown there to be a greater proportion of females among problem drinkers than among severely dependent drinkers (Fillmore, 1988; Sobell, Cunningham, Sobell, Toneatto, & Kozlowski, in preparation; Sobell, et al., 1992).

Several features of these clients' drinking in the year prior to treatment are of interest. Pretreatment drinking, which was assessed using the "Timeline Follow-back" method (see Sobell & Sobell, in press; Sobell, Sobell, Leo, & Cancilla, 1988), revealed that daily drinking was uncommon among this population, as subjects reported drinking on 68.2% of all days during the year. In other words, they were abstinent 1 out of every 3 days. Second, when they did drink, on 38.7% of those days they drank ≤ 4 standard drinks (1 standard drink = 0.6 oz. of pure ethanol). Thus more than one third of all their drinking can be characterized as light drinking. Third, their mean number of standard drinks per drinking day was 6.2 ($SD = 2.7$). Although we lack comparison data, this figure is probably well below the level considered to be heavy drinking by severely dependent drinkers. Finally, the mean percentage of very heavy drinking days (i.e., ≥ 10 standard drinks) was 16.8%. Thus, as a group, these problem drinkers were not extremely heavy drinkers. One reason for this may relate to the fact that clients who reported heavy drinking (i.e., ≥ 12 drinks on ≥ 5 days per week for the 6 months prior to admission) were ineligible for the study. Nevertheless, while this sample may represent lighter-drinking problem drinkers, these individuals perceived themselves as having alcohol problems for which they sought treatment.

In terms of drinking patterns, client profiles were quite varied. The profiles did not fit the traditional stereotypes of daily heavy drinkers or of binge drinkers (i.e., more than one consecutive day of very heavy drinking). In fact, the mean level of consumption defined by these problem drinkers as "heavy" drinking was 7.3 standard drinks (each containing 13 g of absolute ethanol) in a day, and only 10% reported that they were likely to drink heavily on the day following a day of heavy drinking. Even when back-to-back days of heavier drinking did occur, the amounts consumed were typically low enough to ensure that an extended (i.e., several-hour) sober period separated the drinking occasions. The vast majority of timeline drinking pattern profiles showed fluctuations in drinking days and in the amounts consumed. Moreover, 88% of the clients reported having at least some days when they drank 4 or fewer drinks without any adverse consequences. There was a tendency for some clients to drink more heavily in the evenings before days off from work or on special occasions (e.g., on holidays or at sporting events).

In contrast to their pretreatment drinking data, the subjects reported an abundance of pretreatment consequences related to their drinking, supporting the suggestion from Zweben et al.'s (1988) study that persons who voluntarily seek out services are more likely to have suffered consequences related to their drinking. The types of alcohol-related problems reported included interpersonal problems (81%), cognitive impairment (78%), vocational problems (48%), financial problems (47%), health problems (27%), alcohol-related arrests (26%), and alcohol-related hospitalizations (8%). Finally, each client gave a subjective evaluation of the severity of his or her drinking problem during the year prior to treatment using an operationally defined 5-point scale (0 = not a problem to 5 = very major problem). A total of 56% rated their pretreatment problems as "major," meaning they had experienced one serious drinking-related consequence during the year, and an additional 22% rated their pretreatment problems as "very major" (two or more serious consequences). As expected, no one reported that his or her pretreatment drinking was not a problem.

It is not possible from this study to determine whether these subjects were representative of problem drinkers in the general population. This study also does not address what proportion of problem drinkers, as designated in population studies, seek treatment or would be receptive to case finding initiatives. It is an open question whether any important differences will be found between problem drinkers who seek help and those who do not.

What Do We Know About Treating Problem Drinkers?

Before we enter into discussion of the research concerning treatment of problem drinkers, it is important to distinguish between two types of interventions that have been directed at problem drinkers. The first concerns excessive drinkers who have been identified by primary caregivers (usually physicians) and who receive brief interventions. While several studies have reported promising results (e.g., Chick, Lloyd, & Crombie, 1985; Kristenson, Öhlin, Hultén-Nosslin, Trell, & Hood, 1983; Kristenson, Trell, & Hood, 1981; Persson & Magnusson, 1989), these studies and their strategies of case identification are beyond the scope of the present chapter. The second approach concerns persons who self-identify as having alcohol problems and who seek treatment. Such problem drinkers are the focus of this chapter.

There is now considerable evidence that many problem drinkers respond well to nonintensive, outpatient interventions, and even some suggestion that more traditional interventions might be counterproductive with this population. The best-known seminal study, reported by Edwards et al. (1977), involved married males in treatment for alcohol problems. Clients were randomly assigned either to the treatment they would ordinarily receive (including outpatient and, if necessary, inpatient care) or to a single session of advice counseling. The study is best known for its finding that outcomes did not differ between the two groups. However, a lesser-known but key finding was that persons whose problems were less severe did better in the single-session condition than in more intensive treatment, while severely dependent persons showed the opposite pattern (Orford, Oppenheimer, & Edwards, 1976).

A plethora of studies have since investigated brief interventions, the majority aimed at problem drinkers. These studies have been reviewed on several occasions (Babor, Ritson, & Hodgson, 1986; Heather, 1989, 1990; Hester & Miller, 1990; Institute of Medicine, 1990; Saunders & Aasland, 1987; Sobell, Wilkinson, & Sobell, 1990). Characteristically, such treatments usually allow clients to choose their own goals (i.e., reduced drinking or abstinence) and use self-help manuals or include just one or two counseling sessions. Very often these studies have found very brief treatments, and sometimes self-help manuals, to be as effective as more intensive outpatient treatments. In one such study, for example, problem drinkers were assigned to receive either four hours of instruction in the use of a self-help manual or one of three other treatments involving 12 to 16 therapist-directed outpatient sessions (e.g., coping skills training) (Skutle & Berg, 1987). At 1-year follow-up all clients had improved, and there was no difference between the treatments.

Although *no-treatment* control conditions have not been reported in the research literature and would be considered unethical (i.e., treatment should not be denied those seeking it), two studies have compared self-management interventions with a brief waiting list control (e.g., 3 months) and found the treatments to be effective (Alden, 1988; Harris & Miller,

1990). Although waiting list control groups raise the possibility that subjects may postpone initiating behavior change until treatment "begins," they remain the closest approximation to no-treatment controls.

Successful brief interventions with problem drinkers tell us that *treatment of problem drinkers can be highly cost-effective compared with traditional services provided for alcohol problems.* Another inference is that to a large extent *the impact of the interventions must be motivational.* Consider the extreme case where one session of advice/counseling has been found to be as effective as more intensive treatment. Assuming that both approaches are effective, what accounts for the change shown by the group receiving the single counseling session? Surely the change cannot be attributed to any relatively involved procedure such as skills training or problem-solving training. It is more likely that the subjects already had the necessary skills to change their behavior, and that the session served to catalyze their bringing those skills to bear on the problem. That is, the treatment seemed to have increased subjects' commitment to change, and the subjects then enacted the changes themselves. This suggests that interventions that have a motivational focus may have special value for treating problem drinkers. Miller (1990) has described several ways of enhancing clients' motivation.

Perhaps the key feature of successful interventions with problem drinkers is that they frequently involve a moderation rather than an abstinence outcome (Heather, 1990; Heather & Robertson, 1983; Hester & Miller, 1990; Hill, 1985; Sobell & Sobell, 1986-1987). Interestingly, this occurs whether or not moderation is the treatment goal (Polich, Armor, & Braiker, 1981; Sanchez-Craig et al., 1984). That problem drinkers successfully moderate their drinking, regardless of the advice received in treatment, suggests that *offering an alternative to abstinence may be an essential feature of services that hope to attract problem drinkers.* In recent years, some studies have begun offering problem drinkers the opportunity to select their own treatment goals (usually with advice; see Sobell & Sobell, 1986-1987). Theoretically, self- selection of treatment goals could increase motivation to achieve the goals, and many problem drinkers indicate that they would prefer to select their own goals (Sobell, Sobell, Bogardis, Leo, & Skinner, 1992). Alternatives to abstinence and goal self-selection are characteristics of many behavioral treatments for alcohol abusers (Hester & Miller, 1990). Unfortunately, however, most of these treatment approaches have been restricted to the research arena (Miller & Hester, 1986).

Closing the Gap
Between Research and Practice

Based on the above rationale, how could services for problem drinkers be made available on a broad scale? First, *the way the alcohol field currently makes services available to the public is inconsistent with the way most other health care services are provided.* Consider, for example, hypertension. Unless one's blood pressure is dangerously high, the treatment approach is likely to involve a series of possible interventions, beginning with a change in diet and/or exercise. For some cases, this may be all that is necessary. In more serious cases, where dietary controls and increased exercise are not sufficient, medication may be necessary. In fact, in most areas of health care, intensive procedures are used only when clear evidence dictates that the intervention is needed or after less intensive interventions have failed.

Numerous other examples could be culled from the health care field, but they are unnecessary. We have come to expect health care to involve different levels of intervention, with the treatment of choice being one that has a reasonable chance of success while minimizing personal and monetary costs and risks. If the initial intervention is not effective, then the strategy would be to implement more demanding and costly treatments until a positive response occurs. In the addictions field, however, the more intensive interventions have been prescribed for all cases, irrespective of the severity of the problem. Why such a situation developed is another issue, but it developed in the absence of research demonstrating that intensive treatments are effective or for whom such treatments work best.

Conceptually, multiple levels of health care can be considered as "treatment tiering." Such an approach, which is illustrated in Figure 6.2, is not novel but simply reflects a reasoned and systematic strategy for the delivery of cost-effective interventions. Figure 6.2 shows that as people enter the health care system some recover from their problems at each level of intervention. Successful cases require no further action unless problems recur. As interventions become more extensive and costly, the portion needing each successive level of intervention is relatively small compared with those initially entering the system. *The alcohol field is nearly unique as a major area of health care in its absence of a treatment tiering approach.* In fact, the across-the-board intensive treatment approach used by many service providers in the

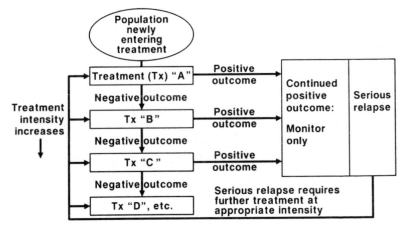

Figure 6.2. Diagrammatic representation of a treatment tiering approach to the delivery of health care services. As treatment intensity increases, the portion of the affected population requiring the more intensive services decreases. Such an approach describes most professional health care practices, but does not guide the alcohol treatment field.

alcohol field (Hansen & Emrick, 1983; Miller & Hester, 1986) can be compared with performing triple-bypass surgery on anyone who complains of chest pains, without regard to the extent of pain, alternative treatments, or the risks or consequences of the operation for the patient.

A costly consequence of not having a treatment tiering approach in the alcohol field is that few appropriate services are available for problem drinkers. The evidence suggests that appropriate services should largely consist of outpatient, nonintensive interventions that incorporate flexible treatment goals and other motivational components. In order to cast a broad net, practitioners must offer services that make sense to and will be used by problem drinkers. In accomplishing such a goal, moderation approaches cannot be ignored. *Nonintensive intervention that offers a choice of goals (moderation or abstinence) should be prominent early in the treatment planning process.* In this regard, Heather (1990) has noted that although nonintensive treatments might raise some concern about the obligations of service providers, "there is nothing unethical or uncaring in offering [brief interventions] . . . provided that safeguards for checking on progress and for offering more intensive treatment when necessary are incorporated into the treatment plan" (p. 96). In essence, treatment is being conceptualized as a process, not a single event.

As of this writing, it has been more than two years since the Institute of Medicine (1990) released its report urging that a broader array of services for alcohol problems be available in the United States, and yet there is little indication that the report has had or will have any noticeable impact on the development of such services. In other health care fields, treatments are based on the research literature. Without the availability of appropriate community services, the research is confined to academic relevance, and problem drinkers are left with no alternative to intensive treatments. How can this identified set of needs be met? Sadly, those who are best placed to respond to those needs (i.e., existing alcohol treatment programs) seem not prepared to reconsider the fundamental *beliefs* guiding their treatment approaches, no matter what the evidence. In our view, the need to provide services for problem drinkers presents both an opportunity and an obligation to everyone working in the alcohol field. If the agenda is to better the fate of alcohol abusers, then there can be no excuse for further delay. The time is past due for policymakers, the alcohol treatment industry, and those working in the clinical arena to take action.

Meeting the Challenge

The first step in meeting the challenge to provide services to problem drinkers would be to offer treatment alternatives that are empirically sound. By itself, however, this would be insufficient, and it could be self-defeating. We need to find ways to influence public policy and to help the public accurately understand the nature of alcohol problems. The general public needs to know that there is a broad array of alcohol problems, and that a great many people have alcohol problems even though they are clearly not chronic alcoholics. The public also needs to recognize that such persons can deal with their problems effectively and often do so by reducing rather than stopping their drinking. Currently, such a view is not widespread. A 1987 Gallup Report, for example, reported that 81% of those polled disagreed with the statement, "A recovered alcoholic can safely return to moderate drinking" (p. 25).

This finding appears in a section of the report titled "Misconceptions About Alcoholism." As long as all varieties of alcohol problems are referred to as "alcoholism," and issues are naively stated, there is little reason for problem drinkers to identify themselves and seek help. A change in public attitudes ironically might also go a long way toward reducing the stigma associated with "alcoholism" (Goldsmith, McCutchen, Sherman, & Reichman, 1984). If the public viewed less serious alcohol problems as "problems" (rather than "alcoholism") and accepted that less serious alcohol problems are in most cases not progressive or irreversible, the stigma that still accompanies the disorder might be effectively diminished.

Miller (1983) has noted that alternative approaches seem to have found much greater acceptance abroad than in the United States. This is not surprising when one considers that services in the United States have been largely of an entrepreneurial nature, whereas in several other countries services are supported by government. However, even where government does not directly pay for alcohol services, third-party payers have become increasingly rigorous in demanding a sound research basis for reimbursable treatments. An excellent example of the stress being placed on the American alcohol treatment system is that as third-party payers have become more discriminating about approving reimbursement for inpatient care, American treatment programs have energetically solicited referrals from some Canadian provinces to bolster their low census (Advisory Committee on Drug Treatment, 1990). Just as we have come to expect that there should be a sound research basis for other treatments (e.g., hospitalization, surgery), there is an increasingly popular view that alcohol treatment services should be justified.

There also is a broader question of how and where services for problem drinkers should be made available. Recently, the Institute of Medicine (1990) recommended that services for alcohol problems should not be provided exclusively by specialized addiction counselors or agencies. Rather, the institute suggests that a valuable role can be played by general health care practitioners, especially those in primary care settings. It has been amply demonstrated that many persons with relatively low severity alcohol problems respond well to brief interventions conducted in primary care settings. Each case that is successfully managed in a general health care setting is one that will not reach specialized addiction services. With respect to the treatment tiering approach described earlier, it is imperative that initial interventions be those that are the least intensive, least intrusive, and most cost-effective, and that have a reasonable chance of success.

A final consideration is how to persuade those who treat or might treat individuals with alcohol problems to embrace a public health approach seriously. A starting place would be to make it widely known to care providers and the public that many people with alcohol problems are not seriously dependent on alcohol, that many can overcome drinking problems with little assistance, and that in some cases problem drinkers can have successful recoveries that involve drinking at nonhazardous levels. For such changes to take place, there must be strong policy leadership. In the United States the leadership should be provided by the NIAAA; however, services for problem drinkers seem a low priority for that organization (compared, e.g., with the search for a genetic basis for severe alcoholism or for biological markers of alcohol consumption). Elsewhere (e.g., Canada, England, and Australia), a public health approach to alcohol problems is being more vigorously pursued.

Implementation of a public health approach to alcohol problems will take more than policy leadership, however. For alcohol problems to be embraced as a health problem similar to other health problems (e.g., smoking, hypertension), the alcohol field must adopt the same level of standards of practice and requirements for research-based treatments that are the foundations of other health care fields. The gulf between research and practice must be bridged.

Conclusion

It is clear that multiple paths and multiple alternatives for recovery from alcohol problems must be recognized. Although the above prescriptions may seem farfetched and unrealistic, one cannot overlook the rapid rise and present atrophying of the multimillion-dollar alcoholism treatment industry, a series of events that a few years ago would have seemed inconceivable. Personal agendas must be set aside by one and all, or the needs of those we claim to care about will continue to be neglected. The proffering of one treatment as suitable for all alcohol abusers has the very real consequence of abetting human suffering. *In other health fields where so much is known, such a circumstance would not be tolerated.* Recognition of multiple paths and multiple alternatives for recovery from alcohol problems is long overdue. Those whose mandate it is to provide services for alcohol problems, from policymakers to therapists, need to set aside their personal biases and see that appropriate treatments are provided for *all* alcohol abusers.

References

Advisory Committee on Drug Treatment. (1990). *Treating alcohol and drug problems in Ontario: A vision for the 90's* (Report to the minister responsible for the Provincial Anti-drug Strategy). Toronto: Provincial Anti-drug Secretariat.

Alden, L. (1988). Behavioral self-management controlled drinking strategies in a context of secondary prevention. *Journal of Consulting and Clinical Psychology, 56,* 280-286.

Atkinson, R. M., Tolson, R., L., & Turner, J. A. (1990). Late versus early onset problem drinking in older men. *Alcoholism: Clinical and Experimental Research, 14,* 574-579.

Atkinson, R. M., Turner, J. A., Kofoed, L. L., & Tolson, R. L. (1985). Early versus late onset alcoholism in older persons: Preliminary findings. *Alcoholism: Clinical and Experimental Research, 9,* 513-515.

Babor, T. R., Ritson, E. B., & Hodgson, R. J. (1986). Alcohol-related problems in the primary health care setting: A review of early intervention strategies. *British Journal of Addiction, 81,* 23-46.

Cahalan, D. (1970). *Problem drinkers: A national survey.* San Francisco: Jossey-Bass.

Cahalan, D. (1987a). Studying drinking problems rather than alcoholism. In M. Galanter (Ed.), *Recent developments in alcoholism* (Vol. 5, pp. 363-372). New York: Plenum.

Cahalan, D. (1987b). *Understanding America's drinking problem: How to combat the hazards of alcohol.* San Francisco: Jossey-Bass.

Cahalan, D., & Room, R. (1974). *Problem drinking among American men.* New Brunswick, NJ: Rutgers Center of Alcohol Studies.

Chick, J., Lloyd, G., & Crombie, E. (1985). Counselling problem drinkers in medical wards: A controlled study. *British Medical Journal, 290,* 965-967.

Edwards, G. (1986). The alcohol dependence syndrome: A concept as stimulus to enquiry. *British Journal of Addiction, 81,* 171-184.

Edwards, G., Orford, J., Egert, S., Guthrie, S., Hawker, A., Hensman, C., Mitcheson, M., Oppenheimer, E., & Taylor, C. (1977). Alcoholism: A controlled trial of "treatment" and "advice." *Journal of Studies on Alcohol, 38,* 1004-1031.

Fillmore, K. (1974). Drinking and problem drinking in early adulthood and middle age. *Quarterly Journal of Studies on Alcohol, 35,* 819-840.

Fillmore, K. M. (1988). *Alcohol use across the life course: A critical review of 70 years of international longitudinal research.* Toronto: Addiction Research Foundation.

Fillmore, K. M., & Midanik, L. (1984). Chronicity of drinking problems among men: A longitudinal study. *Journal of Studies on Alcohol, 45,* 228-236.

Gallup Report. (1987). *Alcohol use and abuse in America* (Report No. 265). Princeton, NJ: Author.

Goldsmith, F., McCutchen, R., Sherman, P., & Reichman, W. (1984). *Analysis of a survey of leadership attitudes toward alcoholism in the United States: Vol. 2. Major findings report.* New York: Christopher D. Smithers Foundation.

Hansen, J., & Emrick, C. D. (1983). Whom are we calling "alcoholic"? *Society of Psychologists in Addictive Behaviors, 2,* 164-178.

Harris, K. B., & Miller, W. R. (1990). Behavioral self-control training for problem drinkers: Components of efficacy. *Psychology of Addictive Behavior, 4,* 82-90.

Hasin, D. S., Grant, B., & Endicott, J. (1990). The natural history of alcohol abuse: Implications for definitions of alcohol use disorders. *American Journal of Psychiatry, 147,* 1537-1541.

Heather, N. (1989). Psychology and brief interventions. *British Journal of Addiction, 84,* 357-370.

Heather, N. (1990). Brief intervention strategies. In R. K. Hester & W. R. Miller (Eds.), *Handbook of alcoholism treatment approaches: Effective alternatives* (pp. 93-116). New York: Pergamon. ·

Heather, N., & Robertson, I. (1983). *Controlled drinking* (2nd ed.). New York: Methuen.

Hester, R. K., & Miller, W. R. (1990). Self-control training. In R. K. Hester & W. R. Miller (Eds.), *Handbook of alcoholism treatment approaches: Effective alternatives* (pp. 141-149). New York: Pergamon.

Hill, S. Y. (1985). The disease concept of alcoholism: A review. *Drug and Alcohol Dependence, 16,* 193-214.

Hilton, M. (1987). Drinking patterns and drinking problems in 1984: Results from a general population survey. *Alcoholism: Clinical and Experimental Research, 11,* 167-175.

Institute of Medicine. (1990). *Broadening the base of treatment for alcohol problems.* Washington, DC: National Academy Press.

Jellinek, E. M. (1946). Phases in the drinking histories of alcoholics. *Quarterly Journal of Studies on Alcohol, 7,* 1-88.

Jellinek, E. M. (1952). Phases of alcohol addiction. *Quarterly Journal of Studies on Alcohol, 13,* 673-684.

Jellinek, E. M. (1960a). Alcoholism, a genus and some of its species. *Canadian Medical Association Journal, 83,* 1341-1345.

Jellinek, E. M. (1960b). *The disease concept of alcoholism.* New Brunswick, NJ: Hillhouse.

Kissin, B. (1983). The disease concept of alcoholism. In R. G. Smart, F. B. Glaser, Y. Israel, H. Kalant, R. E. Popham, & W. Schmidt (Eds.), *Research advances in alcohol and drug problems* (Vol. 7, pp. 93-126). New York: Plenum.

Kristenson, H. (1987). Alcohol dependence and problem drinking in urban middle aged men. *Alcohol and Alcoholism, 1,* 601-606.

Kristenson, H., Öhlin, H., Hultén-Nosslin, M. B., Trell, E., & Hood, B. (1983). Identification and intervention of heavy drinking in middle-aged men: Results and follow-up of 24-60 months of long-term study with randomized controls. *Alcoholism: Clinical and Experimental Research, 7,* 203-209.

Kristenson, H., Trell, E., & Hood, B. (1981). Serum-g-glutamyltransferase in screening and continuous control of heavy drinking in middle-aged men. *American Journal of Epidemiology, 114,* 862-872.

Mandell, W. (1983). Types and phases of alcohol dependence. In M. Galanter (Ed.), *Recent developments in alcoholism* (Vol. 3, pp. 415-448). New York: Plenum.

Miller, W. R. (1983). Alcoholism American style: A view from abroad. *Bulletin of the Society of Psychologists in Addictive Behaviors, 2,* 11-17.

Miller, W. R. (1986-1987). Motivation and treatment goals. *Drugs & Society, 1,* 133-151.

Miller, W. R. (1990). Increasing motivation for change. In R. K. Hester & W. R. Miller (Eds.), *Handbook of alcoholism treatment approaches: Effective alternatives* (pp. 67-80). New York: Pergamon.

Miller, W. R., & Hester, R. K. (1986). The effectiveness of alcoholism treatment: What research reveals. In W. R. Miller & N. Heather (Eds.), *Treating addictive behaviors: Processes of change* (pp. 121-174). New York: Plenum.

Miller, W. R., Sovereign, R. G., & Krege, B. (1988). Motivational interviewing with problem drinkers: II. The drinkers's check-up as a preventive intervention. *Behavioural Psychotherapy, 16,* 251-268.

Miller, W. R., Taylor, C. A., & West, J. C. (1980). Focused versus broad-spectrum behavior therapy for problem drinkers. *Journal of Consulting and Clinical Psychology, 48,* 590-601.

Moorhead, H. H. (1958). Study of alcoholism with onset forty-five years or older. *Bulletin of the New York Academy of Medicine, 34,* 99-108.

National Institute on Alcohol Abuse and Alcoholism (NIAAA). (1971). *First special report to the U.S. Congress on alcohol and health* (DHEW Publication No. [ADM] 74-68). Washington, DC: Government Printing Office.

National Institute on Alcohol Abuse and Alcoholism (NIAAA). (1990). *Seventh special report to the U.S. Congress on alcohol and health* (DHHS Publication No. [ADM] 90-1656). Washington, DC: Government Printing Office.

Orford, J., Oppenheimer, E., & Edwards, G. (1976). Abstinence or control: The outcome for excessive drinkers two years after consultation. *Behaviour Research and Therapy, 14,* 409-418.

Pattison, E. M., Sobell, M. B., & Sobell, L. C. (Eds.). (1977). *Emerging concepts of alcohol dependence.* New York: Springer.

Persson, J., & Magnusson, P.-H. (1989). Early intervention in patients with excessive consumption of alcohol: A controlled study. *Alcohol, 6,* 403-408.

Polich, J. M. (1981). Epidemiology of alcohol abuse in military and civilian populations. *American Journal of Public Health, 71,* 1125-1132.

Polich, J. M., Armor, D. J., & Braiker, H. B. (1981). *The course of alcoholism: Four years after treatment.* New York: John Wiley.

Polich, J. M., & Kaelber, C. T. (1985). Sample surveys and the epidemiology of alcoholism. In M. A. Schuckit (Ed.), *Alcohol patterns and problems* (pp. 43-77). New Brunswick, NJ: Rutgers University Press.

Pomerleau, O., Pertschuk, M., Adkins, D., & Brady, J. P. (1978). A comparison of behavioral and traditional treatment for middle income problem drinkers. *Journal of Behavioral Medicine, 1,* 187-200.

Room, R. (1980). Treatment-seeking populations in large realities. In G. Edwards & M. Grant (Eds.), *Alcoholism treatment in transition* (pp. 205-224). London: Croom Helm.

Sanchez-Craig, M., Annis, H. M., Bornet, A. R., & MacDonald, K. R. (1984). Random assignment to abstinence and controlled drinking: Evaluation of a cognitive-behavioral program for problem drinkers. *Journal of Consulting and Clinical Psychology, 52,* 390-403.

Sanchez-Craig, M., & Wilkinson, D. A. (1986-1987). Treating problem drinkers who are not severely dependent on alcohol. *Drugs & Society, 1,* 39-67.

Saunders, J. B., & Aasland, O. G. (1987). *WHO Collaborative Project on Identification and Treatment of Persons with Harmful Alcohol Consumption* (Doc. WHO/MNH/ DAT/86.3). Geneva: World Health Organization.

Skinner, H. A., & Allen, B. A. (1982). Alcohol dependence syndrome: Measurement and validation. *Journal of Abnormal Psychology, 91,* 199-209.

Skutle, A., & Berg, G. (1987). Training in controlled drinking for early-stage problem drinkers. *British Journal of Addiction, 82,* 493-501.

Sobell, L. C., Cunningham, J., Sobell, M. B., Toneatto, T., & Kozlowski, L. T. (1992). *Recovery from alcohol problems with and without treatment in a general population survey.* Unpublished manuscript.

Sobell, L. C., & Sobell, M. B. (in press). Timeline follow-back: A technique for assessing self-reported ethanol consumption. In J. Allen & R. Z. Litten (Eds.), *Techniques to assess alcohol consumption.* Totowa, NJ: Humana.

Sobell, L. C., Sobell, M. B., Leo, G. I., & Cancilla, A. (1988). Reliability of a timeline method: Assessing normal drinkers' reports of recent drinking and a comparative evaluation across several populations. *British Journal of Addiction, 83,* 393-402.

Sobell, L. C., Sobell, M. B., & Toneatto, T. (1992). Recovery from alcohol problems without treatment. In N. Heather, W. R. Miller, & J. Greeley (Eds.), *Self-control and the addictive behaviours* (pp. 198-242). Botany.Bay, NSW, Australia: Maxwell Macmillan.

Sobell, M. B., & Sobell, L. C. (1986-1987). Conceptual issues regarding goals in the treatment of alcohol problems. *Drugs & Society, 1,* 1-37.

Sobell, M. B., & Sobell, L. C. (1990). *Problem drinkers and self-control treatments: A closer look.* Paper presented at the Fifth International Conference on Treatment of Addictive Behaviors, Sydney, Australia.

Sobell, M. B., Sobell, L. C., Bogardis, J., Leo, G. I., & Skinner, W. (1992). Problem drinkers' perceptions of whether treatment goals should be self-selected or thera-pist-selected. *Behavior Therapy, 23,* 43-52.

Sobell, M. B., Wilkinson, D. A., & Sobell, L. C. (1990). Alcohol and drug problems. In A. S. Bellack, M. Hersen, & A. E. Kazdin (Eds.), *International handbook of behavior modification and therapy* (2nd ed., pp. 415-435). New York: Plenum.

Stall, R. (1987). Research issues concerning alcohol consumption among aging popula-tions. *Drug and Alcohol Dependence, 19,* 195-213.

Vaillant, G. E. (1983). *The natural history of alcoholism: Causes, patterns, and paths to recovery.* Cambridge, MA: Harvard University Press.

Zweben, A., Pearlman, S., & Li, S. (1988). A comparison of brief advice and conjoint therapy in the treatment of alcohol abuse: The results of the Marital Systems Study. *British Journal of Addiction, 83,* 899-916.

PART III

Integrative Treatment
of Addictive Problems

7

Recovery Patterns in Adolescent Substance Abuse

SANDRA A. BROWN

A dolescents entering treatment for alcohol- and drug-related problems are typically experiencing some type of crisis. Families with adolescents whose drug abuse is sufficiently severe to require structured intervention have often exhausted their resources for managing the teens' behavior, and are struggling to cope with the family disruption. Both teens and parents feel at a loss as to how to make life changes effectively to diminish the resultant personal and family problems. Parental attempts to control the teens' drug use have been ineffective, and have resulted in anger and frustration for family members. Parents feel at a loss as to what additional coping efforts could be employed, and are relatively pessimistic regarding the ability of their offspring to make changes.

Professional help for adolescent alcohol and drug abuse is not sought until the alcohol- or drug-related problems come to the attention of authority figures. The majority of teens who enter treatment programs are no longer attending school, either because of their truancy or because they have been suspended or expelled (Brown, Vik, & Creamer, 1989). In addition, teens brought to treatment evidence a variety of emotional and psychiatric problems (including depression, thought disorder, psychotic symptoms, and suicidal ideation) that may prompt the efforts to seek professional help (Brown, Mott, & Stewart, 1992). Teens admitted for treatment may be referred by the courts because of their involvement in illegal activities associated with their drug use. Thus teens entering treatment for alcohol- and drug-related problems typically present with a variety of life problems and at a time when their usual resources for dealing with these difficulties have been eroded.

There has been a dramatic rise in concern over adolescent alcohol- and drug-related problems over the past decade (National Institute on Alcohol Abuse and Alcoholism [NIAAA], 1990). In concert with this accelerated interest in teen drug abuse comes a substantial proliferation in treatment programs available for adolescent substance abusers. While adolescent treatment programs have rapidly developed over the past decade, clinical characteristics of adolescents in treatment and the clinical course following adolescent substance abuse treatment have been relatively unstudied. This chapter will focus on characteristics of adolescents in treatment for alcohol- and drug-related problems and will describe the clinical course of teens following treatment. A review of past adolescent drug treatment outcome evaluations will be presented to highlight unique features of the study of teen addiction. Finally, particular emphasis is placed on the common pathways to improved functioning following teen alcohol and drug treatment.

Clinical Presentation of
Adolescent Substance Abusers

Adolescents with alcohol- and drug-related problems present for treatment in a number of different clinical settings. While it is presumed that substance-abusing teens will be evaluated first in alcohol and drug treatment programs, a large number of teens hospitalized for psychiatric problems and brought in for medical emergencies present with problems that are related to their alcohol and drug use. While the focus of this chapter is on adolescents who enter addiction treatment programs, it is important for the clinician to be sensitive to the fact that difficulties resulting from adolescent alcohol and drug abuse may result in contact with diverse clinical settings.

What are the characteristics of alcohol and drug abuse of teens entering addiction treatment programs? According to the National Household Survey on Drug Abuse, alcohol, tobacco, and marijuana are by far the most commonly used drugs among American adolescents in the 12- to 17-year-old age range (National Institute on Drug Abuse, 1989). Among hard drugs, inhalants, stimulants, cocaine, and analgesics are most frequently used by teens in this age group (3% to 9% of lifetime use). Although these substances are also commonly used by teens in treatment for alcohol- and drug-related problems, there are two important differences between national survey findings and treatment sample drug use characteristics. First, although patterns of drug preferences parallel those in the teen's community, the severity and persistence of substance use within clinical samples vary markedly. In earlier work, my colleagues and I found that teens in treatment initiate alcohol and drug use at an earlier age and progress relatively rapidly from alcohol or marijuana use to involvement with hard drugs (Brown et al., 1992). Virtually all adolescents in treatment for substance abuse report lifetime use of alcohol and marijuana, and more than 95% of clinical samples currently use these substances in addition to two or three other drugs. For example, inhalants have been used by more than 40% of teens entering treatment, whereas the incidence of amphetamine, cocaine (including crack), and hallucinogen use is significantly higher (68% to 97% of treatment samples during the 1980s). Of particular note in terms of potential long-term health outcomes is the finding that approximately 85% of teens entering alcohol and drug treatment regularly smoke cigarettes (Myers & Brown, 1990). Thus prevalence and incidence of use vary markedly from general school samples of adolescents to clinical samples.

A second major difference between national survey findings for adolescents and drug use of clinical treatment samples has to do with ongoing use of multiple substances. Regular use of multiple substances is the norm for teens entering treatment (Brown, Vik, & Creamer, 1989). Hard drug use uniformly overlays a history and current use of alcohol or marijuana in treatment samples. Thus teens entering treatment typically present with heavy use of alcohol and cigarettes and concomitant use of two or three other substances. Our knowledge of the consequences of alcohol and drug use and patterns of changes in use over time that are based on general adolescent populations may be misleading when applied to teens whose alcohol- and drug-related problems are severe enough during early or middle adolescence to require treatment.

Information about clinical presentation and posttreatment clinical course for addiction derived from adult populations may also not be applicable to adolescents in treatment for alcohol and drug abuse. In contrast to adult alcohol and drug treatment samples, adolescents are uniformly polysubstance users and have significantly shorter durations of substance abuse than do adults in treatment. It is not uncommon for teens to have used alcohol regularly for only 3 years and hard drugs for only 1 or 2 years before entering treatment (Brown, Mott, & Myers, 1990). Consequently, adolescent alcohol and drug abuse results in presentation of symptoms and problematic consequences that are different from those found in adult addiction. For example, withdrawal symptoms and medical complications are far less common in the clinical presentation of drug-abusing teens entering treatment than among addicted adults entering treatment.

As shown in Table 7.1, the most prevalent clinical features of adolescents presenting for substance abuse treatment include family disruption, school problems, deviant peer group, emotional disruption, and a constellation of deviant behaviors. Family relations are typically marred by increased conflict, decreased cohesion, reduced expressiveness (Moos, 1986), and a history of alcohol- and drug-related problems for one or both parents (Brown et al., 1992). The majority of teens who enter substance abuse treatment programs are repeatedly truant, and their academic performance has deteriorated or they have been suspended or expelled from school prior to treatment entry. Consequently, their attitudes toward school and academic authorities (teachers) are typically poor.

By the time teens enter treatment for their alcohol and drug use, their social resource networks contain an abundance of peers with heavy alcohol and drug use patterns. Although these teens perceive their social support network as satisfactory or supportive, such peers are likely to be less reliable, consistent, and/or available to provide emotional and instrumental support for an adolescent attempting to change alcohol and drug use patterns. Yet, given the high incidence of alcohol- and drug-related problems within the family, substance-abusing teens in treatment more commonly turn to peers or siblings for support than to their parents (Holden, Brown, & Mott, 1988).

Depending on the specific pattern of recent drug use, substance-abusing teens may present with a variety of psychiatric symptoms (Brown et al., 1992). These symptoms may include suicidal ideation and attempts, severe depression, anger, agitation, and psychotic symptoms (paranoia, thought disorganization, and disorientation of time, place, or person). Such emotional or behavioral disturbances often lead parents or other authority figures to seek psychiatric assistance for treatment of the symptoms. Rapid abatement of such symptomatology without psychotropic intervention

TABLE 7.1 Assessing Teen Alcohol and Drug Abuse: Common Behavioral Correlates of Abuse

Domain of Functioning	Behavioral Correlates	Change
School	attendance:	truancy, suspension, expulsion
	academic performance:	decreased grades, decreased comprehension
	behavior problems:	conflict with authorities and peers
Family	withdrawal:	decreased contact and expressiveness
	conflict:	arguments, runaway, lying
Social	behavior:	fights, decreased communication
	peer group:	change in friends or peer drug use
	sexuality:	promiscuity, teen pregnancy
Activities	work:	absenteeism, firing, walking off job
	school:	decreased participation
	illegal behavior:	theft, property damage
	reckless behavior:	speeding while driving
Health	physical:	accidents, injury, withdrawal symptoms
	emotional:	emotional lability, anxiety, depression or anger, suicidal ideation, psychotic thoughts, decreased motivation

SOURCE: Brown et al. (1992, Table 37.3). Copyright 1992 by John Wiley & Sons, Inc. Reprinted by permission.

may be the first indicator of substance abuse-induced psychiatric disorder (Brown & Schuckit, 1988; Meyer, 1986).

Above and beyond the emotional turbulence and behavioral diversity that are hallmarks of adolescence is the common clustering of a variety of deviant behaviors associated with drug use (Donovan & Jessor, 1985). These include criminal activities (e.g., theft, property damage, selling illegal substances) and conduct disorder-type behaviors that are interpersonally disruptive (e.g., violent or aggressive behavior, repeated defiance of authority). Reckless behaviors that occur while the adolescent is procuring drugs, while under the influence of a substance, or during acute withdrawal add to the risk of a variety of health-related or life-threatening circumstances (e.g., driving while under the influence, sexual promiscuity).

Although conduct disorder-type behaviors are prevalent features of the clinical presentation of teens entering treatment, a significant portion of such behaviors occur as a direct or indirect consequence of drug use and should be considered separate from conduct disorder behaviors that occur independent of or prior to drug use. Thus, despite a relatively short duration of drug use, teens presenting for substance abuse treatment evidence difficulties across a number of important life domains.

Heterogeneity among alcohol- and drug-dependent adults has been noted (e.g., Cloninger, 1987) and has received considerable attention in recent years. Similarly, it is obvious that there is marked heterogeneity of symptoms, behavioral characteristics, and intrapersonal functioning of adolescents entering treatment for alcohol and drug abuse. Although little attention has been paid to the issue of heterogeneity within the adolescent population in drug treatment outcome studies to date, such variability may have important implications for the clinical course of teens following alcohol and drug treatment programs.

Adolescent Treatment Outcome Evaluations

Despite the recent proliferation of adolescent drug treatment programs, only a limited amount is known about effectiveness of therapeutic regimes or long-term clinical course for adolescent substance abusers following treatment (Brown, Mott, & Myers, 1990). Information regarding teen treatment outcome is further complicated by the fact that a significant portion of information available comes from outcome studies conducted during the time when adolescents were treated in adult alcohol and drug treatment programs rather than in separate adolescent programs. For example, according to one report of the National Institute on Drug Abuse (1983), approximately 20% of those in treatment for alcohol and drug abuse in the United States were 19 years of age or younger; however, only 5% of drug treatment programs had teens constituting more than 50% of the clientele. Historically, few residential alcohol and drug treatment programs have been designed for adolescents; teens typically received treatment in the same settings as adults and received the same intervention efforts even when treated separately. The practices of most adolescent treatment programs today are derived from adult studies, with limited information available regarding the effectiveness of intervention efforts for substance-abusing adolescents.

Several systematic efforts have been made to evaluate the effectiveness of adolescent drug treatment. Using the data from the Pennsylvania Data Collection System, Rush (1979) examined potential predictors of teen treatment outcomes at discharge, comparing residential treatment to outpatient programs. The primary outcome measure examined was productivity, which was based on measures of education, training, and employment following discharge for 4,738 teens. Among teens in residential treatment communities, a greater length of treatment was the best predictor of improved productivity. In contrast, teens from outpatient programs who had longer treatment involvement obtained the poorest productivity gains. Rush interprets these findings to mean that teens who remain in outpatient treatment for extended periods are most likely to have the most severe drug dependence problems and to be least capable of achieving gains in productivity. In addition, teens who participate in inpatient residential programs report more heavy drug use involvement prior to treatment and greater incidence of criminal activities. Both of the above noted sample differences limit conclusions that can be drawn about the efficacy of these various treatment modalities.

The Drug Abuse Reporting Program (DARP) studied 5,406 adolescents for four to six years following treatment (Sells & Simpson, 1979). Although the DARP programs were designed for adult opiate abusers, portions of the clientele were 19 years of age or under. Reduction in drug use and criminal activities were evident across the treatment programs surveyed; however, adolescents were found to use alcohol and marijuana extensively one year following treatment. Further highlighting the heterogeneity of treatment samples was the finding that black teens reported increases in their levels of marijuana use, in contrast to constant levels of use reported by Anglo teens. Alcohol use decreased in this population in general following treatment, whereas use of alcohol increased slightly among 18- and 19-year-old blacks.

The Treatment Outcome Prospective Study (TOPS), conducted by Hubbard, Cavanaugh, Graddock, and Rachel (1983), examined 240 adolescents in several cities in the United States and made comparisons between residential and outpatient programs for teens who remained in treatment at least three months. Residential programs reported favorable one-year outcomes for criminal activity and for daily marijuana and alcohol use. Following treatment in outpatient programs, teens were less likely to be engaged in criminal activity and decreased their alcohol use, but a greater proportion of this sample continued to be marijuana users (48% pretreatment compared to 58% posttreatment).

A number of client characteristics have been associated with more positive drug use outcome following adolescent drug treatment. For example, Friedman, Glickman, and Morrisey (1986) conducted a large-scale study of substance-abusing teens participating in outpatient clinics. Decreases in posttreatment drug use were associated with length of time in treatment, fewer previous admissions, drug problems other than marijuana, and Caucasian background. Holsten (1980) found that background characteristics, including being female, coming from a broken home without a biological family history of alcoholism, and experiencing no problems specifically related to alcohol and no legal problems prior to treatment, accounted for 25% of the outcome variance in a Scandinavian study. Benson (1985) examined characteristics associated with poor treatment outcomes for adolescents. Relapsing adolescent males were found to display more school attendance problems, whereas females more commonly reported alcoholic parents; all relapsers were significantly more likely to have poorer school careers, including higher dropout rates and suspensions or expulsions.

Brown, Vik, and Creamer (1989) have reported that adolescent addiction relapse rates in the first six months following treatment are relatively comparable to rates observed among adult addicts (see Figure 7.1). While adolescent relapse rates are relatively high at the one-year point (up to 85% by some estimates), the greatest risk for relapse is in the initial months following treatment. In a replication study, my colleagues and I found that approximately one third of teens participating in inpatient adolescent alcohol and drug treatment programs abstained for the first 6 months following treatment (Brown et al., 1990). Nearly one fourth (24%) of teens were classified as improved, although they had some alcohol and drug use involvement during the 6-month follow-up period. These teens ("minor relapsers") reported time-limited drug use episodes, with no more than a total of 30 days of alcohol or drug use during the first six months following treatment. The remaining adolescents in the study (43%) had significantly poorer drug use outcomes. Teens who had returned to heavy use and reported concurrent problems secondary to their alcohol or drug use drank or used on the average of 110 of the first 180 days following treatment.

Although early relapse appears to be a negative prognostic indicator, not all teens who do poorly in the first six months following treatment continue to have poor outcome during the second six months after treatment (see the discussion of posttreatment drug use patterns below). This fluctuating clinical course has also been noted in adult populations

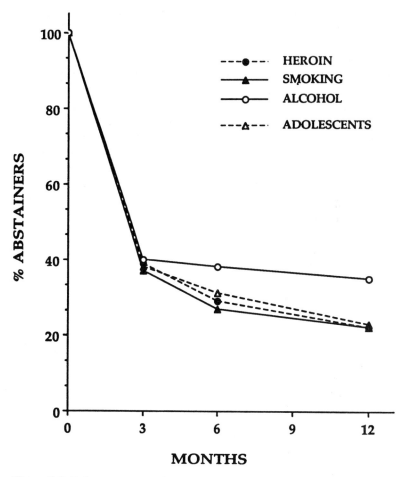

Figure 7.1. Relapse rate over time.

SOURCE: Adolescent data are from Brown, Vik, and Creamer (1989). Adult data are adapted, by permission, from Hunt, Barnett, and Branch (1971).

and highlights the significance of examining clinical populations over extended periods of time. Some authors have suggested that a minimum of four years may be necessary to describe reliably the patterns of typical clinical course for adults (e.g., Nathan & Skinstad, 1987).

In addition, several investigations have begun to examine the patterns of relapse for adolescents in the same fashion that these initial relapses have been examined among adults (e.g., Marlatt & Gordon, 1980; Shiffman & Wills, 1985). While relapse rates for adolescents appear to be relatively comparable to those of adults, the precursors for teen relapse differ from those for adults (Brown, Vik, & Creamer, 1989). Negative emotional states and interpersonal conflict commonly precede adult addiction relapse, whereas direct and indirect social pressure appears to be more salient in adolescent initial relapse situations. For example, in a study examining relapse precipitants among 75 adolescents between the ages of 12 and 18, social factors were found to be salient in these initial relapse experiences, with 90% of relapses occurring in the presence of other people (Brown, Vik, & Creamer, 1989). Further, no abstention models were present in the majority of these situations (73%), and socializing was defined as the most common activity engaged in when the initial relapse occurred (49%). While some of these situations were sought out with the object of drug use (20%), the majority of initial relapses did not fit this pattern. When socializing was the primary activity in the initial situation, in only 44% of these cases did relapses occur in the presence of pretreatment drug-using friends. Further, 60% of the adolescents reported direct social pressure prior to use, whereas only half the adolescents reported any negative affect or interpersonal conflict prior to relapse.

In general, social context appears salient in initial adolescent alcohol and drug use following treatment, whereas negative intrapersonal states and interpersonal situations predominate in the adult relapse picture (Marlatt & Gordon, 1980). Although relatively positive outcomes have been reported in large survey studies of adolescent drug treatment outcome, many studies have been fraught with methodological problems. Information regarding posttreatment substance use is typically based on adolescent self-report, without concomitant verification of posttreatment drug use patterns. In addition, outcome categories typically employed in teen studies have been based on the more extensive treatment program evaluations conducted with adults, and may fail to include aspects of adolescent posttreatment drug involvement or features of functioning (e.g., school) that are specific to teens. Adolescent substance abuse treatment program effectiveness should be considered separately from treatment program outcome evaluations that involve older teens who have participated in adult treatment programs. Presumably, adolescent treatment programs will be better tailored to meet the needs and address the developmental levels of adolescents.

Little information is available regarding drug treatment outcome differences across the adolescent age range. Long-term outcome for individuals who by age 12 or 13 have experienced alcohol- and drug-related problems severe enough to merit treatment may be quite different from adolescents whose first alcohol- or drug-related problems appear at age 18 or 19. In addition, few comparison groups have been incorporated into the longitudinal clinical course evaluations of teen substance abuse. Finally, the extent to which adolescent drug treatment program effectiveness varies as a function of specific type of drug abuse remains an open question.

Special Adolescent Issues

Adolescence is a time of considerable behavioral, emotional, and physical changes (see Table 7.2). Hormonal changes (e.g., gonadotrophin-releasing hormone, follicular stimulating hormone, and luteinizing hormone) produce increased physical size and significant pubertal development, and are accompanied by an acceleration of negative affect (Brooks-Gunn & Warren, 1989). Social behavior is marked by fluctuations in interest in heterosexual involvement, investment in one's peer group, and reduced investment in parent-child relationships. Although the intensity of these changes varies tremendously over the course of adolescence, and onset varies across individuals, an escalation of deviant behaviors is considered a hallmark of adolescent development. Such emotional disruption and behavioral diversity may reflect normal attempts to master the developmental tasks of adolescence. Conversely, many deviant behaviors or significant changes in emotional and behavioral functioning during adolescence may be a result of alcohol and other drug use. Thus discriminating the consequences of alcohol and drug abuse for teens from deviations associated with normal development or various forms of psychopathology is a difficult task. Minimally, evaluation of teen alcohol and drug abuse occurs in the complex matrix of adolescent development, which is in continual fluctuation.

As shown in Table 7.1, there are a variety of emotional and behavioral changes produced by alcohol and drug use that may reflect other problems antedating or co-occurring with teen drug abuse. By some estimates, up to 75% of clinical samples of substance-abusing teens meet criteria for

TABLE 7.2 Developmental Tasks of Adolescence

Biological maturity
sequential changes of puberty

Social maturity
peer relations
family relations
love relations
social roles

Emotional maturity
independence from family
identity development
impulse and affect control
responsible behavior

Intellectual maturity
abstract reasoning
broadening of scope of intellectual activity
reality testing of self-concept
mature peer relations

---

coexisting DSM-III-R disorders (e.g., Bukstein, Brent, & Kaminer, 1989; Windle, 1990). Other studies suggest that up to 50% of adolescents in treatment meet criteria for conduct disorder, 20% meet criteria for affective disorder, and attention-deficit hyperactivity disorder may be evident in up to 20% (Brown et al., 1990). No specific behavioral change during adolescence has been identified as pathognomonic for addiction.

For those in treatment for substance abuse, deviant behaviors may be a direct or indirect effect of alcohol and drug use, a reflection of concomitant psychopathology, or a manifestation of normal adolescent development. For example, while conduct disorder-type behaviors are associated with drug use, certain behaviors occurring without drug involvement (e.g., cruelty to people or animals, starting fights, setting illegal fires, and confrontation during theft) are more suggestive of independent conduct disorders (Brown, Gleghorn, & Schuckit, 1989).

Comorbidity estimates, while highlighting the significance of the heterogeneity of the adolescent substance-abusing population, may be inflated. In particular, most diagnostic clinical assessment is conducted during periods of recent drug use or during acute withdrawal, and consequently may reflect state rather than trait features of behavior

(Brown, Gleghorn, & Schuckit, 1989). In addition, investigators typically fail to exclude behaviors that appear to be direct or indirect products of the drug use (Brown et al., 1992).

Although considerable change takes place during adulthood, the intensity of behavioral and affective changes and the rate at which those changes occur are even greater during adolescence. Thus studies investigating posttreatment functioning of adolescents need to do so with the consideration of typical fluctuations and levels of deviant behavior in comparable samples of nonabusing teens. To date, few investigations have made such comparisons. These comparisons are critical to understanding the extent to which posttreatment changes are a function of maturation versus a reflection of improvement accompanying abstinence from alcohol and drugs.

Several models of teen drug abuse are particularly attentive to the developmental issues of adolescence (e.g., Kandel, Davies, Karus, & Yamaguchi, 1986) and highlight the extent to which adolescent alcohol or drug use produces a diversion from normal developmental tasks. For example, Newcomb and Bentler (1988) have examined the consequences of adolescent drug use in young adulthood. Based on their longitudinal investigation of adolescents, these authors conclude that *alcohol* use during adolescence results in limited negative consequences in young adult functioning. Teen alcohol use was found to decrease social conformity, religious commitment, and college involvement. In addition, alcohol use during adolescence increased perceived social support and deterred property crime, confrontational acts, and relationship problems for young adults. In contrast, adolescent involvement with *hard drugs* was associated with earlier family formation, elevated incidence of family problems, and significant elevation in deviant behaviors during young adulthood. Those using hard drugs during adolescence had greater numbers of sexual partners, decreased likelihood of continuing in the educational process, earlier involvement in the work force, and decreased job stability during young adulthood. An increase in certain emotional and psychological problems, along with decrements in perceived social support, was evident at follow-up. Newcomb and Bentler conclude that adolescent alcohol use has modest negative consequences for young adult functioning. In contrast, hard drug use promotes significant deterioration in young adult functioning by diverting adolescents from accomplishing the critical developmental tasks that promote a more adequate adjustment in young adulthood.

Several other researchers have reported that a significant proportion of adolescent alcohol abusers in school samples mature out of alcohol problems in young adulthood (e.g., Donovan & Jessor, 1985). In particular, problematic alcohol consumption in young adulthood is poorly predicted by levels of alcohol use during adolescence. While a number of authors have argued for examination of drug use patterns in conjunction with the study of adolescent drinking patterns (Pandina & Schuele, 1983), historically few studies have approached investigating the use of alcohol in this manner.

Although much is known about factors that place adolescents at risk for early use of alcohol or drugs, it is less clear which of these factors are most predictive of adult drinking- or drug-related problems. For example, Stein, Newcomb, and Bentler (1987) found that, in their sample, there were different predictors of young adult drug use and problems associated with drug use during the early 20s. While teenage drug use was predictive of young adult drug use, deviant attitudes and drug use role models during adolescence were most predictive of problematic use of drugs for the young adults. Chassin (1984) has suggested that motivations for substance use during adolescence may have long-term negative implications, and outcome expectancies for alcohol have been linked to the onset of both use and abuse during adolescence (Christiansen, Smith, Roehling, & Goldman, 1989). Reinforcement attributed to alcohol and other drugs appears to be intricately linked to use patterns (Schafer & Brown, 1991; see also Goldman, Brown, Christiansen, & Smith, 1991) and persists even after problems emerge (Brown, 1985; Marlatt & Gordon, 1985). While such drug effect expectancies may change with actual experience with substances, the potential for these anticipated effects to influence alcohol- and drug-related decisions as one matures is unquestionable. Clearly, the requirements of adolescent development are quite distinct from developmental demands during adulthood. The significance of school, the shift to a focus on heterosexual relationships, and the development of personal identity while managing one's physical and social maturation are primary during adolescence. To the extent that alcohol or drug involvement produces delays in the mastery of these tasks or impairs attempts at successful completion of tasks, a divergent trajectory is created for teens as they move into young adulthood.

Posttreatment Drug Use Patterns

As adolescent alcohol and drug use develops, a variety of factors influence the establishment of use patterns. As shown in Figure 7.2, a

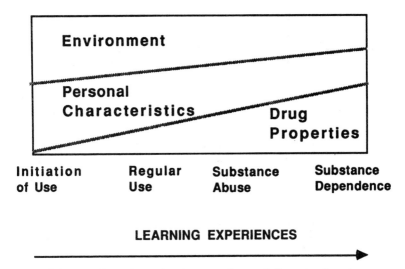

Figure 7.2. Drug dependence development: factors influencing learning.

variety of environmental characteristics, including drug availability, drug cost, and models of drug use and abuse, have been associated with onset of drug use and drug abuse in adolescence. Personal factors such as family history of alcoholism, personality characteristics, and drug effect expectancies may influence the onset and topography of substance use as well as the rate of progression along the substance use continuum (Schafer & Brown, 1991). Similarly, the pharmacologic impact of drugs (e.g., half-life, dosage) also influences the development of dependence and the topography of drug use.

Just as these factors influence the onset and progression of use patterns, they may also be involved in the resolution or persistence of drug problems for teens following treatment. Drug-specific relapse risks as well as personal and environmental resources available following treatment for substance abuse appear to direct the posttreatment clinical course for teens (Brown et al., 1990). For example, the effectiveness of intervention may vary as a function of the posttreatment consequences of pretreatment drug use the teen must face, extent of family history of alcoholism and drug abuse, cognitive and educational resources available, and social activities to which the teen has access.

Based on a series of studies funded by the National Institute of Alcohol Abuse and Alcoholism (NIAAA R01 AA07033, Sandra Brown, principal investigator), detailed analyses of outcome patterns for adolescent alcohol and drug abuse are now available. These results are based on sequential (e.g., 6-, 12-, 24-, and 48-month) multimodal assessments with independent corroborative interviews with a resource person (e.g., parent) to ensure reliability of summary measures.

Results indicate that despite the goal of abstinence from all mind-altering drugs, only a minority of teens appear to maintain abstinence in the first year following treatment. The highest risk period for initial adolescent relapse for alcohol and drug use appears to be in the first month following treatment, and there is reduced but relatively stable risk for survivors ("remaining abstainers") over the next 4 to 5 months (Brown et al., 1990). Of particular significance for adolescents is the finding that more than three fourths of those who remain abstinent in the first 6 months following treatment will continue their abstinence over the next year. In contrast, of teens who use alcohol or other drugs heavily during the first 6 months posttreatment, one third are able to reduce their use or fully abstain in the second 6 months after treatment. Finally, the majority of teens with sporadic, time-limited alcohol or drug use in the first 6 months following treatment continue nonproblematic use or are abstaining by 1 year following treatment (Brown et al., 1990). Thus, although most teens completing alcohol and drug treatment programs will have relapsed by 1 year, it appears that some teens with alcohol or drug involvement following treatment are markedly improved in their total drug use, and do not quickly revert to severe drug use by 1 year after treatment.

Following 1-year posttreatment outcome assessment, discriminant function analyses were used to compare 140 abstaining and relapsing teens on pretreatment drug use history and posttreatment behaviors and personal and environmental characteristics. While pretreatment drug use was not predictive of 1-year outcome, posttreatment factors did predict subsequent alcohol and drug use. Teens who have the poorest drug use outcome at 1 year posttreatment are those with the greatest exposure to alcohol and other drug use in their posttreatment environment and with the least continued involvement in self-help groups such as Alcoholics Anonymous (AA), Narcotics Anonymous (NA), or Cocaine Anonymous (CA). Greater portions of relapsing than abstaining teens return to their pretreatment alcohol- and drug-using peer group and are critical of self-help efforts, including structured groups such as AA. In contrast, teens who are able to abstain during the first year following treatment are more likely to attend self-help groups, to stay in school, and to have improved grades. Whereas those who return to heavy drug use report less emotional distress initially (i.e., first 6 months posttreatment), abstainers are more apt to acknowledge depression and anxiety and to date less than their peers in the first 6 months following treatment.

Although abstaining teens tend to have slightly less drinking and drug use in their immediate families and to develop autonomy more rapidly, there are several major stressors for abstaining teens to manage in the year following treatment. For example, abstaining teens and their families experience significantly more conflict and are more expressive of family problems, some of which are long-term interpersonal consequences of the teen's alcohol and drug use. Further, abstaining teens report higher levels of stress associated with establishing a new group of friends and changes in activities. Fortunately, at 1 year posttreatment, those teens who have continued to abstain report significantly less depression and anxiety than teens who revert to heavy drug involvement.

As one would expect, teens who remain abstinent for 1 year after treatment show marked improvement in functioning in a variety of different domains (Mott, 1990). School-related problems begin to be resolved. In the first 6 months, abstainers are more likely than heavy users to stay in school, and at 1 year they are also more likely to show improvements in grades and more positive attitudes toward school, and to report meeting teachers that they liked. Thus improvement in the academic domain may develop slowly. In terms of social functioning, adolescents who abstain for the year following treatment are less likely to be involved in work and also less likely to be dating than are their relapsing peers. Abstaining adolescents typically begin to establish new groups of friends with less alcohol and drug involvement during the first 6 months following treatment. This process creates increased stress; however, during the second 6 months after treatment, these new friends are perceived as more helpful, and abstaining teens once again report higher levels of interpersonal acceptance. Finally, abstaining peers can expect elevated conflict within their families during the first 6 months after treatment. As the family masters the transition to having a nonabusing teen, family conflict recedes, and by 1 year family members are seen as more helpful.

Although the most prominent posttreatment correlates of poor drug use outcome following adolescent alcohol and drug treatment are exposure to alcohol- and drug-abusing models and reduced involvement in alcohol- or drug-focused support groups, there appear to be other avenues to success for adolescents following treatment. Given that there is considerable heterogeneity in the adolescent treatment population, it is not surprising that subgroups of teens may be at least initially successful despite limited involvement with AA or NA. Historically, there has been little clinical or research focus on such alternative avenues to success for teens following drug treatment. Consequently, our knowledge of viable alternatives for certain types of adolescent clients is quite restricted.

To investigate possible alternative avenues to success following adolescent alcohol and drug treatment, the study examined teens who did not attend self-help groups on a regular basis (i.e., less than 50 times during the year following treatment). Based on alcohol and drug use during the year following treatment, three outcome groups were compared: abstainers, minor relapsers ($\leq$ 30 days alcohol or other drug use each 6 months, M = 16 days per year), and major relapsers. Abstainers and major relapsers attended the fewest self-help group sessions (M = 13.1 and 14.1, respectively), whereas minor relapsers attended an average of 23.4 sessions during the year. Using the same pre- and posttreatment dimensions described above, discriminant function analyses defined two dimensions along which these groups differed. Table 7.3 displays outcome group means of a partial listing of 6-month posttreatment variables that correlated with the discriminant functions.

The two improved groups (i.e., abstainers and minor relapsers) differ from the heavy use outcome group (i.e., major relapsers) both in client characteristics (personal and environmental resources) and in their approach to success following treatment (behavioral efforts). The correlates of the first discriminant function suggest that adolescents who are able to establish abstinent life-styles following alcohol and drug treatment despite little self-help group involvement tend to be younger (M = 15.0 years), come from families with no drug use other than modest alcohol consumption, and have less exposure to drug use, particularly among their closest friends. Although these teens report higher levels of anxiety in the first 6 months of treatment than do teens with poor drug use outcome, they are more likely to persist in school and other structured activities. These teens appear to use the strengths of their families to help master their life-style changes. Families of such teens report conflict surrounding the teens' past drug involvement, but they are more expressive of issues in the family and the teen views the

TABLE 7.3 Characteristics of Adolescents With Low Self-Help Group Attendance Following Treatment[a]

Six Months Posttreatment Characteristics	One Year Abstainers	Outcome Minor Relapsers	Groups Major Relapsers
Total exposure to alcohol	4.14	6.55	6.96
(1 = none, 10 = maximal exposure)	(2.19)	(2.55)	(2.23)
Total exposure to drug use	3.29	4.78	6.79
(1 = none; 10 = maximal exposure)	(2.50)	(2.91)	(2.64)
Closest friends' alcohol use	1.29	2.00	2.82
(1 = nonuser; 6 = problem user)	(0.49)	(0.70)	(1.33)
Closest friends' drug use	1.14	1.55	2.93
(1 = nonuser; 6 = problem user)	(0.38)	(1.01)	(1.74)
New group of friends	.80	.66	.72
(0 = no; 1 = yes)	(0.45)	(0.51)	(0.45)
Parent alcohol use	2.00	4.00	3.43
(1 = nonuser; 6 = problem user)	(0.82)	(1.73)	(1.64)
Parent drug use	1.14	2.56	1.50
(1 = nonuser; 6 = problem user)	(0.38)	(2.19)	(1.07)
Family Relationship Index[b]	12.42	8.22	7.21
(Expression + Cohesion − Conflict)	(2.99)	(4.76)	(5.78)
Parent/Family Stressful	0.71	1.33	1.21
Life Events[c]	(0.95)	(1.73)	(1.13)
Family helpfulness rating	92.86	76.11	67.75
(1 = not helpful; 100 = very helpful)	(11.13)	(17.98)	(32.72)
Attending school	1.20	1.50	1.27
(1 = yes; 2 = no)	(0.45)	(0.55)	(0.46)
Academic grades	4.00	4.10	4.60
(1 = A's; 9 = F's)	(2.91)	(2.45)	(2.11)
Teacher: teen liked	0.62	0.66	0.44
(0 = no; 1 = yes)	(0.54)	(0.51)	(0.50)
Employment	2.86	4.67	3.71
(1 = no; 6 = full-time)	(2.19)	(1.80)	(1.95)
Structured recreation			
(sports, clubs, hobbies)	1.57	2.01	2.14
(1 = none; 3 = weekly)	(1.51)	(1.50)	(1.14)
Activity helpfulness rating	56.57	74.44	46.00
(1 = not helpful; 100 = very helpful)	(33.22)	(26.39)	(34.32)
Report anxiety symptoms	1.00	1.00	1.32
(1 = yes; 2 = no)	(0.00)	(0.00)	(0.48)

a. Mean (standard deviation).
b. Subscales of the Family Environment Scale (Moos, 1986).
c. Subscale of the Life Event Survey (Newcomb, Huba, & Bentler, 1981).

family as helpful in the recovery process (Tammariello & Fulkerson, 1990). Thus one alternative road to success following treatment for adolescents with no family history of drug abuse and minimal drug exposure in their environment is through family support and involvement. While this approach may initially be more stressful, if the teen has the personal and familial resources to persist for 1 year, anxiety symptoms appear to abate and the teen once again appears to become actively involved in school and social activities.

A second pattern associated with marked improvement in posttreatment functioning despite minimal involvement with traditional self-help groups is more common among teens with parental alcohol and drug abuse. These teens perceive their families as less helpful in their attempts to make posttreatment life-style changes. Instead of relying on family support, these teens appear to become more involved in school or recreational activities and work. These experiences allow them less time at home as well as opportunities to participate in self-esteem-enhancing activities outside the family. Such teens are more likely to persist in school and to have better grades by 1 year posttreatment, and to report they have met teachers that they really liked. Although they tend not to change their friends, there is typically only limited drug use in their peer group. This subgroup of teens may evidence intermittent substance use, typically alcohol, but do not exhibit any ongoing alcohol- or drug-related problems. While the long-term course of alcohol or drug use involvement is not known, these teens appear to have adopted very modest drinking habits that persist at least 1 year following treatment. Thus, for a small portion of teens in treatment for alcohol and drug abuse, purposeful engagement in activities outside the home appears to play a protective role during the first posttreatment year. As the long-term outcome of teens pursuing early independence from their families is unknown, it is not clear whether modest alcohol involvement following treatment will degenerate into abuse at a later time.

Conclusion

The arena of clinical outcome research has only begun to appreciate the complexities of the clinical course of adolescent substance abuse. Adolescents' alcohol and drug involvement patterns vary markedly from those of adults, and teens face many formidable developmental tasks in addition to establishing major life-style changes in their post-treatment recovery period. It is not surprising that, although adolescent alcohol and drug treatment programs produce some success, there is also considerable relapse following treatment. It is noteworthy that significant improvement can be attained in major areas of teen functioning with only 1 year of abstinence, and that measurable deterioration in functioning continues when adolescents revert to drug abuse in the year following treatment. While posttreatment factors appear to play a major role in influencing the clinical course of adolescent substance abuse, the heterogeneity of the population and pathways to improved functioning following treatment may be somewhat varied. Clearly, much additional research is necessary to determine prognostic indicators of longer-term course, particularly as adolescents move through young adulthood, which is the highest risk period for alcohol and drug abuse.

References

Benson, G. (1985). Course and outcome of drug abuse and medical and social condition in selected young drug abusers. *Acta Psychiatrica Scandinavica, 71*, 48-66.

Brooks-Gunn, J., & Warren, M. P. (1989). Biological and social contributions to negative affect in young adolescent girls. *Child Development, 60*, 40-55.

Brown, S. A. (1985). Reinforcement expectancies and alcoholism treatment outcome after a one-year follow-up. *Journal of Studies on Alcohol, 46*, 304-308.

Brown, S. A., Gleghorn, A. A., & Schuckit, M. A. (1989). *Conduct disorder among adolescent substance abusers.* Manuscript submitted for publication.

Brown, S. A., Mott, M. A., & Myers, M. A. (1990). Adolescent alcohol and drug treatment outcome. In R. R. Watson (Ed.), *Drug and alcohol abuse prevention* (pp. 373-403). Totowa, NJ: Humana.

Brown, S. A., Mott, M. A., & Stewart, M. A. (1992). Adolescent alcohol and drug abuse. In C. E. Walker (Ed.), *Handbook of clinical child psychology* (2nd ed., pp. 677-693). New York: John Wiley.

Brown, S. A., & Schuckit, M. A. (1988). Changes in depression among abstinent alcoholics. *Journal of Studies on Alcohol, 49*, 412-417.

Brown, S. A., Vik, P. W., & Creamer, V. A. (1989). Characteristics of relapse following adolescent substance abuse treatment. *Addictive Behaviors, 14*, 291-300.

Bukstein, O. G., Brent, D. A., & Kaminer, Y. (1989). Comorbidity of substance abuse and other psychiatric disorders in adolescents. *American Journal of Psychiatry, 146*, 1131-1141.

Chassin, L. (1984). Adolescent substance use and abuse. *Advances in Child Behavioral Analysis and Therapy, 3*, 99-152.

Christiansen, B. A., Smith, G. T., Roehling, P. V., & Goldman, M. S. (1989). Using alcohol expectancies to predict adolescent drinking behavior after one year. *Journal of Consulting and Clinical Psychology, 51*, 249-258.

Cloninger, C. R. (1987). Neurogenic adaptive mechanisms in alcoholism. *Science, 236,* 410-416.

Donovan, J., & Jessor, R. (1985). Structure of problem behavior in adolescence and young adulthood. *Journal of Consulting and Clinical Psychology, 53,* 890-904.

Friedman, A., Glickman, N., & Morrisey, M. (1986). Prediction of successful treatment outcome by client characteristics and retention in treatment in adolescent drug treatment programs: A large scale cross-validation. *Journal of Drug Education, 16,* 149-165.

Goldman, M. S., Brown, S. A., Christiansen, B. A., & Smith, G. T. (1991). Alcohol etiology and memory: Broadening the scope of alcohol expectancy research. *Psychological Bulletin, 110,* 137-146.

Holden, M., Brown, S. A., & Mott, M. (1988). Social support network of adolescents: Relation to family alcohol abuse. *American Journal of Drug and Alcohol Abuse, 14,* 487-498.

Holsten, F. (1980). Repeat follow up studies of 100 young Norwegian drug abusers. *Journal of Drug Issues, 10,* 491-504.

Hubbard, R., Cavanaugh, E., Graddock, S., & Rachel, J. (1983). *Characteristics, behaviors and outcomes for youth in TOPS study* (Report submitted to the National Institute on Drug Abuse, Contract No. 271-79-3611). Research Triangle Park, NC: Research Triangle Institute.

Hunt, W. A., Barnett, L. W., & Branch, L. G. (1971). Relapse rates in addiction programs. *Journal of Clinical Psychology, 27,* 455-456.

Kandel, D. B., Davies, M., Karus, D., & Yamaguchi, K. (1986). The consequences in young adulthood of adolescent drug involvement. *Archives of General Psychiatry, 43,* 746-754.

Marlatt, G. A., & Gordon, J. R. (1980). Determinants of relapse: Implications for the maintenance of behavior change. In P. O. Davidson & S. M. Davidson (Eds.), *Behavioral medicine: Changing health lifestyles* (pp. 410-452). New York: Brunner/Mazel.

Marlatt, G. A., & Gordon, J. R. (1985). *Relapse prevention.* New York: Guilford.

Meyer, R. (1986). *Psychopathology of addictive behavior.* New York: Guilford.

Moos, R. (1986). *Family Environment Scale manual* (2nd ed.). Palo Alto, CA: Consulting Psychologists Press.

Mott, M. A. (1990, April). Adolescent drug treatment outcome and functioning on major life domains. In P. M. Newcomb (Chair), *Adolescent substance abuse: Biopsychosocial characteristics and clinical course.* Symposium presented at the annual meeting of the Society of Behavioral Medicine, Chicago.

Myers, M. G., & Brown, S. A. (1990, April). *Cigarette smoking and health in adolescent substance abusers.* Paper presented at the meeting of the Society of Behavioral Medicine, Chicago.

Nathan, P., & Skinstad, A. (1987). Outcomes of treatment for alcohol problems: Current methods, problems and results. *Journal of Consulting and Clinical Psychology, 55,* 332-340.

National Institute on Alcohol Abuse and Alcoholism (NIAAA). (1990). *Seventh special report to the U. S. Congress on alcohol and health* (DHHS Publication No. [ADM] 90-1656). Washington, DC: Government Printing Office.

National Institute on Drug Abuse. (1983). *Main findings for drug abuse treatment units: Data from the National Drug and Alcoholism Treatment Utilization Survey (NDATUS)*. Rockville, MD: Author.

National Institute on Drug Abuse. (1989). *National household survey on drug abuse: Population estimates 1988* (DHHS Publication No. ADM 89-1636). Rockville, MD: Author.

Newcomb, M. D, & Bentler, P. M. (1988). *Consequences of adolescent drug use*. Newbury Park, CA: Sage.

Newcomb, M. D., Huba, G. J., & Bentler, P. M. (1981). A multidimensional assessment of stressful life events among adolescents: Derivation and correlates. *Journal of Health and Social Behavior, 22,* 400-415.

Pandina, R. J., & Schuele, J. A. (1983). Psychosocial correlates of alcohol and drug use of adolescent students and adolescents in treatment. *Journal of Studies on Alcohol, 44,* 950-973.

Rush, T. (1979). Predicting treatment outcomes for juvenile and young adult clients in the Pennsylvania substance-abuse system. In G. Beschner & A. Friedman (Eds.), *Youth drug abuse: Problems, issues and treatment* (pp. 629-656). Lexington, MA: Lexington.

Schafer, J., & Brown, S. A. (1991). Marijuana and cocaine effect expectancies and drug use patterns. *Journal of Consulting and Clinical Psychology, 59,* 558-565.

Sells, S., & Simpson, D. (1979). Evaluation of treatment outcome for youths in the Drug Abuse Reporting Program (DARP): A follow-up study. In G. Beschner & A. Friedman (Eds.), *Youth drug abuse: Problems, issues and treatment* (pp. 571-628). Lexington, MA: Lexington.

Shiffman, S., & Wills, T. A. (1985). *Coping and substance use*. Orlando, FL: Academic Press.

Stein, J. A., Newcomb, M. D., & Bentler, P. M. (1987). An 8-year study of multiple influences on drug use and drug use consequences. *Journal of Personality and Social Psychology, 53,* 1094-1105.

Tammariello, C., & Fulkerson, J. (1990, April). *Genetic and environmental risk factors following treatment of adolescent substance abuse*. Paper presented at the meeting of the Society of Behavioral Medicine, Chicago.

Windle, M. (1990, June). *Salient issues in the development of alcohol abuse in adolescence*. Paper presented at ISBRA/RSA Symposium, Toronto.

8

The Offender Substance Abuse
Pre-Release Program:
An Empirically Based Model of
Treatment for Offenders

LYNN O. LIGHTFOOT

Surveys in American prison populations have consistently confirmed an association between alcohol/drug use and crime. For example, a survey of 12,000 inmates in U.S. state prisons found that 33% of inmates reported having drunk "very heavily" just before committing the offenses for which they were convicted (U.S. Department of Justice, 1983). Habitual offenders (more than five prior convictions) and those convicted of assault, burglary, and rape were more likely than other inmates to be heavy drinkers. Some 20% reported having drunk heavily *every day* the entire year prior to their entering prison. Use of alcohol has also been found to be strongly linked to recidivism (Goodwin, Crane & Guze, 1971; Lambert & Madden, 1975), to poor halfway house adjustment (Moczydlowski, 1980), and to parole failure (National Council on Crime

---

AUTHOR'S NOTE: This research was supported by grants from Educational and Personal Development, Correctional Services Canada. The views expressed are those of the author, and do not necessarily represent those of Correctional Services Canada.

and Delinquency, 1972). In a survey of Canadian federal offenders, 75%-80% of incarcerated offenders were found to have alcohol- and/or drug-related problems (Lightfoot & Hodgins, 1988). Most (79%) reported having used alcohol and/or drugs on the days they committed the offenses for which they were currently serving time.

These data suggest that the use of alcohol and drugs by offenders is frequently associated with criminal behavior. What is unclear, however, is the nature of the relationship between alcohol/drug abuse and dependence and the commission of crime, particularly violent crime. Are inmates who have substantial to severe degrees of dependence on alcohol and/or drugs more likely to commit crimes of increasing violence, or is it just as likely that acute incidents of use account for the statistical association between alcohol/drug use and violent behavior and apprehension (Collins, 1981)? Although the precise nature of the relationship between substance use and crime is unknown, alcohol and drug abuse and dependence are nonetheless obviously important targets for rehabilitative programming within the criminal justice system.

Despite the consistently documented high prevalence of alcohol and drug problems in offenders (Lightfoot & Hodgins, 1988; Ross & Lightfoot, 1985; U.S. Department of Justice, 1983), there have been few systematic attempts to develop or evaluate programs for this population (Gendreau & Ross, 1987). This chapter describes the development and evaluation of a skills-based cognitive-behavioral program designed to be provided to offenders prior to their release from institutional correctional settings. The program is viewed as the first step in long-term comprehensive alcohol/drug rehabilitative programming, the major goal of which is to provide incarcerated offenders with the opportunity to acquire the knowledge, skills, and attitudes required to cope with the daily pleasures and pains of community living, without relying on the use of chemicals.

The Offender Substance Abuse Pre-Release Program

General Program Content, Models, and Principles

It is a well-accepted truism in the addictions field that substance abusers "deny" that their substance use is a problem. Many programs attempt to break down this denial through head-on confrontation. Recent research on motivation and behavior change suggests that there may be alternative approaches that may be much more productive, particularly with rebellious and antisocial individuals. Miller and Hester (1986) have noted that there has not been a single adequately controlled evaluation of confrontational counseling with alcoholics. Rather, evidence from the general counseling literature suggests that hostile and confrontational group therapy is associated with more negative outcomes (Lieberman, Yalom, & Miles, 1973). A randomized trial with offenders found that those with low self-esteem had higher levels of recidivism following involvement in a confrontational substance abuse program than did those receiving regular institutional care (Annis & Chan, 1983).

A primary premise of the Offender Substance Abuse Pre-Release (OSAP) Program is, therefore, that substance abuse treatment programs have as one of their responsibilities the development of motivation in "unmotivated" individuals. This contrasts with the view underlying some programs, that it is the client's responsibility to be motivated for change before treatment can be effective. It is important to note in this regard that mandatory substance abuse treatment has been found to be as effective as voluntary treatment for clients within the same treatment program (Freedberg & Johnston, 1980; Miller, 1978; Smart, 1974). However, as Miller and Hester (1986, p. 149) point out, although reinforcement and punishment contingencies can be used to enhance program compliance, the ultimate impact on drinking depends on the effectiveness of the program itself. No client will do well in a poorly conceived or badly delivered program.

Prochaska and DiClemente (1982) have proposed a transtheoretical model of the change process that provides a dynamic view of motivation and behavior change. According to this model, behavior change can be thought of as a process involving a series of four stages: precontemplation, contemplation, action, and maintenance. Individuals who are in the precontemplation stage have not yet personally identified a need for change of the "target" behavior, which in this instance is alcohol and drug use. For precontemplators, substance use is viewed as providing valuable outcomes or reinforcements that far outweigh its negative impacts.

The next stage is contemplation, where the individual becomes aware that a change in his or her pattern of substance use may be desirable or necessary. This awareness may arise because the individual experiences a number of negative consequences related to drug use. However, as with the precontemplation stage, individuals may remain in this stage for an indefinite period of time without making any changes in their behavior. Alternatively, the individual may progress to the "action stage," where he or she has made a commitment to change and has started to engage in purposeful activities designed to change his or her drug use behavior.

Once the desired change has been achieved, the individual enters the maintenance phase of the behavior change process. Here the focus is on maintaining the behavioral changes made during the action phase. Many offenders will present for treatment only because they have been advised that treatment participation will greatly improve their chances for parole. The initial phase of the Offender Substance Abuse Pre-Release Program is, therefore, designed to increase and consolidate motivation for change, in order to prepare participants to learn practical skills they will need if they are to achieve the behavioral changes they seek. Later phases of the program are designed to include interventions that are appropriate for each sequential stage of change. As Prochaska and DiClemente (1982) note, different behavior change interventions or "processes" are appropriate at different stages of change. Table 8.1 describes the processes of change that are likely to be effective at each stage of change. These processes of change will be described within the context of the OSAP Program.

Identification of Treatment Components

Treatment outcome studies in the substance abuse field have tended to indicate that effective treatments are those that involve the teaching and practicing of skills (cognitive and behavioral), particularly those that involve modifying or eliminating use of the problem substance (Miller & Hester, 1986). Accordingly, the second phase of the OSAP Program addresses the action stage of change and involves training skills that were assessed to be deficient at the beginning of treatment and are likely functionally related to the maintenance of the substance abuse behavior, such as poor assertiveness and stress management skills.

The last phase of the program provides offenders with the opportunity and challenge of applying their newly learned skills to potential risk situations for alcohol and drug use that they may encounter in the institution and in the community. Relapse prevention and maintenance skills are additional major aspects of the final phase of treatment, all of which are designed to address the maintenance stage of change.

In summary, the OSAP Program is based upon a sequential model of treatment in which specific interventions (or change processes) are

TABLE 8.1 Interventions and Stages of Change

Precontemplation	Stages of Change Contemplation	Action	Maintenance
Consciousness-raising			
	Self-reevaluation		
		Self-liberation	
		Contingency management	
		Helping relationship	
			Counterconditioning
			Stimulus control
			Relapse prevention

SOURCE: Adapted from Prochaska and DiClemente (1986).

employed at different stages of treatment to address the different offender needs that are manifest at different stages of change. Table 8.2 illustrates the way in which the interventions in the OSAP Program are designed to fit with the needs of individuals at different stages of change.

The Process

The program is delivered primarily in a group format. According to the principles of "inductive" adult learning, the group therapy process depends on an interactive discussion facilitated by a group leader who poses a sequence of carefully selected leading questions. In this way, the informational aspect of program content is elicited from participants based upon their past experience and knowledge, and is supplemented where necessary with brief lectures and a variety of audiovisual materials. The format is supportive, nonconfrontational, and mutually respectful. In our experience, this approach has been most effective in creating a climate where trust and personal disclosure can occur. Over time, the group becomes a major source of social support to individual participants.

Referral Screening and Selection

Volume II of the OSAP curriculum manual provides a detailed description of the proposed assessment process for identifying clients for OSAP. The modified Michigan Alcoholism Screening Test (Gunn & Orenstein, 1983) is recommended as a screening instrument for use by

TABLE 8.2 Components of the Offender Substance Abuse Pre-Release Program and Stage of Change

Stage of Change	Goal of Intervention	Program Strategy
Precontemplation	increase motivation	assessment
Contemplation	increase awareness	alcohol and drug education
Action	learn skills to assist in behavior change process	behavioral self-control training; social skills training
Maintenance	apply skills	employment skills refresher; leisure planning; prerelease planning
Relapse	learn skills and attitudes to prevent or reduce severity and frequency of relapses	relapse prevention; relapse management

case management officers who wish to identify substance abuse problems systematically among offenders on their caseloads. Potential candidates for the program are then referred by case managers for a more comprehensive assessment conducted by the OSAP Program staff using a structured interview and a battery of paper-and-pencil tests. A Structured Interview for Selecting Treatment for Inmates (ASIST-I; Lightfoot & Hodgins, 1988) elicits information on alcohol and drug use histories as well as on the inmates' perceptions of the effects of alcohol or other drugs on their lives. The interview assesses the inmate's functioning in seven life areas in the 6 months before incarceration: marital and family relationships, other social relationships, education and employment, finances, legal status, physical health, and emotional health. A study by Hodgins (1986) investigating interviewer reliability on the structured interview has indicated high agreement among interviewers (Hodgins, 1986).

The self-report questionnaires assess a number of additional constructs. The severity of alcohol dependence is measured using the 25-item version of the Alcohol Dependence Scale (ADS; Skinner & Horn, 1984) and severity of problems associated with drug use is measured by the Drug Abuse Screening Test (DAST; Skinner, 1982). The time frame specified for response to these scales was modified from the past 12 months to the 6 months before incarceration to make them comparable to the time frame of the structured interview.

Psychological distress of the subjects is assessed using the 28-item American version of the General Health Questionnaire (GHQ; Goldberg & Hillier, 1979). Cognitive abilities are estimated by using the Shipley-Hartford Institute of Living Scale (Shipley, 1940) and the Trail Making Test (Reitan, 1958). Shipley-Hartford scores are converted to age-corrected WAIS estimates using tables provided by Paulson and Lin (1970).

In earlier work, using a statistical clustering algorithm, we have developed a typology of substance-abusing offenders (Hodgins & Lightfoot, 1988). Five groups were differentiated primarily by the extent of alcohol and drug problems identified. We found a group of offenders who are basically free of alcohol or drug problems and who therefore did not require treatment. A second group abused drugs rather than alcohol and led generally criminal life-styles. The third group abused alcohol rather than drugs and was relatively socially stable. The fourth and fifth groups abused both alcohol and drugs. In addition, the fourth group showed significant emotional distress and the fifth group was neuropsychologically impaired. Both of these last two groups had special needs that went beyond the usual capabilities of substance abuse treatment programs, and available empirical evidence indicates that these offenders would be unlikely to benefit from substance abuse treatment (McLellan, Woody, Luborsky, O'Brien, & Druley, 1983; Rounsaville, Dolinsky, Babor, & Meyer, 1987). Accordingly, offenders whose assessment scores on the GHQ and/or Trails B and Shipley CQ are above cutoff would not be deemed appropriate for the OSAP Program. Instead, we would recommend referral for further specialized neuropsychological and/or psychiatric assessment and treatment prior to involvement in substance abuse treatment.

Overview of the Program

A program curriculum manual provides detailed protocols for each of the 26 three-hour sessions of the Offender Substance Abuse Pre-Release Program (Lightfoot, 1989b). The treatment protocols are based on a group format, with a group size of 8-12 participants, supplemented by a minimum of three individual counseling sessions. The program is divided into the following nine units: Introduction, Alcohol and Drug Education, Self-Management Skills Training, Social Skills Training,

TABLE 8.3 Program Overview

Individual Assessment Interviews
Unit I: Introduction (2 sessions)
Individual Counseling Session I
Unit II: Alcohol and Drug Education (5 sessions)
Unit III: Self-Management Skills Training (7 sessions) (self-control training, problem solving, assertion training)
Individual Counseling Session II
Unit IV: Social Skills Training (3 sessions)
Unit V: Job Skills Refresher (2 sessions)
Unit VI: Leisure and Life-Style (1 session)
Unit VII: Pre-Release Planning (2 sessions)
Unit VIII: Relapse Prevention and Management (2 sessions)
Unit IX: Posttesting and Graduation (2 sessions)
Individual Counseling Session III

Job Skills Refresher, Leisure and Life-Style Planning, Pre-Release Planning, Relapse Prevention and Management, and Posttesting and Graduation. Table 8.3 provides an overview of the program elements and the number of sessions devoted to each.

The Introduction phase of the program consists of two sessions. The first session is an orientation to the substance abuse treatment program. It is intended to provide participants with an overview of the program, including a shared understanding of the objectives of the program and the philosophical and conceptual basis for the program in the framework and terminology of social learning theory.

In the second session of the Introduction unit, all participants complete a standard set of pretests. This information is used as the baseline against which posttreatment test performance is compared in order to evaluate the client's progress in treatment and the program. The information obtained in pretesting is also important in developing individualized treatment goals for each participant. Finally, pretest information is considered in determining which goals are most appropriate for each participant during the skills training phase of treatment. Participants are also provided with an overview of the program and the social learning model of addictions upon which it is based. A treatment contract is then presented for review and discussion, and this provides the formal opportunity for participants to consent to and contract for treatment.

The primary intent of the Alcohol and Drug Education unit of the program is not to increase knowledge about alcohol and drugs, but rather to increase motivation for those offenders who may not yet have identified that they have problems with alcohol and drugs. We use the terminology of the stages of change model referred to earlier, and the intention is to stimulate offenders with low motivation to move from the precontemplation phase into the contemplation phase of the process. The program is designed to enlist precontemplators in an exercise in which they begin to assess the relative advantages (short-term positive consequences) and disadvantages (long-term negative consequences) of their substance use behavior. For those inmates who entered the correctional facility already concerned about their alcohol and/or drug use, the objective of this unit is to consolidate their motivation and to push them forward into the action phase.

The Alcohol and Drug Education unit consists of five sessions or modules. Two modules focus on alcohol use, two focus on psychoactive drug use, and the final session is used for review. Scientifically accurate and factual information regarding acute and chronic effects of substance use is presented and discussed. Implications for functioning in all major life areas, including physiological, psychological, social, and legal, are discussed. The education sessions are designed to provide participants with an opportunity to assess the extent to which alcohol and drug use has had negative impact on their lives and on others. This increased awareness is intended to create a state of cognitive dissonance that, properly directed, will provide the motivation for active change.

In the skills training phases of treatment (Self-Management Skills Training, Social Skills Training, Job Skills Refresher, and Leisure and Life-Style), participants acquire a broad repertoire of skills that will enable them to modify and/or abstain from substance use. Consistent with the empirical literature on substance abuse treatment, offenders who are younger, unmarried, relatively socially stable, and have problem drinking histories of less than 10 years may be most effectively treated in a program that teaches responsible drinking skills rather than one that leads to total abstinence (Sanchez-Craig, 1980; Sanchez-Craig, Annis, Bornet, & MacDonald, 1984; Sanchez-Craig & Lei, 1986). For others, the literature encourages us to target complete abstinence as a goal in treatment. In the first edition of the treatment manual it was recommended that participants be divided into these two streams for this phase of treatment. In the current edition of the manual, based on the results of field tests, a combined program that can address the needs of participants in both groups is presented as a cost-effective alternative. During skills training participants are introduced to a variety of strategies they can use to deal with risk situations, including self-management (Alden, 1988), problem solving, cognitive coping, behavioral coping (Sanchez-Craig, 1984), communication skills (Chaney, 1989), assertiveness skills, interpersonal skills, employment skills and their relationship to substance use and abuse, and leisure and life-style skills. Participants first identify high-risk situations for alcohol and drug abuse using the Inventory of Drinking Situations (Annis, 1982). They are introduced to a simple ABC (antecedents, behavior, consequences) model of behavior for understanding how antecedents (triggers) and consequences (payoffs) influence their use of alcohol and drugs. Strategies for identifying alternative ways to achieve the payoffs provided by alcohol and drugs are identified through use of Miller's New Roads exercises (Miller & Pechacek, 1987).

The Pre-Release Planning phase of treatment is designed to form a bridge between the theoretical knowledge acquired in the skills training sessions and situations likely to be encountered in postrelease community living. Participants systematically review all areas of their lives and, using paper-and-pencil exercises and role-play rehearsals, they then apply the skills they have learned in treatment to achieve their personal goals. Feedback from other members of the group as well as from the group facilitators provides an opportunity for participants to fill gaps or address limitations identified in their initial plans. Participants are provided with information about the array of addiction treatment resources available in the community and are encouraged to identify and make contact with appropriate community aftercare services and resources.

Finally, the Relapse Prevention and Management unit addresses skills needed to avoid relapse or to manage it if it occurs. The purpose of these two sessions is to introduce participants to a cognitive-behavioral model of the relapse process using the ABC model previously described. We have relied heavily on the work of Marlatt and colleagues (Marlatt & George, 1984; Marlatt & Gordon, 1985) and Annis and Davis (1989a, 1989b) in the development of this component of the treatment program. The relationship between risk situations and relapse is illustrated, and participants are invited to apply their problem-solving skills to the identification of preventive strategies for dealing with their high-risk situations. This is particularly challenging for offenders who have successfully maintained abstinence while incarcerated. They find it difficult to imagine that a return to community living will mean a return to situations previously highly associated with heavy use (triggers) that may contribute to a "lapse" or a "slip." A realistic appraisal of the broad array of reintegration stresses is essential preparation for a return to community living. A variety of slip prevention strategies are identified by the individual and evaluated within the group.

A second major component of this unit is the recognition that a slip, lapse, or even a full-blown relapse may well occur, particularly within the first three months after release. Through group brainstorming exercises, participants identify a broad range of strategies that can be employed to reduce the length and severity of a lapse as much as possible. Every effort is made to encourage offenders to view lapses not as failures but as experiences they can learn from, while at the same time not providing "permission" for lapses to occur.

Another major focus is the relationship of a lapse or relapse to the risk of reoffending. For extremely high-risk offenders, those who have committed violent offenses while under the influence of a substance, a preventive detoxification or hospital (crisis unit) admission is strongly encouraged as one of the relapse prevention strategies.

The final phase of treatment is devoted to posttesting, followed by a graduation exercise designed to provide recognition to participants for the commitment and effort they have expended in completing the treatment program.

Individual Counseling

For reasons of efficiency and cost-effectiveness, a group format is used for delivering the bulk of the treatment program. However, because offender needs vary widely, and because some participants may have difficulty discussing particular problems in a group setting, individual counseling is considered an essential component of the treatment program. Each participant receives a minimum of one individual counseling session in the orientation phase of treatment, a second midway through the program, and a third during the prerelease phase of treatment. In addition to this minimum requirement for individual counseling, program staff advise participants that staff are available for additional assistance whenever necessary. When program staff identify that a participant is having a problem, or could benefit from referral to another institutional program, they will intervene in the context of individual counseling sessions.

Program Goals and Objectives

A goal statement and a specific set of behavioral objectives have been developed for each session of the program. Development of specific behavioral objectives provides concrete benchmarks against which progress of individual participants can be assessed and the program evaluated.

How Effective Is the Program?

The Offender Substance Abuse Pre-Release Program has been systematically developed over the past six years on the basis of a comprehensive program of research and evaluation, in contrast to most correctional alcohol and drug programs (Gendreau & Ross, 1987). The program was designed empirically, on the basis of a needs assessment survey of Ontario region offenders (Hodgins & Lightfoot, 1988; Lightfoot & Hodgins, 1988) and a thorough review of the treatment outcome literature (Ross & Lightfoot, 1985). The program was field tested (Lightfoot & Barbaree, 1988), and results of the evaluation were used to revise and modify the program. A second field test was conducted in 1989, and the results of that evaluation were used to make the most recent changes to the format and content of the program (Lightfoot & Barker, 1989). A comprehensive curriculum was subsequently published in 1989 by Correctional Services Canada (Lightfoot, 1989a, 1989b). A staff training manual was prepared and used in a pilot project later that year (Lightfoot & Matthews, 1989). Staff trained in this way have been involved in a third pilot study of the program in a medium-security institution (Lightfoot, 1992).

Within the correctional system, the long-term goal of rehabilitation programs is to reduce recidivism. Substance abuse is thought to be a criminogenic risk factor (Ross & Lightfoot, 1985)—that is, it increases the risk of reoffending, at least for some offenders—and is therefore a reasonable target for rehabilitation programming. However, most treatment programs have short-term (secondary) targets, such as increases in problem-solving skills or assertiveness, which are assumed to be intervening behaviors, and that must be altered if long-term changes in targeted behaviors (i.e., drinking/drug use, crime) are to be achieved. Because of its developmental nature, our program evaluations to date have focused primarily on these secondary targets.

To this end, a battery of pretests has been developed that targets alcohol and drug knowledge and attitudes, assertiveness skills, communication skills, responsible drinking skills, problem-solving skills, employment skills, and relapse prevention-related knowledge and skills. A summary of the pre-posttest battery is provided in Table 8.4.

In general, the program evaluations described above have focused on the immediate impact of the program on alcohol- and drug-related knowledge and attitudes and skills that are thought to mediate alcohol and drug use behavior. These content domains can be considered "secondary targets" for the purpose of program evaluation. Results of these field test evaluations indicate that the program is increasingly successful in changing offender attitudes toward alcohol and drugs to a more negative orientation. Increases in alcohol- and drug-related knowledge, relapse prevention and management skills, and problem-solving and employment skills were also found following participation in the program.

Although all offenders complete the battery of tests prior to and following treatment participation, each exhibits a unique pattern of knowledge and skills at the outset of treatment. These large individual differences at treatment initiation present a major challenge to program evaluation, which usually looks at group change from pre- to posttreatment compared with changes seen in a control or comparison group (Campbell & Stanley, 1966).

Recently in our laboratory an innovative approach to this evaluation conundrum was developed (Barker, 1990). Thirteen federal inmates completing the 80-hour OSAP Program were compared with a no-treatment comparison group on the pre-posttest battery previously described. Following psychometric evaluation of the test instruments, groups were compared on alcohol and drug attitudes, communication skills, problem solving, employment, and relapse prevention attitudes and knowledge. Within- and between-group analyses were conducted, and these indicated that treated group subjects' attitudes toward alcohol and drug use

TABLE 8.4 Offender Substance Abuse Pre-Release Program Pre-Posttreatment Assessment Battery

Content Assessed	Test Name
(1) Alcohol knowledge	Consequences of Alcohol Use (adapted from Gunn & Orenstein, 1983)
(2) Drug knowledge	Consequences of Drug Use (adapted from Gunn & Orenstein, 1983)
(3) Alcohol and drug attitudes	How Much Do They Matter? (adapted from Gunn & Orenstein, 1983)
(4) Assertiveness skills	Drinking & Assertiveness (adapted from Gunn & Orenstein, 1983)
(5) Communication skills	Communicating About Drinking (adapted from Gunn & Orenstein, 1983)
(6) Responsible drinking	Using Alcohol Responsibly (adapted from Gunn & Orenstein, 1983)
(7) Problem-solving skills	Decision-Making (adapted from Gunn & Orenstein, 1983)
(8) Personal goals in treatment	Personal Goal Review (Post) (Lightfoot, 1989b)
(9) Consumer satisfaction	Consumer Satisfaction Rating Scale (posttreatment only) (Larsen, Attkisson, Hargreaves, & Nguyen, 1979)
(10) Employment knowledge and attitudes *and* relapse knowledge and attitudes	Substances, Employment & Relapse Questionnaire (Barker, 1990)

were significantly more negative than those of controls, and their problem-solving and responsible drinking skills were significantly greater than those of controls following treatment.

An analysis of individual change scores on each of the scales was then made using a regression equation based on available normative data (Lord & Novick, 1968). A z score was calculated to determine whether the actual posttest score differs significantly from the predicted posttest score for each program participant. Table 8.5 summarizes the

TABLE 8.5 Individual Change Score Distribution for Participants in the OSAP Treatment Group

Number of Significant Outcome Measure Change Scores (max = 4)	Number of Treatment Group Participants	%	Cumulative %
0	1	7.69	7.69
1	5	38.46	46.15
2	1	7.69	53.84
3	4	30.77	84.61
4	2	15.39	100.00
4	13	100.00	

SOURCE: Adapted from Barker (1990).

distribution of individual change scores for treated offenders. More than half (51.92%) of posttest scores were significantly higher than predicted posttest scores. Most participants (12/13) made at least one significant change, and most (50%) made two or more changes.

Although long-term evaluation is necessary to assess the impact of the program on postrelease alcohol and drug use, which are of course the ultimate targets of the program, these early findings are very encouraging. Few programs have been systematically and empirically developed to ensure that they are actually achieving the kinds of changes in participants for which they are designed. In addition, it is important to note that few programs have been as thoroughly documented as OSAP, and the documentation now includes a detailed curriculum guide, an assessment manual, and a staff training manual, providing for a superior level of quality assurance and maintenance of program integrity over time.

References

Alden, L. E. (1988). Behavioral self-management controlled-drinking strategies in a context of secondary prevention. *Journal of Consulting and Clinical Psychology, 56,* 280-286.

Annis, H. M. (1982). *Inventory of drinking situations*. Toronto: Addiction Research Foundation of Ontario.

Annis, H. M., & Chan, D. (1983). The differential treatment model. *Criminal Justice and Behavior, 10(2)*, 159-173.

Annis, H. M., & Davis, C. S. (1989a). Relapse prevention. In R. K. Hester & W. R. Miller (Eds.), *Handbook of alcoholism treatment approaches* (pp. 170-182). New York: Pergamon.

Annis, H. M., & Davis, C. S. (1989b). Relapse prevention training: A cognitive-behavioral approach based on self-efficacy theory. *Journal of Chemical Dependency Treatment, 2*, 81-103.

Barker, J. (1990). *An evaluation of the substance abuse pre-release program at Joyceville Institution*. Unpublished master's thesis.

Campbell, D. T., & Stanley, J. C. (1966). *Experimental and quasi-experimental designs for research*. Skokie, IL: Rand McNally.

Chaney, E. (1989). Social skills training. In R. K. Hester & W. R. Miller (Eds.), *Handbook of alcoholism treatment approaches*. New York: Pergamon.

Collins, J. J. (1981). *Drinking and crime: Perspectives on the relationship between alcohol consumption and criminal behavior*. New York: Guilford.

Freedberg, E. J., & Johnston, W. E. (1980). Outcome with alcoholics seeking treatment voluntarily or after confrontation by their employer. *Journal of Occupational Medicine, 22*, 83-86.

Gendreau, P., & Ross, R. H. (1987). Revivification of rehabilitation: Evidence from the 1980s. *Justice Quarterly, 4(3)*, 349-406.

Goldberg, D. P., & Hillier, V. F. (1979). A scaled version of the general health questionnaire. *Psychological Medicine, 9*, 139-145.

Goodwin, D. W., Crane, J. B., & Guze, S. B. (1971). Felons who drink: An 8-year follow-up. *Quarterly Journal of Studies on Alcohol, 32*, 136-147.

Gunn, W. J., & Orenstein, D. (1983). *An evaluation handbook for health education programs in alcohol and substance abuse*. Atlanta, GA: Centers for Disease Control.

Hodgins, D. C. (1986). *An alcohol and drug use typology of male prison inmates*. Unpublished doctoral thesis.

Hodgins, D. C., & Lightfoot, L. O. (1988). Types of male alcohol- and drug-abusing incarcerated offenders. *British Journal of Addiction, 83*, 1201-1213.

Lambert, L. R., & Madden, P. G. (1975). *Adult female offenders before, during and after incarceration: Summary, conclusions and recommendations*. Toronto: Ontario Ministry of Correctional Services.

Larsen, D. L., Attkisson, C. C., Hargreaves, W. A., & Nguyen, T. D. (1979). Assessment of client/patient satisfaction: Development of a general scale. *Evaluation and Program Planning, 2*, 197-207.

Lieberman, M. A., Yalom, I. D., & Miles, M. B. (1973). *Encounter groups: First facts*. New York: Basic Books.

Lightfoot, L. O. (1989a). *A substance abuse pre-release program for federal offenders* (Vol. 1). Ottawa: Correctional Services Canada.

Lightfoot, L. O. (1989b). *A substance abuse pre-release program for federal offenders: Vol. 2. Assessment materials*. Ottawa: Correctional Services Canada.

Lightfoot, L. O. (1992). *Short-term evaluation of a substance abuse program for offenders*. Unpublished manuscript.

Lightfoot, L. O., & Barker, J. (1989). *A field test of the revised Substance Abuse Pre-Release Program: Joyceville Institution.* Ottawa: Correctional Services Canada.

Lightfoot, L. O., & Barbaree, H. (1988). *The Substance Abuse Pre-Release Program: A descriptive report of the Joyceville institution field test.* Ottawa: Correctional Services Canada.

Lightfoot, L. O., & Hodgins, D. (1988). A survey of alcohol and drug problems in incarcerated offenders. *International Journal of the Addictions, 23*(7), 687-706.

Lightfoot, L. O., & Matthews, M. (1989). *A substance abuse pre-release program for federal offenders: Staff training manual.* Ottawa: Correctional Services Canada.

Lord, F. M., & Novick, M. R. (1968). *Statistical theories of mental test scores.* Reading, MA: Addison-Wesley.

Marlatt, G. A., & George, W. H. (1984). Relapse prevention: Introduction and overview of the model. *British Journal of Addiction, 79,* 261-273.

Marlatt, G. A., & Gordon, J. R. (Eds.). (1985). *Relapse prevention: Maintenance strategies in the treatment of addictive behaviors.* New York: Guilford.

McLellan, A. T., Woody, G. E., Luborsky, L., O'Brien, C. P., & Druley, K. A. (1983). Increased effectiveness of substance abuse treatment: A prospective study of patient-treatment "matching." *Journal of Nervous and Mental Disease, 171*(10), 597-605.

Miller, W. R. (1978). Behavioral treatment of problem drinkers: A comparative outcome study of three controlled drinking therapies. *Journal of Consulting and Clinical Psychology, 46,* 74-86.

Miller, W. R., & Hester, R. K. (1986). Matching problem drinkers with optimal treatments. In W. R. Miller & N. Heather (Eds.), *Treating addictive behaviors: Processes of change* (pp. 175-203). New York: Plenum.

Miller, W. R., & Pechacek, T. F. (1987). New roads: Assessing and treating psychological dependence. *Journal of Substance Abuse Treatment, 4,* 73-77.

Moczydlowski, K. (1980). Predictors of success in a correctional halfway house for youthful and adult offenders. *Corrective and Social Psychiatry and Journal of Behavior Technology Methods and Therapy, 26*(2), 59-72.

National Council on Crime and Delinquency, National Probation and Parole Institutes. (1972, January). *Uniform Parole Reports Newsletter.*

Paulson, M. J., & Lin, T. (1970). Predicting WAIS IQ from Shipley-Hartford scores. *Journal of Clinical Psychology, 26,* 453-461.

Prochaska, J. O., & DiClemente, C. C. (1982). Transtheoretical therapy: Toward a more integrative model of change. *Psychotherapy: Theory, Research and Practice, 19,* 276-288.

Prochaska, J. O., & DiClemente, C. C. (1986). Toward a comprehensive model of change. In W. R. Miller & N. Heather (Eds.), *Treating addictive behaviors: Processes of change* (pp. 3-27). New York: Plenum.

Reitan, R. M. (1958). Validity of the trail making test as an indicator of organic brain damage. *Perceptual and Motor Skills, 8,* 271-276.

Ross, R. R., & Lightfoot, L. O. (1985). *Treatment of the alcohol abusing offender.* Springfield, IL: Charles C Thomas.

Rounsaville, J., Dolinsky, Z. S., Babor, T. F., & Meyer, R. E. (1987). Psychopathology as a predictor of treatment outcome in alcoholics. *Archives of General Psychiatry, 44,* 505-513.

Sanchez-Craig, M. (1980). Random assignment to abstinence or controlled drinking in a cognitive-behavioral program: Short-term effects on drinking behavior. *Addictive Behaviors, 5,* 35-39.

Sanchez-Craig, M. (1984). *Therapist's manual for secondary prevention of alcohol problems.* Toronto: Addiction Research Foundation.

Sanchez-Craig, M., Annis, H. M., Bornet, A. R., & MacDonald, K. R. (1984). Random assignment to abstinence and controlled drinking: Evaluation of a cognitive-behavioral program for problem drinkers. *Journal of Consulting and Clinical Psychology, 52*(3), 390-403.

Sanchez-Craig, M., & Lei, H. (1986). Disadvantages to imposing the goal of abstinence on problem drinkers: An empirical study. *British Journal of Addiction, 81,* 505-512.

Shipley, W. C. (1940). A self-administering scale for measuring intellectual impairment and deterioration. *Journal of Psychology, 9,* 371-377.

Skinner, H. A. (1982). The drug abuse screening test. *Addictive Behaviors, 7,* 363-371.

Skinner, H. A., & Horn, J. L. (1984). *Alcohol dependence scale user's guide.* Toronto: Addiction Research Foundation.

Smart, R. G. (1974). Employed alcoholics treated voluntarily and under constructive coercion: A follow-up study. *Quarterly Journal of Studies on Alcohol, 34,* 196-209.

U.S. Department of Justice. (1983). *Prisoners and alcohol* (Bureau of Justice Statistics Bulletin). Washington, DC: Government Printing Office.

9

Adult Marijuana Dependence

ROBERT S. STEPHENS
ROGER A. ROFFMAN

In the past few years adult marijuana dependence has emerged as a significant problem. Recent clinical perspectives recognize the need for assessment and intervention with this population of drug users (Miller & Gold, 1989; Tennant, 1986; Zweben & O'Connell, 1988), but there are few empirical studies upon which to base clinical strategies. In this chapter, we discuss the evidence for a significant population of adults who are dependent on marijuana, review research concerning clinically relevant characteristics of these individuals, and present an overview of the cognitive-behavioral group treatment we use with this drug-dependent population (Roffman, Stephens, Simpson, & Whitaker, 1988).

Unfortunately, there are no studies that directly address the prevalence of marijuana dependence in the general population. The 1990 National Household Survey on Drug Abuse found that marijuana continues to be the drug most commonly used for nonmedical purposes in the United States (National Institute on Drug Abuse, 1991). As has been

AUTHORS' NOTE: Preparation of this manuscript was supported by NIDA Grant DA03586.

the case with most other forms of nonmedical drug use, marijuana use has been declining. Yet, in 1990, 20.5 million Americans used marijuana and more than one fourth (5.5 million) of these users reported using it one or more times per week. As we will discuss below, high frequency use is not the same as dependence, but if even 10% of weekly users manifest signs of dependence, there are potentially more than one-half million persons for whom treatment may be beneficial.

Marijuana Dependence and the Need for Treatment: Fact or Fiction?

We have speculated that several misconceptions may have contributed to the relative inattention to marijuana dependence in the research and clinical literature (Roffman et al., 1988). First, data from nontreatment samples (e.g., Grupp, 1972; Kandel, 1984) and publicly funded drug treatment centers (Kleinman, Wish, Deren, & Rainone, 1984) show that heavy marijuana use is related to lifetime use of multiple drugs. Some investigators have interpreted these findings to mean that marijuana dependence is unlikely to occur in the absence of concurrent dependence on one or more other substances (see, e.g., Kleinman et al., 1984). The perception that marijuana dependence occurs primarily in conjunction with polydrug dependence appears to obviate the need for assessment and treatment specific to marijuana. However, this assumption is based on data that do not distinguish substance use from substance abuse or dependence. Although it is true that most marijuana-dependent users have used other psychoactive substances, it is not necessarily true that they show concurrent dependence on them.

In two studies relying on marijuana-specific research advertisements to attract subjects, we have found that only about 20% of adult marijuana users who are interested in treatment report current abuse of other drugs (Roffman & Barnhart, 1987; Stephens, Roffman, & Simpson, in press). Another 43% of these dependent marijuana users have abused other drugs in the past but are not doing so currently (i.e., in the last 90 days), and 38% have never abused or been dependent on a drug other than marijuana (Stephens et al., in press). Our data clearly show that some adult users, without concurrent alcohol or other drug dependencies, perceive themselves to be dependent on marijuana and in need of treatment.

A second possible reason for the lack of clinical studies of marijuana dependence is an assumption that treatment for the problem is unnecessary. Recognizing that withdrawal from marijuana is unlikely to present anything other than mild and short-term physiological symptoms (Jones, Benowitz, & Herning, 1981; Nowlan & Cohen, 1977), researchers might conclude that users who become dependent will be able to stop easily on their own and will not be likely to seek help in abstaining. Once again, we have found that the volume of individuals who seek professional assistance for overcoming marijuana dependence and the chronicity of their problems suggest that this phenomenon is worthy of clinical inquiry. In an initial 1985 survey of users who were "concerned about their marijuana use," 225 telephone interviews were logged in a two-week period, and more than 90% of the callers were interested in treatment (Roffman & Barnhart, 1987). Two years later, we received 382 applications *in less than two months* for our treatment intervention trial (Stephens et al., in press). These treatment-seeking marijuana users averaged more than 10 years of daily use and more than six serious attempts at quitting in the past. Further, their use often persisted in the face of multiple forms of impairment (e.g., social, psychological, physical), and most perceived themselves as unable to stop.

Finally, the paucity of attention given to the development of treatments for marijuana dependence may result from a belief that existing drug abuse services are sufficient. We believe that in many respects the process of overcoming marijuana dependence is similar to that entailed in changing other addictive behavior patterns. However, we also believe there are some important reasons for offering and tailoring treatment specific to the adult who is solely dependent on marijuana. As noted above, adult marijuana users interested in treatment readily responded to publicity specific to marijuana dependence, but few of these individuals reported previous participation in drug abuse treatment programs (Roffman & Barnhart, 1987; Stephens et al., in press). Marijuana-specific treatment programs may reach individuals whose perceptions of their needs are inconsistent with enrolling in community drug treatment programs.

Several historical influences may be contributing to this phenomenon. Many of the men and women struggling with marijuana dependence today began using in the more socially and legally tolerant decades of the 1960s and 1970s. Marijuana use was closely linked with a "counterculture" life-style (Grupp, 1972; Erickson, 1989) and became a normative social behavior for many others during these years (Johnston, O'Malley, & Bachman, 1986). The past few decades have seen consider-

able public debate concerning the pros and cons of marijuana decriminalization and legalization (Himmelstein, 1986). The effects of marijuana have often been described as relatively harmless in such discussions,
perhaps inviting the inference that it is not addictive. The absence of
life-threatening or severe physiological consequences associated with
marijuana use (see Hollister, 1986, for a review), its integration into
normative social behavior, and its association with strongly held coun-
tercultural values may make it unlikely that individuals will see their
difficulties with the drug as necessitating help. Now in their 30s and
40s, many of the people who find themselves unable to stop smoking
marijuana are faced with threats of urine screening on the job, fears of
modeling inappropriate behavior for their children, seeing fewer of
their friends continuing to use marijuana, and being aware that there is
now far less acceptance of illicit drug use, marijuana included. Nonetheless, marijuana remains for many of these individuals a powerful
symbol of political and cultural values and perspectives.

A marijuana-specific counseling program may be likely to attract
individuals who feel conflicted about the changes in societal norms and
the reevaluation of drug use it entails. Potential clients are more likely
than those entering other treatment programs to expect that therapists
and other group treatment members will be sensitive to these issues,
that they will not be inappropriately grouped with "hard" drug users,
and, perhaps, that treatment staff will be less judgmental about a lengthy
history of excessive marijuana use. In turn, the treatment program needs
to be responsive to these values and perspectives. Assisting the client
in identifying and coming to terms with the losses and transitions
inherent in these societal changes becomes an important and unique
component of the intervention. Therefore, a marijuana-specific counseling
program must attend substantially to the early processes of motivation
building and goal setting through educational and consciousness-raising
exercises concerning the personal meaning of marijuana use and the
idiosyncratic manifestations of psychosocial impairment.

The Marijuana-Dependent Adult:
Clinical Characteristics and Diagnostic Issues

In this section we review what is known about the characteristics of
adult marijuana users and attempt to derive a picture of the marijuana-

dependent adult. Several recent studies have specifically targeted adult marijuana users and provide the only systematic data on the subject. One of the first attempts to look at indices of addiction in adult marijuana users adapted research diagnostic criteria for alcoholism and applied them to a volunteer sample of 97 white, middle-class marijuana users who had been using marijuana for about 10 years (Weller & Halikas, 1980). Only nine of the subjects (less than 10%) met criteria for marijuana abuse by reporting problems in at least three of the following four areas: adverse physiological effects, control problems, interpersonal/social problems, and adverse opinions of use (e.g., feeling guilty, significant others object). The most frequently reported symptoms were panic anxiety reactions, early morning use, traffic arrests, feeling addicted, and health problems. However, only 26% of the subjects in this nontreatment sample were daily marijuana users, and 38% used only once per month. The relatively infrequent use in this sample is also seen in the fact that only 1% felt unable to stop marijuana use. As we will discuss later, the reliance on physiological and social problem indices in this study also may have contributed to the low rate of diagnosable abuse.

Hendin and colleagues studied a group of 150 self-identified *daily* marijuana users and concluded that they rarely reported adverse consequences, at least in comparison with the number of positive effects they experienced (Haas & Hendin, 1987; Hendin, Haas, Singer, Ellner, & Ulman, 1987). Overall, the subjects were more pleased with the effects of marijuana than concerned, yet two thirds complained of impaired memory and nearly one half noted difficulty concentrating, motivational problems, and concerns about physical health. One half indicated that they would like to cut down or stop using. In-depth psychodynamic interviews and assessment studies of 15 cases suggested that marijuana played a significant role in difficulties at work or in relationships with others. The authors were careful not to conclude that marijuana caused the observed dysfunction and highlighted how its use often served to help subjects avoid, deny, or minimize already-existing problems. Their work suggests that marijuana may produce subtle signs of dependence that do not manifest themselves in the more extreme social and physical problems of other drug abuse.

Another attempt to study the incidence of marijuana-related problems in a nontreatment sample of adults ($n = 99$) suggested that almost half had experienced some adverse consequences (Rainone, Deren, Kleinman, & Wish, 1987). The largely white male sample was composed primarily

of daily or near-daily users who responded to newspaper announcements of a study of "heavy" marijuana users. The most frequently
reported problems included reduced level of energy or motivation,
impairment of concentration or memory, and financial problems. Although only 10% had ever sought treatment for drug-related problems,
another 28% had considered contacting treatment professionals. Among
this heavier-using sample there was an indication of greater awareness
of adverse physical, psychological, and social problems.

Similarly, Roffman and Barnhart's (1987) phone interviews with
marijuana users who were concerned about their use yielded an average
of 4.5 self-reported problems related to the use of marijuana. These data
provided the impetus for our first treatment study of marijuana dependence. We assumed that anyone who was interested in treatment aimed
at marijuana cessation would represent the client population of interest.
Rather than attempting to diagnose and screen for marijuana dependence formally, we offered treatment free of charge and observed the
characteristics of individuals who showed up. Several screening criteria, a refundable deposit, and a lengthy pretreatment assessment
process ensured that we were including only adults who sincerely desired
help in stopping marijuana use and who were not abusing other substances
(see Roffman et al., 1988, for the study design and screening process).

Of the 382 men ($n = 290$) and women ($n = 92$) who completed
screening questionnaires, only 73 (19%) reported abuse of alcohol or
other substances in the past 90 days and are, therefore, excluded from
the data reported below (Stephens et al., 1991). The resulting sample
was primarily white (95%), male (76%), and reasonably well educated
(mean years of school completed = 13.8). They were 31 years of age on
average and had been using marijuana for 15 years. They reported using
marijuana an average of 79 of the past 90 days and almost all of them
used multiple times each day. The most commonly reported negative
consequences were feeling bad about using (87%), procrastinating because of use (85%), loss of self-esteem (76%), memory impairment (66%),
withdrawal symptoms (50%), spouse/parental complaints (47%), other
medical concerns (40%), and financial problems (38%). Almost all
subjects had made multiple attempts to quit in the past, and most
reported feeling unable to stop their use of marijuana.

It is important to remember that the self-selected nature of the
samples studied may limit the generalizability of the findings. In particular, none of the studies was conducted in a preexisting clinical
setting, and few ethnic minority individuals were recruited. Although

we have argued that adults with marijuana-related concerns may be reluctant to approach drug treatment programs, it is unclear to what extent the samples studied in these nontreatment, research contexts represent the entire population of adults who may want or need treatment (see Kleinman et al., 1984). Both epidemiological research and studies in clinical settings are needed to further our understanding of the characteristics of marijuana-dependent adults and the consequences of prolonged heavy marijuana consumption.

With this caveat in mind, the picture of marijuana dependence that emerges from the studies reviewed is generally consistent with the "dependence syndrome" concept (Edwards, 1986; Edwards & Gross, 1976). First described in relation to alcohol use and later incorporated into diagnostic criteria for other substance dependence (American Psychiatric Association, 1987; Kosten, Rounsaville, Babor, Spitzer, & Williams, 1987), the dependence syndrome concept captures the essential features of marijuana dependence. The proposed unidimensional syndrome is characterized by increased salience of drug taking, a compulsion to use, tolerance to the drug's effects, a drug-specific withdrawal syndrome, and use of the drug to relieve or avoid withdrawal symptoms. A major advantage of the dependence syndrome concept is its assumption of a continuum rather than an all-or-none categorization. Drug users are seen as falling on a continuum of dependence, with more dependent users exhibiting more symptoms.

The salience of drug use is perhaps best operationalized in terms of the amount of time spent obtaining, using, and recovering from the drug and the associated decrements in participation in other activities (American Psychiatric Association, 1987). Although none of the studies reviewed above systematically employed measures of this aspect of the dependence syndrome, evidence for the salience of marijuana use can be inferred from the sheer frequency of use and associated problems. The modal subject seeking treatment aimed at marijuana cessation used multiple times each day (Stephens et al., in press). In addition, procrastination was one of the most commonly reported consequences of use, suggesting that participation in other important activities was avoided or reduced. Similarly, in Hendin et al.'s (1987) study of daily users there was evidence that marijuana use allowed individuals to avoid responsibilities and interpersonal and intrapersonal conflicts. Although the combination of daily use and avoidance of other activities provides some evidence for the increased salience of marijuana use in those adults seeking or needing treatment, it is important to note that not all daily users reported related problems or a desire to reduce use (Hendin et al., 1987; Rainone et al., 1987). Daily use alone may not be a good indicator of the salience of marijuana use (e.g., daily use may be restricted to a single occasion each evening when it does not replace other important activities) and is not, therefore, a sufficient condition for the diagnosis of dependence.

There is more direct evidence for the compulsive aspect of marijuana dependence. Almost all subjects seeking treatment reported feeling unable to stop their use of marijuana; most had made several prior attempts at reducing use, with limited success (Stephens et al., in press). All of these individuals were continuing to use daily despite self-reported problems associated with use, further suggesting some loss of control. Similar evidence of compulsive use was found in subsamples of users not in treatment who reported negative consequences and an interest in reducing use (Hendin et al., 1987; Rainone et al., 1987).

Continued drug use in the face of adverse consequences is an important marker of dependence that clearly seems to occur in relation to marijuana use. Interestingly, the studies converge on the most frequently reported adverse consequences. By most indices these are well-functioning, employed people who feel held back by their reliance on marijuana to cope with daily living. They do not report major legal, occupational, or social problems. Concerns about memory loss and other health problems are evident, but it seems to be the progressive increase in personal dissatisfaction that brings individuals closer to treatment. We suspect that this increased self-examination process results from both changes in societal tolerance for drug use and developmental processes within the individual. Of importance for the assessment of marijuana dependence is the increased probability that these subtler, intrapersonal consequences of marijuana use may elude or be minimized by both the prospective client and the clinician.

Two aspects of the dependence syndrome, salience and compulsion, clearly apply to marijuana dependence. However, modification of other aspects of standard dependency criteria may be necessary to characterize marijuana dependence correctly. For most drugs, tolerance, withdrawal, and use to avoid withdrawal are indicators of more severe levels of dependence and occur at later stages in the development of the dependence syndrome. However, psychometric analyses of the reporting of these symptoms in relation to marijuana use suggests that they are less consistently experienced (Kosten et al., 1987). Only 50% of our heavy-using treatment sample reported withdrawal symptoms in relation to marijuana cessation (Stephens et al., in press), and it is unclear what proportion of these subjects may have been misattributing normal fluctuations in emotional and physical signs to marijuana cessation. These findings are consistent with laboratory investigations of marijuana's ability to produce tolerance and withdrawal. Although evidence of tolerance and withdrawal has been found (Jones et al., 1981; Nowlan & Cohen, 1977), it is mild in nature and brief in duration.

Some investigators hypothesize that because THC is stored in fat cells and later metabolized, the withdrawal syndrome may be delayed (e.g., Tennant, 1986), leading the user to misattribute the symptoms to nonspecific causes (e.g., to a cold or the flu). The purported effects of THC stored in fat cells have yet to be demonstrated, leaving the validity of this hypothesis in doubt at this time. Unless more convincing objective evidence of a reliably experienced marijuana withdrawal syndrome is found, we believe that tolerance and withdrawal phenomena are less important criteria for a diagnosis of marijuana dependence and probably do not discriminate those with more severe levels of dependence. However, insomnia and mild flulike symptoms may follow cessation of marijuana use for a subset of users and, therefore, are important clinical targets for the development of coping strategies in the early weeks of cessation.

A Group Treatment Model
for Adult Marijuana Dependence

Treatment interventions based on a disease conceptualization of marijuana dependence and incorporating 12-step fellowship participation have been suggested (Miller, Gold, & Pottash, 1989; Zweben & O'Connell, 1988), but we know of no tests of their efficacy. In 1986 we obtained funding from the National Institute on Drug Abuse to develop and test group treatment protocols for marijuana-dependent adults. An initial study has been completed and another study is under way. In this final section we describe the basic components of the primary group treatment intervention tested in these two studies.

Three overlapping models shaped our development of the group intervention for adults dependent on marijuana. The first model, relapse prevention, is a cognitive-behavioral approach that places emphasis on identifying, anticipating, and coping with the intrapersonal and interpersonal determinants of drug use (Marlatt & Gordon, 1985). It provides an integrative framework for bringing cognitive, motivational, and behavioral intervention strategies to bear on the problem. Second, a stages of change model (Prochaska & DiClemente, 1983) emphasizes the need for different interventions at different points in the change process and guides the sequencing of intervention strategies. Third, the legacy of group support in behavior change (e.g., Alcoholics Anonymous) indicates the need to involve others in the change process. In this section, we provide a brief overview of these models and their relation to our treatment approach.[1]

Relapse prevention, as articulated by Marlatt and Gordon (1985), follows from social learning theory and assumes that drug dependence is an acquired behavior pattern learned in the same way as other nondrug-related behaviors (Abrams & Niaura, 1987). The direct reinforcing properties of intoxication, parental and peer attitudes and pressures, and vicarious sources of positive information about drug use combine to foster initial experimentation. As use continues, various coping functions are served and further reinforce the behavior pattern. For instance, marijuana use may become the means for releasing creativity, socializing with friends, reducing stress, avoiding unpleasant tasks, or perhaps dealing with deep-seated insecurity. Although there is little concrete evidence of specific vulnerability factors, it is proposed that individuals who are deficient in the skills needed to cope with a variety of life situations and/or who function within an environment supportive of drug use will be more likely to rely on drug use for coping. Reliance on drugs to cope results in the atrophy or failed development of alternative coping behaviors and increases the value of drug use to the individual. This pattern of increasing reliance on drug use is consistent with the dependence syndrome continuum.

Relapse prevention is an appropriate approach for the dependent marijuana user on both philosophical and clinical grounds. At the philosophical level it is a nonjudgmental, compensatory helping model (Brickman et al., 1982) that does not hold the client responsible for the development of the problem. This view of the nature of marijuana dependence is more likely to be consistent with the experience of users who escalated their use in a more accepting social and political climate than a perspective that emphasizes a physiologically based loss of control with the implication of an inherent weakness or defect in the user. At the clinical level, the relapse prevention approach targets the functional role that drug use plays in the individual's life. Clients learn to identify the antecedent feelings, thoughts, and situations that precipitate use and then are helped to generate and master alternate responses (Marlatt & Gordon, 1985). The theme of anticipating and avoiding relapse clearly conveys that the client must take personal responsibility for changing behavior. Self-monitoring and debriefing encounters with recent high-risk situations aid the identification of antecedents to use, and coping strategies are sampled from a list that includes relaxation techniques, positive imagery, distraction, assertiveness, physical exercise, positive self-statements, and cognitive restructuring. The choice of specific coping strategies is idiosyncratic to the individual and his or her situation, allowing even the most individualistic client the room to feel unique. The therapist uses role playing, modeling, and instruction to assist the client in practicing and ultimately mastering techniques for avoiding and/or coping with high-risk situations.

The relapse prevention approach also works at a more molar level by encouraging life-style changes that will decrease encounters with high-risk situations. Daily marijuana users are particularly in need of attention to life-style issues because the relatively mild effects of marijuana intoxication allow it to be interwoven throughout their social, occupational, and familial roles. Monitoring of daily "shoulds" and "wants" (i.e., stresses and rewards) is used to identify life-style imbalances (Marlatt & Gordon, 1985) that may foster stress, boredom, or other negative affective states that precipitate marijuana use. Clients are encouraged to build frequent rewards into their daily or weekly schedules in order to offset the loss of a potent reinforcer. More comprehensive changes in life-style are fostered by helping the client set both proximal and distal life-style goals and by identifying manageable steps to take in reaching them.

The action-oriented techniques of relapse prevention are nested within a stage conceptualization of the change process. Prochaska and DiClemente (1983; DiClemente & Prochaska, 1982, 1985) propose a sequence of stages common to both self-change and therapy-assisted change. In their model, individuals move from precontemplation to contemplation, to decision making, to action, and finally to maintenance of change or relapse. Data from cigarette smokers suggest that different processes are important at different stages (Prochaska & DiClemente, 1983). For instance, consciousness-raising and self-reevaluation appear to be crucial to someone in the contemplation stage, whereas techniques for managing the environment and urges are more important for individuals in the action and maintenance stages.

Individuals in the precontemplation stage, by definition, will not seek treatment because they are not yet considering behavior change. Awareness of the problem or need for change must first increase through some combination of education, social pressure, and self-reevaluation. It is possible, for instance, that the media advertisements we used to attract subjects to our projects (e.g., "If you are an adult who is concerned about your marijuana use and would like some help in stopping, call . . . ") may have helped move some people along the road to the contemplation stage by increasing awareness.

The contemplation stage probably describes the majority of marijuana-dependent adults who approach treatment with highly conflicted feelings. According to Prochaska and DiClemente (1983), subjects in the contemplation stage are weighing the pros and cons of the change, and they need information, feedback, and the opportunity to reflect on their personal dissatisfaction in order to "tip the scales" in favor of change. Many of the subjects in the surveys of adult marijuana users reviewed above appear to hold mixed feelings regarding the benefits and costs of continued use versus cessation (e.g., Hendin et al., 1987) and, therefore, fall into this contemplating category. Although they have rarely sought help in the past, they are increasingly noticing adverse consequences, are feeling dissatisfied, and are considering seeking treatment. It is important that early therapy sessions facilitate this self-examination process by providing additional information about the effects of marijuana, fostering discussion of feelings of dependence, generating and examining reasons for quitting, and providing a vision of the benefits of life without marijuana. An attempt to jump directly into behavior change efforts without fostering the client's sense of resolve and motivation for change is likely to engage the client's defenses and be countertherapeutic (Miller & Rollnick, 1991).

Eventually a decision-making point must be reached. Making personal and social commitments to the change process and focusing on feelings of liberation from marijuana dependence may be most important at this time. Quit ceremonies and contracts are used to formalize commitment as the individual prepares to take action.

During the action stage, coping strategies and life-style issues take precedence as the client attempts to identify alternative reinforcers, manage the environmental and personal stimuli associated with prior use, and engage in unfamiliar behaviors. These strategies and techniques remain useful as the successful quitter moves into an indefinite maintenance stage. However, motivational issues may reemerge and need to be addressed. Our data suggest that marijuana smokers may be at risk for relapse for as long as two to three years after quitting (Roffman, Stephens, & Simpson, 1990). Marlatt and Gordon (1985) offer two strategies for combating relapse during the maintenance phase. First, they emphasize vigilance and self-examination to identify rationalizations that justify a return to the addictive behavior. Second, if a "slip" into marijuana use occurs, cognitive restructuring of the experience may be needed in order to avoid a full-blown relapse. This restructuring takes the form of objectifying the experience and consequences of the lapse in order to minimize the negative self-evaluations and emotional concomitants that foster further use. Clients are helped to view the slip as a learning experience rather than a failure. The therapist helps the client focus on waning motivation, poor preparation, or needed coping skills in order to avoid similar future slips.

The final element in our treatment approach is social support. The numerous self-help support groups targeting addiction are testimony to the appeal of this component. Group interventions therefore may be particularly powerful because they provide multiple opportunities for support. In fact, in our first treatment outcome study, subjects' posttreatment ratings of various treatment components indicated that "having time available to discuss issues related to marijuana use" and "being encouraged to discuss concerns with other group members" were judged to be as helpful as learning new coping techniques. During initial sessions, the sharing of common concerns about marijuana use is a powerful form of consciousness-raising that may help to shatter myths regarding the potential for dependence and to strengthen resolve. Work on stages of change suggests that helping relationships may also be particularly important during the action phase (Prochaska & DiClemente, 1983), perhaps because recent quitters face strong urges when alternative rewards and skills are not yet in place. During this phase, the group becomes an environment in which the individual can share frustrations, receive encouragement, and celebrate successes as he or she grapples with implementing new coping strategies and making life-style changes. In our current group treatment protocol we are attempting to help the therapist-led groups make the transition to an ongoing self-help group. Although the efficacy of this approach is yet to be determined, the provision of group support during a lengthy maintenance phase is a promising idea.

In addition to the support inherent in groups, the relapse prevention approach directly targets social support by encouraging clients to identify and enlist support from network members outside the intervention context (Marlatt & Gordon, 1985). Support from others may take many forms, including encouraging words, participation in alternate entertainment strategies, and even being left alone to relax at the end of a stressful day. Clients are encouraged to identify the ways in which significant network members can aid the quit effort. Role plays are used to model and practice the process of negotiating support from others. In addition, in our most recent study we are exploring the utility of relapse prevention training groups for "supporters" of our clients. These brief four-session groups consist of spouses, partners, friends, and relatives identified by clients and who want to be helpful in the change process. Therapists educate supporters about the change process and then lead clients and supporters through exercises designed to facilitate communication and develop supporter-assisted coping techniques for urges to use.

An initial test of this group treatment model, without the "supporters" groups or ongoing self-help components, demonstrated the efficacy of the relapse prevention approach. Of 106 subjects who were randomly assigned to receive the relapse prevention intervention in a controlled clinical trial (Roffman et al., 1988; Stephens, Roffman, Simpson, & Whitaker, 1988), 75 completed the 10 weekly group sessions. Follow-up assessments indicated that treatment completers reduced their monthly frequency of marijuana use from a pretreatment average of 27 days to an average of 9 days per month at the 3-month posttreatment assessment and to 12 days per month at the 6-month posttreatment assessment. Almost 40% of the completers were abstinent at the 3-month posttreatment assessment, and 25% remained abstinent at the 6-month posttreatment assessment. Another 25% of the subjects maintained reduced use (i.e., used less than 2 days per week on average) at each follow-up, so that a total of 50% of the treatment completers could still be classified as substantially improved six months after treatment (Stephens et al., 1988).

A 1-year posttreatment assessment showed some continued deterioration of abstinence rates in this sample (17% were abstinent for the preceding three months), but a total of 40% of the treatment completers had substantially reduced their use and remained free of problems related to marijuana (Roffman et al., 1990). Although these outcomes remain less than ideal, they demonstrate clinically meaningful improvements in a substantial minority of individuals who were dependent on marijuana. They therefore provide initial support for the efficacy of the relapse prevention and stages of change models as applied to this population of substance users. It is interesting to note that outcomes in this first study are comparable to those found in the treatment of nicotine and alcohol dependence, further suggesting that marijuana dependence is a formidable problem requiring treatment and, perhaps, multiple attempts to quit.

Summary and Conclusions

It now seems clear that a significant adult marijuana-dependent population exists and is in need of treatment intervention. Most of these individuals do not appear to be abusing alcohol or other drugs, although epidemiological studies are needed to address the prevalence of both marijuana and polydrug problems. A specific treatment focus on marijuana dependence may be more attractive to marijuana users because it avoids negative connotations associated with community drug abuse treatment programs. It also allows attention to issues that may be relatively unique to marijuana dependence.

Marijuana-dependent clients are likely to be struggling to reconcile beliefs and feelings about drug use that developed in the more tolerant decades of the 1960s and 1970s with the current "war on drugs." Although this conflict probably affects most users of drugs, it is particularly insidious among marijuana users. The demographic characteristics and types of problems reported by marijuana users seeking treatment suggest a largely functional group, perhaps held back by their sole reliance on marijuana for coping, who nonetheless experience little objective evidence of the negative effects of marijuana in their lives. Treatments, therefore, need to foster greater awareness of the personal dissatisfaction with marijuana use and the significant ways in which it limits the life-styles of those dependent on it.

Our relapse prevention support groups for marijuana-dependent adults are based primarily on a cognitive-behavioral model that emphasizes the acquisition of coping skills to deal with high-risk situations and the modification of life-style to reduce temptation. However, this active change phase is preceded by consciousness-raising exercises designed to increase motivation and commitment to the change process. Similarly, it is followed with increased attention to rationalization and denial processes that may set the individual up for a relapse and to the cognitive-affective aftermath of a single lapse that may further promote relapse. Throughout each of these stages, social support processes are enlisted to bolster motivation and establish alternative reward systems.

An initial study of outcomes following participation in this relapse prevention group treatment supports its efficacy.

Note

1. More detailed therapist manuals for our treatment programs may be obtained from Robert S. Stephens, Department of Psychology, Virginia Polytechnic Institute and State University, Blacksburg, VA 24061-0131.

References

Abrams, D. B., & Niaura, R. S. (1987). Social learning theory. In H. T. Blane & K. E. Leonard (Eds.), *Psychological theories of drinking and alcoholism* (pp. 131-180). New York: Guilford.

American Psychiatric Association. (1987). *Diagnostic and statistical manual of mental disorders* (3rd ed., rev.). Washington, DC: Author.

Brickman, P., Rabinowitz, V. V., Karuza, J., Coates, D., Cohn, E., & Kidder, L. (1982). Models of helping and coping. *American Psychologist, 37,* 368-384.

DiClemente, C. C., & Prochaska, J. O. (1982). Self-change and therapy change of smoking behavior: A comparison of processes of change in cessation and maintenance. *Addictive Behaviors, 7,* 133-142.

DiClemente, C. C., & Prochaska, J. O. (1985). Processes and stages of self-change: Coping and competence in smoking behavior change. In S. Shiffman & T. A. Wills (Eds.), *Coping and substance use* (pp. 319-343). New York: Academic Press.

Edwards, G. (1986). The alcohol dependence syndrome: A concept as stimulus to enquiry. *British Journal of Addiction, 81,* 171-183.

Edwards, G., & Gross, M. M. (1976). Alcohol dependence: Provisional description of a clinical syndrome. *British Medical Journal, 1,* 1058-1061.

Erickson, P. G. (1989). Living with prohibition: Regular cannabis users, legal sanctions, and informal controls. *International Journal of the Addictions, 24,* 175-188.

Grupp, S. E. (1972). Multiple drug use in a sample of experienced marijuana smokers. *International Journal of the Addictions, 7,* 481-491.

Haas, A. P., & Hendin, H. (1987). The meaning of chronic marijuana use among adults: A psychosocial perspective. *Journal of Drug Issues, 17,* 333-348.

Hendin, H., Haas, A. P., Singer, M. D., Ellner, M., & Ulman, R. (1987). *Living high: Daily marijuana use among adults.* New York: Human Sciences Press.

Himmelstein, J. L. (1986). The continuing career of marijuana: Backlash within limits. *Contemporary Drug Problems, 13,* 1-21.

Hollister, L. E. (1986). Health aspects of cannabis. *Pharmacological Reviews, 38,* 1-20.

Johnston, L. D., O'Malley, P. M., & Bachman, J. G. (1986). *Drug use among American high school students, college students, and other young adults: National trends through 1985.* Rockville, MD: National Institute on Drug Abuse.

Jones, R. T., Benowitz, N. L., & Herning, R. I. (1981). Clinical relevance of cannabis tolerance and dependence. *Journal of Clinical Pharmacology, 21,* 143S-152S.

Kandel, D. B. (1984). Marijuana users in young adulthood. *Archives of General Psychiatry, 41,* 200-209.

Kleinman, P. H., Wish, E. D., Deren, S., & Rainone, G. A. (1984, August). *The "pure" marijuana using client: Where?* Paper presented at the annual meeting of the American Psychological Association, Toronto.

Kosten, T. R., Rounsaville, B. J., Babor, T. F., Spitzer, R. L., & Williams, J. B. W. (1987). Substance-use disorders in DSM-III-R: Evidence for the dependence syndrome across different psychoactive substances. *British Journal of Psychiatry, 151,* 834-843.

Marlatt, G. A., & Gordon, J. R. (Eds.). (1985). *Relapse prevention: Maintenance strategies in the treatment of addictive behaviors.* New York: Guilford.

Miller, N. S., & Gold, M. S. (1989). The diagnosis of marijuana *(cannabis)* dependence. *Journal of Substance Abuse Treatment, 6,* 183-192.

Miller, N. S., Gold, M. S., & Pottash, A. C. (1989). A 12-step treatment approach for marijuana *(cannabis)* dependence. *Journal of Substance Abuse Treatment, 6,* 241-250.

Miller, W. R., & Rollnick, S. (1991). *Motivational interviewing: Preparing people to change addictive behavior.* New York: Guilford.

National Institute on Drug Abuse. (1991). *National household survey on drug abuse: 1990 population estimates.* Washington, DC: Government Printing Office.

Nowlan, R., & Cohen, S. (1977). Tolerance to marijuana: Heart rate and subjective "high." *Clinical Pharmacology and Therapeutics, 22,* 550-556.

Prochaska, J. O., & DiClemente, C. C. (1983). Stages and processes of self-change of smoking: Toward an integrative model of change. *Journal of Consulting and Clinical Psychology, 51,* 390-395.

Rainone, G. A., Deren, S., Kleinman, P. H., & Wish, E. D. (1987). Heavy marijuana users not in treatment: The continuing search for the "pure" marijuana user. *Journal of Psychoactive Drugs, 19,* 353-359.

Roffman, R. A., & Barnhart, R. (1987). Assessing need for marijuana dependence treatment through an anonymous telephone interview. *International Journal of the Addictions, 22,* 639-651.

Roffman, R. A., Stephens, R. S., & Simpson, E. E. (1990, November). *Relapse prevention and the treatment of marijuana dependence: Long-term outcomes.* Paper presented at the annual meeting of the Association for Advancement of Behavior Therapy, San Francisco.

Roffman, R. A., Stephens, R. S., Simpson, E. E., & Whitaker, D. L. (1988). Treatment of marijuana dependence: Preliminary results. *Journal of Psychoactive Drugs, 20,* 129-137.

Stephens, R. S., Roffman, R. A., & Simpson, E. E. (In press). Adult marijuana users seeking treatment. *Journal of Consulting and Clinical Psychology.*

Stephens, R. S., Roffman, R. A., Simpson, E. E., & Whitaker, D. L. (1988, August). *Treatment of marijuana abuse: Six month outcomes.* Paper presented at the Ninety-sixth Annual Convention of the American Psychological Association, Atlanta, GA.

Tennant, F. S. (1986). The clinical syndrome of marijuana dependence. *Psychiatric Annals, 16,* 225-242.

Weller, R. A., & Halikas, J. A. (1980). Objective criteria for the diagnosis of marijuana abuse. *Journal of Nervous and Mental Disease, 168,* 98-103.

Zweben, J. C., & O'Connell, K. (1988). Strategies for breaking marijuana dependence. *Journal of Psychoactive Drugs, 20,* 121-127.

10

A Comprehensive and
Integrated System for
Treating Alcohol and
Drug Problems in Alberta

LEONARD M. BLUMENTHAL

J. ROBERT HUNTER

EDWARD SAWKA

Over recent years, the Alberta Alcohol and Drug Abuse Commission (AADAC) has made significant strides in establishing a comprehensive and integrated system for treating alcohol and drug problems. This chapter will describe this treatment system in relation to the historical development of the AADAC, its conceptual framework, its range of services, and the key organizational structures that support the operation and continued refinement of this treatment system. Major challenges to maintaining this system will also be discussed.

Historical Development of AADAC

AADAC provides addictions treatment and prevention services throughout the western Canadian province of Alberta, which has a population of 2.46 million people and an area of 255,285 square miles, roughly the size of Texas. The commission is an agency of the government of the province of Alberta. Its beginnings can be traced to the work of a committee established by the College of Physicians and Surgeons of Alberta in the early 1950s to examine services available to alcoholics in the province. The recommendations of this committee led in 1951 to the granting of a provincial charter establishing the Alcoholism Foundation of Alberta. Staff were hired and offices were opened in Edmonton, the capital city of Alberta, and Calgary, the other of Alberta's two largest cities. The treatment approach was closely tied to the pioneering work of Alcoholics Anonymous, and since that time clients have been introduced to AA during their treatment with AADAC and encouraged to maintain attendance as part of their recovery.

During the 1960s a virtual revolution occurred in how many North Americans used and viewed psychoactive substances. Since that time, more people have been presenting for treatment at earlier ages with a broader range of problems, and the system has evolved to meet these changes. In part as a reflection of this change, the Alcoholism Foundation was restructured in 1965 and became the Division of Alcoholism within the Alberta Department of Public Health. This demonstrated a stronger commitment on the part of the Alberta government to recognize alcohol and drug problems as a legitimate health concern. It also moved the organization closer to the mainstream of government-supported services.

In 1970, another major reorganization of provincial alcoholism services occurred with the creation of the Alberta Alcoholism and Drug Abuse Commission. This was supported by legislation, with a mandate to address not only alcohol problems but also the abuse of drugs other than alcohol. AADAC still received its funding from the provincial government and was directed by a commission board consisting of up to 12 citizens selected from communities throughout Alberta. This arrangement retained the vehicle of provincial funding while enhancing the commission's scope for more independent action.

In the late 1970s the provincial government appointed a member of the provincial legislature as chairman of the commission board, a practice continued to the present day. The current chairman is Mr. Stan Nelson, who represents the constituency of Calgary-McCall.

Since 1970, AADAC has expanded it services and has undergone a minor name change to the Alberta Alcohol (the *ism* was dropped) and

Drug Abuse Commission, again to reflect the broad range of alcohol and drug problems that AADAC had to deal with.

From a base originally confined to Alberta's major urban centers, offices have now been opened in approximately 25 locations, and funding has been granted to approximately 30 community agencies. Between its own direct services and those of its funded agencies, AADAC provides for more than 30 local outpatient and community education offices and in excess of 800 residential beds operating in more than 65 service centers throughout the province.

Thus AADAC's treatment services have evolved to form a province-wide network serving all of Alberta. The agency has from the start featured strong local and regional management, and its programs have reflected the specialized needs of these communities. AADAC has made the transition from a two-office operation in the 1950s to a provincewide system in the 1990s with combined direct service and funded agency admissions totaling more than 36,500 in 1989-1990.

AADAC's Clientele

The nature of alcohol and drug problems has been a matter of great debate. However, in the past 15 to 20 years the literature indicates that a general consensus has been reached that alcohol/drug problems are not a unitary concept (Glaser, 1980; Institute of Medicine, 1990; McLellan, Luborsky, Woody, & O'Brien, 1980; Pattison, Sobell, & Sobell, 1977). In fact, alcohol/drug problems show a great diversity both in their presentation and in the clients who experience them. This view is supported by AADAC's 40 years of experience in the treatment of alcohol and drug problems. The consumption levels, the types of associated problems, the severity, and the number of problems that any one individual may have can all be quite different. The clients who present with these problems again demonstrate great diversity on numerous characteristics such as age, sex, socioeconomic status, cultural and educational background, family history of alcohol/drug problems, physical health characteristics, motivation to change, and more. In order to respond to this multiplicity of needs, AADAC has developed a comprehensive and integrated system of treatment delivery. It is worth noting that this system incorporates many of the ideas recently advanced in the Institute of Medicine (1990) report, *Broadening the Base of Treatment for Alcohol Problems.*

A comprehensive treatment system is one that can respond effectively to this variety of problems. This multiplicity of people and problems demands a system that is equally diverse. As an agency with province-wide scope, AADAC has been able to use economies of scale to assist in the provision of these diverse services. Although every community in the province many not have all of the elements of a comprehensive system in its location, the individuals in those communities do have relatively easy access to all of the elements of the system. Later sections of this chapter describe these elements.

Six Characteristics of a Comprehensive and Integrated Treatment System

AADAC's experience suggests that there are six characteristics critical to effective and efficient functioning of a comprehensive and integrated treatment system:

(1) a sound and clear vision
(2) a means to deliver programs consistent with the vision
(3) a standardized comprehensive assessment system
(4) a variety of specialized treatment services for alcohol and drug problems
(5) other complementary treatment services
(6) community treatment for alcohol and drug problems

A Sound and Clear Vision

Development of AADAC's Vision of Services

AADAC's roots are in treatment. Treatment was the motivation for the formation of the original Alcoholism Foundation, and the need for treatment was the reason the provincial government continued to increase its support to AADAC, in its various forms, during those early years. Even with the establishment of AADAC's community education offices the treatment focus was clearly evident. One of their initial tasks was to educate helpers in the community so that they could recognize individuals with alcohol and drug problems more readily and refer them appropriately.

In the mid-1970s, as AADAC expanded its treatment role, it became clear to the agency that treatment was not sufficient in addressing alcohol and drug problems. It was recognized at that time that prevention must become a larger part of the organization's work. AADAC wanted to develop an approach to prevention that, ideally, would be consistent with its treatment efforts.

At the time, AADAC's conceptual framework for treatment practice was more pragmatic than theoretical, more implicit than explicit. It borrowed understandings from the self-help community and from the behavioral sciences. But one aspect of this approach was clear: Alcohol and drug problems were seen primarily as people issues rather than as substance issues. Drugs were recognized as part of the individual's environment. However, the focus was on the dynamics of the individual's use of substances and not on the specific properties of the drugs themselves. As a result, the focus in both belief and practice was on strengthening the capabilities of people with alcohol or drug problems so that they could better avoid these problems in the future. This treatment perspective proved to be compatible with a major innovative prevention effort undertaken by AADAC during the 1980s to increase the competence development of adolescents and enhance their social and physical environments.

In the early 1980s, as AADAC was planning its prevention program for adolescents, health and addictions practitioners elsewhere were vigorously developing the concepts of prevention (Kessler & Albee, 1975; Lalonde, 1975; Low, 1978) and health promotion (World Health Organization, 1984). AADAC planners saw that many of these ideas could be applied to the Alberta situation. Indeed, health promotion concepts became an integral part of the multifaceted and multidisciplinary framework (Skirrow & Sawka, 1987) that evolved to guide AADAC's successful prevention initiative (Thompson & Huebert, 1990).

Within this framework, health promotion is understood as the process of enabling people to increase control over, and to improve, their own health. It is aimed at involving people in the enhancement of their physical, mental, and social health, rather than solely the elimination of disease. Health promotion, then, is consistent with AADAC's long-held perspective on strengthening people's capacities to anticipate, interpret, and manage their environment without abusing drugs.

Soon after the adolescent prevention program was implemented, AADAC planners began to understand that the health promotion process, and its associated premises, was not only relevant to prevention but could also be useful in developing a conceptual framework for treatment. Since 1985, health promotion concepts, especially as they relate to client relevance and client participation in the development and delivery of programs, became increasingly evident throughout AADAC's treatment programs and resources.

This led to the adoption of the following four premises as the conceptual framework for AADAC's programming (Alberta Alcohol and Drug Abuse Commission, 1988; Kearns, 1988), which remains congruent with the most recent developments in health promotion theory and practice (Epp, 1987; International Conference on Health Promotion, 1987; Kickbusch, 1989).

(1) *Understand the client's experience.* It is important to pay close attention to people and to understand their unique experiences. It is important to understand people in their day-to-day lives, to determine how they perceive problems, and what meaning such difficulties have for the individuals involved.

(2) *Assess the client's current status and future aspirations.* There is a need to assess people's perceptions and aspirations. It is critical to understand people's views of where they are and where they would like to be.

(3) *Help clients to act on their own behalf.* The empowerment of people to act energetically on their own behalf is important. Enabling people to act in their own self-interest requires working with individuals to help them to see that their own actions make a meaningful difference in their lives.

(4) *Help to develop health-enhancing environments for clients.* In order for people to achieve their aspirations, one of the necessary conditions is the existence of a supportive social environment.

AADAC's efforts to articulate its conceptual framework led to the understanding that treatment needed to focus on enhancing the individual's competence at managing the wide range of his or her daily experiences and emotions. Equally important is the interaction of the individual's competence and the supports and restrictions of the environment to expanding those skills. The purpose of treatment is to provide the client with reasonable satisfaction in being able to meet his or her daily needs without having to rely on drugs.

Mission Statement

AADAC's mission statement is an important part of the expression of its vision of treatment and prevention. The process of development of AADAC's mission statement reflected the agency's adherence to the above key concepts. It involved extensive consultation with AADAC staff, detailed knowledge of the clientele served, and consultation with the community, through surveys, focus groups, and related research. AADAC's mission statement, revised 1990, reads as follows:

> The mission of the Alberta Alcohol and Drug Abuse Commission is to encourage and assist Albertans in achieving personal, family and community health, free from alcohol and drug abuse.

Stemming from the mission statement are the three corporate objectives:

> To assist individuals in achieving a greater degree of control over their lives without reliance on alcohol or drugs.
>
> To support the development of environments that encourage responsible decisions about alcohol and drugs.
>
> To provide and support a credible, effective and coordinated system of addictions treatment, prevention and information services.

Program Services Values

To ensure that AADAC's ideas of health promotion have impact, they must be stated at various levels throughout the organization. Therefore, in addition to the mission statement, AADAC's Program Services Branch (the branch responsible for all treatment and prevention programming in the organization) worked on developing a set of values for treatment and prevention that were consistent with the health promotion approach. Again, extensive participation of staff was crucial in the development of these values.

The central or key stated values that guide the operation of AADAC Program Services are as follows:

- that individuals, families, and communities are involved in decisions regarding the development and implementation of services to ensure that services remain relevant to those for whom they are designed

- that programs remain of high quality and demonstrate sound planning based on the best available research and evaluation
- that AADAC's programs are provided at a level that is consistent with assessed need
- that services value people, treat them with respect, and safeguard their basic human rights and freedoms
- that services are provided in a positive, dependable, and accountable manner to the agency's clients and the public served
- that staff are encouraged and supported to be creative, to take initiative, and to achieve excellence

Means to Deliver Programs Consistent With the Vision

Importance of an Infrastructure

The second characteristic of a comprehensive and integrated treatment system is the presence of an infrastructure upon which treatment services are delivered consistent with the agency's vision. This was of particular importance to AADAC as the agency implemented its conceptual framework of treatment, for the following reasons.

First, although this approach does not dictate a specific therapeutic approach, it involved a significant shift in thinking for many program and management staff. It meant moving from a somewhat paternalistic approach to treatment to one that is client centered. It meant moving from a view of the client as someone who is damaged, who does not know what he or she needs or how to get it, and requires firm direction to get better, to understanding the client as an individual who at some level knows what he or she needs and wants, wants to manage his or her life successfully, and thus is in charge of his or her own treatment. This meant shifting from *doing to or for* to *facilitating or empowering* clients to *do for themselves.* There had to be a shift in focus from the counselor to the client; a shift from asking, What do I think the client needs? and What do I do about it? to What does the client want? and How can I help the client get what he or she wants? Finally, it meant increased emphasis on building healthy environments, which, in an immediate sense, meant a focus on the treatment environment to ensure that it was consistent with the key premises of treatment.

Second, AADAC believed that these concepts had to become part of the organizational culture. Lip service to these concepts would not be enough.

Third, the key premises of the treatment approach had to be applied to staff. This approach had to be sensitive to and understand the experience of staff; it had to take into account the staff's perceptions and aspirations; it had to empower staff to use the concepts; and it had to provide and encourage a supportive environment in which the use of these concepts could flourish. A simple imposition would work against the desired results and be counterproductive to the principles.

The agency could have attempted to ensure the consistency of programs by establishing standards and regulations. This approach was rejected, however, because of the belief that such an approach would result in minimum effort to the lowest common standard. Instead, AADAC developed a system with the features described below.

Recruitment of High-Quality Staff. One component of the infrastructure underlying program delivery concerns recruitment of new staff. AADAC has paid particular attention to, and has made considerable investment in, the recruitment of high-quality staff. The agency has established minimum recruitment standards and developed an addictions counselor and office support technical series for promotion and development. In addition, AADAC looks at the personnel being recruited to see whether they share AADAC's vision of treatment or are willing to learn to work within this approach.

Training and Professional Development. Another important structure behind AADAC's programming is its Training and Professional Development Division. This division supported the implementation of AADAC's conceptual framework for treatment and continues to support its maintenance in three ways. First, division personnel ensure that all of the division's courses reflect the conceptual framework. Second, they plan courses based on input from all levels of AADAC staff. They consider not only organizational needs but staff needs also. Third, the division provides the opportunity for professional development of AADAC and AADAC's funded agency staff.

Compatible Program Materials. To ensure the compatibility of program service delivery with its vision, AADAC provides staff with high-quality, highly usable program materials that are based on the organization's conceptual framework. Examples include AADAC's two assessment packages and its relapse prevention package. Additional packages are being developed in the treatment area.

Decentralized Management System. An important feature of AADAC's operation is the considerable authority given to local management—consistent with a philosophy of empowerment. At the same time, field management receives a great deal of central support, as mentioned above. All senior field managers participate in the executive committees of the commission and have full and active parts in all decisions affecting the organization. This relatively flat hierarchy helps to ensure that programs are delivered in a manner consistent with the vision of AADAC.

Management Information Systems. Computerized information systems are yet another part of the infrastructure that AADAC uses to support its treatment framework. AADAC operates several of these systems. They are client focused and provide the necessary client intake, assessment, and discharge information, with each client assigned a unique identifier, to assist in monitoring the operation of the treatment system. Separate systems are maintained to monitor AADAC direct services and funded agency services for adult treatment clients and collaterals; adolescent treatment clients (under age 18), and their collaterals; impaired driving program clients—first offenders; impaired driving program clients—repeat offenders; and community education and prevention projects.

This ongoing information source is used by program evaluators and management to assess treatment service utilization, monitor trends in client characteristics, determine optimum resource allocation, and to assist with issues of program development and program accountability. AADAC's information systems help guide operational decision making.

Reports are distributed on a regular basis. In addition, AADAC provides for the capacity to respond to individual managers' ad hoc requests regarding the data collected. These regular and ad hoc reports help AADAC to understand its clients and their presenting problems better.

Program Research. Program research represents another structural element supporting treatment framework. The goal of program research in AADAC is to help improve the programs and services offered to the public. There are two aspects to this research. First is the research that precedes program implementation, involving needs analysis, social marketing research, and literature searches to ensure that the program being implemented is using the most recent information available and that it is consistent with AADAC's treatment approach. The second aspect of program research is program evaluation. Treatment evaluation is important for two main reasons: It provides feedback to program managers and staff so that changes in program components or procedures can be based on systematic data as well as on clinical observation, and it is important for demonstrating treatment effectiveness. Program evaluations provide crucial feedback for the treatment system as well as periodic information to support strategic decision making.

The first step in designing a treatment evaluation study is ascertaining and clarifying the specific questions that need to be addressed in the study. The requirements of program managers, program staff, clients, and other decision makers will vary depending on local and regional priorities and circumstances. A single evaluation study will not answer all questions that could be raised about a program, but should provide information relevant for decision making on selected, important questions.

Evaluation research is important not only for existing programs, but also for program planning. Needs assessment surveys and research on proposed target groups and the feasibility of proposed programs are examples of this type of program planning evaluation research. This research helps AADAC to understand its clientele and to match services to the potential client population appropriately.

A Standardized Comprehensive Assessment Protocol

A central characteristic of a comprehensive and integrated treatment system is a standardized assessment protocol. Assessment is an important part of any treatment system because it is necessary first to understand the problems, goals, and strategies involved before clients' needs can be matched to resources. Furthermore, a standardized assessment helps to improve communication among various parts of the system by creating a common language. This in turn helps to facilitate clients' movement through the system. Consistent with the four premises of AADAC's approach to treatment, assessment is viewed as a mutually cooperative process between client and counselor. The purpose of assessment is to develop realistic and achievable goals for treatment and plans that will lead to realization of those goals. The client must be actively involved in assessment and treatment planning, because such involvement helps to enhance commitment.

At AADAC, three levels of assessment are used: screening, basic assessment, and specialized assessment (Skinner, 1981). Screening determines whether alcohol or drug use is a problem. Basic assessment focuses on the problems in the major life areas related to alcohol or drug use. It provides an overall assessment of the problem and flags specific areas, such as mental health disturbances or family problems, that need further assessment. The third level, specialized assessment, provides a more detailed investigation of the specific areas of functioning flagged as problematic in the basic assessment. Although specialized assessment may require the skills of other professionals, such as psychologists or physicians, it can also be directed by counseling staff.

With the principles of its treatment approach in mind, AADAC planners conducted a major literature review to find appropriate assessment instruments (Hunter, 1988). Two packages, incorporating several instruments, were developed: the AADAC Assessment Package for Adults is for those 18 and over; the AADAC Adolescent Assessment Package is for those 12 to 17 years of age.

The screening instruments used in the adult package are the Alcohol Dependence Scale (ADS; Skinner & Allen, 1982) and the Drug Abuse Screening Test (DAST; Skinner, 1982). The adolescent package uses the Personal Experience Screen Questionnaire (PESQ; Winters, 1988). The basic assessment instrument used in the adult package is the Addiction Severity Index (ASI; McLellan et al., 1980); the adolescent package uses the Adolescent Problem Severity Index (PSI; Metzger, 1990). Both are structured interviews that involve the client in a very active manner. Clients are asked questions not only about their use of alcohol and drugs but about other major life areas, such as physical health; psychological functioning; marital, family, and social relationships; legal involvement; employment; and leisure. In addition, clients are asked about their perceptions of how troubled they are about the problems in each life area and how much they want treatment for the problems identified. This is done well before the counselor discusses with the client his or her own perceptions on these issues. Clients also complete the Treatment Goals Checklist, which asks them to select and prioritize their treatment goals. Again, clients are actively involved in directing their own treatment.

These instruments were chosen because of their soundness as assessment tools, their ease of use, and their compatibility with AADAC's approach. They not only assist AADAC with understanding what clients need and what their situations are, they allow clients to have direct input into the assessment and treatment planning process.

After selection of the instruments, the assessment packages were pilot tested, extensive staff input was solicited, and significant modifications were made based on this input. The packages were then implemented provincewide. A provincewide training program was conducted to ensure that staff have the skills to use the packages. The client information systems have also been modified to collect assessment information.

Variety of Specialized Treatment Services for Alcohol and Drug Problems

The fourth characteristic of a comprehensive and integrated treatment system is that it must possess a variety of specialized treatment services. As mentioned above, AADAC and its funded agencies operate more than 65 service centers across the province. Following are descriptions of the specialized services these services centers represent.

Outpatient Services. Services vary in each office depending on community demand and resources. Typically, an information series, assessment and treatment for alcohol and drug problems, aftercare, referral to aftercare treatment, and treatment for family members are available at each office. Therapy groups with a variety of different foci are often available at these offices as well.

Intensive Day Treatment Programs. Three of AADAC's urban outpatient clinics operate day programs. These intensive treatment programs offer assessment, information, group therapy, experiential learning techniques, leisure skills training, and individual counseling. The programs are 2 to 3 weeks long and operate between 8 a.m. and 4 p.m., Monday through Friday.

Detoxification. The purpose of AADAC's detoxification centers is to provide care and support to see clients safely through the physical symptoms of alcohol or other drug withdrawal. They provide assessment and referral to other services for ongoing treatment. Meals, accommodations, and help with reorientation to everyday living skills are provided. There is 24-hour nursing care and a medical consultant visits each center three times a week. Medications are used minimally. Clients requiring medical interventions are sent to their own physicians or to general hospitals.

Short-Term Intensive Residential Treatment. AADAC operates two short-term residential treatment programs, the Henwood Treatment Center in Edmonton and the Lander Treatment Center in Claresholm. These highly intensive, 2- to 3-week programs are intended for clients who need intensive inpatient treatment for serious problems with alcohol or drugs. These programs involve assessment, information groups, group therapy, experiential workshops, individual counseling, leisure counseling, and leisure programming as well as a 1-week aftercare program and referral to other services, including community support and aftercare. Programming is flexible so as to attend to the individual needs of clients. The intent is to help clients understand their problems, particularly their use of substances, to encourage them to change, and to teach them the skills they require to manage their experiences and emotions without using alcohol or drugs.

Adolescent Treatment. Recognizing the gap in addiction services for adolescents, the Alberta government made funds available, in 1989, to AADAC to start the provincewide Adolescent Treatment Program. This program is built on the awareness that there is no single type of intervention that is capable of responding to the requirements of all youth. Each AADAC office in the province has an adolescent specialist who performs assessments and outpatient counseling and refers clients, when appropriate, to other adolescent treatment programs. In addition, intensive day treatment and residential support programs for adolescents are operated in both Edmonton and Calgary. These programs operate Monday through Friday, 9:00 a.m. to 9:00 p.m., and last for approximately 12 weeks. Assessment, workshops, groups, lectures, leisure programming, school, and individual counseling, aftercare, and referral to other services are all used to help clients develop the skills they need to help them manage their lives without relying on alcohol or drugs. Residential support is also available to adolescents requiring it through placement with a carefully selected number of families in Edmonton and Calgary, who provide homelike settings for a maximum of two clients per home.

Opiate Dependency Program. AADAC operates a program for treatment and rehabilitation of opiate-dependent clients in Edmonton. Clinical assessment, urinalysis, and a thorough medical examination determine the diagnosis of opiate dependency. Clients attend the clinic or community pharmacies daily to receive methadone, a synthetic narcotic, which reduces their involvement with illicit opiates. Individual counseling is available for clients who desire it. A physician attends the clinic to provide medical care for the clients. Random urinalysis is done to help ensure that clients are not using unauthorized drugs. The purpose of the program is to stabilize clients' lives and assist them in assuming more normal and responsible roles in society.

Treatment for Women. AADAC has also established specialized programming for women. There are several women's groups running throughout the province, attending to the special needs of women who have problems with alcohol and or drugs. As well, the Henwood Treatment Center, one of the commission's intensive residential treatment centers, offers a 3-week program for women on an ongoing basis.

Family/Collateral Treatment. Family or collateral treatment is available for those who are close to an individual with an alcohol or drug problem. This is done on a one-to-one basis at any AADAC clinic, through various groups at the larger clinics, or at the family programs offered at residential treatment centers. These programs are appropriate for individuals whose significant others are experiencing problems with alcohol or drugs. It is not necessary for the substance abusing person to be currently in treatment.

Drinking Decisions. AADAC has established a program in Edmonton called Drinking Decisions, which is designed to assist people who are beginning to experience drinking problems. Through an educational format it helps individuals assess their drinking habits and learn more appropriate methods of managing their drinking. This is not a program for clients who are dependent on alcohol. The program consists of 10 weekly counseling sessions arranged at the convenience of the client.

Programs for Impaired Drivers. AADAC operates two programs for impaired drivers. The first, Planning Ahead, is a 1-day educational program for first-time convicted impaired drivers. The second program, IMPACT, is for drivers who have had two or more impaired driving convictions in the past 5 years. IMPACT is a weekend residential program that focuses on having drivers assess their use of alcohol and drugs and motivating them to seek further treatment, if necessary. Completion of the appropriate program is necessary for the reinstatement of a suspended Alberta driver's license.

Self-Help Groups. AADAC has always had a close working relationship with various self-help groups that are concerned with substance abuse. Therefore, AADAC not only refers clients to and recommends that many client attend these groups, it also arranges for meetings run by Alcoholics Anonymous, Narcotics Anonymous, Women for Sobriety, Al-Anon, and Alateen on AADAC premises.

Programs for Native Persons. AADAC provides funding to a number of programs that are located in and operated by Native communities. These programs cover a full range of services aimed directly at meeting the special needs of these groups.

Other Complementary Treatment Services

In addition to the specialized treatment that individuals with substance use problems require, many other services are often needed. Many clients may require long-term medical attention, psychiatric services, vocational counseling, or family counseling. AADAC continues to facilitate access of clients to these types of services in the province. Efforts to strengthen working relationships with allied professionals continue to be a priority at AADAC.

Community Treatment of Alcohol and Drug Problems

The Institute of Medicine (1990) has noted that a significant part of any comprehensive treatment system is "community treatment." The role of the community agency is to identify individuals with alcohol problems, briefly intervene with those experiencing mild to moderate problems, and refer those with substantial to severe problems to specialized treatment services. This treatment takes place in a variety of settings, such as health care facilities, social services agencies, the workplace, educational settings, and the criminal justice system.

AADAC has been actively engaged in this area for many years. Staff have worked with educational institutions to help prepare students to deal with drug- and alcohol-related problems. AADAC personnel work with numerous groups, such as municipal boards of health, social services, and correctional services, helping these agencies to develop the knowledge and skills to perform this kind of function. Recent figures show that approximately 30% of AADAC's community education function is spent working with these professionals.

AADAC has for many years consulted with organizations both private and public to assist in setting up employee assistance programs. It has developed significant resources in this area and operates an employee assistance program for AADAC staff.

This is an area in which progress is difficult, as other organizations have their own agendas and most are operating within restricted budgets. Still, effort and small successes continue.

Challenges of Tomorrow

Past success, of course, includes no guarantees about the future. AADAC management and staff recognize that in order to sustain success the organization will, like most other health care services, face continuing challenges to its ability to survive and remain effective.

Outpatient Versus Inpatient Treatment. The high costs of residential treatment are of concern in light of mounting evidence that outpatient treatment may be as effective as residential treatment (Bonstedt, Ulrich, Dolinar, & Johnson, 1984; Greenstreet, 1988; Willson, White, & Lange, 1978). AADAC is left with the challenge of determining how best to allocate scarce resources to ensure that costly and intensive residential treatment is appropriately provided to Albertans in the face of strong community pressure that such services be widely distributed throughout the province.

Dual-Diagnosis Clients. In recent years AADAC and other care providers have come to understand that substantial numbers of clients suffer not only from substance use problems but also from some form of significant psychiatric disturbance. Clients in this group often go undiagnosed, and even when properly identified they are difficult to treat successfully. Currently, AADAC is working with the dual diagnosis program at the Foothills Hospital in Calgary, but more needs to be done to enable us to understand and treat this group of clients effectively.

Specialization by Target Group. As mentioned earlier, AADAC has begun to respond to the demands of various sectors of the population, by age, gender, cultural background, and other specialized needs, to provide them with better treatment. The attempt is to differentiate treatment so as to provide individualized care for these clients. It is clear that this trend will continue. AADAC is facing the challenge of learning more about the populations currently served and of identifying other potential target groups. Although this will result in more effective treatment to greater numbers of people, it can be done only by drawing on ever-dwindling resources. Part of the response will have to be to secure funding from sources other than government—the community itself and corporate sources, for example.

Treatment Evaluation. Evaluation of treatment methods and approaches will remain of utmost importance in the ongoing task of refining and extending the treatment system. Much remains to be learned about the effectiveness of treatment programs, about how to understand and define success better. The challenge is to undertake stronger client-centered research as opposed to program-focused research. Outcomes beyond the cessation of use need to be carefully considered, so there is better measurement of a broad range of health outcomes and better matching of client needs and treatment goals.

Stronger Community Partnerships. AADAC must continue to develop partnerships with other community agencies, both public and private, in order to facilitate the development of a communitywide approach to the problems associated with alcohol and other drugs. This means forging closer working relationships with other social service agencies, business, and police forces in order to sustain such a cooperative vision.

Trend Mapping. The information base of the addictions field has improved significantly over recent years. However, more complete research needs to be done, especially in the areas of standardized studies of alcohol and drug use at the national, provincial, and community levels; of epidemiological studies of the range of effects of alcohol and drug abuse; and of sensitive needs-assessment methods for selected communities. By collating and mapping the results of these research efforts over time, AADAC and other addictions agencies will be in a much better position to forecast and specify community needs for treatment and prevention services and to put the most applicable programs in place.

Policy Advocacy. Addictions agencies such as AADAC should be prepared to advocate policy positions more vigorously on behalf of clients served. In this way, legislators and other care providers can improve their understanding of the issues, which will enable them collectively to respond more effectively to community problems.

Shrinking Resources. The last challenge concerns, as might be expected, finances. AADAC's programs, like those of other government agencies, must compete with the full range of government priorities. Several rounds of budget cuts have already occurred as the provincial government confronts the issues associated with the high costs of public services. Agencies such as AADAC find it increasingly difficult to maintain current programs, let alone to develop new ones for special needs groups. There will be no easy solutions here either; however, AADAC believes that they lie in part in securing new funding sources, as in the private sector; in encouraging community participation and ownership of services; and in better harmonizing the various components in the broad spectrum of health care services.

Summary

This chapter has reviewed the six characteristics of a comprehensive and integrated treatment system operated by the Alberta Alcohol and Drug Abuse Commission: a sound and clear vision, a system to facilitate program delivery that is consistent with the vision, a standardized assessment system, a variety of specialized treatment services for alcohol and drug problems, other complementary treatment services, and community treatment of alcohol and drug problems. Although this organization's experience has been specific to Alberta, much of what is being done in Alberta is undoubtedly of interest to service providers in other jurisdictions.

References

Alberta Alcohol and Drug Abuse Commission. (1988, June). *Decisions on health for Albertans: Making healthy choices the easier choices.* Submission to the Premier's Commission of Future Health Care for Albertans, Edmonton.

Bonstedt, T., Ulrich, D. A., Dolinar, L. J., & Johnson, J. (1984). When and where should we hospitalize alcoholics? *Hospital and Community Psychiatry, 35,* 1038-1042.

Epp, J. (1987). Achieving health for all: A framework for health promotion. *Health Promotion, 1,* 419-428.

Glaser, F. B. (1980). Anybody got a match? Treatment research and the matching hypothesis. In G. Edwards & M. Grant (Eds.), *Alcoholism treatment in transition* (pp. 178-196). London: Croom Helm.

Greenstreet, R. L. (1988). *Cost-effective alternatives in alcoholism treatment.* Springfield, IL: Charles C Thomas.

Hunter, J. R. (1988). *Assessing alcohol and drug troubled people: A proposed battery.* Unpublished master's thesis, University of Alberta, Edmonton.

Institute of Medicine. (1990). *Broadening the base of treatment for alcohol problems.* Washington, DC: National Academy Press.

International Conference on Health Promotion. (1987). Ottawa Charter for Health Promotion. *Health Promotion, 1,* iii-iv.

Kearns, B. (1988, July). *Where's the beef? The meaning of AADAC's prevention and treatment programs.* Paper presented at the Alberta Alcohol and Drug Abuse Commission Institute, Calgary.

Kessler, M., & Albee G. W. (1975). Primary prevention. In M. R. Rosenzweig & L. W. Porter (Eds.), *Annual review of psychology* (pp. 557-591). Palo Alto, CA: Annual Reviews.

Kickbusch, I. (1989). Approaches to an ecological base for public health. *Health Promotion, 1,* 265-268.

Lalonde, M. (1975). *A new perspective on the health of Canadians: A working document.* Ottawa: Information Canada.

Low, K. (1978). Prevention. In L. A. Phillips, C. R. Ramsey, L. Blumenthal, & P. Crawshaw (Eds.), *Core knowledge in the drug field* (Vol. 5). Ottawa: National Health and Welfare Canada, Non-Medical Use of Drugs Directorate.

McLellan, A. T., Luborsky, L., Woody, G. E., & O'Brien, C. P. (1980). An improved diagnostic evaluation instrument for substance abuse patients: The Addiction Severity Index. *Journal of Nervous and Mental Disease, 168,* 26-33.

Metzger, D. (1990). *Problem Severity Index: Version 3.* Philadelphia: University of Pennsylvania/VA Medical Center.

Pattison, E. M., Sobell, M. B., & Sobell L. C. (1977). *Emerging concepts of alcohol dependence.* New York: Springer.

Skinner, H. A. (1981). Assessment of alcohol problems: Basic principles, critical issues, and future trends. In Y. Israel, F. B. Glaser, H. Kalant, R. E. Popham, W. Schmidt, & R. G. Smart (Eds.), *Research advances in alcohol and drug problems* (Vol. 6, pp. 319-369). New York: Plenum.

Skinner, H. A. (1982). The drug abuse screening test. *Addictive Behaviors, 7,* 363-371.

Skinner, H. A., & Allen, B. A. (1982). Alcohol dependence syndrome: Measurement and validation. *Journal of Abnormal Psychology, 91,* 199-209.

Skirrow, J., & Sawka, E. (1987, Summer). Alcohol and drug abuse prevention strategies: An overview. *Contemporary Drug Problems,* pp. 147-241.

Thompson, J., & Huebert, K. (1990). *Making the most of you: A decade of success.* Edmonton: Alberta Alcohol and Drug Abuse Commission.

Willson, A., White, J., & Lange D. E. (1978). Outcome evaluation of a hospital-based alcoholism treatment programme. *British Journal of Addiction, 73,* 39-45.

Winters, K. (1988). *Personal experience screen questionnaire (PESQ) manual.* St. Paul, MN: Adolescent Assessment Project.

World Health Organization (1984). *Health promotion: A discussion document on the concept and the principles.* Copenhagen: Author.

PART IV

Policy Issues

11

Harm Reduction:
Reducing the Risks of Addictive Behaviors

G. ALAN MARLATT

SUSAN F. TAPERT

> Habit is habit and not to be flung out of the window by any man, but coaxed
> downstairs one step at a time. (Mark Twain, *Pudd'nhead Wilson's Calendar*)

Definitions and Overview

The terms *harm reduction, harm minimization,* and *risk reduction* are often used interchangeably in the addictive behaviors literature. Although they refer to the same general approach or model, Europeans (particularly the Dutch) call it harm reduction, the British refer to harm minimization, and Americans are more likely to prefer risk reduction. In this chapter, we define harm reduction as the application of methods designed to reduce the harm (and risk of harm) associated with ongoing or active addictive behaviors.

AUTHORS' NOTE: We would like to thank Jewel Brien for the outstanding graphics preparation for this chapter.

We agree with the *Webster's New World Dictionary* (1986) definitions of *harm* ("hurt, injury, damage") and *risk* ("chance of injury, damage, or loss"). *Webster's* also defines *addiction* as "the condition of being addicted (to a habit)" and the verb *to addict* as "to give (oneself) up (to some strong habit)." We would like to note the emphasis on "habit" as the key construct in these definitions. This same dictionary defines *habit* as "a thing done often and hence, usually, done easily; a pattern of action that is acquired and has become so automatic that it is difficult to break." Clearly the emphasis is on acquired ongoing behaviors (habits, patterns of action) rather than on an internal "condition" or disease.

Active addictive behaviors are indicated here by continued engagement in high-frequency behaviors (characterized by intense immediate rewards), despite increased risk of harm. What do we mean by "high-frequency behaviors characterized by intense immediate rewards"? Here we refer to habits that occur frequently in an individual's life-style—behaviors that range from one or more times per week or month (e.g., unsafe sexual practices) to many times a day (e.g., cigarette smoking). Engaging in these habits provides intense immediate rewards, including both positive reinforcement (euphoric mood, feeling "high") and negative reinforcement (tension reduction, relief of dysphoric mood or withdrawal discomfort). These outcomes occur immediately (usually within seconds) and are often intensely rewarding, despite the increased risk of long-range negative consequences.

Addictive behaviors include habits associated with drug use (smoking, excessive drinking, substance abuse), but also other habits not associated with drug taking: unsafe or harmful sex, excessive eating or gambling, and so on. Some prefer the adjective *excessive* to *addictive* in describing these behaviors (Mule, 1981; Orford, 1985), on the grounds that words such as *addiction* imply an internal condition or trait that one either has or does not have (e.g., whether or not one is an "addict"). *Webster's* defines *excessive* as "characterized by excess; being too much or too great" and *excess* itself is defined as "action or conduct that goes beyond the usual, reasonable or lawful limit; lack of moderation; intemperance, overindulgence; an amount or quantity greater than is necessary, desirable, usable." This definition refers to a behavioral continuum ranging from moderate to excessive frequency of occurrence of a particular habit.

It is noteworthy that the above definition of *excess* equates it with "intemperance" and "lack of moderation." For many people, the term *temperance* is associated with abstinence, as in the nineteenth-century temperance movement that culminated in the national prohibition of alcohol. Again the dictionary informs us that temperance includes both moderation *and* abstinence as points along the same continuum: "Temperance: 1. The state or quality of being temperate; self-restraint in conduct, expression, indulgence of the appetites, etc.; moderation. 2. Moderation in drinking alcoholic liquors *or* total abstinence from alcoholic liquors." One of the definitions of *temperate* given is "neither very hot nor very cold; said of climate." Note the same root is used in the words *temperate* and *temperature* (*temp* originally meant "span"), again indicative of an underlying continuum, as in a thermometer indicating a range or span of degrees of temperature. To moderate is to temper one's tendency toward excess; this is often contrasted with "losing one's temper" in terms of expressing anger or "loss of control" in terms of drug use. The distinction between abstinence and temperance was made long ago by Aristotle, who wrote: "We become temperate by abstaining from indulgence, and we are better able to abstain from indulgence after we have become temperate."

Harm reduction methods are based on the assumption that habits can be placed on a similar continuum, ranging from temperate to intemperate use along with associated risks for harm. Figure 11.1 represents this continuum; the left side represents excess, the middle part moderation, and at the farthest point to the right is abstinence. The risk of harm increases to the left and decreases to the right along this continuum. The goal of harm reduction programs is to move the individual with excessive behavior problems from left to right: to begin to take "steps in the right direction" to reduce the harmful consequences of the habit. It is important to note that this continuum model accepts abstinence as the ideal or ultimate risk-reduction goal. With the exception of eating habits, abstinence greatly reduces or entirely eliminates the risk of harm from most excessive behaviors. But the harm reduction model promotes *any* movement in the right direction along this continuum as progress, even if total abstinence is not attained.

As explained by Allan Parry (1989), a leader of harm reduction approaches to drug addiction and AIDS prevention in Liverpool, England:

> Harm reduction takes small steps to reduce, even to a small degree, the harm caused by the use of drugs. If a person is injecting street heroin of unknown potency, harm reduction would consider it an advance if the addict were prescribed safe, legal heroin. A further advantage if he stopped sharing needles. A further advance if he enrolled in a needle-exchange scheme. A much further advance if he moved on to oral drugs or to smoked drugs. A

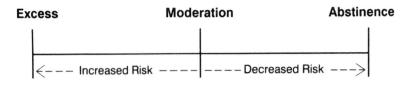

Figure 11.1. Continuum of excess, moderation, and abstinence.

further advance in harm reduction if he started using condoms and practicing safe sex practices. A further advance if he took advantage of the general health services available to addicts. A wonderful victory if he kicked drugs, although total victory is not a requirement as it is in the United States. (p. 13)

We believe that harm reduction provides a conceptual umbrella that covers a variety of previously unrelated programs and techniques in the addictive behaviors field, including needle exchange programs for injection drug users (IDUs), methadone maintenance for opiate users, nicotine replacement methods for smokers, weight management programs for the obese, controlled drinking for problem drinkers, and safe-sex programs (e.g., condom distribution in high schools) to reduce the risk of HIV infection and AIDS.

The organization for this chapter is as follows. First, we draw upon the "Dutch model" as an illustration of harm reduction principles currently utilized in the Netherlands. Other examples of harm reduction programs and ongoing research follow this section. The chapter concludes with a brief discussion of political issues and professional conflicts associated with the harm reduction model, particularly as it applies to American drug policy and the addiction treatment industry in the United States.

The Dutch Model of Harm Reduction

In the summer of 1990, the senior author was invited to Holland to give a series of workshops on relapse prevention to the staff at the

Jellinekcentre (named after E. M. Jellinek, the American alcoholism scholar), the main addiction treatment agency in Amsterdam. During his visit of 6 weeks, he was hosted by a psychologist who serves as director of the Jellinekcentre, Dr. Jan Walberg. Thanks to the hospitality and expertise of Dr. Walberg and his professional staff, he learned the basic elements of the Dutch model of harm reduction (Van de Wijngaart, 1991). The approach is based on a pragmatic philosophy and embraces a public health view of addictive behavior. As stated by sociologist E. L. Engelsman (1989), a leading exponent of Dutch drug policy:

> The Dutch being sober and pragmatic people, they opt rather for a realistic and practical approach to the drug problem than for a moralistic or over-dramatized one. The drug abuse problem should not be primarily seen as a problem of police and justice. It is essentially a matter of health and social well-being. (p. 212)

This "realistic and practical" approach is readily apparent to any informed visitor to the Netherlands. Their pragmatic public health philosophy extends to a variety of high-risk behaviors, from drug use to sex. Visitors to Amsterdam's red light district soon observe that otherwise "taboo" behaviors such as sexual contact with prostitutes and smoking marijuana are readily available and openly tolerated. Prostitutes can be viewed sitting in their parlor rooms along many streets, beckoning to prospective "window-shopping" clients through the glass. Pornography shops and "live sex" shows are predominant throughout the district. Police on bicycles patrol the streets, providing protection for both prostitutes and their customers.

Prostitution is both a legal and a respected profession in Amsterdam's red light area. Condom use is required, as are frequent tests for HIV infection among prostitutes. By providing health resources and licensing prostitution, the Dutch hope that any problems otherwise associated with illicit sex can be brought under public health control. By placing sexuality and the risk of HIV infection squarely on the table for public inspection, harm reduction methods (e.g., mandatory condom use) can more easily be applied and monitored. Along similar lines, Dutch public health campaigns use sexually explicit videos and other training materials to promote safe-sex practices for high-risk populations (e.g., gays and adolescents). As one Dutch psychologist put it, "The message we want to give our young people is: Sex is no big deal, but do it safely if you choose to do it at all."

In America, where prostitution is for the most part illegal, injection drug-using prostitutes are at high risk for contracting HIV. Drug addicts are often forced into the sex industry by the economic expense of their drug habit. When the price of drugs increases, users become more desperate to raise cash. A glut of prostitution develops, and the price and safe-sex negotiating power of each sex worker decreases. Therefore, risk of disease transmission increases when the price of drugs increases. Availability of substitute drugs such as methadone as well as outreach programs geared toward this population may reduce this risk (Schuler & McBride, 1990).

The Dutch policy regarding cannabis is similar to the Dutch view of sex: Both are considered "no big deal" as long as the risks are "out in the open" and can be monitored from a public health perspective. In Amsterdam as in other large Dutch cities, marijuana and other cannabis products are readily available in many coffee shops and youth centers. Although not legalized, possession of small amounts of marijuana (up to 30 g) for personal use is decriminalized and tolerated. The Dutch make a distinction between "soft drugs" (e.g., alcohol and cannabis) and "hard drugs" (e.g., cocaine and heroin). One premise for this decision is that the existing scientific and medical literature clearly shows that abuse of hard drugs increases the risk of harm compared with use of soft drugs. Dutch officials reason that by making this distinction, they enhance the credibility of educational programs geared toward youth. An informed citizenry is more likely to realize the differential risks involved between smoking a marijuana cigarette and injecting heroin with a shared needle. To equate all drug use as equally dangerous and illegal (as in the current American drug policy) is misleading and may lead to excessive punishments that the Dutch try to avoid:

> The Dutch do care about the related health hazards and therefore try to address the next obvious question: What policy could lead to the lowering of drug consumption? In this regard the Dutch prove very pragmatic and try to avoid a situation in which consumers of cannabis suffer more damage from the criminal proceedings than from the use of the drug itself. (Engelsman, 1989, p. 213)

Another reason the Dutch differentiate between drugs presenting unacceptable risks (opiates, cocaine, amphetamines) and soft drugs such as hashish and marijuana is to separate the markets for the sales of both types of drugs. Since only cannabis products are sold in designated coffee shops, users are not tempted to buy even stronger drugs;

strict penalties apply to the sale of hard drugs in these locations. Educational programs geared toward harm reduction also distinguish between cannabis and hard drugs:

> Much attention to cannabis is paid in education programs, albeit as a part of an integrated approach aimed at a healthy life-style. Learning how to cope with risk involving behavior (including alcohol and tobacco use) and how to be responsible for one's behavior and choices, is better than simply deterring and warning people. (Engelsman, 1989, p. 215)

According to Engelsman's (1989) review, "The policy of de facto decriminalization of cannabis does not produce more drug use and has proven to be very successful" (p. 213). He cites government statistics showing that, despite the implementation of decriminalization in 1976, the prevalence of cannabis use in the Netherlands is low. For youth in the Netherlands between the ages of 10 and 18, only 4.2% have ever used cannabis (lifetime prevalence); the number of daily users appears to be no more than one in a thousand. In a 1987 household survey conducted in Amsterdam (where drug use is considered to be higher than the national average), the last-month prevalence of cannabis use was reported to be 5.5% (with the highest last-month use reported by persons in the 23-24 age bracket).

What about hard drug use? In Amsterdam (population 640,000), estimates of the number of drug addicts range from 4,000 to 7,000; one 1987 household survey showed the prevalence of heroin use to be 0.4% and cocaine use to be 0.6% (Sandwijk, Westerterp, & Musterd; cited by Engelsman, 1989). Despite the reputation of Amsterdam as an "open drug market" city, crack cocaine use has remained low, possibly because public health warnings about the dangers of crack addiction have been treated seriously as credible information by the public.

The Dutch endorse a *normalization policy* in dealing with their addict population. Instead of criminalizing drug abuse, along with labeling and stigmatizing drug abusers (which may enhance the excitement and glamour of being a deviant person in the eyes of young people), the Dutch model attempts to eliminate the sensational and emotional overtones of the addict life-style. Under a normalization policy, "drug takers or even addicts should neither be seen as criminals, nor as dependent patients, but as 'normal' citizens of whom we make 'normal' demands and to whom we offer 'normal' opportunities. Addicts should not be treated as a special category" (Engelsman, 1989, p. 215).

This normalization policy also extends to the treatment of addiction. Prior to this change in policy, addiction treatment in Holland (as in most other countries) was carried out in both outpatient facilities and addiction clinics (most often drug-free therapeutic community programs). These programs required an initial commitment on the addict's part to total abstinence. As a result, addicts who did not feel the need to abstain or who were not willing or able to do so as a prerequisite of gaining entrance to treatment were not coming into contact with the health care system. How could these isolated and alienated addicts be reached? Could treatment access be made more "user friendly" to the addict population? In the 1980s, the Dutch changed their policy to reach out to the otherwise hidden addict population by adopting *low-threshold policies* that do not insist upon lifelong abstinence as a "high-threshold" barrier to treatment access:

> In the eighties a new treatment philosophy emerged which stressed the socially backward position of most drug addicts. Increasing encouragement by the Government has been given to forms of aid which are not primarily intended to end addiction as such, but to improve addicts' physical and social well-being and to help them to function in society. At this stage the addicts' (temporal) inability to give up drug use was being accepted as a fact. This kind of assistance may be defined as harm reduction or more traditionally: secondary and tertiary prevention. Its effectiveness can only be ensured by low-threshold facilities and accessible help, which are the key concepts in Dutch drug policy. (Engelsman, 1989, p. 216)

Low-threshold programs of harm reduction have replaced traditional programs geared only toward drug abstinence. At the Jellinekcentre, the senior author observed many such programs based on this outreach model, including the use of mobile methadone clinics (the "methadone bus") to reach addicts in their own neighborhoods, fieldwork in the streets and in hospitals and jails, and open-door centers for prostitutes, along with programs that provide material support and social rehabilitation opportunities. Brief courses or weekend seminars in changing addictive behaviors (e.g., a two-day intensive course on changing drinking behavior) are available, as are more outpatient and intensive inpatient treatment facilities. Low-threshold programs do not require a commitment to abstinence or drug testing as a requirement of admission. All they ask of the addict is a willingness to show up and, it is hoped, to begin taking steps in the direction of reducing harm.

On one afternoon during his visit to Amsterdam, the senior author traveled as a visitor on one of the two methadone mobile buses run by the Jellinekcentre. This experience allowed him to see how the low-threshold approach works in actual practice. Addicts can obtain methadone in the bus only if they have regular contact with a medical doctor and are enrolled in the central methadone registration file (both easily arranged for the addict). The staff on the bus consisted of the driver and two male nurses. During the 2 hours that the bus was parked in one downtown area, approximately 50 addicts came by for their methadone (administered orally; no "take home" doses are allowed). The nurses seemed to know most of the addicts by name and exchanged social pleasantries with them during their brief visits. There was a receptacle for "dirty needles," which were promptly replaced with new, sterile needles. The nurses also handed out condoms and first-aid materials upon demand. In one exchange with a young couple and their child, the staff agreed to provide help with fixing the couple's apartment, which was badly in need of repair. An arrangement was made to send a team of volunteer helpers (including a plumber) to assist the family later in the week. Once public health officials are in contact with addicts in this helpful and respectful manner, bridges can be built that may lead these persons to seek help in the future.

Addicts have even formed their own "junkie unions" in the Netherlands and have been able to exert their influence on shaping drug policies and treatment program development. Members of these unions have had considerable impact on the development of better attitudes on the part of local and national authorities toward individuals who have ongoing drug problems. Along these lines, Engelsman (1989) notes that the "Dutch policy of normalization seems to have produced a context where the addict more resembles an unemployed Dutch citizen than a monster endangering society" (p. 217).

One of the most significant results of this easy-access, low-threshold treatment philosophy is that the Dutch claim to be in contact with a majority of the addict population. "In Amsterdam about 60-80% are being reached by any kind of assistance. This percentage is certainly higher in less urbanized regions" (Engelsman, 1989, p. 217). Such a high rate of contact is very useful in terms of AIDS prevention and other public health programs. Data are available that support the harm reduction approach with injection drug users. Studies show, for example, that the average age of hard drug users is rising (in Amsterdam, from 26.8 to 30.1 years between 1981 and 1987), and that people who use injection drugs for the first time tend to be older (Buning & Brussel cited in Engelsman, 1989). In Amsterdam, the proportion of drug users aged 21 and younger decreased from 14.4% in 1981 to 4.8% in 1987. Another index of success is the finding that the number of injecting drug addicts seeking treatment in Amsterdam alone has tripled in recent years, from 600 in 1981 to 1,800 in 1988. In 1988, only 8% of AIDS patients in Holland were drug addicts, and the prevalence of HIV-positive cases among high-risk injection addicts in Amsterdam was reported to be 30% (Houweling cited in Engelsman, 1989).

Comparison of Dutch
and American Drug Policies

In summarizing the main principles of the Dutch harm reduction model, we would like to highlight how this approach contrasts with comparable American drug policy. Documentation of current drug policy in the United States is based on publications by the Office of National Drug Control Policy (e.g., 1990). Four main points emerge in this comparative analysis.

Low- Versus High-Threshold Access
to Prevention and Treatment Programs

In contrast to the low-threshold approach favored by the Dutch, American policy appears to place a high threshold on treatment access. Despite the fact that "treatment on demand" is often advocated for the addict population in the age of AIDS, U.S. funding for public addiction treatment programs lags far behind funding expended on interdiction programs (police and military) designed to remedy the "supply side" of the drug problem. According to a report released in June 1991 by the Inter-American Commission on Drug Policy, interdiction efforts have had little impact on the price and availability of drugs sold in the United States. "Since 1985, U.S. federal budget funds spent annually on interdiction have increased by $1 billion, an investment not justified by past or current results," the report concludes. In the 1992 federal budget, 70% of $11.68 billion in federal drug program funds is allotted to interdiction and law enforcement, whereas only 30% is earmarked for education and treatment programs.

Evidence for an American high-threshold policy is further illustrated by the following points. First, given that the vast majority of drug treatment programs in the United States require abstinence (or at least detoxification) as a requirement for treatment admission, many addicts who are unable or unwilling to meet this "absolute abstinence barrier" are barred from entry (see Figures 11.2 and 11.3). Second, needle exchange programs are rarely available to American IDUs because they have been declared illegal in many cities and states (based on conservative views that easy access to needles will appear to condone drug use and increase addiction rates). In addition, because many addicts fear arrest and imprisonment as a result of their illegal drug use, Americans are less likely to seek treatment of any kind (including addicted mothers of "crack babies," who fear they will be prosecuted for child abuse). Also, methadone maintenance programs may become less available due to budget cuts coupled with professional ambivalence concerning this approach to addiction treatment. Finally, resistance to typical American addiction treatment based on the predominant "disease model" and "12-step programs" (with their required quasi-religious belief in a "higher power") may keep many addicts from seeking help.

The end result of these high-threshold policies is that the majority of addicts in the United States are out of touch with *any* public or private treatment programs. Although recent reports estimate that there are currently between 5 and 6 million Americans with diagnosable addiction problems (excluding alcohol and tobacco addiction; National Institute on Drug Abuse, 1991), only 350,000 addicts were in treatment in one recent year (1989), a mere 6% of the addict population. Contrast this low figure with the estimate given by Dutch authorities that 60%-80% of their addict population is registered in some kind of program. New York City has an estimated 200,000 IDUs but only 38,000 publicly funded treatment slots. More than 107,000 people in the United States are estimated to be on drug treatment waiting lists (National Commission on AIDS, 1991). Getting off drugs greatly reduces the risk of contracting HIV, but for addicts to get into treatment, treatment must be available, without barriers, and with options to suit individual needs.

Public Health Versus
Criminal Justice Approaches to Drug Addiction

In the United States, addicts are both victimized and stigmatized by current drug policies and theories of addiction causation (Mieczkowski,

Figure 11.2. High-threshold route: absolute abstinence barrier.
SOURCE: Jewel Brien. Reprinted with permission.

1992). On the one hand, illegal drug use is strictly punished by law, as advocated by the ongoing "War on Drugs" policy. As a result, the American prison population is now the highest (per capita) of any country in the world (more than a million people currently are housed in state and federal prisons, the majority for drug-related offenses).

LOW THRESHOLD ROUTE

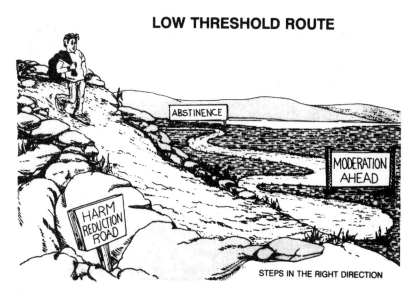

Figure 11.3. Low-threshold route.
SOURCE: Jewel Brien. Reprinted with permission.

Incarceration poses increased risk of many problems, including HIV transmission (Stimson, 1990). Sterile injection equipment is not allowed in prisons, but drug use occurs commonly. Because drugs are relatively easy to smuggle in but injection equipment is not, very high-risk methods of drug administration are employed. Making syringes available could pose security problems, but increased availability of substitution drugs may alleviate this problem. Many incarcerated individuals may benefit more from drug treatment-oriented sentences rather than standard prison sentences (Schuler & McBride, 1990). Male-to-male sex is also common in prisons, but condoms are not usually made available (Beers, 1992).

Educational programming acknowledging the presence of these behaviors coupled with skills training and prevention tools may help reduce the high risk of contracting HIV in prison and the subsequent spread to sexual partners and children once prisoners are released. Prison incarceration may increase the harm of addiction in terms of the following factors. First, ongoing injection and other drug use, along with unprotected sex, occurs frequently in the prison population. Second, inmates with drug problems often receive no treatment for their abuse or dependence problems while in prison (although the Federal Bureau of Prisons is beginning to provide support for such programs). Third, recidivism rates are high and often the incentive to pursue a drug-free life is nonexistent, because "ex-cons" are discriminated against in terms of employment and rehabilitation. Finally, there are huge profits to be made from drug trafficking, and drug pushers model an antisocial life-style with an emphasis on money, guns, and power; it is little wonder that inner-city youth are at great risk for involvement in drug-related activities leading to contact with the criminal justice system.

The Dutch policy, as reviewed above, favors a public health approach rather than relying on the courts and the prisons to control and punish addicted citizens. Engelsman (1989) notes:

It should be emphasized that the role of the penal system and law enforcement in the Netherlands is not as prominent as in many other countries. Dutch people favor a policy of encirclement, adaptation and integration. Although Dutch drug legislation is still a part of criminal law, it is generally considered as an instrument of social control, the results of which should be assessed for each case, and it should not be considered as a mouthpiece for passing moral judgment. Drug legislation remains supplementary to the (informal) social control, which has for centuries been established on traditionally tight family structures conforming with a Calvinistic life-style. (p. 212)

Tolerance Versus Zero Tolerance

Unlike the Dutch, who tolerate the use of soft drugs such as cannabis, American policy is strictly intolerant of any illegal drug use, from marijuana to morphine. Consistent with a total-abstinence policy when it comes to treatment goals, the principle of zero tolerance insists on an absolute dichotomy between no (zero) use and any use whatsoever. This all-or-none dichotomy equates all drug use as equally criminal and harmful and fails to distinguish between light and heavy use or degrees of harmful use. Along similar lines, individuals subjected to drug testing as a condition of employment will fail because the tests (e.g., urinalysis, hair analysis, blood tests) are evaluated as either "clean" or "dirty." According to this pass/fail criterion based on zero-tolerance policy, you are equally "dirty" whether you once smoked a single marijuana cigarette or smoked crack cocaine on a daily basis for months. American drug policy is based on the assumption that there can be no such thing as occasional or "casual" use of drugs; any use equals abuse.

Normalization Versus Denormalization Policies

The Dutch attempt to normalize drug use and to avoid the notoriety and special appeal of a deviant drug life-style, motivated in part by a desire to avoid moral double standards. According to Engelsman (1989), "The Dutch government wants to remain credible and does not want to encourage messages to youngsters such as 'your drugs are killers, but ours are pleasures'" (p. 215). In contrast, current American policy adopts a "denormalization" stance. Herb Kleber, a psychiatrist who served as Director of Demand Reduction in the White House Drug Policy Office (under the direction of former "drug czar" William Bennett), in a public symposium on drug policy at the 1990 conference of the American Psychological Association, stated the basic credo of the denormalization policy: "The user is the loser." Kleber stated that casual users of "soft drugs" are targeted for criminal prosecution (even more than heavily addicted users of narcotics) because the government wants to send the message that absolutely no drug use will be tolerated, particularly in individuals who might otherwise be viewed as "role models" for young people. Most drug arrests in the United States are for marijuana use and sales in the middle-class population. No drug use is to be viewed as safe or normal in any segment of society in this movement toward denormalization.

The differences between the Dutch and American drug policies were pointed out to the senior author during his Amsterdam visit by another international visitor to the Jellinekcentre, a drug specialist from India who was visiting centers in both the United States and Europe during a fact-finding tour to review programs and policies on both sides of the Atlantic. The specialist summarized his impressions during one conversation:

> In America, you have a big governmental hierarchy with the Drug Czar at the top of the heap who tells the addicts what to do and what not to do, and if the addict fails to comply, he is put in prison or jail. In Holland, in comparison, the approach is quite different; someone from this center sits down next to the addict on the park bench and asks, "How can we help you return to a productive life in our society?"

Harm Reduction Methods
and Areas of Application

Harm-reduction methods can be employed in three main areas: (a) AIDS prevention (e.g., safe-sex and condom-use programs, needle exchange for IDUs); (b) treatment of ongoing, active addictive behaviors (e.g., methadone maintenance for opiate addiction, nicotine replacement therapy for tobacco smokers); and (c) prevention of harmful addictive or excessive behaviors (e.g., controlled drinking, moderation of excessive food intake). Examples of each of these areas are provided below, followed by a summary of the harm reduction methods involved.

AIDS Prevention

AIDS prevention is one of the most critical examples of harm reduction. Public health officials around the world are acknowledging that the crisis of AIDS is more pressing than the threat of drug addiction or premarital sex, and several harm reduction measures can be taken to reduce the spread of HIV, including needle exchange, methadone maintenance treatment programs, and educational prevention programs. harm reduction approaches offer at-risk populations simple behavior changes that reduce the harm of high-risk activities, often with abstinence as the end point, but accepting that abstinence is not a realistic goal for all people. As relapse is common, people need skills to prevent harm if a relapse should occur. harm reduction approaches work to empower rather than to marginalize high-risk groups.

Needle Exchange

History. Needle exchange was first started in the Netherlands in 1984, prompted by the "Junky Union." In 1986, needle exchanges also started in the United Kingdom and Sweden (Christensson & Ljungberg, 1991; Lart & Stimson, 1990). The first American needle exchange was started in Tacoma, Washington, in August 1988 by Dave Purchase, a drug treatment counselor. The program received funding from the Tacoma-Pierce County Health Department in January 1989 as an opportunity to reduce some of the problems associated with drug use (Sorge, 1990).

Tacoma's needle exchange served as a model for other American communities. By 1990, San Francisco, Seattle, New Haven, Portland,

Spokane, Boulder, Honolulu, New York, Berkeley, Fairbanks, and a few other cities around the country also offered needle exchanges, operating either legally through health departments or clinics or illegally by AIDS activists. New York City did not begin successful legal operation of needle exchanges until June 1992, after former prohibitive policies were reexamined in light of encouraging findings from other needle exchanges. New York's needle exchanges will continue to be operated by the activists who set up the first successful needle exchange in that city (Navarro, 1992). Canada, New Zealand, Australia, Thailand, Nepal, and most European nations also have needle exchanges.

Rationale. Some 32% of all U.S. AIDS cases are now related to injection drug use. Fully 71% of all female cases and 58% of all pediatric cases are related to injection drug use, directly (through personal injection use) or indirectly (prenatally or through sexual contact; Centers for Disease Control, 1992). Lack of syringe availability has been associated with increased HIV prevalence in a number of studies. Nelson et al. (1991) found that nondiabetic illicit IDUs were almost three times more likely to be HIV positive than were diabetic illicit IDUs, despite similar patterns of drug use, because of diabetics' open access to clean needles.

Injection-related infections pose additional risk to the IDU population. Many things can go wrong when one injects drugs, such as skin infections or abscesses, "cotton fever," and vein deterioration. The Exeter Drugs Project in England has published a pamphlet for people who choose to inject drugs (Preston, Armsby, & the Exeter Drugs Project, 1990). This pamphlet illustrates how to inject safely, things that can go wrong, and certain body locations to avoid, as well as how to prevent contracting HIV and hepatitis. Injecting drugs is a very high-risk activity, but as more than 3 million people in the United States alone are estimated to have injected drugs (National Institute on Drug Abuse, 1991), such useful information should be made available to reduce not only the harm individuals cause themselves but also the cost to society. Furthermore, some individuals may be willing to "step up" from the risks of injection to methadone maintenance or other treatment programs.

By providing a much-needed service with a nonjudgmental attitude, needle exchanges have the capacity to reach a population not yet ready to seek treatment for drug problems. Needle exchanges provide a simple format from which sterile injection equipment, safer injection education, AIDS prevention education, bleach, condoms, HIV testing, drug treatment referral, and even primary medical care, housing referral, legal advocacy, clothing, and food can be disseminated. Needle exchanges give drug users the often unique opportunity of contact with nonusers, providing examples of other ways of living. With the shortage of available treatment slots and difficulty in getting people to abstain for long periods of time, needle exchange provides a simple and practical behavior change that can help many people reduce their risk of contracting HIV.

How It Works. Needle exchanges operate in a number of different formats, including using folding tables on the street, vans, storefronts, clinics, drive-throughs, and cafes. Some exchanges offer "starter kits" for beginning clients, which may contain information, bleach, condoms, alcohol prep pads, and sometimes syringes. Some programs require registration prior to participation, which aids in data collection, whereas other programs require no registration or identification. Used syringes are dropped into "sharps containers" that are disposed of through medical disposal services. The exchange format also serves to keep used syringes off the streets and out of parks and public trash receptacles, where they could puncture others.

Staff and volunteers are encouraged to treat clients with respect and without judgment. Problems sometimes arise when a client has no syringe to exchange but is in a situation requiring a syringe. Only bleach for disinfecting a syringe can be offered in these instances. Police harassment is often a deterrent for clients, as police seeing an individual using a needle exchange may assume that person is a drug user or dealer.

Many needle exchanges utilize the experience of former or current IDUs in tailoring the program to the needs of the community. Current users can serve as peer counselors or outreach workers (Stimson, 1990). Former users are often placed in situations with a high risk for relapse, and programs must offer special support for these staff members.

Effectiveness. In Scotland, two cities with similar injection drug use epidemics handled syringe availability differently and had quite different outcomes (Brettle, 1991). Edinburgh made syringes illegal to purchase without a prescription in 1981 as an attempt to reduce drug use. This led to considerable needle sharing. More than 50% of all IDUs in Edinburgh were HIV positive by 1984, and an epidemic of hepatitis B occurred simultaneously. Glasgow had a larger number of IDUs, but did not restrict syringe availability and did not suffer an HIV or hepatitis B epidemic, with only 5% of the city's IDUs testing HIV positive. Cities such as St. Louis (Compton, Cottler, Decker, Mager, & Stringfellow, 1992) and Seattle (Calsyn, Saxon, Freeman, & Whittaker, 1991), which have allowed syringes to be purchased without prescription since before the AIDS epidemic, have suffered lower rates of HIV among IDUs (about 3%) than New York or New Jersey (50%-60%), where syringe purchase is illegal (Des Jarlais & Friedman, 1990). In some parts of New York City, 80%-90% of IDUs are HIV positive (Centers for Disease Control, 1990), compared with less than 1% in Liverpool, another center of injection drug use, but that instigated a harm reduction approach early on in the epidemic.

Cities with needle exchanges have shown decreasing incidence rates; that is, a decrease in the number of new cases each year (Buning, 1991; Hart et al., 1989; Stimson, Donoghoe, Alldritt, & Dolan, 1988). The New Haven needle exchange was evaluated for effectiveness by members of the Yale School of Medicine (Kaplan, O'Keefe, & Heimer, 1991). Estimates of HIV prevalence were made from tests on returned syringes. The New Haven needle exchange is estimated to have reduced new infections of HIV among clients by 33%, and this finding has encouraged public health officials in other cities to reconsider prohibitive policies.

The most common argument against needle exchanges is that they will encourage or increase illicit drug use. This fear has not been supported by the data. In 1986, a Sydney methadone clinic added a syringe exchange and reported no increase of illicit drugs in urine specimens of clinic clients compared with clients of a methadone clinic without a syringe exchange (Wolk, Wodak, Guinan, Macaskill, & Simpson, 1990). A San Francisco study found a decrease in frequency of injecting by IDUs corresponding temporally to the initiation of San Francisco's needle exchange. They also found a slowly aging population of drug injectors (Watters, Cheng, Clark, & Lorvick, 1991). An evaluation of a London needle exchange also failed to show an increase in drug use (Hart et al., 1989).

The most successful needle exchanges are user friendly and administer services in locations, times, and manners appropriate for the clientele. For example, one needle exchange in Boulder, Colorado, is located near a gymnasium to target steroid injectors (Keller, 1992). Amphetamine injection is often associated with gay IDUs, who have additional risk factors. Amphetamine and cocaine injectors seem at be at higher risk for HIV than heroin injectors, perhaps because these drugs tend to be injected more frequently and are often associated with high-risk sexual activity. HIV rates also tend to be much higher among blacks, Latinos, and low-income individuals in the United States (Schilling et al.,

1989; Stimson, 1992). Women of ethnic minorities who inject drugs often tend to have greater difficulty in negotiating safe sex (Schilling, El-Bassel, Gilbert, & Schinke, 1991), and are at greater risk for HIV. These differences and particular risk factors need to be addressed by AIDS prevention programs.

AIDS Prevention and Sex Education

Open sex education is another controversial form of harm reduction. Sex education for students in primary and secondary schools has long been a topic of controversy. The nature of HIV transmission often calls for explicit sex education to inform students, who may or may not be sexually active, about how HIV is transmitted and how they can protect themselves and others. Sex education that deals with socioenvironmental influences on behavior (Walter et al., 1991), ideally accompanied by condom distribution, has been suggested as a major prevention effort for underage students. However, many school administrators choose to advocate abstinence from sex, despite the fact that more adolescents are reporting having had sex and are reporting more partners than was the case 10 years ago (Anderson et al., 1990). A 1989 national survey of ninth through twelfth graders found that 58.5% reported having had sexual intercourse (Anderson et al., 1990). A recent national high school sample found that 2.7% reported having ever injected illicit drugs. Students who reported having learned about HIV in school were significantly less likely to report having ever injected drugs and having ever shared needles, had fewer sexual partners, and were more likely to use condoms (Holtzman et al., 1991). Approximately 20% of U.S. AIDS cases to date are in the 20-29 age bracket, and many of these may have contracted HIV during teenage years (Centers for Disease Control, 1990). An open sex education/HIV prevention program that does not encourage sexual activity but acknowledges its presence among people of all ages while providing useful information and skills along with the tools necessary to have safe sex (condoms) could help stem the spread of AIDS.

Other Examples of Harm Reduction in Addiction Treatment and Prevention

harm reduction methods can be applied to the treatment of addiction problems in addition to AIDS prevention. Nonabstinent goals to reduce risk of harm include (a) changing the route of drug administration, (b) providing alternative "safer" substances, and (c) reducing the frequency and/or intensity of ongoing addictive behaviors. Although space does not permit a full discussion of each of these goals here, brief descriptions of some examples may help clarify these methods.

One goal is to reduce the harm of ongoing addictive behavior by changing the route of administration of the substance or drug. In AIDS prevention, needle exchange is the most obvious example: Clean needles and syringes are used to administer injection drugs in place of "dirty" or shared needles. Other examples include smoking or orally consuming drugs instead of using the injection method of administration. In the Merseyside region of northwestern England, pharmacists provide drug clinics with noninjectable drugs in the form of "reefers" (herbal or tobacco cigarettes injected with heroin, methadone, cocaine, or amphetamine). Reefers are prescribed through drug dependency units located in Liverpool and other Merseyside hospitals or in self-contained units near town centers. For those who cannot immediately give up injecting drugs, a combined injection and reefer prescription can be given. For users who are able to move toward stabilizing on oral drugs, a combined oral and reefer prescription can be used (Canadian Center on Substance Abuse, 1991). The "Liverpool model" of harm reduction has pioneered in the policy of making illicit drugs available to addicts on a controlled basis (Marks, 1992).

A related treatment method for nicotine dependence is *nicotine replacement therapy* (Benowitz, 1988). Nicotine replacement changes the route of administration of nicotine from smoking to either nicotine gum or a transdermal nicotine patch. The risk of cancer associated with smoking is thereby reduced by changing the method of drug ingestion. Although this form of treatment is recommended as a method of reducing withdrawal symptoms associated with smoking cessation with the eventual goal of abstinence, some smokers may maintain ongoing use with these replacement strategies or use them as a way of reducing intake or tapering down (Gross & Stitzer, 1989; Russell, 1991).

A second goal of nonabstinence harm reduction methods is the provision of a safer alternative substance or drug to replace the more harmful substance. The Dutch approach to decriminalizing cannabis use is an illustration of this approach. Here the rationale is that if "soft drugs" are provided as a means of allowing experimentation with intoxicating substances, users will not turn to substances of higher risk such as cocaine or heroin. The same argument applies to alcohol: Programs that recommend moderate consumption of beverages low in alcohol content (e.g., wine and beer) promote alternatives to the excessive use of stronger brews (e.g., distilled spirits).

Perhaps the most widely known example of this method is *methadone maintenance* as an alternative to injection opiate/heroin use. Methadone reduces risks associated with illicit substance use and injection, and provides a realistic option for some drug users; many clients report preferring this form of treatment to drug-free treatments (Chaney & Roszell, 1985; Mavis, DeVoss, & Stoffelmayr, 1991). Methadone dispensing programs utilizing contingency contracting interventions (urinalysis to test for illicit drug use) have been shown to be most successful in keeping clients from using illicit drugs (Dolan, Black, Penk, Robinowitz, & DeFord, 1985; Higgins, Stitzer, Bigelow, & Liebson, 1986). Positive reinforcement by increasing methadone dosages for negative urinalysis has been found to reduce dropout rates (Stitzer, Bickel, Bigelow, & Liebson, 1986).

Methadone maintenance treatment programs have also shown success in reducing risks of contracting HIV, delaying onset of AIDS-related illnesses, and reducing withdrawal, crime, and other negative effects associated with injection opiate use. A controlled study in Thailand randomly assigned 240 heroin addicts to drug-free detox or to methadone maintenance, and found that those in the methadone group were significantly less likely to have used heroin during the span of treatment or to drop out, suggesting methadone maintenance as a viable AIDS prevention measure in helping users avoid injection of illicit opiates (Vanichseni, Wongsuwan, Staff of BMA Narcotics Clinic No. 6, Choopanya, & Wongpanich, 1991). Methadone maintenance has been shown to be most effective when coupled with other services such as counseling (Calsyn, Saxon, Freeman, & Whittaker, 1990; Childress, McLellan, Woody, & O'Brien, 1991; McLellan, Luborsky, & Woody, 1986). However, methadone treatment does not offer any solutions for cocaine and amphetamine injectors. Treatment options for these substances need to be researched and implemented.

The third goal of harm reduction applies to both prevention and treatment of addictive behaviors: to reduce the frequency and/or intensity (quantity, dose level) of the target behavior. Risk-reduction programs based on moderation or "responsible use" principles have been applied in prevention programs geared toward alcohol use (described below). Similar principles have been applied in promoting moderate food consumption for individuals who are overweight or who have binge eating problems (see Brownell & Foreyt, 1986). In addition, sex education for AIDS prevention may focus on reducing the frequency of high-risk sexual activity (e.g., promoting monogamous sex, reducing the number of unsafe sexual episodes, or moving toward less risky forms of sex).

One of the most controversial harm reduction strategies is controlled or moderate drinking as an alternative to abstinence for people with alcohol problems (Heather & Robertson, 1983; Marlatt, 1983; Sobell & Sobell, 1978). In the treatment of alcohol dependence in the United States, in contrast with other countries (e.g., Canada, Australia, and many European countries), controlled drinking programs are rarely available. The bulk of the resistance to this approach stems from abstinence advocates of the medical model, who view alcoholism as a progressive disease that cannot be cured (i.e., moderation can never be attained by "recovering" alcoholics). Abstinence is the only acceptable goal for both treatment and prevention—no amount of moderation training can stem the tide of this insidious disease, according to these critics.

One of the apparent paradoxes of controlled drinking programs for problem drinkers is that many clients exposed to this approach eventually end up abstaining from alcohol (Miller, Leckman, Delaney, & Tinkcom, 1992). From the perspective of harm reduction theory, such a "paradoxical" outcome is not surprising. Problem drinkers who might otherwise resist the high-threshold commitment to abstinence as a precondition for treatment or participation in an abstinence-based self-help group may well be attracted by a moderation program instead. Once they have entered such a low-threshold program and are "taking steps in the right direction," it is little wonder that many of these clients eventually end up abstinent. Many of the skills and coping strategies employed in these cognitive-behavioral programs can be used to foster both moderation and abstinence goals (see Nathan & McCrady, 1987). The greater the options available to the large mass of otherwise unreachable problem drinkers, the more people will be motivated to seek help for their drinking. Instead of requiring that clients uniformly quit in a "cold turkey" approach, harm reduction provides the client with options to taper off gradually, to opt for a "warm turkey" alternative route to quitting (Miller & Page, 1991).

Consider the three teams represented in the "Recovery Playoffs" (Figure 11.4). The majority of people in the United States with active drug problems currently play on the D Team. Players on the D Team are those at highest risk: They include those who Deny they have a problem

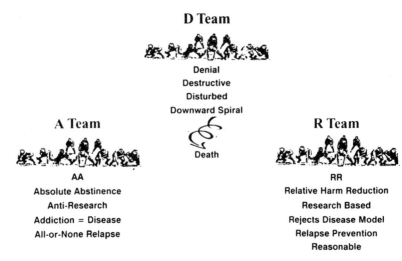

D Team

Denial
Destructive
Disturbed
Downward Spiral

Death

A Team

AA
Absolute Abstinence
Anti-Research
Addiction = Disease
All-or-None Relapse

R Team

RR
Relative Harm Reduction
Research Based
Rejects Disease Model
Relapse Prevention
Reasonable

Figure 11.4. Recovery Playoffs.
SOURCE: Jewel Brien. Reprinted with permission.

or need help; their ongoing addictive behavior may be Destructive to self and/or others, in some cases leading to a Downward spiral that may eventuate in Death (e.g., an addict dies of AIDS contracted from a shared needle). In short, players on the D Team are often Disturbed, Dangerous, and Disappointing in their unwillingness to change their harmful behavior. The biggest challenge for society is to move people off the D Team. What other teams are there to attract them?

The traditional alternative is, of course, to play on the A Team. However, it is not easy to get on the A Team. The requirements are severe: Absolute Abstinence for a lifetime, based on the assumption that Addiction is a disease that cannot be controlled (admission of powerlessness). Advocates of AA are often Anti-research, particularly when this research questions or challenges their dogmatic beliefs. Any consumption of alcohol, even a single drink, is a violation of Abstinence, leading to an All-or-none view of relapse. Anyone who claims to play on the R Team is seen as in denial by members of the A Team. It is not permissible to switch from the A Team to either the D Team or the R Team without risking the loss of one's Higher Power.

Relative harm reduction is represented by players on the R Team. Abstinence is the ideal goal, as reflected by those members who belong to Rational Recovery (RR), a self-help group patterned after the principles of Rational-Emotive Therapy (Trimpey, 1992). Research based, the R Team Rejects the disease model and embraces learning-based approaches such as Relapse Prevention (RP) and Recovery Training to assist those who are unable to attain or maintain abstinence. Although A Team members consider this team to be Radical and Rebellious, R Team players see themselves as more Reasonable than their A Team counterparts. For one thing, although R Team players are free to transfer to the A Team whenever they wish, the opposite exchange is not possible. Those on the A Team must remain there or else be dropped to the D Team.

The point of the Recovery Playoffs discussion is that we need to offer more alternatives to the D Team players, to move them from "pre-contemplation" to contemplating "action" in terms of the stages of change model described by Prochaska and DiClemente (1986). Although both the A Team and the R Team offer abstinence as the ideal goal, the harm reduction philosophy represented by the R Team offers low-threshold access to beginning the process of habit change. To join the R Team, all it takes is a commitment to begin making changes, one step at a time, in the direction of reduced risk for harm.

How does relapse prevention (Marlatt & Gordon, 1985) fit in with the harm reduction approach? In the treatment of alcohol dependence, in programs with an abstinence goal, RP can be applied as a maintenance-stage strategy to prevent relapse (e.g., training clients to cope with high-risk situations). If relapse occurs, RP methods can be employed to interrupt the relapse process (e.g., taking steps to prevent the escalation of an initial lapse or slip into a full-blown relapse). With ongoing relapse problems, RP programs are designed for relapse management: to reduce the frequency and intensity of relapse episodes, to keep the client involved in the treatment process, and to motivate renewed efforts toward behavior change. Applied to relapse management, RP represents a tertiary prevention approach to harm reduction, designed to reduce the magnitude of relapse.

Harm reduction also is congruent with secondary prevention programs designed to reduce risks associated with ongoing behaviors. An application of this approach to high-risk drinking in young adults by our research group at the University of Washington is described elsewhere in this volume (see Baer, Chapter 5). Our secondary prevention program is designed to reduce the risk of harmful drinking or alcohol abuse in the college population. Based on prior studies by our group showing that excessive drinking behavior can be reduced significantly by the application of brief intervention programs based on cognitive-behavioral principles (Baer et al., 1992; Kivlahan, Marlatt, Fromme, Coppel, & Williams, 1990), our current research is evaluating a stepped-care approach for harm reduction. Patterned after stepped-care models in the treatment of borderline hypertension (Sobell & Sobell, Chapter 6, this volume), our secondary prevention program is designed to increase the intensity of prevention programming progressively through a series of stepped interventions until the desired harm reduction effect is attained. Our programs begin with high-risk drinkers receiving a single hour of professional feedback concerning their drinking risks coupled with advice on how to reduce harm by adopting moderation skills. If this brief motivational interview (Miller & Rollnick, 1991) leads to a significant stable reduction in drinking risks, no additional interventions are necessary. If, on the other hand, risk behavior continues during subsequent follow-up assessments, the student is encouraged to "take the next step" by participating in a more intensive prevention program (e.g., taking a course in habit change for credit, or joining an ongoing prevention support group). Other more intensive steps (individual counseling or even inpatient treatment) are applied only if previous steps are ineffective. Stepped-care programs are consistent with the harm reduction philosophy in that the "first step" is an easy-access, low-threshold single session of feedback and advice.

The Politics of Harm Reduction in the United States

Americans are a safety-conscious people. With today's emphasis on health and fitness, the American populace has made giant strides in decreasing health risks such as giving up smoking (only one out of four Americans still smokes, down from almost one out of two Americans two decades ago), increasing exercise, and eating healthier foods. In addition, consumer advocacy and public health policy have combined to reduce the risks of accidents and injury: Laws that require the use of automobile seat belts and helmets for bicycle riders, and safer highways with separate pedestrian and bike paths are now commonplace. Requiring safety precautions for injury prevention is entirely consistent with the harm reduction approach described in this chapter. So why is there such opposition to harm reduction methods applied to drug addiction and AIDS prevention?

The National Drug Policy currently in effect in the United States is clear in its opposition to harm reduction programs for drug addicts, despite the increased prevalence of AIDS among IDUs. Consider the following evaluation of needle exchange programs provided in the 1990 White Paper *Understanding Drug Treatment* published by the Office of National Drug Control Policy:

> What Doesn't Work: Needle Exchange. Although it is not touted as treatment, the high rate of HIV transmission among intravenous drug users has prompted some to call for the free distribution of hypodermic needles. The rationale most frequently given is that these addicts won't share needles if clean ones are provided for them, and informal studies done in Holland are often cited as evidence. . . . No matter what addicts promise when they aren't on drugs, they may still share needles when they shoot up heroin or cocaine. In many cases it is simply part of the ritual of taking drugs that accompanies an illicit and socially condemned activity. More often, drug-induced stupefaction overwhelms rational thinking. Many addicts know that they can gets AIDS from dirty needles. Yet hazards to their health—even deadly ones—do not weigh heavily on their minds, especially when they are strung out. We have to remind ourselves that drug addicts are primarily concerned with the instant gratification of drugs; their time horizons are extremely limited. . . . Today the best way to help drug addicts escape the AIDS virus is to either make drugs unavailable to them or get them into treatment. Needle exchange programs may also confound a community's anti-drug efforts by implicitly condoning the intravenous use of illegal drugs. (p. 29)

Until recently, American drug policy prohibited the use of federal research funds (e.g., from the National Institute of Drug Abuse) to evaluate the effectiveness of needle exchange programs for IDUs. In 1992, funding was made available by the National Centers for Disease Control in Atlanta to support the establishment of limited needle exchange programs. Clearly, the conservative American opposition to addiction, homosexuality, and other "immoral" behaviors is gradually responding to the threat of AIDS as a potential epidemic among the general population. The pressing need for effective AIDS prevention strategies is fueling the fire for increased harm reduction programs. Political opposition to current American drug policy is mounting. Leadership and political activism to oppose existing policy and to advocate for "kinder,

gentler" alternatives to the "War on Drugs" is supported by the Drug Policy
Foundation in Washington, DC (Trebach & Zeese, 1990a, 1990b).

References

Anderson, J. E., Kann, L., Holtzman, D., Arday, S., Truman, B., & Kolbe, L. J. (1990).
HIV/AIDS knowledge and sexual behavior among high school students. *Family
Planning Perspective, 22,* 252-255.

Baer, J. S., Marlatt, G. A., Kivlahan, D. R., Fromme, K., Larimer, M., & Williams, E.
(1992). An experimental test of three methods of alcohol risk-reduction with young
adults. *Journal of Consulting and Clinical Psychology, 60,* 974-979.

Beers, D. (1992, January). Making sense on drugs. *Progressive Review,* pp. 1-2.

Benowitz, N. L. (1988). Drug therapy: Pharmacologic aspects of cigarette smoking and
nicotine addiction. *New England Journal of Medicine, 319,* 1318-1330.

Brettle, R. P. (1991). HIV and harm reduction for injection drug users. *AIDS, 5,* 125-136.

Brownell, K. D., & Foreyt, J. P. (Eds.). (1986). *Handbook of eating disorders.* New York:
Basic Books.

Buning, E. C. (1991). Effects of Amsterdam needle and syringe exchange. *International
Journal of the Addictions, 26,* 1303-1311.

Calsyn, D. A., Saxon, A. J., Freeman, G., Jr., & Whittaker, S. (1990). Effects of education
on high risk HIV transmission behaviors. *NIDA Research Monograph, 105,* 482-483.

Calsyn, D. A., Saxon, A. J., Freeman, G., Jr., & Whittaker, S. (1991). Needle-use practices
among intravenous drug users in an area where needle purchase is legal. *AIDS, 5,*
187-193.

Canadian Center on Substance Abuse. (1991). Harm reduction strategies: Smokable drugs
help reduce spread of HIV in Merseyside. *News Action, 11*(4), 7.

Centers for Disease Control. (1990). *HIV/AIDS surveillance report.* Atlanta, GA: Center
for Infectious Diseases, AIDS Program.

Centers for Disease Control. (1992). *HIV/AIDS surveillance report.* Atlanta, GA: Center
for Infectious Diseases, AIDS Program.

Chaney, E. F., & Roszell, D. K. (1985). Coping in opiate addicts maintained on methadone.
In S. Shiffman (Ed.), *Coping and substance use* (pp. 267-292). Orlando, FL: Academic Press.

Childress, A. R., McLellan, A. T., Woody, G. E., & O'Brien, C. P. (1991). Are there
minimum conditions necessary for methadone maintenance to reduce intravenous
drug use and AIDS risk behaviors? *NIDA Research Monograph, 106,* 167-177.

Christensson, B., & Ljungberg, B. (1991). Syringe exchange for prevention of HIV
infection in Sweden: Practical experiences and community reactions. *International
Journal of the Addictions, 26,* 1293-1302.

Compton, W. M., III, Cottler, L. B., Decker, S. H., Mager, D., & Stringfellow, R. (1992).
Legal needle buying in St. Louis. *American Journal of Public Health, 82,* 595-596.

Des Jarlais, D. C., & Friedman, S. R. (1990). The epidemic of HIV infection among
injecting drug users in New York City: The first decade and possible future

direction. In J. Strang & G. V. Stimson (Eds.), *AIDS and drug misuse* (pp. 86-94). London: Tavistock/Routledge.

Dolan, M. P., Black, J. L., Penk, W. E., Robinowitz, R., & DeFord, H. A. (1985). Contracting for treatment termination to reduce illicit drug use among methadone maintenance treatment failures. *Journal of Consulting and Clinical Psychology, 53,* 549-551.

Engelsman, E. L. (1989). Dutch policy on the management of drug-related problems. *British Journal of Addiction, 84,* 211-218.

Gross, J., & Stitzer, M. L. (1989). Nicotine replacement: Ten-week effects on tobacco withdrawal symptoms. *Psychopharmacology, 98,* 334-341.

Hart, G. J., Carvell, A. L. M., Woodward, N., Johnson, A. M., Williams, P., & Parry, J. V. (1989). Evaluation of needle exchange in central London: Behaviour change and anti-HIV status over one year. *AIDS, 3,* 261-265.

Heather, N., & Robertson, I., (1983). *Controlled drinking.* London: Methuen.

Higgins, S. T., Stitzer, M. L., Bigelow, G. E., & Liebson, I. A. (1986). Contingent methadone delivery: Effects on illicit-opiate use. *Drug and Alcohol Dependence, 17,* 311-322.

Holtzman, D., Anderson, J. E., Kann, L., Arday, S. L., Truman, B. I., & Kolbe, L. J. (1991). HIV instruction, HIV knowledge, and drug injection among high school students in the United States. *American Journal of Public Health, 81,* 1596-1601.

Inter-American Commission on Drug Policy. (1991). *United States drug policy toward Latin America.* Washington, DC: Woodrow Wilson Center, Latin American Program.

Kaplan, E. H., O'Keefe, E., & Heimer, R. (1991). *Evaluating the New Haven needle exchange program.* Paper presented at the meeting of the International Conference on AIDS, Florence, Italy.

Keller, I. E. (February, 1992). Needle exchange: HIV prevention takes on the law. *Exchange of the National Lawyers Guild AIDS Network.*

Kivlahan, D. R., Marlatt, G. A., Fromme, K., Coppel, D. B., & Williams, E. (1990). Secondary prevention with college drinkers: Evaluation of an alcohol skills training program. *Journal of Consulting and Clinical Psychology, 58,* 805-810.

Lart, R., & Stimson, G. V. (1990). National survey of syringe exchange schemes in England. *British Journal of Addiction, 85,* 1433-1443.

Marks, J. (1992). The practice of controlled availability of illicit drugs. In N. Heather, W. R. Miller, & J. Greeley (Eds.), *Self-control and the addictive behaviours* (pp. 304-316). Botany Bay, NSW, Australia: Maxwell Macmillan.

Marlatt, G. A. (1983). The controlled drinking controversy: A commentary. *American Psychologist, 38,* 1097-1110.

Marlatt, G. A., & Gordon, J. R. (Eds.). (1985). *Relapse prevention: Maintenance strategies in the treatment of addictive behaviors.* New York: Guilford.

Mavis, B. E., DeVoss, G. H., & Stoffelmayr, B. E. (1991). The perceptions of program directors and clients regarding the efficacy of methadone treatment. *International Journal of the Addictions, 26,* 769-776.

McLellan, A. T., Luborsky, L., & Woody, G. E. (1986). *Is the counselor an "active ingredient" in methadone treatment?* Unpublished manuscript, University of Pennsylvania.

Mieczkowski, T. (Ed.). (1992). *Drugs, crime, and social policy.* Needham Heights, MA: Allyn & Bacon.

Miller, W. R., Leckman, A. L., Delaney, H. D., & Tinkcom, M. (1992). Long-term follow-up of behavioral self-control training. *Journal of Studies on Alcohol, 53,* 249-261.

Miller, W. R., & Page, A. C. (1991). Warm turkey: Other routes to abstinence. *Journal of Substance Abuse Treatment, 8,* 227-232.

Miller, W. R., & Rollnick, S. (1991). *Motivation interviewing: Preparing people for change.* New York: Guilford.

Mule, S. J. (1981). *Behavior in excess: An examination of the volitional disorders.* New York: Free Press.

Nathan, P. E., & McCrady, B. S. (1987). Bases for use of abstinence as a goal in the behavioral treatment of alcohol abusers. *Drugs & Society, 1,* 109-131.

National Commission on AIDS. (1991, July). *Report: The twin epidemics of substance use and HIV.* Washington, DC: Author.

National Institute on Drug Abuse. (1991). *National household survey on drug abuse: Main findings 1990* (DHHS Publication No. [ADM] 91-1788). Washington, DC: Government Printing Office.

Navarro, M. (1992, May 14). New York City resurrects plan on needle swap. *New York Times,* pp. A1, A15.

Nelson, K. E., Vlahov, D., Cohn, S., Lindsay, A., Solomon, L., & Anthony, J. C. (1991). Human immunodeficiency virus infection in diabetic intravenous drug users. *Journal of the American Medical Association, 266,* 2259-2261.

Office of National Drug Control Policy. (1990, June). *White paper: Understanding drug treatment.* Washington, DC: Author.

Orford, J. (1985). *Excessive appetites: A psychological view of addictions.* New York: John Wiley.

Parry, A. (1989). Harm reduction [Interview]. *Drug Policy Letter, 1*(4), 13.

Preston, A., Armsby, T., & the Exeter Drugs Project. (1990). *What works? Safer injecting guide* (2nd ed.). Exeter, UK: Exeter Drugs Project.

Prochaska, J. O., & DiClemente, C. C. (1986). Toward a comprehensive model of change. In W. R. Miller & N. Heather (Eds.), *Treating addictive behaviors: Processes of change* (pp. 3-27). New York: Plenum.

Russell, M. A. H. (1991). The future of nicotine replacement. *British Journal of Addiction, 86,* 653-658.

Schilling, R. F., El-Bassel, N., Gilbert, L., & Schinke, S. P. (1991). Correlates of drug use, sexual behavior, and attitudes toward safer sex among African-American and Hispanic women in methadone maintenance. *Journal of Drug Issues, 21,* 685-698.

Schilling, R. F., Schinke, S. P., Nichols, S. E., Zayas, L. H., Miller, S. O., Orlandi, M. A., & Botvin, G. L. (1989). Developing strategies for AIDS prevention research with Black and Hispanic drug users. *Public Health Reports, 104,* 2-11.

Schuler, J. T., & McBride, A. (1990). Notes from the front: A dissident law-enforcement perspective on drug prohibition. *Hofstra Law Review, 18,* 893-942.

Sobell, M. B., & Sobell, L. C. (1978). *Behavioral treatment of alcohol problems.* New York: Plenum.

Sorge, R. (1990, Fall). A thousand points: Needle exchange around the country. *Health PAC Bulletin,* pp. 16-22.

Stimson, G. V. (1990, June). *The prevention of HIV injection in injecting drug users: Recent advances and remaining obstacles.* Paper presented at the meeting of the International Conference on AIDS, San Francisco.

Stimson, G. V. (1992). Drug injecting and HIV infection: New directions for social science research. *International Journal of the Addictions, 27,* 147-163.

Stimson, G. V., Donoghoe, M., Alldritt, L., & Dolan, K. (1988). HIV transmission risk behaviour of clients attending syringe-exchange schemes in England and Scotland. *British Journal of Addiction, 83,* 1449-1455.

Stitzer, M. L., Bickel, W. K., Bigelow, G. E., & Liebson, I. A. (1986). Effect of methadone dose contingencies on urinalysis test results of polydrug-abusing methadone-maintenance patients. *Drug and Alcohol Dependence, 18,* 341-348.

Trebach, A. S., & Zeese, K. B. (1990a). *Drug prohibition and the conscience of nations.* Washington, DC: Drug Policy Foundation.

Trebach, A. S., & Zeese, K. B. (1990b). *The great issues of drug policy.* Washington, DC: Drug Policy Foundation.

Trimpey, J. (1992). *The small book.* New York: Delacorte.

Van de Wijngaart, G. F. (1991). *Competing perspectives on drug use.* Amsterdam: Swets & Zeitlinger.

Vanichseni, S., Wongsuwan, B., Staff of BMA Narcotics Clinic No. 6, Choopanya, K., & Wongpanich, K. (1991). A controlled trial of methadone maintenance in a population of intravenous drug users in Bangkok: Implications for prevention of HIV. *International Journal of the Addictions, 26,* 1313-1320.

Walter, H. J., Vaughan, R. D., Gladis, M. M., Ragin, D. F., Kasen, S., & Cohall, A. T. (1991). Factors associated with AIDS risk behaviors among high school students in an AIDS epicenter. *American Journal of Public Health, 81,* 528-532.

Watters, J. K., Cheng, Y. T., Clark, G. L., & Lorvick, J. (1991, June). *Syringe exchange in San Francisco: Preliminary findings.* Paper presented at the meeting of the International Conference on AIDS, Florence, Italy.

Webster's New World Dictionary (2nd ed.). (1986). New York: Prentice-Hall.

Wolk, J., Wodak, A., Guinan, J. J., Macaskill, P., & Simpson, J. M. (1990). The effect of a needle and syringe exchange on a methadone maintenance unit. *British Journal of Addiction, 85,* 1445-1450.

12

Women's Issues
in Alcohol Use
and Cigarette Smoking

R. LORRAINE COLLINS

Although women are portrayed as using a variety of addictive substances, alcohol and tobacco are the ones they use most commonly. As such, these substances will be the focus of this chapter. This review of the literature on women's use of alcohol and tobacco will focus on (a) prevalence and consumption patterns, (b) the initiation of use, (c) health-related consequences, and (d) treatment.

Prevalence of Alcohol Use
and Cigarette Smoking

Alcohol Consumption Patterns of Women

Current data suggest that in every age group in the United States, 18 to 60+ years, more men than women drink alcohol, and men consume

AUTHOR'S NOTE: Preparation of this chapter was supported in part by grant R01-DA05852 from the National Institute on Drug Abuse. I would like to thank Gerard Connors and Elizabeth Morsheimer for their comments on an earlier draft of the manuscript.

more alcohol than do women. For example, at ages 18-29 approximately 7% of women are heavy drinkers, whereas approximately 27% of men are heavy drinkers. More men than women report problems related to alcohol use (Hilton, 1987), and problem-related drinking patterns tend to occur later in life for women (the decade of their 30s) than for men (the decade of their 20s) (Fillmore, 1987). Trends in women's drinking behavior suggest no major increases or convergence with men's drinking rates over the past 10 years (NIAAA, 1987). However, some convergence has been noted among college students (Mercer & Khavari, 1990).

Statistics from general population surveys of levels of consumption in the United States indicate that as of 1985, the majority of women either abstained from drinking alcohol or defined themselves as light drinkers (NIAAA, 1987). However, there are variations in the drinking patterns of women related to a range of sociodemographic characteristics, such as age and life roles (Fillmore, 1987; Hilton, 1987; NIAAA, 1990; Wilsnack & Cheloha, 1987), ethnicity (NIAAA, 1990), marital status (Wilsnack, Wilsnack, & Klassen, 1985), and socioeconomic status (encompassing education and employment; Wilsnack et al., 1985). Generally, being younger, being divorced, having more education, and being employed are independently associated with higher levels of alcohol consumption in women. African-American women report higher rates of abstention and tend to drink less at all age levels compared with European-American women (NIAAA, 1990).

Tobacco Smoking Among Women

Approximately 30% of adults in the United States currently smoke cigarettes: 34% of men and 28% of women (Fiore et al., 1989). This represents a decrease in the smoking rates of men and women from the high levels achieved during the early 1960s. However, men have shown a greater rate of decrease over the past decade (from 43% in 1974 to 34% in 1985, mean rate of −0.91% per year) than have women (from 31% in 1974 to 28% in 1985, mean rate of −0.33% per year), such that the difference in smoking prevalence of women and men is becoming smaller (Fiore et al., 1989). Further, although men's smoking prevalence is currently higher than that of women, the rate of smoking initiation among young women is remaining constant while the rate of initiation among young men is decreasing (Pierce, Fiore, Novotny, Hatziandreu, & Davis, 1989a). If current rates of initiation and cessation continue into the next century, the smoking rate for women (projected at

23%) will surpass the rate for men (projected at 20%) (Pierce, Fiore, Novotny, Hatziandreu, & Davis, 1989b). However, differences in the smoking topography (e.g., depth of inhalation, number of cigarettes smoked per day) suggest that men's nicotine intake is greater than women's (Grunberg, Winders, & Wewers, 1991).

As with alcohol consumption, there are variations in smoking rates among different subgroups of women defined by sociodemographic characteristics such as ethnicity and education. For example, in 1985 approximately 32% of African-American women smoked, while 27% of European-American women smoked (Fiore et al., 1989). Young women (20-24 years) who were high school graduates or less had a smoking prevalence rate of 44% in 1985 (an increase from 39% in 1974), while those with at least some college education had a prevalence rate of 20% in 1985 (a decrease from 24% in 1974; Pierce et al., 1989a). Initiation rates for cigarette smoking are decreasing more rapidly among young men than among young women. However, rates for use of smokeless tobacco products, particularly chewing tobacco, are increasing among young men, with negligible levels of use by young women (Chassin, Presson, Sherman, & Margolis, 1988; Jacobs, Neufeld, Sayers, Spielberger, & Weinberg, 1988).

In sum, prevalence data for adult women's substance use, relative to men's, indicate that levels of alcohol use have remained relatively stable over time while women's levels of smoking have declined more slowly than men's. The latter phenomenon is attributable in part to relatively high rates of smoking initiation among young women. However, within gender, there are variations in prevalence rates for drinking and smoking, based on demographic characteristics such as age, employment, education, and ethnicity. Clearly, factors related to the initiation of use of these two substances will have a major impact on prevalence. In examining initiation of use, it will become apparent that although drinking and smoking have a number of features in common, factors unique to the development of alcohol problems and smoking also exist.

Initiation of Substance Use

The Role of Social Influence Processes

Social learning approaches highlight commonalities among factors linked to the initiation of alcohol use and smoking. These factors include the role of cultural and familial norms (Barnes, 1990; Bennett & Wolin, 1990; Fawzy, Coombs, & Gerber, 1983; Feinhandler, 1986), beliefs about the effects of the substance (Bauman & Chenoweth, 1984; Leigh, 1989), and peer influences (Collins & Marlatt, 1981; Hover & Gaffney, 1988; Jessor & Jessor, 1975). Modeling of drinking behavior is thought to serve as a mechanism for the transmission of a variety of social influences, such that offspring from families where the parents drink heavily are more likely to become heavy drinkers and the offspring of light drinkers are more likely to become light drinkers (Barnes, 1990). Peers influence consumption patterns and amounts consumed (Collins & Marlatt, 1981; Jessor & Jessor, 1975). Family influences on smoking, particularly mother's smoking, have been reported (Fawzy et al., 1983). With regard to peer influences, young women report more peer pressure to smoke than do young men (Silverstein, Feld, & Kozlowski, 1980) and young women who smoke tend to have more friends who smoke (Hover & Gaffney, 1988).

Women's movement into heavier drinking has been linked to having heavy-drinking partners. This suggests that exposure to such partners alters norms for drinking and/or that these women may participate in companionable drinking with their husbands (Hammer & Vaglum, 1989; Thom, 1986; Wilsnack et al., 1985; R. W. Wilsnack & S. C. Wilsnack, 1990). However, social influences on drinking behavior are not always directly apparent among women, as is evident from research that has shown (a) that men conform to peer modeling of drinking behavior more so than women (Cooper, Waterhouse, & Sobell, 1979; Lied & Marlatt, 1979), (b) that men conform more to group norms and pressures to drink than do women (Aitken, 1985; Budd & Spencer, 1984), (c) that cultural norms about women not drinking predominate over exposure to heavy-drinking male models (Roman, 1988), and (d) that exposure to the negative consequences of problem-drinking husbands inhibits the drinking of their female spouses (Wilsnack, Wilsnack, & Klassen, 1987).

Social Influences of Advertising. Advertising serves as another source of social influence to initiate or maintain use of alcohol and cigarettes. Many advertising and marketing campaigns designed to encourage women to use substances have co-opted themes of women's liberation and independence (e.g., the "You've come a long way, baby" advertising campaign for Virginia Slims cigarettes) to present substance use as a positive way of expressing modern femininity. Although there is controversy as to whether advertising really has any impact on substance use (Davis, 1987; Smart, 1988), expenditures for advertising alcohol and cigarettes are high, and more and more advertisements are being specifically targeted to young people and women (Davis, 1987).

The impact of advertising is complemented by the design and marketing of alcohol and cigarette products that appeal directly to women. For example, the alcohol industry has developed products such as wine coolers (sweeter, lower in alcohol content, and less expensive than regular wines) and light beers (lower in calories and alcohol content than regular beers) that ease the initiation into drinking. The cigarette industry has developed a number of brands with names, colors, and sizes designed to appeal to women (e.g., Virginia Slims, Eve, Satin) and introduced low-nicotine cigarettes that may make it easier for young women to cope with their greater sensitivity to nicotine as they initiate smoking (Silverstein et al., 1980). The images in advertising are reinforced by presentation of substance use in other forms of media, all of which are representative of gender stereotypes in the culture (Grunberg et al., 1991). To the extent that such media presentations, specialized products, and advertising campaigns are successful, they serve to influence young women to initiate and maintain use of alcohol and cigarettes.

The social influences just described could have an impact on the initiation and maintenance of substance use of all individuals, regardless of gender. However, there are other initiation factors that either are specific to women and/or predominate among women. Two such factors that will be discussed are (a) childhood sexual victimization, which recent research suggests plays a role in the development of problem drinking among women, and (b) concern about weight as a factor in the initiation of smoking among women.

Victimization as a Factor in Women's Alcohol Abuse

Among those who have examined the effects of victimization, Miller and colleagues have documented a relationship between various forms of victimization and alcohol problems in women (Downs, Miller, & Gondoli, 1987; Miller, Downs, & Gondoli, 1989; Miller, Downs, Gondoli, & Keil, 1987; Miller, Downs, & Testa, 1990). Based on retrospective reports, alcoholic women were more likely to have been involved in delinquent activities when compared with a nonalcoholic household sample of women (Miller et al., 1989) and to have experienced childhood sexual abuse in greater frequency, duration, and variety than had nonalcoholic women (Miller et al., 1987). Alcoholic women also were more likely to have experienced moderate to serious violence and more father-to-daughter negative verbal interactions than either a nonalcoholic household sample (Downs et al., 1987; Miller et al., 1990) or a sample of nonalcoholic women either in treatment for mental health problems or receiving services for battering (Miller et al., 1990). Miller and colleagues (1990) suggest that as a result of their victimization experiences women develop "negative feelings about themselves and their lives, including lack of control, setting the stage for substance abuse as a coping strategy" (p. 1).

Although based on retrospective reports, these findings are compelling because they occur even when controls for a variety of confounds (e.g., demographic characteristics, alcohol problems of parents) have been implemented. In addition, they form part of a growing body of literature in which childhood victimization is being linked to a variety of negative psychological and behavioral outcomes, including substance abuse (Browne & Finkelhor, 1986; Hurley, 1991).

Concern About Weight as a Factor in Women's Initiation of Smoking

The trend for young women to evidence greater rates of smoking initiation than young men is disturbing. Among the factors that might explain this trend is the belief that smoking is an effective method for controlling weight, a belief seemingly based on fact. Since social norms emphasizing thinness have made weight control an important concern for many adolescent girls and young women, the likelihood that smoking could lessen weight creates a compelling reason to initiate and maintain smoking. Klesges, Meyers, Klesges, and La Vasque (1990) reviewed 70 cross-sectional and longitudinal studies on smoking and body weight and reported that in most of the cross-sectional studies smokers weighed significantly less than nonsmokers, with a tendency for moderate smokers (10-20 cigarettes per day) to weigh the least. Six of the eight studies in which main effects for gender were found indicated that weight differences were greater among women than among men, suggesting that women achieve more of the weight-control benefits of smoking. Similarly, in prospective studies of weight change related to smoking cessation, the results for 31 of 41 studies indicated that individuals who quit smoking gained weight to levels that were higher that those of nonsmokers (Klesges et al., 1990).

Although there is a paucity of research on the direct role of weight control in smoking initiation, there are studies that suggest such a relationship. Heavier-smoking adolescents, particularly girls, are more likely to agree that smoking controls weight (Charlton cited in Klesges et al., 1990). Among young women (ages 18 to 20 years) there are significantly more weight concerns among regular smokers than among nonsmokers (Feldman, Hodgson, & Corber, 1985). Overweight college women are more likely to report starting smoking for weight-control reasons than are normal-weight women (Klesges & Klesges, 1988), and women are more likely to intend to smoke than men (Page cited in Klesges et al., 1990).

The cigarette industry has reinforced these beliefs and tendencies by advertising and marketing cigarettes geared to women. Such products may have names that connote slimness (e.g., Virginia Slims, Silva Thins), have a longer, slimmer, profile than regular cigarettes, and/or have advertisements that feature slim, attractive, female models. Clearly these products represent attempts to capitalize on women's perception that smoking can assist in attempts to control their weight.

Health-Related Consequences
of Alcohol and Tobacco Use

Since appeals based on negative health effects of alcohol use and smoking are serving as the basis for public policy and prevention programs targeted at women, it is important to examine the current state of knowledge concerning the correlates and consequences of women's use of these substances. Health effects in three areas unique and/or important to women will be examined: risk for gynecologic and obstetric problems, fetal effects, and risk for coronary heart disease (CHD).

Health and Alcohol Consumption

While it is clear that at least two thirds of women consume alcoholic beverages, the health-related consequences of alcohol use have been much more extensively studied in men than in women. Much of the existent research on alcohol effects in women's health has focused on alcoholic samples. Alcoholic women share many of the health-related consequences experienced by men who engage in high levels of alcohol use (e.g., central nervous system damage, liver cirrhosis). However, women may suffer more severe health consequences of alcohol use than men, even though males typically have consumed more alcohol for longer durations (Hill, 1984). Even with significantly lower levels of alcohol intake than their male counterparts, female alcoholics have been found to experience greater mortality from a variety of health-related causes (cirrhosis, digestive disorders, hypertension) (Ashley et al., 1977; Hill, 1984; Saunders, Davis, & Williams, 1981).

Whether alcohol per se or alcohol's relationship to other risk factors mediates women's vulnerability to health problems is not clear. Alcohol consumption occurs within a life-style context that includes other health-related behaviors. Health-related behavioral risk factors related to the misuse of alcohol include being a heavy smoker and deviating from normal weight (Bradstock et al., 1988). Since smoking is implicated in the risk for a number of health problems (lung cancer, coronary heart disease), it is clear that women who drink are likely to engage in other behaviors that place them at risk for health problems.

Although the health consequences of problem/alcoholic drinking can be severe, research concerning the health effects of women's social drinking is the focus here. Examination of this topic seems timely because the majority of women are social drinkers, the move to assessing health effects of social drinking in women is gaining momentum, and there is an emerging sense that even nonalcoholic levels of drinking may increase a woman's vulnerability to health problems. The areas to be discussed are risk for gynecologic and obstetric problems, fetal effects of alcohol, and risk for coronary heart disease.

Alcohol Use and Risk for
Gynecologic and Obstetric Problems

Research indicating elevated levels of a variety of gynecologic and obstetric problems in alcoholic women has been a staple of the literature on alcohol abuse for the past few years. This research generally indicates that female alcoholics tend to experience menstrual problems (Beckman, 1979), have difficulty becoming pregnant (Beckman, 1979; Wilsnack 1973), have more hysterectomies (Morrissey & Schuckit, 1978), and have increased pregnancy and birth complications (e.g., spontaneous abortions, stillbirths) (Harlap et al., Kaminski et al., Sokol et al., all cited in Wilsnack, 1982).

Researchers also have examined levels of gynecologic problems in samples of nonalcoholic women. Wilsnack, Klassen, and Wilsnack (1984) studied reproductive problems in a representative national sample of 917 social-drinking women. Menstrual problems (e.g., painful menstruation, heavy flow) were related to increasing levels of alcohol use. However, rates of hysterectomy were lower among women who reported consuming 2 oz. of absolute alcohol (three to four drinks) per day. Rates of obstetric disorders (e.g., infertility, miscarriage) increased at higher levels of consumption (six or more drinks/day, three or more times/week). However, temporary abstainers (infrequent drinkers who had not consumed alcohol in the past 30 days) were the most likely to have reproductive problems. Wilsnack et al. speculate that these women may have chosen to abstain (temporarily) either because their gynecologic problems increased their concerns regarding their health or they found alcohol consumption to be less pleasant. They conclude that drinking and reproductive dysfunction are related in a general population, particularly in heavier drinkers, and propose a cycle in which gynecologic problems are both a consequence of heavy drinking and a contributor to such drinking.

An alternative approach to the question of the nature of the relationship between alcohol use and gynecologic problems is to examine levels of alcohol use in obstetric-gynecologic samples. Russell and Bigler (1979) reported that 11% of their sample of obstetric patients and 19% of their gynecologic patients were "probable or potential problem drinkers" (p. 8). Russell and Coviello (1988) reported that 17% of their sample of gynecologic outpatients were heavy drinkers. High levels of alcohol abuse also have been reported in women seeking gynecologic care (12%) and experiencing premenstrual syndrome (21%; Halliday, Bush, Cleary, Aronson, & Delbanco, 1986).

The rates of heavy drinking in gynecologic and obstetric samples (11% to 21%) are much higher than rates reported in the general population (3% to 7%). The consistency of findings from the studies just reviewed suggest that even in nonalcoholic general population samples, there is a positive relationship between heavy drinking and various reproductive problems. However, to date there is no evidence that light to moderate levels of alcohol consumption are related to reproductive problems.

Fetal Effects of Alcohol

Fetal alcohol syndrome (FAS) involves a variety of physical (e.g., facial dysmorphology) and psychological (e.g., retardation) effects seen in the offspring of women who consume large amounts of alcohol during pregnancy (Little & Ervin, 1984; NIAAA, 1987, 1990). Long-term follow-ups of FAS children suggest that effects, including low IQ, poor intellectual and academic functioning, physical anomalies, and maladaptive behavior, continue into adolescence and adulthood (Streissguth et al., 1991). These more dramatic FAS effects occur to children born of alcoholic mothers who drink excessively during pregnancy. Less dramatic fetal alcohol effects (FAEs) are said to occur with heavy drinking during pregnancy. Descriptions of the correlates and developmental deficits of FAS and FAE have led to an increasing interest in the fetal effects of light to moderate levels of alcohol consumption during pregnancy.

Due to the inception of a federal law in late 1989, alcoholic beverages now carry labels (and some drinking establishments display signs) that are designed to remind women that alcohol can adversely affect the fetus. These warnings have brought new attention to the issue of fetal effects related to the consumption of light to moderate amounts of alcohol. Generally, the research indicates that fetal effects occur along a continuum; the more severe consequences occur for offspring of mothers who drink excessively and more subtle effects occur as drinking decreases (NIAAA, 1987, 1990). For example, Streissguth and colleagues have followed a cohort of 500 children born to a sample of predominantly European-American, married, middle-class women, some of whom drank during pregnancy. The newborn offspring of heavy-drinking mothers showed impairments in areas such as central nervous system development and less vigorous body activity (Martin, Martin, & Streissguth, 1979; Streissguth, Barr, & Martin, 1983). Although physically normal, these children have continued to show some cognitive deficits at follow-ups conducted at 4 years (reduced attention and slower information processing; Streissguth, Martin, Barr, & Sandman, 1984) and 7 years of age (deficits in vigilance, reaction times, and distractibility; Streissguth et al., 1986). A number of cautions should be observed in interpreting these findings. Measures of alcohol intake were averaged across days, and therefore did not represent differing patterns of consumption (e.g., binge versus steady drinking; Streissguth et al., 1983). In addition, some of the effects were so subtle that statistical significance could be achieved only when large numbers of children were tested. These findings overall suggest that cognitive deficits occur for the offspring of heavy-drinking mothers, but no effects were reported for offspring of mothers at the lighter end of the drinking range.

The results of these and other studies (e.g., Gusella & Fried, 1984; Little, Asker, Sampson, & Renwick, 1986) suggest that fetal alcohol effects range widely from the more subtle cognitive deficits that occur as a result of heavy drinking during pregnancy to the physical anomalies evident in FAS. Research findings also suggest complex relationships among the woman's preexisting physiological state (e.g., nutrition), topography of drinking behavior, period of gestation, and fetal effects. For example, cases of FAS occur in much lower frequency than would be expected based on reports of excessive drinking in pregnant women. Sokol, Miller, and Reed (1980) reported only 5 FAS cases (2.5%) among 204 alcohol-abusing pregnant women. However, rates for a variety of fetal alcohol effects were high (50%), and smoking contributed independently to negative birth outcomes. If alcohol is uniformly teratogenic, then the FAS rate should be higher, suggesting that other factors, including the use of other substances, must be considered in determining the impact of alcohol use during pregnancy.

The alcohol-related variables that must be considered in understanding alcohol effects on the fetus include the mother's pattern of consumption (e.g., steady versus binge drinking), the amounts typically consumed, the peak blood alcohol level achieved, and individual differences in alcohol distribution and metabolism (NIAAA, 1987, 1990). In addition, characteristics of the mother and the pregnancy, such as the trimester of pregnancy during which drinking occurs, have some impact on alcohol effects. As Roman, Beral, and Zuckerman (1988) conclude in their critique of research on fetal alcohol effects:

> The evidence suggests that if alcohol does exert an adverse effect on pregnancy and prenatal development it is most likely to do so if consumed in large quantities by susceptible individuals. On balance the evidence for a dose-response relation is not convincing. Even with high levels of maternal alcohol consumption the strength and specificity of the association between alcohol intake and pregnancy outcomes remains to be clarified, as does the role of many potential confounding factors such as socioeconomic status, diet, prenatal infections, the use of other drugs, and the effects of home environment and upbringing. (p. 231)

Although FAS is associated with alcohol abuse during pregnancy, the evidence concerning fetal effects at lower levels of alcohol intake is inconclusive, and the consumption limit for no risk to the fetus cannot yet be specified. Specification of a level of minimal risk will be difficult, but it is an important issue for both public policy and public behavior. For example, the National Organization for Women (NOW) joined with restaurant and tavern owners in New York State to oppose a bill that required all establishments that served alcohol to display signs warning of the dangers of drinking during pregnancy (Sack, 1991). NOW's objections to the bill included the unfair focus on women's drinking and the implicit suggestion that the rights of the fetus override those of the pregnant woman. The bill passed in the State Assembly, and New York joined a number of other states and cities in which such laws exist. In Spring 1991 there was also a national debate about a case in which a pregnant woman (one week beyond her delivery date) ordered a strawberry daiquiri in a Seattle restaurant. Two waiters (a male and a female) recommended that, given her pregnancy, she should not consume alcohol. The woman, who says she had refrained from drinking during her pregnancy, had her drink and also complained to the restaurant management. Both waiters were fired. One week after the incident, the woman delivered a healthy baby.

Such cases raise myriad moral and legal issues, among which are whether the rights of the fetus outweigh the rights of the pregnant woman, and whether women's reproductive functions should be used as a means of controlling their substance use behavior (Kantrowitz, Quade, Fisher, Hill, & Beachy, 1991). It is not difficult to imagine guidelines suggesting that women trying to become pregnant refrain from alcohol use because of the potential dangers to the fetus during the time between fertilization and confirmation of the pregnancy. Perhaps all sexually active women of childbearing age should refrain from drinking because of the possibility of harm to the fetus in unplanned pregnancies. These scenarios may seem farfetched; however, once women's alcohol use is regulated based only on the *possibility* of fetal effects, decisions about women's individual rights become blurred.

Alcohol Use and Risk for Coronary Heart Disease

Women have a lower risk of coronary heart disease than do men, but their levels of risk are increasing. The role of alcohol consumption in

CHD risk is complex. There is consistent information that excessive drinking is associated with increased risk for CHD in both men and women (NIAAA, 1990). In addition, heavy alcohol use is positively related to life-style factors such as heavy smoking, which could interact with heavy drinking to potentiate CHD.

Rosenberg et al. (1981) studied relative risk for CHD in 513 women experiencing their first myocardial infarction (MI) and 918 control subjects, all less than 50 years of age. After the results were controlled for major confounds (e.g., smoking status, other medical conditions, education), current drinkers (86% of the sample drank on fewer than 4 days/week) were found to have a lower estimated relative risk of MI (0.7) compared with women who never drank. The relative risk did not vary significantly in relation to drinking frequency, although effects varied for different types of beverages, with a significantly lower level of risk (0.5) being evident for wine. Rosenberg et al. conclude that current drinkers have a significantly reduced risk of first infarction relative to those who never drink.

Stampfer, Colditz, Willett, Speizer, and Hennekens (1988) employed a prospective design to assess risk for CHD in a sample of 87,526 nurses. Consistent with general population surveys, 32% of the sample were abstainers, the majority of the sample were light to moderate drinkers, and less than 2% were heavy (three drinks/day) drinkers. After controlling for various confounds, the researchers found that risk for CHD was lower for drinkers relative to nondrinkers. Within drinkers, there was a decreased risk for CHD (0.6 to 0.4) as alcohol consumption increased. Given the prospective design and the consistency of their findings with previous research, Stampfer et al. speculate that the association between moderate alcohol use and lowered risk for CHD is causal.

These two examples of research on alcohol use and CHD risk among women are representative of the research to date. The findings of numerous studies suggest that moderate levels of alcohol consumption (one to two drinks per day) are related to lower risk for CHD in women (e.g., LaVecchia, Franceschi, Decarli, Pampollona, & Tognoni, 1987; Rosenberg et al., 1981; Stampfer et al., 1988). The mechanism for this "protective" function of alcohol is not clear. Alcohol increases plasma levels of high-density lipoprotein (HDL) and may thereby decrease CHD risk. There is evidence to suggest that alcohol's effects on HDL may occur at lower levels of alcohol consumption in women compared with men (Weidner et al., 1991), but further study of this phenomenon is warranted.

Health and Cigarette Smoking

Currently, almost equal proportions of men and women smoke, and men and women experience similar negative health consequences of smoking (e.g., increased risk of lung cancer and coronary heart disease). As with alcohol, more research on the health consequences of smoking is available for men than for women. However, given the recent trend for higher rates of smoking initiation among females, there is increased concern that over time negative health effects for women will occur with greater severity and will affect a greater proportion of female smokers. Such is the case with lung cancer, which has replaced breast cancer as the leading cause of cancer deaths among women (American Cancer Society, 1991). Smoking is also related to life-style factors (e.g., sexual activity, alcohol consumption) that may in and of themselves be related to health outcomes (Pederson & Stavraky, 1987). As more of the health consequences of smoking have become apparent, the trend in public policy has been to suggest that any amount of smoking increases vulnerability to a variety of health problems and that women therefore should not smoke.

Smoking and Risk for
Gynecologic and Obstetric Problems

One of the most common gynecologic effects of smoking is reduced fertility. When compared with women who never smoked, smokers have decreased likelihood of conceiving even when intending to become pregnant (Baird & Wilcox, 1985; Howe, Westhoff, Vessey, & Yeates, 1985). There also is evidence to suggest that smokers have greater risk for ectopic pregnancies and spontaneous abortions, but failure to control for potential confounds such as the occurrence of sexually transmitted diseases, which also affect these pregnancy outcomes, lessens confidence in these findings.

Women who smoke also have been found to reach menopause at earlier ages (average 1-2 years) than women who never smoked, with ex-smokers showing average increases of only 0.2 to 0.5 years (U.S. DHHS, 1990). Since menopause is linked to risk for serious health problems such as heart disease, osteoporosis, and cancers of the reproductive system, early menopause can represent increased health risk. As with many other negative health effects, stopping smoking decreases relative risk for gynecologic and obstetric problems such that with increased duration of cessation, the relative risk for former smokers becomes similar to that for women who never smoked.

Fetal Effects of Smoking

Although the prevalence of smoking during pregnancy has decreased (Kleinman & Kopstein, 1987), approximately 21% of pregnant women continue to smoke during pregnancy (Williamson, Serdula, Kendrick, & Binkin, 1989). In addition, smoking rates are said to be higher in groups of pregnant women who are unmarried, adolescents, and/or have fewer years of education (Kleinman & Kopstein, 1987), as well as in older women (35 years or older) and European Americans (Williamson et al., 1989). Common fetal effects of smoking are low birth weights, retarded fetal growth, and premature birth (U.S. DHHS, 1990). Mechanisms for smoking effects on pregnancy and pregnancy outcome seem to involve nicotine toxicity and carbon monoxide toxicity. As with alcohol, fetal effects of smoking appear related to dosage, such that the offspring of women who smoke more heavily during pregnancy show more effects than the offspring of women who smoke less and/or stop smoking, particularly if they stop smoking earlier in the pregnancy.

Birth weights of the babies of women who smoke are reduced by an average of approximately 200 grams, and smoking is said to double the likelihood of having a low-birth-weight baby (U.S. DHHS, 1990). Smoking is believed to have a causal relationship with low birth weight as well as low fetal growth, and various mechanisms have been postulated to account for this relationship. For example, carbon monoxide in cigarette smoke can cross the placenta and combine with hemoglobin to produce carboxyhemoglobin, which reduces the blood's ability to carry oxygen. Smoking is also said to decrease the blood flow to the placenta because it leads to constriction of the arteries in the umbilical cord. Many of these effects are reversible. For example, oxygen availability to the fetus has been shown to increase in as little as 48 hours after pregnant women stop smoking (Davies, Latto, Jones, Veale, & Wardrop, 1979).

It also has been postulated that some weight-gain deficits of the babies of mothers who smoke are related to impairment in the mother's ability to gain weight. When women have stopped smoking before the onset of pregnancy or during pregnancy, both they and their babies have experienced weight gains, in some studies registering even greater average weight gain during pregnancy than that found for women who never smoked (Kuzma & Kissinger, 1981; U.S. DHHS, 1990). Since most fetal growth takes place in the third trimester, the babies of women who stop smoking early in their pregnancies are less likely to show birth-weight and growth deficits.

Smoking and Risk for Coronary Heart Disease

Cigarette smoking serves as one of the three traditional risk factors for coronary heart disease, the other two being elevated levels of plasma cholesterol and hypertension. Reports of the increased risk for CHD among women seem related to the prevalence of cigarette smoking among women. In one of the most comprehensive studies of this issue, Willett et al. (1987) followed a sample of 119,404 female nurses for 6 years. Participants began the study between the ages of 30 and 55. At the start of the study, 30% of the sample were current smokers and all were free of a CHD diagnosis. During the follow-up, 242 women had nonfatal myocardial infarctions (MI) and 65 had CHD-related fatalities. Women who smoked had higher risk for CHD than women who never smoked. For example, women who smoked 25 or more cigarettes per day had a relative risk of 5.4 for fatal CHD compared with women who never smoked, and their risk for nonfatal MI was 5.8. Further, even light smoking (1-4 cigarettes per day) led to an increased relative risk of 2.4 when compared with not smoking. Rates rose progressively through the heaviest (more than 45 cigarettes per day) smokers, whose risk for CHD was 10.8. Approximately 58% of CHD in the lightest smokers and 91% of CHD in the heaviest smokers was attributable to smoking. Overall, rates attributable to smoking were 54% for nonfatal MI and 46% for fatal CHD. Relative risk for ex-smokers was virtually identical to that for women who never smoked. Across the entire sample, smoking also added to CHD risk for those women who already possessed a risk factor (e.g., parental history of MI, overweight). Willett et al.'s findings are consistent with a number of studies that indicate that women who smoke are at increased risk for CHD (U.S. DHHS, 1980, 1990) and provide support for the conclusion that smoking plays an important role in negative health outcomes for women.

Treatment of Alcohol Abuse and Smoking

Women's Issues in Treatment for Alcohol Abuse

Barriers to Seeking Treatment. As of 1987, approximately 24% of persons in treatment for alcohol abuse were female (NIAAA, 1990).

These data are consistent with the prevalence data indicating that fewer women than men have alcohol problems, but also has been interpreted as suggesting that women may not become involved in alcoholism treatment as readily as men. This is because women with alcohol problems face a number of barriers to treatment that may affect treatment initiation, the course of recovery, and maintenance of treatment gains (Beckman & Amaro, 1984, 1986; Duckert, 1987; Thom, 1986). First, based on traditional social norms, women who have drinking problems are more stigmatized than are men with such problems, and tend to fear such stigmatization (Thom, 1986). Women may face family issues, particularly those related to their role as homemaker and/or mother, which make it more difficult and disruptive for them to be involved in certain forms of treatment, such as inpatient programs (Beckman & Amaro, 1986). There are reports that the husbands of alcohol-abusing women are less supportive/tolerant than are wives of alcohol-abusing men (Beckman & Amaro, 1986). These husbands often fail to seek help for their wives, possibly because of their concerns about their own social stigmatization. Thus women often enter treatment as self-referrals or are brought into treatment by their parents, children, or other relatives (Beckman & Amaro, 1986; Thom, 1987).

Women's lower social position and/or lack of support from spouses may leave them to face treatment with fewer social and financial resources. There also is a lack of knowledge about alcohol abuse by women and/or a reluctance on the part of health professionals to diagnose women as having drinking problems. This is compounded by the fact that women, more so than men, tend to seek treatment from physicians and other health professionals, and cite problems other than alcohol as their presenting complaints (Marsh & Miller, 1985; Thom 1986). Availability of treatment also may be an issue; many facilities do not make provisions for women (Beckman & Amaro, 1984).

Given these barriers to treatment, it has been suggested that special efforts be made to recruit and treat women (Dahlgren & Willander, 1989). Others have suggested that the development of specific treatment approaches and/or the provision of ancillary services, such as child care, might result in better treatment outcome for women (Dahlgren & Willander, 1989; Duckert, 1987; Marsh & Miller, 1985). However, even marital and family approaches that seem tailored to meet women's treatment needs have tended to give little or no attention to women's issues (Collins, 1990). Aspects of alcohol treatment services that attract women include the provision of long-term treatment and aftercare services, psychiatric treatment for children, home visits, employment counseling, a casual social atmosphere, and availability of child care (Bander, Stilwell, Fein, & Bishop, 1983; Beckman & Amaro, 1984, 1986; Dahlgren & Willander, 1989). However, client characteristics such as social stability and higher functioning at intake have been the best predictors of abstinence over time (Bander et al., 1983).

Treatment Efficacy. Although female problem drinkers clearly bring a number of unique issues to treatment, most studies of alcoholism treatment outcome are based on programs in which men and women are treated in a similar fashion. Reviews of treatment outcomes report that a majority of studies show no gender differences in the efficacy of alcoholism treatment (Annis & Liban, 1980; Duckert, 1987; Toneatto, Sobell, & Sobell, in press; Vannicelli, 1984). For example, Annis and Liban's (1980) comprehensive review of all English-language studies conducted between 1950 and 1978 found that of 23 studies, 15 (65%) showed no significant gender differences in remission rates, 5 (22%) showed higher improvement rates in women, and 3 (13%) showed higher rates in men. Although many of these studies suffered from a variety of methodological ills (e.g., lack of randomization to treatment, small samples of women, failure to consider pretreatment characteristics of subjects), they are indicative of a general trend for men and women to react similarly to the same interventions.

Vannicelli's (1984) review of research from 1975 to 1979 found that 12 of 15 studies (80%) showed no significant gender differences in treatment outcome, 2 (13%) showed greater improvement in women, and 1 (7%) showed greater improvement in men. Most recently, Toneatto et al. (in press) examined 110 outcome studies on treatment for different forms of substance abuse. Most (84%, $n = 32$) of the 39 studies that focused on alcohol treatment included men and women, but only 13 (33%) of these studies reported on gender differences in outcome. Of these 13 studies, the majority showed women to function better than men, and the remainder showed no gender differences in outcome. In no case was men's functioning better than women's functioning. Interestingly, although appropriate numbers of women were being included in treatment studies, many researchers failed to analyze for gender effects. This continued failure to examine gender differences precludes definitive conclusions concerning the role of gender in alcohol treatment outcome.

Assessment of gender differences often can help to identify factors that predict women's response to alcohol treatment. Annis and Liban's

(1980) review indicates a variety of prognostic factors from single studies, but these factors do not tend to form a consistent pattern. Some studies have indicated a tendency for married female alcoholics to show greater improvement and for women who abused alcohol in addition to other substances to show less improvement. Women have tended to show greater ability to drink moderately following treatment (Helzer et al., 1985; Miller & Joyce, 1979; Sanchez-Craig, Leigh, Spivak, & Lei, 1989), even if treatment did not include a moderation goal (Helzer et al., 1985). Women also show increased ability to maintain moderation goals, even without formal treatment. Sobell, Cunningham, Sobell, Toneatto, and Kozlowski (1992) found that among Canadians reporting recovery from an alcohol problem on a national survey, 74% of the women and 54% of the men had returned to moderate drinking without receiving formal treatment. Similarly, among another sample of 120 individuals who had recovered from alcohol problems without formal treatment, more women (38%) returned to moderate drinking than to abstinence (13%). The opposite was true for men; a significantly greater percentage of men reported abstinence rather than moderate drinking following recovery (Sobell, Sobell, & Toneatto, 1992).

Pregnancy and Treatment for Alcohol Abuse. Pregnancy may provide a unique opportunity to intervene with women's drinking problems because concern about alcohol effects on the fetus can be a potent source of motivation to stop drinking. In addition, some pregnant women report revulsion at the taste and smell of alcohol, which sometimes lead to self-initiated cessation or reduction in alcohol use. Spontaneous abstinence rates as high as 45% have been reported in women interviewed during the second trimester of their pregnancy (Smith, Lancaster, Moss-Wells, Coles, & Falek, 1987). Among the predictors of continued drinking during pregnancy are a longer drinking history, alcohol-related problems, and drinking with family members.

Given the natural opportunity for intervention that pregnancy presents, and the identification of characteristics that potentially place women at risk for alcohol abuse, it is surprising that only a few studies of treatment for pregnant alcohol abusers exist in the literature, and most of these are at the level of demonstration projects or pilot studies. Rosett, Weiner, Zuckerman, McKinlay, and Edelin (1980) describe a program in which pregnant, heavy-drinking women participated in individual counseling focused on reducing their drinking. Approximately 36% (25 of 69) of the participants achieved either abstinence or significant reductions in drinking prior to the third trimester and maintained them through delivery. Pregnancy outcomes (e.g., baby's head size) were better for those who responded to the intervention.

Little and colleagues (1985) describe a demonstration project in which 304 pregnant women were treated. Approximately 38% of the women ($n = 115$) reported no problems with alcohol during the initial contact. Women with moderate to severe problems (35%, $n = 107$) were more likely to drink during pregnancy, to drink on a daily basis, and to use other drugs such as stimulants and marijuana. The intervention program focused on stopping drinking or reducing alcohol consumption during pregnancy. Dependent on need, participants received a variety of interventions, ranging from individualized counseling and group support to detoxification and inpatient alcoholism treatment. Although contact with the program tended to be brief (women with alcohol problems tended to keep an average of five appointments), the results indicated a steady decline in drinking, with particular lessening of heavy episodic drinking as pregnancy progressed. Increases in knowledge about alcohol effects on the fetus and decreases in anxiety and guilt also were reported. Pregnancy outcomes were more positive (bigger babies, higher Apgar scores) for those women who responded to the interventions. However, at the termination of their contact with the program, approximately 44% of the participants were still judged as having alcohol problems.

These innovative programs were relatively successful, even with seemingly modest interventions (Rosett et al., 1980) and limited contact (Little et al., 1985). Their results indicate that pregnancy can be a propitious time for intervening with female alcohol abusers and that benefits accrue to the pregnant women and their offspring. However, more research, involving better-controlled intervention programs, is needed.

Women's Issues in Smoking Cessation

The slower decline in women's smoking rates relative to men's has raised the possibility that women have more difficulty quitting smoking and/or maintaining abstinence. The apparent gender differences in quit rates may not reflect the true state of affairs. Jarvis (1984) has argued that men's higher rates of quitting may actually be a function of gender differences in the preference for different tobacco products. That is, men are more likely to switch from cigarettes to other tobacco products, such as pipes, cigars, or chewing tobacco. When cessation rates are adjusted to account for the secondary smoking of other tobacco products, the differences between genders become negligible (Jarvis, 1984; U.S. DHHS, 1990), suggesting the need for a more comprehensive definition of smoking cessation. Nonetheless, it seems worthwhile to consider those factors that might lessen the likelihood that women will attempt to quit smoking and/or successfully maintain abstinence from cigarettes.

Barriers to Smoking Cessation. First, women may see themselves as more addicted to smoking, and this may affect the frequency and success of their quit attempts. For example, Eiser and Van der Pligt (1986) assessed smokers' perceptions of their own smoking behavior and reported that although men and women had similar tendencies to see themselves as "sick" (i.e., concerned about health consequences), more women than men tended to perceive themselves as "hooked" on cigarettes (i.e., needed smoking to help cope and lacked confidence in their motivation and ability to quit smoking).

Some of these perceptions may be realistic; there is evidence that certain physiological mechanisms may make smoking more addictive for women than for men. One such mechanism involves gender differences in the metabolism and depletion of nicotine. There is some evidence that nicotine metabolism is accelerated by increasing the acid/base balance in the body, so that when smokers receive an acidifying agent (or an agent that lowers their urinary pH), they will increase their rate of smoking to maintain a constant blood nicotine level (Schachter, 1978; Schachter, Kozlowski, & Silverstein, 1977). This effect is more pronounced in women than in men (Silverstein, Kelly, Swan, & Kozlowski, 1982). In addition, women (smokers and nonsmokers) excrete nicotine more rapidly than do men (Grunberg et al., 1991), implying a need to maintain smoking as a means of forestalling negative withdrawal symptoms. Differential metabolism of nicotine, possibly related to variations in the menstrual cycle, also could have some impact on women's success in smoking cessation (O'Hara, Portser, & Anderson, 1989; Steinberg & Cherek, 1989).

Among the factors that can mediate the relationship between urinary pH and smoking is the experience of stress (Schachter, Silverstein, Kozlowski, Herman, & Liebling, 1977), and there is evidence that women are more inclined to use smoking as a strategy for coping with stress than are men (Biener, 1987). Due to their social position vis-à-vis men, women often have less control over the outcomes of stressful events and the resources needed to cope with stressors (Solomon & Rothblum, 1986). This could help to explain the reported tendency for women to use more emotion-focused coping strategies, including smoking and alcohol use, when faced with stressful situations (Biener, 1987; Eiser & Van der Pligt, 1986; Swan et al., 1988; Thom, 1986). More women than men use smoking as a way of handling negative affect (Ikard & Tomkins, 1973), some of which may be related to stress, and negative affect is related to smoking relapse (Cummings, Gordon, & Marlatt, 1980; O'Connell & Shiffman, 1988).

The societal emphasis on being slim, and other issues related to weight control, have already been cited as a factors in the initiation of smoking by female adolescents. Weight gain is a common sequela of quitting smoking (Grunberg, 1990; Klesges et al., 1989). Concerns about weight may affect many women's reluctance to attempt to stop smoking (Klesges et al., 1989) and their relapse following smoking cessation (Klesges & Klesges, 1988). Interestingly, actual weight gain following smoking cessation has not been predictive of relapse (Emmons, Emont, Collins, & Weidner, 1988; Hall, Ginsberg, & Jones, 1986). These barriers to quitting and to maintenance of abstinence must be addressed if smoking cessation programs are to treat women more successfully.

Treatment Efficacy. Men and women seem to differ in their attempts to quit smoking, as indicated by the following findings from the most recent surgeon general's report on smoking: (a) Overall, a larger proportion of women smokers (27%) had never tried to quit smoking, compared with men (22%); (b) although more women than men quit for at least one day, women's efforts to quit were less likely to be successful over the long term; and (c) significantly fewer women (18%) than men (24%) were able to maintain abstinence for 5 years or more (U.S. DHHS, 1990). These differences occur in spite of evidence that women participate in smoking cessation programs at higher rates than men (Orlandi, 1986).

Overall, the pattern of outcome for smoking cessation indicates high levels of success at posttreatment and poor maintenance over time (U.S. DHHS, 1990). Research on the efficacy of smoking cessation programs for women has produced inconsistent findings. For example, a review in which studies were categorized according to the nature of the intervention (e.g., physician's advice, behavior modification) reported that, although some studies showed no gender difference in treatment outcome, overall, women tended to have less successful long-term outcomes than did men (U.S. DHHS, 1980). Gritz (1980), who employed a similar categorization strategy, reports that most studies have shown no differences in the abstinence rates of men and women, at posttreatment and long-term follow-up. However, there have been cases in which men had more success than women, at posttreatment and long-term follow-up. Orlandi (1986) notes that men exhibited more success at stopping smoking through the 1970s. Since then, cessation trends for men and women have become more similar. The gender differences that occur seem related to the tendency for young women (ages 21 to 24) to be less successful at maintaining abstinence from cigarettes. Toneatto et al.'s (in press) review reports no gender differences in outcome, although in a few cases women had more success than men.

These reviews of treatment outcome suggest that although women may possess certain barriers to successful abstinence from smoking, their short-term responses to a variety of smoking cessation strategies are similar to men's responses. To the extent that there are gender differences in the long-term efficacy of smoking cessation programs, they may be related to women's inclination to cut down on smoking rather than to quit entirely, their tendency to make fewer sustained (longer than 1 week) attempts to quit (Blake et al., 1989), and younger women's failure to maintain abstinence (Orlandi, 1986).

Based on the research to date, interventions that might enhance women's maintenance of abstinence include (a) a focus on lessening initial withdrawal symptoms, for example, by using nicotine gum (Emont & Cummings, 1987); (b) training in the use of alternative, nonsubstance-related strategies for effectively coping with stress (Shiffman, Read, Maltese, Rapkin, & Jarvik, 1985); and (c) a focus on minimizing weight gain related to smoking cessation by using behavioral strategies (Klesges et al., 1989) and/or nicotine gum (Emont & Cummings, 1987).

Pregnancy and Smoking Cessation. As with alcohol abuse, pregnancy provides a unique opportunity for intervening with women smokers, particularly because of increased motivation related to concern about fetal effects of smoking. Spontaneous quitting rates for pregnant smokers have ranged from 22% (Windsor et al., 1985) to 40% (Aaronson, Ershoff, & Danaher, 1985; Quinn, Mullen, & Ershoff, 1991). Quinn et al. (1991) report that, compared with continuing smokers, spontaneous quitters in their sample had stronger beliefs in the harmful effects of maternal smoking, were more likely to have been lighter smokers, and were less likely to be exposed to other smokers in their homes. Most spontaneous quitters maintained abstinence through their pregnancies, resulting in an overall abstinence rate of 32% for the entire sample. This rate of abstinence, achieved without any formal intervention, was higher than the 10%-22% rate achieved with prenatal interventions (Ershoff, Mullen, & Quinn, 1989; Windsor & Orleans, 1986), suggesting that interventions to prevent relapses among pregnant abstainers would be an effective strategy for helping some women to stop smoking.

The Sociocultural Context of
Research on Women's Alcohol and Tobacco Use

Although many gains have been made in research on women's use of alcohol and tobacco, there is a need to study topics ranging from the role of genetic influences to the efficacy of different forms of treatment for women (Lex, 1991; S. C. Wilsnack & R. W. Wilsnack, 1990). Some of the limitations in the research to date can be addressed both by including women in research in sufficient numbers so that gender-based analyses can be conducted and by conducting analyses based on gender. All too often, the former occurs but the latter does not (see Toneatto et al., in press). In addition, the heterogeneity among women must be acknowledged. Sources of heterogeneity can vary from demographic characteristics (e.g., age, ethnicity, education) to gender identity and life roles. Although all of these considerations cannot be incorporated into every study, increased awareness of the role of these factors in alcohol use and smoking among women will lead to improvements in the conceptual and methodological rigor of research.

More specific to substance use, the inconsistencies in the findings in many areas suggest a need to define what constitutes the levels of consumption at which beneficial versus harmful effects are most likely to occur. There are striking differences in this realm for alcohol versus tobacco. Throughout history, most of the individuals who have consumed alcohol have done so as light to moderate social drinkers who experience positive social and psychological benefits without reporting untoward psychological or health-related consequences. Research on risk for CHD even suggests that light to moderate alcohol consumption may confer health benefits. Thus prospects for defining the specific levels at which beneficial versus harmful health effects of alcohol occur seem more varied. Consideration must be given to alcohol's physical effects as well as to the combination of alcohol use and other demographic or life-style factors that may increase risk for negative health outcomes. Clearly, efforts to preempt the move to heavy and/or abusive drinking are very important, and women should be encouraged to lessen their alcohol intake while pregnant and lactating.

Although the intermittent use of cigarettes by individuals without signs of nicotine dependence (so-called "chippers") has been described (Shiffman, 1989), such individuals are relatively rare. Thus the prospects for social use of cigarettes without developing an addiction to nicotine, and/or experiencing other negative health outcomes, are slim. For the most part, the research on women and smoking leads one to conclude that although tobacco use may confer benefits related to stress release and weight control, the health costs are great. Future prospects of designating a harmless level of tobacco use are likely to be limited; therefore, efforts to help women stop smoking must continue.

For both alcohol and tobacco use, it is important to consider the sociocultural context in which research is conducted and consumed, because it may flavor the interpretation of research findings on women. Given the moral reactions to alcohol consumption by women, sociocultural factors may predominate over empirical findings. For example, implicit in the conclusions of some of the research reviewed in this chapter (e.g., fetal effects of alcohol) and in the current social zeitgeist is the need for *all* women to lessen their consumption of alcohol. This is evident despite the fact that light to moderate levels of social drinking by women do not seem to represent a general hazard to physical health. It is possible that factors other than concern for the health consequences of women's alcohol use serve as the source of motivation for some of these strictures. One source of such motivation is the fact that alcohol consumption by women is still seen as representing a social hazard. In particular, women's deviation from their nondrinking roles may be seen as having the potential to destabilize the traditional (i.e., patriarchal) social order.

A case in point, brought to our attention by Fillmore (1984), is the fact that although epidemiological evidence concerning trends in women's drinking behavior has remained stable, interpretations of this evidence have either understated or overstated the problem as the cultural and political climate vis-à-vis women has varied. For example, research in the 1960s and 1970s found support for the notion that women who drank excessively were in conflict about their sex role (i.e., excessive drinking served as a masculine activity in which "feminine" women did not engage). More recent research has found alcohol consumption to be most strongly related to sex-role behaviors, not sex-role conflict (Chomak & Collins, 1987).

In the 1990s, appeals for maintenance of the social order via sustaining traditional sex roles are likely to be less persuasive than appeals/warnings based on scientific findings concerning negative health effects. Within this context, pronouncements on the health hazards of moderate drinking, even if based on equivocal empirical evidence, can serve as a social control on women's drinking behavior. To paraphrase Fillmore (1984): In a day when women are allegedly going through a social revolution by moving away from what are regarded as traditional female roles, the scientific establishment and the social ideology are clearly warning them that their drinking will retaliate in defiance of this movement. As we conduct and consume research on women's issues in alcohol use and smoking, it is important that we maintain an awareness of the sociocultural context in which women exist.

References

Aaronson, N. K., Ershoff, D. H., & Danaher, B. G. (1985). Smoking cessation in pregnancy: A self-help approach. *Addictive Behaviors, 10,* 103-108.

Aitken, P. P. (1985). An observational study of young adults' drinking groups: II. Drink purchasing procedures, group pressures and alcohol consumption by companions as predictors of alcohol consumption. *Alcohol & Alcoholism, 20,* 445-457.

American Cancer Society. (1991). *Cancer facts and figures: 1991.* Atlanta, GA: Author.

Annis, J. M., & Liban, C. D. (1980). Alcoholism in women: Treatment modalities and outcomes. In O. J. Kalant (Ed.), *Alcohol and drug problems in women: Research advances in alcohol and drug problems* (pp. 385-422). New York: Plenum.

Ashley, M. J., Olin, J. S., le Riche, W. H., Kornaczewski, A., Schmidt, W., & Rankin, J. G. (1977). Morbidity in alcoholics: Evidence for accelerated development of physical diseases in women. *Archives of Internal Medicine, 137,* 883-887.

Baird, D. D., & Wilcox, A. J. (1985). Cigarette smoking associated with delayed conception. *Journal of American Medical Association, 253,* 2979-2983.

Bander, K. W., Stilwell, N. A., Fein, E., & Bishop, G. (1983). Relationship of patient characteristics to program attendance by women alcoholics. *Journal of Studies on Alcohol, 44,* 318-327.

Barnes, G. M. (1990). Impact of the family on adolescent drinking patterns. In R. L. Collins, K. E. Leonard, & J. S. Searles (Eds.), *Alcohol and the family: Research and clinical perspectives* (pp. 137-161). New York: Guilford.

Bauman, K. E., & Chenoweth, R. L. (1984). The relationship between the consequences adolescents expect from smoking and their behavior: A factor analysis with panel data. *Journal of Applied Social Psychology, 14,* 28-41.

Beckman, L. J. (1979). Reported effects of alcohol on the sexual feelings and behavior of women alcoholics and nonalcoholics. *Journal of Studies on Alcohol, 40,* 272-282.

Beckman, L. J., & Amaro, H. (1984). Patterns of women's use of alcohol treatment agencies. In S. C. Wilsnack & L. J. Beckman (Eds.), *Alcohol problems in women* (pp. 319-348). New York: Guilford.

Beckman, L. J., & Amaro, H. (1986). Personal and social difficulties faced by women and men entering alcoholism treatment. *Journal of Studies on Alcohol, 47,* 135-145.

Bennett, L. A., & Wolin, S. J. (1990). Family culture and alcoholism transmission. In R. L. Collins, K. E. Leonard, & J. S. Searles (Eds.), *Alcohol and the family: Research and clinical perspectives* (pp. 194-219). New York: Guilford.

Biener, L. (1987). Gender differences in the use of substances for coping. In R. C. Barnett, L. Biener, & G. K. Baruch (Eds.), *Gender and stress* (pp. 330-349). New York: Free Press.

Blake, S. M., Klepp, K. I., Pechacek, T. F., Folsom, A. R., Luepker, R. V., Jacobs, D. R., & Mittelmark, M. B. (1989). Differences in smoking cessation strategies between men and women. *Addictive Behaviors, 14,* 409-418.

Bradstock, K., Forman, M. R., Binkin, N. J., Gentry, E. M., Hogelin, G. C., Williamson, D. F., & Trowbridge, F. L. (1988). Alcohol use and health behavior lifestyles among U.S. women: The behavioral risk factor surveys. *Addictive Behaviors, 13,* 61-71.

Browne, A., & Finkelhor, D. (1986). Impact of child sexual abuse: A review of the research. *Psychological Bulletin, 99,* 66-77.

Budd, R. J., & Spencer, C. P. (1984). Predicting undergraduates' intentions to drink. *Journal of Studies on Alcohol, 45,* 179-183.

Chassin, L., Presson, C. C., Sherman, S. J., & Margolis, S. (1988). The social image of smokeless tobacco use in three different types of teenagers. *Addictive Behaviors, 13,* 107-112.

Chomak, S., & Collins, R. L. (1987). Relationship between sex-role behaviors and alcohol consumption in undergraduate men and women. *Journal of Studies on Alcohol, 48,* 194-201.

Collins, R. L. (1990). Family treatment of alcohol abuse: Behavioral and systems perspectives. In R. L. Collins, K. E. Leonard, & J. S. Searles (Eds.), *Alcohol and the family: Research and clinical perspectives* (pp. 285-308). New York: Guilford.

Collins, R. L., & Marlatt, G. A. (1981). Social modeling as a determinant of drinking behavior: Implications for prevention and treatment. *Addictive Behaviors, 6,* 233-239.

Cooper, A. M., Waterhouse, G. J., & Sobell, M. B. (1979). Influence of gender on drinking in a modeling situation. *Journal of Studies on Alcohol, 40,* 562-570.

Cummings, C., Gordon, J. R., & Marlatt, G. A. (1980). Relapse: Prevention and prediction. In W. R. Miller (Ed.), *The addictive behaviors* (pp. 291-321). New York: Pergamon.

Dahlgren, L., & Willander, A. (1989). Are special treatment facilities for female alcoholics needed? A controlled 2-year follow-up study from a specialized female unit (EWA) versus a mixed male/female treatment facility. *Alcoholism: Clinical and Experimental Research, 13,* 499-504.

Davies, J. M., Latto, I. P., Jones, J. G., Veale, A., & Wardrop, C. A. J. (1979). Effects of stopping smoking for 48 hours on oxygen availability from the blood: A study on pregnant women. *British Medical Journal, 2,* 355-356.

Davis, R. M. (1987). Current trends in cigarette advertising and marketing. *New England Journal of Medicine, 316,* 725-732.

Downs, W. R., Miller, B. A., & Gondoli, D. M. (1987). Childhood experiences of parental physical violence for alcoholic women as compared with a randomly selected household sample of women. *Violence and Victims, 2,* 225-240.

Duckert, F. (1987). Recruitment into treatment and effects of treatment for female problem drinkers. *Addictive Behaviors, 12,* 137-150.

Eiser, J. R., & Van der Pligt, J. (1986). "Sick" or "hooked": Smokers' perceptions of their addiction. *Addictive Behaviors, 11,* 11-15.

Emmons, K. M., Emont, S. L., Collins, R. L., & Weidner, G. (1988). Relapse prevention versus broad spectrum treatment for smoking cessation: A comparison of efficacy. *Journal of Substance Abuse, 1,* 79-89.

Emont, S. L., & Cummings, K. M. (1987). Weight gain following smoking cessation: A possible role for nicotine replacement in weight management. *Addictive Behaviors, 12,* 151-155.

Ershoff, D. H., Mullen, P. D., & Quinn, V. P. (1989). A randomized trial of a serialized self-help smoking cessation program for pregnant women in an HMO. *American Journal of Public Health, 79,* 182-187.

Fawzy, F. I., Coombs, R. H., & Gerber, B. (1983). Generational continuity in the use of substances: The impact of parental substance use on adolescent substance use. *Addictive Behaviors, 8,* 109-114.

Feinhandler, S. J. (1986). The social role of smoking. In R. D. Tollison (Ed.), *Smoking and society: Toward a more balanced assessment* (pp. 167-187). Lexington, MA: Lexington.

Feldman, W., Hodgson, C., & Corber, S. (1985). Relationship between higher prevalence of smoking and weight concern amongst adolescent girls. *Canadian Journal of Public Health, 76,* 205-206.

Fillmore, K. M. (1984). "When angels fall": Women's drinking as cultural preoccupation and as reality. In S. C. Wilsnack & L. J. Beckman (Eds.), *Alcohol problems in women* (pp. 7-36). New York: Guilford.

Fillmore, K. M. (1987). Women's drinking across the adult life course as compared to men. *British Journal of Addiction, 82,* 801-811.

Fiore, M. C., Novotny, T. E., Pierce, J. P., Hatziandreu, E. J., Patel, K. M., & Davis, R. M. (1989). Trends in cigarette smoking in the United States: The changing influence of gender and race. *Journal of the American Medical Association, 261,* 49-55.

Gritz, E. R. (1980). Problems related to the use of tobacco by women. In O. G. Kalant (Ed.), *Alcohol and drug problems in women* (pp. 487-543). New York: Plenum.

Grunberg, N. E. (1990). The inverse relationship between tobacco use and body weight. In L. T. Kozlowski, H. M. Annis, H. D. Cappell, F. B. Glaser, M. S. Goodstadt, Y. Israel, H. Kalant, E. M. Sellers, & E. R. Vingilis (Eds.), *Research advances in alcohol and drug problems* (Vol. 10, pp. 273-315). New York: Plenum.

Grunberg, N. E., Winders, S. E., & Wewers, M. E. (1991). Gender differences in tobacco use. *Health Psychology, 10,* 143-153.

Gusella, J. L., & Fried, P. A. (1983). Effects of maternal social drinking and smoking on offspring at 13 months. *Neurobehavioral Toxicology and Teratology, 6,* 13-17.

Hall, S. M., Ginsberg, D., & Jones, R. T. (1986). Smoking cessation and weight gain. *Journal of Consulting and Clinical Psychology, 54,* 342-346.

Halliday, A., Bush, B., Cleary, P., Aronson, M., & Delbanco, T. (1986). Alcohol abuse in women seeking gynecologic care. *Obstetrics & Gynecology, 68*, 322-326.

Hammer, T., & Vaglum, P. (1989). The increase in alcohol consumption among women: A phenomenon related to accessibility or stress? A general population study. *British Journal of Addiction, 84*, 767-775.

Helzer, J. E., Robins, L. N., Taylor, J. R., Carey, K., Miller, R. H., Combs-Orme, T., & Farmer, A. (1985). The extent of long-term moderate drinking among alcoholics discharged from medical and psychiatric treatment facilities. *New England Journal of Medicine, 312*, 1678-1682.

Hill, S. Y. (1984). Vulnerability to the biomedical consequences of alcoholism and alcohol-related problems in women. In S. C. Wilsnack & L. J. Beckman (Eds.), *Alcohol problems in women* (pp. 121-154). New York: Guilford.

Hilton, M. E. (1987). Drinking patterns and drinking problems in 1984: Results from a general population survey. *Alcoholism: Clinical and Experimental Research, 11*, 167-174.

Hover, S. J., & Gaffney, L. R. (1988). Factors associated with smoking behavior in adolescent girls. *Addictive Behaviors, 13*, 139-145.

Howe, G., Westhoff, C., Vessey, M., & Yeates, D. (1985). Effects of age, cigarette smoking, and other factors on fertility: Findings in a large prospective study. *British Medical Journal, 290*, 1697-1700.

Hurley, D. L. (1991). Women, alcohol and incest: An analytical review. *Journal of Studies on Alcohol, 52*, 253-268.

Ikard, F. F., & Tomkins, S. (1973). The experience of affect as a determinant of smoking behavior: A series of validity studies. *Journal of Abnormal Psychology, 81*, 172-181.

Jacobs, G. A., Neufeld, V. A., Sayers, S., Spielberger, C. D., & Weinberg, H. (1988). Personality and smokeless tobacco use. *Addictive Behaviors, 13*, 311-318.

Jarvis, M. (1984). Gender and smoking: Do women really find it harder to give up? *British Journal of Addiction, 79*, 383-387.

Jessor, R., & Jessor, S. L. (1975). Adolescent development and the onset of drinking: A longitudinal study. *Journal of Studies on Alcohol, 36*, 27-51.

Kantrowitz, B., Quade, V., Fisher, B., Hill, J., & Beachy, L. (1991, April 29). The pregnancy police. *Newsweek*, pp. 52-53.

Kleinman, J. C., & Kopstein, A. (1987). Smoking during pregnancy, 1967-80. *American Journal of Public Health, 77*, 823-825.

Klesges, R. C., & Klesges, L. M. (1988). Cigarette smoking as a weight loss strategy in a university population. *International Journal of Eating Disorders, 7*, 413-419.

Klesges, R. C., Meyers, A. W., Klesges, L. M., & La Vasque, M. E. (1989). Smoking, body weight, and their effects on smoking behavior: A comprehensive review of the literature. *Psychological Bulletin, 106*, 204-230.

Kuzma, J. W., & Kissinger, D. G. (1981). Patterns of alcohol and cigarette use in pregnancy. *Neurobehavioral Toxicology and Teratology, 3*, 211-221.

LaVecchia, C., Franceschi, S., Decarli, A., Pampollona, S., & Tognoni, G. (1987). Risk factors for myocardial infarction in young women. *American Journal of Epidemiology, 125*, 832-843.

Leigh, B. C. (1989). In search of the seven dwarves: Issues of measurement and meaning in alcohol expectancy research. *Psychological Bulletin, 105*, 361-373.

Lex, B. W. (1991). Some gender differences in alcohol and polysubstance users. *Health Psychology, 10*, 121-132.

Lied, E. R., & Marlatt, G. A. (1979). Modeling as a determinant of alcohol consumption: Effect of subject sex and prior drinking history. *Addictive Behaviors, 4,* 47-54.

Little, R. E., Asker, R. L., Sampson, P. D., & Renwick, J. H. (1986). Fetal growth and moderate drinking in early pregnancy. *American Journal of Epidemiology, 123,* 270-278.

Little, R. E., & Ervin, C. H. (1984). Alcohol use and reproduction. In S. C. Wilsnack & L. J. Beckman (Eds.), *Alcohol problems in women* (pp. 155-188). New York: Guilford.

Little, R. E., Streissguth, A. P., Guzinski, G. M., Uhl, C. N., Paulozzi, L., Mann, S. L., Young, A., Clarren, S. K., & Grathwohl, H. L. (1985). An evaluation of the pregnancy and health program. *Alcohol Health and Research World, 10,* 44-59.

Marsh, J. C., & Miller, N. A. (1985). Female clients in substance abuse treatment. *International Journal of the Addictions, 20,* 995-1019.

Martin, D. C., Martin, J. C., & Streissguth, A. P. (1979). Sucking frequency and amplitude in newborns as a function of maternal drinking and smoking. In M. Galanter (Ed.), *Currents in alcoholism* (Vol. 5, pp. 359-366). New York: Grune & Stratton.

Mercer, P. W., & Khavari, K. A. (1990). Are women drinking more like men? An empirical examination of the convergence hypothesis. *Alcoholism: Clinical and Experimental Research, 14,* 461-466.

Miller, B. A., Downs, W. R., & Gondoli, D. M. (1989). Delinquency, childhood violence, and the development of alcoholism in women. *Crime & Delinquency, 35,* 94-108.

Miller, B. A., Downs, W. R., Gondoli, D. M., & Keil, A. (1987). The role of childhood sexual abuse in the development of alcoholism in women. *Violence and Victims, 2,* 157-172.

Miller, B. A., Downs, W. R., & Testa, M. (1990, August). *Relationship between women's alcohol problems and experiences of childhood violence.* Paper presented at the annual meeting of the American Psychological Association, Boston.

Miller, W. R., & Joyce, M. A. (1979). Prediction of abstinence, controlled drinking, and heavy drinking outcomes following behavioral self-control training. *Journal of Consulting and Clinical Psychology, 47,* 773-775.

Morrissey, E. R., & Schuckit, M. A. (1978). Stressful life events and alcohol problems among women seen at a detoxification center. *Journal of Studies on Alcohol, 39,* 1559-1576.

National Institute on Alcohol Abuse and Alcoholism (NIAAA). (1987). *Sixth special report to the U.S. Congress on alcohol and health* (DHHS Publication No. [ADM] 87-1519). Washington, DC: Government Printing Office.

National Institute on Alcohol Abuse and Alcoholism (NIAAA). (1990). *Seventh special report to the U.S. Congress on alcohol and health* (DHHS Publication No. [ADM] 90-1656). Washington, DC: Government Printing Office.

O'Connell, K. A., & Shiffman, S. (1988). Negative affect smoking and smoking relapse. *Journal of Substance Abuse, 1,* 25-33.

O'Hara, P., Portser, S. A., & Anderson, B. P. (1989). The influence of menstrual cycle changes on the tobacco withdrawal syndrome in women. *Addictive Behaviors, 14,* 595-600.

Orlandi, M. A. (1986). Gender differences in smoking cessation. *Women and Health, 11,* 237-251.

Pederson, L. L., & Stavraky, K. M. (1987). Relationship of smoking to lifestyle factors in women. *Women and Health, 12,* 47-66.

Pierce, J. P., Fiore, M. C., Novotny, T. E., Hatziandreu, E. J., & Davis, R. M. (1989a). Trends in cigarette smoking in the United States: Educational differences are increasing. *Journal of the American Medical Association, 261,* 56-60.

Pierce, J. P., Fiore, M. C., Novotny, T. E., Hatziandreu, E. J., & Davis, R. M. (1989b). Trends in cigarette smoking in the United States: Projections to the year 2000. *Journal of the American Medical Association, 261,* 61-65.

Quinn, V. P., Mullen, P. D., & Ershoff, D. H. (1991). Women who stop smoking spontaneously prior to prenatal care and predictors of relapse before delivery. *Addictive Behaviors, 16,* 29-40.

Roman, E., Beral, V., & Zuckerman, B. (1988). The relation between alcohol consumption and pregnancy outcome in humans. *Issues and Reviews in Teratology, 4,* 205-235.

Roman, P. M. (1988). *Women and alcohol use: A review of the research literature* (DHHS Publication No. [ADM] 88-1574). Washington, DC: Government Printing Office.

Rosenberg, L., Slone, D., Shapiro, S., Kaufman, D. W., Miettinen, O. S., & Stolley, P. D. (1981). Alcoholic beverages and myocardial infarction in young women. *American Journal of Public Health, 71,* 82-85.

Rosett, H. L., Weiner, L., Zuckerman, B., McKinlay, S., & Edelin, K. C. (1980). Reduction of alcohol consumption during pregnancy with benefits to the newborn. *Alcoholism: Clinical and Experimental Research, 4,* 178-184.

Russell, M., & Bigler, L. (1979). Screening for alcohol-related problems in an outpatient obstetric-gynecologic clinic. *American Journal of Obstetrics and Gynecology, 134,* 4-12.

Russell, M., & Coviello, D. (1988). Heavy drinking and regular psychoactive drug use among gynecological outpatients. *Alcoholism: Clinical and Experimental Research, 12,* 400-406.

Sack, K. (1991, April 5). Unlikely union in Albany: Feminists and liquor sellers. *New York Times,* pp. B1, B5.

Sanchez-Craig, M., Leigh, G., Spivak, K., & Lei, H. (1989). Superior outcome of females over males after brief treatment for the reduction of heavy drinking. *British Journal of Addiction, 84,* 395-404.

Saunders, J. B., Davis, M., & Williams, R. (1981). Do women develop alcoholic liver disease more readily than men? *British Medical Journal, 282,* 1140-1143.

Schachter, S. (1978). Pharmacological and psychological determinants of smoking. *Annals of Internal Medicine, 88,* 104-114.

Schachter, S., Kozlowski, L. T., & Silverstein, B. (1977). Effects of urinary pH on cigarette smoking. *Journal of Experimental Psychology: General, 106,* 13-19.

Schachter, S., Silverstein, B., Kozlowski, L. T., Herman, C. P., & Liebling, B. (1977). Effects of stress on cigarette smoking and urinary pH. *Journal of Experimental Psychology: General, 106,* 24-30.

Shiffman, S. (1989). Tobacco "chippers": Individual differences in tobacco dependence. *Psychopharmacology, 97,* 539-547.

Shiffman, S., Read, L., Maltese, J., Rapkin, D., & Jarvik, M. E. (1985). Preventing relapse in ex-smokers: A self-management approach. In G. A. Marlatt & J. R. Gordon (Eds.), *Relapse prevention: Maintenance strategies in the treatment of addictive behaviors* (pp. 472-520). New York: Guilford.

Silverstein, B., Feld, S., & Kozlowski, L. T. (1980). The availability of low-nicotine cigarettes as a cause of cigarette smoking among teenage females. *Journal of Health and Social Behavior, 21,* 383-388.

Silverstein, B., Kelly, E., Swan, J., & Kozlowski, L. T. (1982). Physiological predisposition toward becoming a cigarette smoker: Experimental evidence for a sex difference. *Addictive Behaviors, 7,* 83-86.

Smart, R. G. (1988). Does alcohol advertising affect overall consumption? A review of empirical studies. *Journal of Studies on Alcohol, 49,* 314-323.

Smith, I. E., Lancaster, J. S., Moss-Wells, S., Coles, C. D., & Falek, A. (1987). Identifying high-risk pregnant drinkers: Biological and behavioral correlates of continuous heavy drinking during pregnancy. *Journal of Studies on Alcohol, 48,* 304-309.

Sobell, L. C., Cunningham, J., Sobell, M. B., Toneatto, T., & Kozlowski, L.T. (1992). *Recovery from alcohol problems with and without treatment in a general population survey.* Unpublished manuscript.

Sobell, L. C., Sobell, M. B., & Toneatto, T. (1992). Recovery from alcohol problems without treatment. In N. Heather, W. R. Miller, & J. Greeley (Eds.), *Self-control and the addictive behaviours* (pp. 198-242). Botany Bay, NSW, Australia: Maxwell Macmillan.

Sokol, R. J., Miller, S. I., & Reed, G. (1980). Alcohol abuse during pregnancy: An epidemiologic study. *Alcoholism: Clinical and Experimental Research, 4,* 135-145.

Solomon, L. J., & Rothblum, E. D. (1986). Stress, coping, and social support in women. *The Behavior Therapist, 9,* 199-204.

Stampfer, M. J., Colditz, G. A., Willett, W. C., Speizer, F. E., & Hennekens, C. H. (1988). A prospective study of moderate alcohol consumption and the risk of coronary disease and stroke in women. *New England Journal of Medicine, 319,* 267-273.

Steinberg, J. L., & Cherek, D. R. (1989). Menstrual cycle and cigarette smoking behavior. *Addictive Behaviors, 14,* 173-179.

Streissguth, A. P., Aase, J. M., Clarren, S. K., Randels, S. P., LaDue, R. A., & Smith, D. F. (1991). Fetal alcohol syndrome in adolescents and adults. *Journal of the American Medical Association, 265,* 1961-1967.

Streissguth, A. P., Barr, H. M., & Martin, D. C. (1983). Maternal alcohol use and neonatal habituation assessed with the Brazelton scale. *Child Development, 54,* 1109-1118.

Streissguth, A. P., Barr, H. M., Sampson, P. D., Parrish-Johnson, J. C., Kirschner, G. L., & Martin D. C. (1986). Attention, distraction and reaction time at age 7 years and prenatal alcohol exposure. *Neurobehavioral Toxicology and Teratology, 8,* 717-725.

Streissguth, A. P., Martin, D. C., Barr, H. M., & Sandman, B. M. (1984). Intrauterine alcohol and nicotine exposure: Attention and reaction time in 4-year-old children. *Developmental Psychology, 20,* 533-541.

Swan, G. E., Denk, C. E., Parker, S. D., Carmelli, D., Furze, C. T., & Rosenman, R. H. (1988). Risk factors for late relapse in male and female ex-smokers. *Addictive Behaviors, 13,* 253-266.

Thom, B. (1986). Sex differences in help-seeking for alcohol problems: 1. The barriers to help seeking. *British Journal of Addiction, 81,* 777-788.

Thom, B. (1987). Sex differences in help-seeking for alcohol problems: 2. Entry into treatment. *British Journal of Addiction, 82,* 989-997.

Toneatto, T., Sobell, L. C., & Sobell, M. B. (in press). Gender issues in the treatment of alcohol, nicotine, and other drug abusers. *Journal of Substance Abuse.*

U.S. Department of Health and Human Services (U.S. DHHS). (1980). *The health consequences of smoking for women: A report of the surgeon general.* Washington, DC: Government Printing Office.

U.S. Department of Health and Human Services. (1990). *The health benefits of smoking cessation: A report of the surgeon general* (DHHS Publication No. [CDC] 90-8416). Washington, DC: Government Printing Office.

Vannicelli, M. (1984). Treatment outcome of alcoholic women: The state of the art in relation to sex bias and expectancy effects. In S. C. Wilsnack & L. J. Beckman (Eds.), *Alcohol problems in women* (pp. 369-412). New York: Guilford.

Weidner, G., Connor, S. L., Chesney, M. A., Burns, J. W., Connor, W. E., Matarazzo, J. D., & Mendell, N. R. (1991). Sex differences in high density lipoprotein cholesterol among low-level alcohol consumers. *Circulation, 83,* 176-180.

Willett, W. C., Green, A., Stampfer, M. J., Speizer, F. E., Colditz, G. A., Rosner, B., Monson, R. R., Stason, W., & Hennekens, C. H. (1987). Relative and absolute excess risks of coronary heart disease among women who smoke cigarettes. *New England Journal of Medicine, 317,* 1303-1309.

Williamson, D. F., Serdula, M. K., Kendrick, J. S., & Binkin, N. J. (1989). Comparing the prevalence of smoking in pregnant and nonpregnant women, 1985-1986. *Journal of the American Medical Association, 261,* 70-74.

Wilsnack, R. W., & Cheloha, R. (1987). Women's roles and problem drinking across the lifespan. *Social Problems, 34,* 231-248.

Wilsnack, R. W., & Wilsnack, S. C. (1990, June). *Husbands and wives as drinking partners.* Paper presented at the Sixteenth Annual Alcohol Epidemiology Symposium of the Kettil Bruun Society for Social and Epidemiological Research on Alcohol, Budapest.

Wilsnack, R. W., Wilsnack, S. C., & Klassen, A. D. (1987). Antecedents and consequences of drinking and drinking problems in women: Patterns from a U.S. national survey. In P. C. Rivers (Ed.), *Nebraska Symposium on Motivation 1986: Alcohol and addictive behavior* (pp. 85-157). Lincoln: University of Nebraska Press.

Wilsnack, S. C. (1973). Sex role identity in female alcoholism. *Journal of Abnormal Psychology, 82,* 253-261.

Wilsnack, S. C. (1982). Alcohol, sexuality, and reproductive dysfunction in women. In E. L. Abel (Ed.), *Fetal alcohol syndrome: Vol. 2. Human studies* (pp. 22-46). Boca Raton, FL: CRC.

Wilsnack, S. C., Klassen, A. D., & Wilsnack, R. W. (1984). Drinking and reproductive dysfunction among women in a 1981 national survey. *Alcoholism: Clinical and Experimental Research, 8,* 451-458.

Wilsnack, S. C., & Wilsnack, R. W. (1990). Women and substance abuse: Research directions for the 1990s. *Psychology of Addictive Behaviors, 4,* 46-49.

Wilsnack, S. C., Wilsnack, R. W., & Klassen, A. D. (1985). Drinking and drinking problems among women in a U.S. national survey. *Alcohol Health and Research World, 9,* 3-13.

Windsor, R. A., Cutter, G., Morris, J., Reese, Y., Manzella, B., Bartlett, E. E., Samuelson, C., & Spanos, D. (1985). The effectiveness of smoking cessation methods for smokers in public health maternity clinics: A randomized trial. *American Journal of Public Health, 75,* 1389-1392.

Windsor, R. A., & Orleans, C. T. (1986). Guidelines and methodological standards for smoking cessation intervention research among pregnant women: Improving the science and art. *Health Education Quarterly, 13,* 131-161.

13

The Codependency Movement:
Issues of Context and Differentiation

JUDITH R. GORDON

KIMBERLY BARRETT

The codependency movement has developed a huge self-help following and created multimillion-dollar markets in both the publishing
and treatment industries. Codependence has been described both as a
national epidemic affecting 96% of the population (Wegscheider-Cruse,
1985) and as "the chic neurosis of our time" (Lyon & Greenberg, 1991).
The construct of codependence has been attacked by significant seg-
ments of the professional and academic communities and by a wide
range of social commentators. Major criticisms are that it is conceptually weak and empirically unsubstantiated (Gomberg, 1989; Harper &
Capdevila, 1990; Katz & Liu, 1991; Peele, 1989), therapeutically iatrogenic (Haaken, 1990; Schnarch, 1991), simplistic (Gomberg, 1989;
Watson, 1991), ethnocentric (Brown, 1990; Ehrenreich, 1989; Kaminer,
1990, 1992; Luff, 1990; Rapping, 1990; Rieff, 1991; Tallen, 1990), and
insensitive to gender issues (Asher & Brisett, 1988; Brown, 1990; Gilligan,
1982; Haaken, 1990; Harper & Capdevila, 1990; Jordan, Kaplan, Miller,
Stiver, & Surrey, 1991; Lerner, 1989; Luff, 1990; Tavris, 1990; Walters,
1990). The concept of codependence raises questions about such

fundamental human values as caring, empathy, altruism, and interdependence. We believe it is important to understand the impact of this movement on the beliefs and behavior of its followers and members of the helping professions (including ourselves), and on broader cultural assumptions about healthy psychological development, relationships, and the nature of the self.

In two workshops that focused on issues of codependence in clinical practice (Gordon & Barrett, 1991), therapists expressed their frustration and concern regarding these issues in a discussion of ways in which their clients had presented problems related to codependent behaviors, dysfunctional families, and the "child within." Many personal questions regarding professional codependency issues also came up. Following are some anecdotal examples presented by clinicians in the group that illustrate some of the confusion around what codependence is:

- A young woman expressed anger in her therapy session because her college professor could not recognize her "inner child" during a meeting that involved selecting a topic for a research paper.
- A husband insisted that his marital unhappiness was due to his wife's "disease" of codependence and her need to control others, which he said she had developed through growing up in an alcoholic family. He felt that couple's therapy would be useless unless his wife attended an adult children of alcoholics or codependency group. He also questioned the therapist's personal beliefs and attitudes about the codependency model.
- A 42-year-old patient in a physical rehabilitation clinic reported a family history of alcohol and drug abuse. Although he himself was a very light and occasional drinker and reported no previous drug use, staff members were suspicious of a possible addiction to Tylenol and codeine, which had been prescribed following the patient's recent back surgery.
- A mother brought her 16-year-old daughter in for therapy because she was caught drinking after a high school football game. The mother described herself as an adult child of an alcoholic and stated with certainty that her daughter is now an alcoholic. She was considering hospitalizing her daughter in a 30-day treatment unit for adolescents. The daughter reported that her drinking occurred only at parties with friends about once a month, saying that her grades were excellent, and that she did not feel that her drinking is abnormal.
- A psychologist with a behavioral orientation had recently become a staff member for an inpatient drug treatment program. Her colleagues felt it important for her to examine her own issues of codependence as they emerged at work. This was a regular topic at weekly staff meetings for all

staff members. When she told her supervisor that she was not codependent, her supervisor stated that the staff as a group could help her work through her denial in order for her to be able to see and seek support in changing her codependent behaviors.

In this chapter we will describe the codependency movement, discuss why it has such appeal, and summarize controversies over relationship dynamics and models of addiction from sociopolitical, theoretical, empirical, and family systems perspectives. Finally, we will describe alternative explanatory models of phenomena the codependency construct refers to and provide treatment recommendations. Several excellent critiques of codependence have already been published (see, e.g., Brown, 1990; Haaken, 1990; Harper & Capdevila, 1990; Katz & Liu, 1991; Peele & Brodsky, 1991), so we will place greater emphasis in this chapter on perspectives from family systems theory and clinical research that have not been covered as extensively elsewhere.

Definitions and Brief History

The concept of codependence emerged from the traditional alcoholism treatment field. Wives of alcoholics had formerly been called highly negative names, such as Provocatrix, Controlling Catherine, Suffering Susan, Wavering Winnie, and Punitive Polly, referring to the neurotic, enabling role they presumably played in their spouses' addictive behavior. Al-Anon and 12-step alcoholism treatment settings were the first to apply the less judgmental terms *co-alcoholic, para-alcoholic,* and finally *codependent* to all members of any family with a chemically dependent member (Harper & Capdevila, 1990). Wegscheider-Cruse (1985) describes the predicament of those close to addicted individuals: "In many respects, the frantic and unremitting efforts to reach the addict become as compulsive as the behavior of the lost person" (p. xiii).

Codependence is considered to be a disease entity similar to substance addiction, except that in this case the sufferer is addicted to or preoccupied and obsessed with a relationship with another person instead of a mood-altering substance or behavior. "A codependent person is one who has let another person's behavior affect him or her and who is obsessed with controlling that person's behavior" (Beattie, 1987, p. 31). Application of the term *codependence* has broadened considerably beyond spouses of alcoholics. Whitfield (1992) sees codependence as a spiritual disease that is

> the most common of all addictions: the addiction to looking elsewhere. We believe that something outside of ourselves—that is, outside of our True Self—can give us happiness and fulfillment. The "elsewhere" may be people, places, things, behaviors, or experiences. Whatever it is, we may neglect our own selves for it. (p. 29)

Individuals vulnerable to this "disease" of "compulsive caretaking" include COAs (children of alcoholics), people in relationships with persons who are emotionally or mentally disturbed or chronically ill, parents of children with behavior problems, and professionals in the chemical dependency field and the helping professions (Beattie, 1987; Schaef, 1986; Wegscheider-Cruse, 1985). Hundreds of characteristics listed in the popular literature reveal a broad range of problems, including low self-worth, repression, obsession, compulsivity, need for control, denial, dependency, weak boundaries, lack of trust, anger, sexual problems, frozen feelings, perfectionism, and rigidity (Beattie, 1987; Mellody, 1989; Schaef, 1986; Wegscheider-Cruse, 1985).

Cermak (1986, 1991) has made the most rigorous attempt to develop psychiatric criteria to establish codependence as a mixed personality disorder (American Psychiatric Association, 1987) with characteristics similar to alcohol dependence, dependent personality disorder, borderline personality disorder, histrionic personality disorder, and PTSD. Since codependent personality traits are "widespread, just as narcissistic traits are virtually universal" (Cermak, 1991, p. 270), diagnosis of a personality disorder should be made only "in the face of identifiable dysfunction resulting from excessive rigidity or intensity associated with these traits" (Cermak, 1986, p. 16). Cermak (1986, pp. 16-17) proposes the following diagnostic criteria:

(1) continual investment of self-esteem in the ability to influence/control feelings and behavior in self and others in the face of obvious adverse consequences
(2) assumption of responsibility for meetings others' needs to the exclusion of acknowledging one's own
(3) anxiety and boundary distortions in situations of intimacy and separation
(4) enmeshment in relationships with personality-disordered, drug-dependent, and impulse-disordered individuals

(5) exhibits at least three of the following: constriction of emotions with or without dramatic outbursts, depression, hypervigilance, compulsions, anxiety, excessive reliance on denial, substance abuse, recurrent physical or sexual abuse, stress-related illness, and/or a primary relationship with an active substance abuser for at least 2 years without seeking outside support

In Cermak's (1986) model, codependence is a "disease of relationships" with the same core dynamics as narcissism, each arising from defective parental mirroring during early differentiation that impairs the capacity for healthy self-confidence and empathy (the pathological results of which are narcissism and codependence, respectively). Cermak (1991) hypothesizes that codependents and narcissists interact in symmetric, synergistic ways that reinforce both of them continuing to focus on the needs of the narcissistic member, as exemplified by the relationship between an alcoholic and his or her spouse.

To summarize, codependence as generally defined is thought to involve basing one's sense of identity, purpose, worth, and security on significant others, and perceiving their needs, wishes, thoughts, and feelings as more important than one's own. It is characterized by hypervigilance to interpersonal cues that is so compelling that it overshadows self-awareness, and a sense of responsibility for others that is so great that caretaking of others supersedes self-care. This preoccupation with others creates a tendency to try to control or manipulate their responses and behaviors. The codependent individual may suppress feelings, harbor anger and resentment, suffer from low self-esteem, and be trapped in the belief that there is no way out of the conflicted interpersonal web that would not be destructive to self or others.

Why is codependence so popular? Although the definitions are so broad and overinclusive that they perhaps create a Barnum effect, this is not enough to account for the phenomenal appeal of this latest offspring of the recovery movement. Our view is that the "symptoms" and diagnostic criteria for codependence do refer to common personal and relationship conflicts that many individuals experience and are attempting to cope with, but that rather than originating in dysfunctional families, these problems reflect certain late twentieth-century American sociocultural phenomena that are largely unacknowledged and unaddressed by proponents. These include issues related to power dynamics embedded in our culture, severe economic stresses and inequities, ethnocentricity, gender socialization, changes in the family and community, the decline of spirituality, and enormous shifts and disruptions in life-styles and values. There are also important theoretical and conceptual debates involving the disease model upon which all recovery movement groups are based. In the next section we review some of the major critiques pointing out the shortcomings and problematic implications of the codependency model.

Critical Issues Related to Codependence

Sociopolitical Perspectives

According to the sociology of deviance, what gets defined as illness is often constructed as a form of social control that reinforces cultural norms (Asher & Brisett, 1988; Sontag, 1978; Szasz, 1971) or avoids confronting larger cultural problems. Stein (1985), for example, views alcoholism as an "American cultural disorder" that functions as a group symptom formation directing our attention away from underlying conflicts in our society. In his interpretation, it is a disguised expression of repressed pain and anger associated with being part of an unresponsive political and cultural system. Proponents of codependence argue that whether or not the disease model of addictions is entirely accurate, and even if it is applied to codependence only as a metaphor, a medical diagnosis is beneficial because it allows for treatment expenses to be reimbursed by insurance. However, applying a medical model to emotional or behavioral problems too broadly has the potential to pathologize responses to an unhealthy environment, labeling them as symptoms of illness at the risk of stigmatizing "healthy but vulnerable people and miss[ing] the mark in terms of the development of genuine solutions" (Horn, 1991, p. 1).

Ehrenreich (1989), Kaminer (1990, 1992), Rapping (1990), and Tallen (1990) indict the recovery movement in general as a middle-class preoccupation with the problems of excess related to privilege while ignoring the true victims of substance addictions who live in poverty, suffer from sexism, racism, and other social inequities, and require much more complex institutional, social, and political changes. Similarly, Rieff (1991) discusses the "politics of victimhood" and criticizes the basic premise of the "recovery gurus to insist that we are all victims (mostly of bad parents) . . . thus diverting our attention from the true victims in our society" (p. 49).

The deviantizing of certain interpersonal behaviors as addictive and pathological and the devaluing of feminine-valued behaviors of caring and empathy have been particularly singled out by feminist critics, who charge that the codependency movement pathologizes, privatizes, and depoliticizes relationship problems that are rooted in larger sociocultural patriarchal structures (Luff, 1990). Brown (1990), Haaken (1990), and Miller (1986) note that all nondominant groups display behavior patterns involving extreme sensitivity and attention to the dominant group as a survival strategy. To blame women and other marginalized individuals for these patterns is tantamount to victim blaming. Having a problem should not be equated with being the problem. Walters (1990) argues that codependence blurs the power differential between the doer (e.g., the addict or the abuser) and the one allowing or even enabling the doing, holding women equally responsible for creating dysfunctional family patterns even though they do not have equal power to effect change. Women usually stay in bad relationships for economic and child-related reasons, not because they are neurotic or codependent: "The powerlessness that is falsely called codependency is the reality of survival in the alcoholic/addict home" (Van Wormer, 1989, p. 62).

Our most revered spiritual and world leaders are characterized by lives of altruism and self-sacrifice. We surely do not want to eliminate caring behaviors, sensitivity to others' needs and feelings, or the practice of generosity. Are there ways of understanding the descriptions of codependence without automatically assuming pathology? The popular descriptions seem to refer to a large domain of contradictory needs for individuality and togetherness that are at the core of all of our significant relationships with each other and the rest of the world. The difficulty of balancing individual needs and self-care with mutuality and altruism presents an ongoing challenge that becomes more complex when an adult member of a family, partnership, or communal group is unavailable to share mutual responsibilities. This lack of participation could be a result of physical illness or handicap, mental or emotional disturbance, or demanding external commitments such as work and career, and it could also include, for example, adults whose addictive disorders interfere with responsible parenting or partnership behaviors.

Another source of lack of balance in relationships is endemic to our society, which institutionalizes power differentials based on sex, race, economics, and related factors, and creates relationships at every level that are inherently unequal. Gender socialization within a patriarchal system is particularly relevant to codependence. Women are expected to be emotional and cooperative, to take responsibility for the interpersonal aspects of relationships, and to perform the caretaker role as their primary identity, with little emphasis placed on self-development and meeting their own individual needs. Men are trained to be instrumental, competitive, and autonomous, and receive little reinforcement for recognizing the emotional needs of themselves or others, prioritizing relationship needs, or actively fostering interdependence.

Such unbalanced relationships can engender one-sided caretaking that becomes increasingly excessive as the person in the caretaker role compensates by overfunctioning. The codependency movement recognizes the destructive effects of this dynamic and focuses on modifying the attitudes and behavior of the overfunctioners, but does not emphasize the interrelated necessity for change in the underfunctioners beyond perhaps working on their addictions. Women in general, caregivers of any age or sex, and members of marginalized, nondominant groups who engage in behaviors that are sex role linked, situationally adaptive, or survival oriented are at risk of being diagnosed with the disease of codependence, which Haaken (1990) suggests "describes the emotional condition of the oppressed" (p. 397). Bepko and Krestan (1990) comment:

> Women have always adapted, accommodated, and focused on others. To now label all forms of this behavior a sickness seems to blame women for doing too much of what they've been taught to do. . . . Rather than labeling these behaviors sick, we need to see them as potentially good behaviors that go to an unbalanced extreme in certain situations and become hurtful rather than helpful to everyone concerned. (p. 9)

How did these dynamics become so inextricably linked with addictive disorders and the recovery movement? A multiplicity of forces and developments in mainstream American culture have prepared a fertile ground for the emergence of a recovery group for individuals suffering from problems related to but not limited to addictive disorders. The increasing sense of alienation, absence of community, disillusionment with the American dream, lack of meaning, and feelings of helplessness regarding economics, politics, and the environment seem ubiquitous. Just as Alcoholics Anonymous developed in response to feelings of individual powerlessness over alcohol, it has become a prototype of 12-step self-help groups for people feeling powerless to end their suffering, as evidenced by the proliferation of all kinds of anonymous groups for people feeling out of control of a variety of behaviors. The benefits of such groups are that the existence of a common problem is the only membership requirement, they provide instant belonging and support nationwide and in some instances worldwide, they offer a spiritual as well as a human connection, they meet frequently and regularly, and they are nonhierarchical, nonprofessional, and free (Luff, 1990). As a whole, the recovery movement has been significantly more "user friendly" than the mental health field in terms of access, support, and providing simple explanations of human suffering (Treadway, 1990).

Because codependence originated out of Alcoholics Anonymous, it incorporated the disease model of addictions, which serves as the explanatory theory underlying the entire recovery movement and also provides the groundwork for medical or psychiatric diagnoses. But the application of the conceptualizations, etiology, assumptions, and terminology of addiction, disease, and recovery to relationships creates its own problems as well as bringing existing controversies over models of addiction into the codependence debate. We turn next to a consideration of controversies surrounding the disease model and the implications for codependency.

The Disease Model Controversy

The disease model of addictive behaviors that underlies codependence developed as an antidote to a moral approach, which indicted the addict as having a flawed character, lacking in self-discipline and willpower, and being entirely to blame for having the problem and responsible for recovering from it (Brickman et al., 1982). The disease model attempts to remove the blame and shame associated with having an addiction that one is unable to overcome. If addiction is a disease with biological causation, then the person is responsible neither for having the problem nor for its cure, but only for accepting powerlessness and seeking recovery by accepting outside help. Some members of AA view the disease concept as a metaphor for a spiritual "dis-ease" rather than a biological disorder, but the basic assumptions are the same and they are incorporated in all traditional recovery programs, including Codependents Anonymous, whose 12 steps are identical to the 12 steps of AA, except that the word *relationships* is substituted for the word *alcohol* (Beattie, 1987).

The traditional disease model rests on several basic assumptions. First, addiction is a progressive, irreversible disease from which there is no permanent recovery. Second, one is powerless over the disease and cannot recover on one's own but requires help from a higher power or spiritual redemption. Third, denial is a hallmark symptom of the disease, so individuals who resist viewing their problem in this framework are essentially manifesting the presence of the disease. Fourth, relapse is seen as a reemergence of the disease. Thus the individual must accept being in lifelong recovery and relying on help from an external source such as a higher power or a 12-step support group.

The popularity and proliferation of 12-step groups attest to their power in providing support to large numbers of people with addictive disorders, who presumably find the disease model assumptions helpful or at least acceptable. However, other individuals have difficulty reconciling these assumptions with taking personal responsibility for making choices and learning new behavior patterns. Whether seen as a metaphor or not, the disease model can be iatrogenic because it attributes the cause of the problem to internal unchangeable factors and locates the power to change outside the personal domain of the sufferer; this can be used by some individuals to rationalize not taking personal responsibility for their actions (Fingarette, 1988; Marlatt & Gordon, 1985; Peele, 1989; Peele & Brodsky, 1991; Schnarch, 1991). Another risk is that the assumption of chronicity and the need for lifelong recovery increases the probability that the addiction will function as a primary source of identity and the underlying context and cause of the addict's behavior and life generally, rather than being seen as a problem existing within the larger context of the individual's life (Peele, 1989).

Scientific controversies over the disease model and debates over its limitations have been covered elsewhere (see, e.g., Fingarette, 1988; Marlatt & Gordon, 1985; Peele, 1989), and it is not the focus of this chapter to review them. However, when this model is applied to relationship dynamics and interpersonal behaviors the problems become even more complex. It is hard to imagine what chronic disease could underlie relationships, or how such a disease could be worsening progressively if the individuals are no longer engaging in the problematic behaviors. When people identify strongly with the popular descriptions of codependence that overgeneralize from biological models of substance abuse, they unknowingly adopt all of the underlying disease model assumptions and philosophy without understanding the implications of these beliefs for their growth and development. Even the view that problematic or maladaptive interpersonal dynamics and behaviors are addictive, without any reference at all to the disease model, is problematic. While there is disagreement over whether or not "true" addictions must involve substance abuse, the common understanding of addictive behaviors is that they involve some sort of "quick fix" to gain immediate gratification or avoid emotional pain or the discomfort of physiological withdrawal from substances. The characteristic behavior patterns associated with codependence are indeed deeply ingrained, habitual ways to cope with difficult relationships and interpersonal situations that may be maladaptive, but they hardly look like quick fixes, providing neither instant gratification nor relief. It is stylish these days to see every problematic habitual behavior as an addiction, but the label is a serious one whose implications should not be taken lightly.

Empirical Questions and Data

The impact of a deviant or underfunctioning family member is always a source of stress in families, but this situation does not always create dysfunctional family members (Gomberg, 1989). There are no data to support diagnosing a personality disorder solely on the basis of being a member of a family in which there is substance abuse (Gomberg, 1989; Littrell, 1991). Nor is there empirical support for the common supposition that the spouse of an alcoholic will decompensate when the alcoholic stops drinking (Cronkite, Finney, Nekich, & Moos, 1990).

For example, Moos, Finney, and Cronkite (1990) found that a supportive family milieu and effective coping skills were related to the alcoholic's success in maintaining remission. Alcoholics with supportive families also demonstrated a broader range of coping responses. Active spousal coping responses, such as a wife's pleading with her husband to stop drinking, were related to a reduction in the husband's drinking. Moos and his colleagues (1990) found no support for theories of underlying personality disorders in wives of alcoholics or a worsening in their functioning as a result of remission in their husbands. These researchers describe spouses of alcoholics as "basically normal individuals trying to cope with disturbed marriages and dysfunctional partners" (Cronkite et al., 1990, p. 321). Children of alcoholic parents who were in remission were found to demonstrate physical and emotional functioning that was comparable to children in control families. The authors conclude that the negative effects of alcoholism on the family resolve after the family has benefited from a two-year period of sobriety.

Stress and social support appear to be critical issues for both alcoholics and their spouses. Cronkite et al. (1990), Jacob, Dunn, Leonard, and Davis (1985), and Steinglass (1981) found spousal impairments such as depression and physical complaints to be related to the alcoholic's psychological impairment and psychosocial dysfunction. Moos et al. (1990) also cite high levels of life stressors and low levels of social support as having negative impact on the alcoholic's recovery as well as spousal functioning.

The role of alcohol in family interaction presents an additional and complex set of variables seldom addressed in writings about codependence. For example, an increase in the expression of either positive or negative affect in the interactions of married couples has been found when the alcoholic is drinking (Littrell, 1991), and short-term problem solving, positive events, and experiences occur in families where steady-state drinking occurs. High degrees of marital satisfaction have been reported by some alcoholic spouses (Dunn, Jacob, Hummon, & Seilhamer, 1987; Jacob, Dunn, & Leonard, 1983; Moos et al., 1990). Jacob et al. (1983) found wives of steady-drinking alcoholics to be healthy and highly adaptive individuals, as opposed to wives of binge drinkers who exhibited more symptomatology, as did their binge-drinking husbands. The adaptive role of drinking in stabilizing the family unit is described by Steinglass, Bennett, Wolin, and Reiss (1987), and a contextual view of the role of alcoholic interaction as an attempt to cope with sociocultural stress is provided by Stein (1985) and Marlatt and Barrett (in press).

Two recent studies provide some of the first empirical data regarding codependent etiology and functioning. Lyon and Greenberg (1991) found in a study of college students that, compared with females from nonalcoholic families, daughters of alcoholic fathers were significantly more likely to volunteer to help an exploitative experimenter than a nurturing experimenter, not because they liked him but because he seemed to need nurturing. Lyon and Greenberg conclude that "codependents may not necessarily be lacking in self-esteem but may simply derive their self-worth from maladaptive relationships" (p. 438), and observe that the codependency phenomenon "is not a new one, but an old one dressed up in new language" (p. 436) originally identified by Horney (1942) as "morbid dependence." While these results do suggest differences between daughters from alcoholic families and those from nonalcoholic families, they neither establish the existence of pathology nor support the hypothesized characteristic of low self-esteem. Examination of such women's actual relationship choices outside of analog laboratory experiments would lend more weight to these findings. Further, such patterns of caretaking may be the result of growing up with persons with all kinds of needs, rather than alcoholism per se. Therefore, it would be illuminating to add a third group consisting of daughters from families with a parental dysfunction other than alcoholism. An older sample needs to be studied as well.

A study by Bensley and Spieker (1992) found that COA status may be an advantage in generating not dysfunctional but positive caretaking behaviors. When these researchers compared the parenting behavior of COAs and non-COAs within a sample of adolescent mothers, COAs and their children consistently scored higher than their peers on three observational measures across two points in time. The assessment instruments they used were the Nursing Child Assessment Teaching Scale, measuring mother-child interactions in a teaching situation; the Child's Game/Parent's Game/Cleanup, measuring mother-child interactions in a structured play situation; and a behavioral measure of attachment security. They conclude that, at least for this group, caretaking qualities that may have been developed in response to a dysfunctional parent serve some adaptive function rather than being pathological. An adolescent girl who has been required to care for herself and possibly a dysfunctional parent from an early age may be better prepared than her peers for the early responsibility of teen parenthood.

Family Systems Perspectives

Although the use of the term *dysfunctional family* has linked the codependency movement to a family systems model, there are several clear distinctions between a *family disease* view of addiction (Black, 1981; Bradshaw, 1988; Brown, 1990; Cermak, 1991; Schaef, 1986) and a *family systems* view of addiction (Bennett & Wolin, 1990; Jacob, Ritchey, Cvitkovic, & Blane, 1981; Kaufman & Kaufmann, 1979; Stanton & Todd, 1982; Steinglass et al., 1987). It is noteworthy that family systems theory has evolved through over 30 years of clinical work, detailed family observation and research, and ongoing theoretical dialogue by major systems theorists such as (Don) Jackson, Bateson, Bowen, Haley, Madanes, Minuchin, Stanton, Steinglass, Weakland, and Watzlawick.

Steinglass et al. (1987) review the basic tenets of family systems theory and homeostasis:

> The family is constantly being subjected to a potentially overwhelming series of challenges. . . . aware of this multiplicity of internal and external stresses, the observer of family behavior cannot help but be impressed by the ability of the family to manage and control these challenges. Despite

living in a constantly changing environment, and despite sudden and unpredictable encounters, the family is able to maintain a sense of balance, a coherence, a regularity to its life. (p. 49)

Steinglass et al. discuss Don Jackson (1957), who first used the term "family homeostasis" to describe how specific mechanisms or behaviors enable families to respond to disruptive internal or external forces such as job stress, illness, financial hardship, depression, and marital conflict. Coping strategies and problem-solving behaviors help the family return to a state of balance and healthy functioning. Family problems arise when there is a malfunction in one or more homeostatic mechanisms, which Steinglass et al. (1987) refer to as "family regulatory mechanisms." Steinglass et al. caution, however, that these regulatory mechanisms are not concrete, observable structures (such as family boundaries), but are really only metaphors that can be used to describe family behavior. They state that if these metaphors are described as actual properties of the family, "they are being misused" (p. 53). An example of how family regulatory mechanisms operate in a homeostatic manner is illustrated in the following case example.

A family requested therapy for their 12-year-old daughter, Susan, because she frequently feigned illness and refused to go to school. A previously excellent student, Susan also regularly failed to turn in her homework, even when she had completed it to her parents' satisfaction, and flunked tests that she was well prepared for. Her parents, both busy professionals, were frequently called to school for conferences, and had become very involved in helping Susan to resolve her problem. The therapist learned that Susan's father had suffered a heart attack in recent months, yet refused to slow down at work and reduce his stress level. Both parents continued to maintain excessively demanding social and professional lives, despite the father's weakened physical condition. Susan, however, had succeeded in "slowing down" their schedules through her self-initiated "vacation" from school. The therapist reframed Susan's behavior by saying that Susan was "on strike" in response to the family's stressful life-style. Next, the therapist asked Susan when her father had last spent a Saturday morning in his pajamas. No one in the family could remember the last time he had even been at home on a Saturday morning. An assignment was given to him to stay home in his pajamas the following Saturday morning. Two weeks later, the family returned to therapy, with Susan and her father holding hands and laughing. Susan smiled from ear to ear as she told the therapist, "My daddy spent a whole weekend in his pajamas, and we made a deal that if he works a little less, I will work a little harder in school!"

In this case example, Susan's parents failed to utilize coping mechanisms and problem-solving behaviors that would help the father and the family adapt to his heart condition. Susan's attempts to get her family to slow down are an example of homeostatic regulatory mechanisms (or behaviors) that were used in the absence of appropriate responses from her mother and father. Although of negative consequence to her, Susan achieved the development of a new balance or focus in the family system that took her parents away from their work schedules, and "helped" her father to stay healthy by spending more time at home with her.

In family systems theory (Haley, 1976; Madanes, 1981; Steinglass et al., 1987), many problematic family behaviors, including alcohol use, can be viewed as problem-solving behaviors. For example, if a couple has difficulty communicating and expressing anger, the introduction of drinking into the evening's activities may lead to an angry encounter about drinking in which many emotions are expressed and other disagreements can be resolved. Or the symptom of drinking may be a distraction from a more serious problem, such as chronic depression in a spouse or other family member.

Cermak's (1986) use of the term "family systems approaches" and his descriptions of the family disease of alcoholism are lacking in both the detail and conceptual coherence that integrates the traditional family systems-based theory of alcoholism and addiction (Kaufman & Kaufmann, 1979; Steinglass, 1981). Cermak discusses unspoken rules, implicit roles, identity disturbances, and the development of a "false self" in his "systemic" description of family dysfunction. Roles are described in a few limited caricatures (also used by Black, 1981; Wegscheider-Cruse, 1985). It is not made clear how these terms relate to the actual functioning of a family system. However, the use of terms for "roles" calls attention to the warnings of Steinglass et al. (1987), who caution against labeling family behaviors as concrete structures. Cermak's disease model criteria exclude explorations of functionality, adaptability, or coping in the family. The etiology of the disease is not defined, yet the family is designated as the transmitter, for "the disease passes through the family as a whole" (Cermak, 1986b, p. viii). Cermak also quotes Schaef's description of a "systems" theory—codependence as a "disease that has many forms and that grows out of a disease process that is inherent in the system in which we live" (p. viii).

Bradshaw (1988) has resurrected the concept of shame as "the essence of codependency," one of many syndromes in his diagnostic criteria for shame-based disorders. Bradshaw has had perhaps the greatest public impact of the movement leaders, producing several books, television specials, and auditorium-sized road shows on "the family." The family system is the source of shame and is headed by needy, shame-based parents who cannot take care of their own children. Bradshaw coins his own brand of family homeostasis, saying that "shame-based families operate according to the laws of social systems" and that dysfunctional families "take care of the system's need for balance" (p. 26). Bradshaw's ideas of balance and homeostasis do not take into account the families' attempts to adapt, cope, and stay together as a family unit (Orford, 1990). Instead, the type of balance alluded to by Bradshaw is described as a balance attained only for the sake of balance rather than for the purpose of maintaining the family. This distorts family systems theory and reverses the principle that families develop their own systems, heterogeneous in nature, in order to negotiate life tasks that are continuous and changing, both inside and outside of the family environment. Families utilize interrelated behaviors that facilitate a process of growth and development, while maintaining cohesion and togetherness. Though sometimes maladaptive, these behaviors are attempts to meet the needs of the family and its members, rather than designed to take care of the needs of a "system" as though it had a life of its own.

In an attempt to capture and exhibit the rigid and static nature of dysfunctional families, Bradshaw (1988) and other popular proponents of the disease model of addiction and codependence have been overly rigid in their portrayal of what are considered the "inescapable dynamics" of addiction. Their vast generalities and overly inclusive criteria for "diagnosis" have labeled and homogenized the identities of millions of individuals and thousands of families. The product of this reduction is the "dysfunctional family," a highly profitable commodity for the treatment community. They have packaged the use of genograms, family maps, structural diagrams, and terminology "borrowed" from the work of the traditional family systems theorists, adding disease model labels and paraphrasing definitions and terms. Such materials, previously developed for careful use by professionals in order to form flexible, clinical hypotheses with the purpose of understanding and treating the dynamics of family problems, have now been set in print for the public to use in self-diagnosis or cocktail party family therapy. Unfortunately, knowing how to describe a family dynamic does not provide the tools and methods that are necessary to facilitate change.

Potter-Efron and Potter-Efron (1989a) make an attempt to clarify the definition of codependence, using an alcoholic family model as a "paradigm from which to gather information about co-dependency" (p. 38). As with Bradshaw's criteria, strengths, coping skills, and attempts at adaptive family interaction are not recognized. Despite their emphasis on the family dynamics of addiction and utilization of a family model, treatment in their program is based on an individual orientation, on the assumption that the codependent can change "without regard to whether or how the alcoholic changes" (Potter-Efron & Potter-Efron, 1989b, p. 151). The program "neither requires nor anticipates participation from the alcoholic or other family members" (p. 151). This is quite contrary to traditional systemic family models. A major treatment goal that Potter-Efron and Potter-Efron describe is working toward detachment, used as an Al-Anon term, but related to Bowen's theory of individuation and differentiation. This detachment involves establishing a sense of independence while working toward interdependence. The authors state that independence must be established before interdependence can occur, but given that "most active alcoholics are incapable of interdependence" (1986b, p. 161) new relationship skills must be practiced with "others" deemed healthier than the alcoholic.

This treatment philosophy reflects a divide-and-conquer attitude toward addictive families (see Steinglass et al., 1987). Family members are often squeezed into program components designed to fit preconceived notions about alcoholics and their family members. For example, Asher and Brisett (1988) found that the self-labeling of codependent women was initiated, guided, and legitimated through attendance in treatment programs. This kind of labeling obscures a woman's personal sense of self and redefines coping behaviors as deviant rather than cooperative.

Family therapist David Treadway (1990) observes that "the strength of the codependency movement is that instead of describing interactive processes between components of a system, it portrays the thoughts and feelings of people in terms they can relate to emotionally" (p. 42), in contrast to family therapy, which never developed a popular language that caught on. But developing a "popular language" has not been a major goal of family therapy. Rather, the recognition that interactions between people have a significant impact on the emotional development and processes of each individual has been the major theoretical, clinical, and investigative thrust in a paradigm that offers treatment for individuals as well as for families. The "language" of traditional family therapy reflects a philosophy that minimizes labeling, discourages use of diagnostic categories, and argues against the deviantizing of troublesome behaviors. Treadway's assumption that there is an "ongoing integration of the chemical dependency field and family therapy" (p. 42) can be questioned in that most assumptions of codependent models are antithetical to family systems theories and practice.

In a close examination of codependency theories and the family, there is a great potential to promote blame, to fuel anger and guilt, to follow a narrow focus on pathology and inadequacy, and to reduce individuality and heterogeneity among families touched by addiction and trauma. Perhaps the most serious issue is that the codependency movement may serve to divide family members who are already extremely discouraged about their relationships and personal competence, and to seed doubts in family members of alcoholics who have been resilient, maintaining a high degree of social and psychological competence despite significant stress. This is not a model that builds on the strength and integrity of the family, or that examines social interactions in an environmental context, but rather a model that judges family and individual processes from a medical and deviance perspective.

Alternatives to Codependence

Family Systems and Family Coping Approaches

In contrast to the views posited by disease model approaches, a summary of family systems and stress and coping models of alcoholism as presented by Orford (1990) describes the use of alcohol in the family as "purposive, adaptive, and meaningful." Orford outlines research findings from major studies conducted since 1976 that demonstrate the functionality of alcohol use from interactional and coping perspectives. Family systems models, as described above, view alcohol use and patterns of alcoholic family interaction as attempts at problem solving and maintaining family stability. Coping models (Marlatt, 1992; Marlatt & Gordon, 1985; Moos et al., 1990; Wills, 1985) discuss the use of alcohol as a method of coping with sociocultural and psychological stressors. In that interactional models deemphasize the importance of the stressors experienced by the alcoholic family, and stress and coping models often ignore the interactional nature of family dynamics, Orford urges consideration of both models, suggesting an integration of stress and coping and family systems theories. Such an integrated model could take into consideration both internal and external family stressors, the use of alcohol in coping with stress, and the family's attempts to cope with the stress of living with an alcoholic. Orford points to the work of Moos and Finney (1983), Moos et al. (1990), and Wilson (1983) as the most parsimonious alternative. An integrative model could thus accommodate a broad range of family dynamics, incorporating the individual characteristics of family members, environmental stresses, interfamily stresses, and degrees of alcohol use into methods of diagnosis and treatment.

The issue of family heterogeneity is specifically addressed by several family researchers who have studied the differences that emerge through the observation of familial patterns of addiction (Bennett, Wolin, & Reiss, 1988; Bennett, Wolin, Reiss, & Teitelbaum, 1987; Jacob et al., 1981, 1983; Moos et al., 1990; Stanton & Todd, 1982; Steinglass, 1981; Steinglass et al., 1987). Three major areas of investigation have yielded results that support the notion of subgroups and variability in family styles and in individual coping responses to alcohol problems. These areas include descriptions of (a) variability in the mental health status of the alcoholic, family members, and types of family interactions; (b) a developmental model of the tasks and stages in family life in relation to addiction; and (c) the risk and protective factors that have a role in determining the intergenerational transmission of alcoholism.

In the presentation of the family life history model of alcoholism, Steinglass et al. (1987) state that there is little evidence to suggest that clinicians are approaching alcoholism with a "sophisticated sense of family dynamics or family systems principles," or with an appreciation for the heterogeneity of families that are being served. Twelve-step models are criticized for creating a "separate but equal" mode of intervention, separating family members into their own treatment groups. Despite promising outcomes in the limited family therapy studies that exist, the inclusion of the family vis-à-vis a traditional family therapy approach has not been a primary aspect of traditional alcohol treatment programs, though such programs often include treatment for codependence.

Steinglass et al.'s (1987) family life history model offers diagnostic criteria that utilize family systems theory in a developmental framework that draws a distinction between alcoholic families and "families with alcoholic members." This distinction recognizes the importance of family heterogeneity in both diagnosis and treatment of families affected by alcoholism. When alcohol has invaded three critical areas of family functioning, identified as short-term problem solving, daily routines, and family rituals, the family is seen as needing more extensive treatment. Treatment is also geared specifically to the developmental phase in the family life cycle. Using some of the terminology from the progressive disease model, in early-phase alcoholism, problems are related to the development of the new family identity, through a new family's process of differentiation from the families of origin. Middle-phase treatment focuses on alcohol's functioning in short-term problem solving and family rigidity, and late-phase treatment addresses issues of transmission of values to the next generation. Steinglass et al. are careful to emphasize the danger of treatment approaches that "plug each family member into a standard treatment package." They advocate therapy that addresses the developmental phases and needs of each family and each family member. Like Moos, Jacob, and others, Steinglass et al. point out that many families successfully cope with alcoholic members, protect the family environment from the demands of alcoholism, and actively exclude drinking alcoholics from important family activities and rituals.

Similarly, Bennett et al. (1987, 1988) and Steinglass et al. (1987) found that the development of a coherent family identity is a protective factor in the transmission of alcoholism from one generation to the next. Daughters or sons of alcoholics who selectively disengage from negative aspects of alcoholic family life, and who are active in planning and carrying out family rituals and routines, are less likely to carry the problem of alcoholism into their nuclear families. Bennett et al. (1988) found that children from alcoholic families in which a high degree of organization, routine, and ritual were observed were highly functional socially, emotionally, and intellectually, compared with children in highly disrupted alcoholic or control group families where routine and ritual were not maintained. The process of consciously planning and carrying out rituals and traditions is termed "deliberateness" and has been found to be a significant protective factor in minimizing the risk of intergenerational transmission of alcoholism.

The potential for adverse effects of alcoholism on the family is undisputed (see Littrell, 1991; Moos et al., 1990; Orford, 1990), but the variability in family characteristics and interactional patterns, positive outcomes related to adaptive coping and resilience in family members, and protective factors related to disruption of intergenerational transmission of alcoholism are not discussed in the codependency literature.

Family systems and coping models offer methods of diagnosis and treatment that are far more specific than disease models in their understanding of family dynamics and in the assessment of the stresses that contribute to drinking. Family members are better respected and served when met with a view that posits health and coping resources rather than assuming illness or diagnosable characteristics such as codependence.

Biopsychosocial Model of Addictive Behaviors

An alternative model of addictions is the biopsychosocial or relapse prevention model (Marlatt, 1992; Marlatt & Gordon, 1985; Peele, 1989). This empirically based model assumes that addictive behaviors are not a result of either weakness of character or disease, but are essentially like bad habits that result from a complex interaction of biological propensities, psychosocial and cultural influences, pharmacological effects, and learning principles. These factors contribute to the development of unconscious, automated, habitual styles of reacting and coping, and addictive behaviors are viewed as maladaptive attempts to cope with problematic situations. Individuals are not to blame for developing these compulsive, overlearned responses, but are responsible for learning and practicing new, more adaptive habits and modifying their life-styles to support them.

Goals are not imposed from the outside, but are based on individually determined needs, values, and choices. Change occurs, with or without outside help, as a function of awareness, learning, and taking responsibility. In contrast to the need to accept powerlessness that is emphasized in 12-step programs, relapse prevention focuses on the development of self-efficacy, or the feeling of competence and self-confidence that one can cope effectively with specific high-risk situations. Such confidence develops as one learns to respond effectively and succeeds in doing so over time. Numerous studies have shown that self-efficacy is related to reduced rates of relapse (Marlatt & Gordon, 1985). Relapses are viewed as lapses into old ways of coping that are mistakes that can be learned from, signs that motivation needs rekindling, or indications that goals may need revision. Problem behaviors are not assumed to be permanent or to justify automatically a psychiatric diagnosis or a lifetime identity as an addict, a victim, or a survivor.

Relapse prevention principles have recently been integrated with behavioral marital and family therapy (Cawthra, Borrego, & Emrick, 1991; O'Farrell & Cowles, 1989). It is hypothesized that treatment outcomes can be improved for both alcoholics and their family members when the entire family is involved in understanding and preventing the relapse process (Marlatt & Barrett, in press; McCrady, 1989). Rather than blaming family members for their participation in an alcoholic's drinking cycles, or assuming collusion, enabling, or codependence, relapse prevention models in conjunction with behavioral marital therapy (Murphy, O'Farrell, Floyd, & Connors, 1991) offer an active approach to teaching family members about the relapse process and how to prevent it. This includes learning to recognize the signals that point to a risk of relapse and then practicing new adaptive behaviors to cope with high-risk situations. For example, negative emotional states, particularly anger and conflict in relationships, are both well-known triggers for relapse (Marlatt & Gordon, 1985). Assertiveness, communication, and negotiation skills can be learned and utilized to minimize conflict and anger, and hence prevent relapse.

Behavioral and family systems models of therapy have much in common. They both emphasize the importance of recognizing and building on strengths and resources that already exist within individuals and families. They focus on the capacity for new learning in the development of more effective coping skills. And they normalize problems as attempts to cope, believing that pathologizing tends to disempower and discourage people. The strength of the relapse prevention approach lies in its specificity of behavioral assessment and focused interventions. The strength of family systems models is the detailed focus on interpersonal processes. Thus there is great potential for cross-fertilization between these two frameworks in the treatment of families with addictive members.

Differentiation, the Relational Self, and the Morality of Care

A separate aspect of family systems theory that is particularly helpful in understanding and depathologizing the construct of codependence involves Bowen's ideas about differentiation of self and togetherness, key elements of the emotional system he conceptualizes to explain people in relationships and families (Kerr & Bowen, 1988).

> Family systems theory assumes the existence of an instinctually rooted life force [individuality] . . . in every human being that propels the developing child to grow to be an emotionally separate person, an individual with the

ability to think, feel, and act for himself. Also assumed is the existence of an instinctually rooted life force (togetherness) that propels child and family to remain emotionally connected and to operate in reaction to one another. . . . Differentiation describes the process by which individuality and togetherness are managed by a person and within a relationship system. (Kerr & Bowen, 1988, p. 95)

Similar to attachment, a related biological survival mechanism underlying behaviors that promote bonding and connectedness is togetherness, which

propels an organism to follow the directives of others, to be a dependent, connected, and indistinct entity. . . . The level of stability, cohesiveness, and cooperation in a group is affected by the interplay of individuality and togetherness [that] results in emotionally significant relationships existing in a state of . . . dynamic equilibrium. (p. 65)

An alternative to what is currently lumped together into a global pathological construct of codependence is a continuum of differentiation on which, theoretically, every human being is constantly balancing. According to Bowen's theory, at lower levels of differentiation, togetherness needs are stronger and "the individuality of a very poorly differentiated person is practically nonexistent" (Kerr & Bowen, 1988, p. 65). The poorly differentiated person is "so responsive to cues from the other and his internal reactions are so intense that he is a complete 'emotional prisoner' of the relationship" (p. 69).

At this point in the discussion, the poorly differentiated person starts to sound more and more like the descriptions of the codependent. "The competing forces of attachment and separation . . . [often result] in what feels like both an addiction to the other and a chronic urge to flee" (Kerr & Bowen, 1988, p. 77), and in attempts to adapt to the other to preserve harmony and relieve anxiety, the one who adapts more loses self, or "de-selfs" (p. 84). Finally, "the more a person adapts to preserve harmony in the system, the more likely he is to feel that his own functioning is out of control and that his well-being depends on the way others respond" (p. 86).

Bowen believes that it is extremely difficult to increase one's level of differentiation without intensive effort; parents "transmit" their own level of differentiation to their offspring, resulting in multigenerational transmission, and most people thus remain at fairly low levels. Recognition of the vast potential of most human beings for further emotional development is a nonpathologizing alternative to the statement that 96% of the American population is codependent.

To us, codependent behavior patterns look like manifestations of the developmental process of differentiation that evolves along a continuum of balancing individuality and togetherness needs. This dynamic is present in all of our relationships and is most visible in the domains of intimate relationships and resulting self-esteem. Pathologizing the entire continuum of differentiation and offering help based on shared pathology can actually work against developing the sense of personal empowerment and self-efficacy necessary to becoming more highly differentiated. In his application of Bowen's theory to relationship therapy, Schnarch (1991) accuses the entire recovery movement of actually impeding differentiation: "Calling oneself an 'addict' offers an identity to people with little solid-self: the label also offers instant acceptance, group membership" (p. 519), and actually works against differentiation from that group. He continues:

> "Healing the wounded child" enshrines childhood narcissism, vulnerability, and dependency as the paradigm of intimacy and eroticism . . . ; the codependence movement reduces grown men and women to "adult children." . . . [Its] answer to the emotional immaturity of adult children is to encourage more child-ness. (p. 520)

Perhaps 12-step programs actually create codependence by fostering a new lifelong dependency on the group and a higher power.

A limitation of Bowen's theory is that it does not specifically address gender differences in carrying out the tasks of differentiation, or deal with the cultural prejudices that place less value on the togetherness side of the balance and greater value on the individuality side. A new "self- in-relation" development model suggests that we all function in a vast web of interrelatedness, and that humans are best understood not as separate selves but rather as relational selves (Chodorow, 1978; Gilligan, 1982; Jordan et al., 1991; Miller, 1986). Surrey (1991) integrates Bowen's concepts with these recent conceptualizations and proposes a "relationship-differentiation" theory to describe a developmental growth process that goes beyond separation-individuation in which the self is understood as developing in the context of specific relationships. Relational empowerment and interdependence form the ongoing ground for continuing self-development, and values of affiliation, connection, mutuality, and empathy are essential in the development of a healthy self (Miller, 1986).

Gilligan and Wiggins (1987), in their examination of the origins of morality in early childhood relationships, offer a conceptual breakthrough toward the understanding of gender differences in attitudes toward caretaking behavior that is directly relevant to the codependency construct. They propose that the universal childhood experiences of inequality and attachment, along with the associated fears of being oppressed or abandoned, lay the groundwork for two "moral visions"—one of justice and one of care. These lead to two different moral injunctions—not to treat others unfairly and not to turn away from someone in need—and these two themes become organized and expressed differently in male and female development as a function of gender role socialization. The "justice orientation" and the "care orientation" that result entail distinct and often conflicting notions of morality, conceptions of emotions, and values placed on relationship behaviors.

> Detachment, which is highly valued as the mark of mature moral judgment in the justice framework, becomes in the care framework a sign of moral danger, a loss of connection with others. The sharp subject-object distinction that is considered essential to development in most psychological theories thus is called into question and a more fluid conception of self in relation to others is tied to the growth of affective imagination, namely, the ability to enter into and understand through taking on and experiencing the feelings of others. (p. 287)

In this model, these gender differences do not imply either the moral superiority of one sex or a biological basis of moral behavior, but illuminate the "paradigmatic human moral problems . . . that arise when demands of equality and demands of attachment clash" (p. 283). In our culture the archetypally male morality of justice has been considered morally superior, and women have been judged morally inferior. Women tend to follow an archetypally female ethic of care rather than abstract principles of justice in relationships. We would argue that this assumption of the inferiority of the morality of care may be an unconscious underpinning of the codependency construct, which perpetuates the devaluing of care.

Gilligan and Wiggins (1987) adopt a term from the Czechoslovakian writer Milan Kundera, "co-feeling," which denotes a type of compassion that is "the art of emotional telepathy," or an act of affective imagination that connects self with others. Without this capacity, the individual becomes egocentric, loses contact with the feelings of others, and reacts based on egocentric judgments. Gilligan and Wiggins suggest that we must value and develop both the morality of justice and the morality of care in both men and women, or "as men and women we can become both cold and sentimental when genuine attachments fail" (p. 303). Especially in this culture, we need to recognize and value co-feeling if we are to encourage greater empathy and responsibility in all our relationships.

Along these lines, we suggest shifting away from the pathologizing emphasis of codependence, with its implied disavowal of dependency needs and disregard for tendencies toward compassion and empathy, toward an exploration into how to develop and cultivate the capacity for co-feeling in all of us as a basis for true interdependence and psychological health.

Recommendations for
Mental Health Professionals

Although most leaders of the codependency movement advocate self-help group treatment for their patients (Bradshaw, 1988; Cermak, 1986; Schaef, 1986), the clinicians working in a variety of mental health settings are the ones who must face the nuts and bolts of treatment. They must address the newly, often self-diagnosed codependents, adult children of alcoholics, and other shadows of addiction that appear in their practice. Treadway (1990) writes, "Lately, in my practice, it seems like every day is codependency day" (p. 40). It is essential when recommending interventions to differentiate among different individuals who are currently being indiscriminately grouped together as codependent.

Codependency proponents challenge therapists to examine their own levels of codependence and to engage in necessary treatment in order to be effective in their work. Cermak (1986), Schaef (1986), and Treadway (1990) make strong statements of inclusion when it comes to seeing the mental health profession as part of a large group of "practicing" codependents. Treadway (1990) feels that the concept may be "threatening" to therapists, and speculates that, "in fact, the therapy profession may have a higher proportion of codependents than any other field" (p. 42). Cermak (1986) states that codependent therapists need therapy "often as long as two years or more" in order to reduce "active" codependence on the job (p. 94). If you come from a chemically dependent family, becoming a treatment professional puts you at greater risk for having unresolved codependency tendencies "activated." Cermak goes on to describe how the very nature of our work also leads to active codependence, listing every major task, role, skill, frustration, reward, and dynamic of the therapist and the therapy relationship as being a potential mine field for codependent behavior and feelings. Thus for the general clinician, as well as for those who are working more directly with addictions treatment and research, clarity about codependence is essential on both personal and professional levels.

In our view, the broad acceptance of the terminology and construct of codependence by the popular culture is unfortunate, because it conceptually links several extremely complex spheres of human experience without determining whether and how they might be interrelated: relationship dynamics, developmental processes, sociopolitical structures, addictive disorders, and spirituality. Codependence stigmatizes individuals, particularly women, blames families for being dysfunctional, and distracts us all from gaining a deeper understanding of and developing more effective ways of coping with normal developmental tasks, relationship and intimacy issues, larger social and cultural issues, and the suffering of the true victims of addiction. While it may be too late to delete the word from our vocabulary, we can encourage those who identify with descriptions of codependence to distinguish between their own experiences and extraneous conceptual baggage and beliefs. Such material can deflect clients from their goals for authentic connection and genuine empowerment and interfere with a natural movement toward interdependence.

For the general clinician, as well as for those who are working more directly with addictions treatment and research, the tasks and practicalities of treatment and investigation become threefold. First, it is important to undertake a balanced study of the current issues, empirically based outcome and etiological research, and various clinical approaches in the field of addictions, including consideration of the social contexts and stresses in which family patterns of addiction occur. Second, it is important to become clear about one's own theoretical orientation and personal position in respect to the topics of addiction and codependence; this orientation can be used both as a diagnostic framework for work with clients and as a tool for self-reflection in order to be clear regarding one's role as a "helper." Third, it is important to develop flexible strategies that allow one to integrate one's orientation and personal stance into work with clients and/or research subjects in a way that still allows room to explore beliefs that may be different from one's own. For example, if a clinician's theoretical orientation is in disagreement with the 12-step philosophy and a client presents who attends a 12-step group and finds it helpful, the therapist must attempt to integrate the two viewpoints in treatment. If a client is self-diagnosing as codependent, it is important for the therapist to find out what beliefs and meanings the individual associates with this label, and to provide some education about alternative views and models that might broaden the client's understanding and open up more options. This could result in the client's dropping the self-diagnosis, but it could also result in the therapist's accepting the client's label but working with the client to redefine underlying assumptions and associated goals and change strategies. In terms of research, an understanding of conflicting models can lead to empirical studies and papers that attempt to substantiate or refute popular notions of codependence, addiction, and treatment success or failure, rather than blindly accepting or rejecting them due to investigator or author bias.

As our discussion of sociocultural critiques makes clear, some of what is currently being diagnosed as codependence and addiction calls for intervention at societal levels that go beyond the individual and the family (Barrett, 1992; Peele, 1989; Stein, 1985). Clinicians must not ignore victims of power inequities, sexism, racism, and poverty through an exclusive focus on personal and family pathology. Rather, clinicians can actively address issues that warrant political action and social change and create an awareness of those issues for clients as they become relevant in therapeutic exchanges. Clinicians can also encourage clients to become active in helping to change the sociological conditions that create problems in their lives. Ewart (1991) discusses the effectiveness of social action as a therapeutic tool as well as a viable means for promoting social change.

In the absence of clear, empirically based diagnostic criteria, it is essential to avoid overgeneralizing all presenting problems that seem related to addiction or popular definitions of codependence. Most of the examples presented in the beginning of this chapter illustrate the current tendency to see codependence everywhere, especially if an individual has a family member with an addiction problem, or does a lot of caretaking, or is a member of the helping professions, or has shaky self-esteem or relationship problems.

We acknowledge the important contribution made by the codependency movement in capturing public attention and raising awareness about issues related to psychological and emotional health of individuals and families. However, it is now time to get back to the work of evaluating, assessing, discriminating, and intervening in ways that are conceptually more coherent and thorough and empirically more amenable to careful investigation and study.

Concluding Remarks

Controversies over codependence reflect essential dilemmas of late twentieth-century America regarding the relationship between self and other, problems of helping and caring and caretaking, gender dynamics, and institutionalized power differentials. The basic survival value of dependency needs often goes unacknowledged in our Western search for independence and autonomy. Counterdependence, or the denial of healthy dependency needs, is culturally acceptable, and instead codependence is diagnosed when compensatory unreciprocated and nonmutual caring behaviors become excessive. New developmental models question whether it is even possible for individuals to achieve a clear sense of an autonomous or "true" self distinct from and independent of significant others. A related issue is whether the Western notion of a separate self is a social construction and, as Eastern philosophy has long contended, an illusion. We have a long way to go toward developing effective models of healthy interdependence that can guide us in our relationships with ourselves, one another, and the global environment with which we coexist.

People in all cultures have struggled for millennia with the dilemmas of balancing togetherness and individuality, caretaking of self and others, and the morality of justice and care, and will surely continue to do so forever. We close with an ancient story, related by Thich Nhat Hahn (1987):

> There is a story . . . about a father and a daughter who performed in the circus. The father would place a very long bamboo stick on his forehead, and his daughter would climb to the top of the stick. When they did this, people gave them some money to buy rice and curry to eat. One day the father told the daughter, "My dear daughter, we have to take care of each other. You have to take care of your father, and I have to take care of you, so that we will be safe. Our performance is very dangerous." Because if

she fell, both would not be able to earn their living. If she fell, then broke her leg, they wouldn't have anything to eat. "My daughter, we have to take care of each other so we can continue to earn our living."

The daughter was wise. She said, "Father, you should say it this way: 'Each one of us has to take care of himself, or herself, so that we can continue to earn our living.' Because during the performance, you take care of yourself, you take care of yourself only. You stay very stable, very alert. That will help me. And if when I climb I take care of myself, I climb very carefully, I do not let anything wrong happen to me. That is the way you should say it, Father. You take good care of yourself, and I take good care of myself. In that way we can continue to earn our living." (pp. 35-36)

References

American Psychiatric Association. (1987). *Diagnostic and statistical manual of mental disorders* (3rd ed., rev.). Washington, DC: Author.

Asher, R., & Brisett, D. (1988). Codependency: A view from women married to alcoholics. *International Journal of Addictions, 23,* 331-350.

Barrett, K. (1992). Addiction treatment: Solution or problems. *Family Dynamics of Addiction Quarterly, 2*(2), 33-43.

Beattie, M. (1987). *Codependent no more: How to stop controlling others and start caring for yourself.* New York: Harper/Hazelden.

Bennett, L. A., & Wolin, S. J. (1990). Family culture and alcoholism transmission. In R. L. Collins, K. E. Leonard, & J. S. Searles (Eds.), *Alcohol and the family: Research and clinical perspectives* (pp. 194-219). New York: Guilford.

Bennett, L. A., Wolin, S. J., & Reiss, D. (1988). Deliberate family process: A strategy for protecting children of alcoholics. *British Journal of Addiction, 83,* 821-829.

Bennett, L. A., Wolin, S. J., Reiss, D., & Teitelbaum, H. A. (1987). Couples at risk for transmission of alcoholism: Protective influences. *Family Process, 26,* 111-129.

Bensley, L. S., & Spieker, S. (1992, July). *Parenting behavior of adolescent children of alcoholics.* Paper presented at the National Conference on Research in Women's Health and Perinatal Nursing, Seattle, WA.

Bepko, C., & Krestan, J. (1990). *Too good for her own good.* New York: Harper & Row.

Black, (1981). *It will never happen to me.* New York: Ballantine.

Bradshaw, J. E. (1988). *Healing the shame that binds you.* Deerfield Beach, FL: Health Communications.

Brickman, P., Rabinowitz, V. C., Karuza, J., Jr., Coates, D., Cohn, E., & Kidder, L. (1982). Models of helping and coping. *American Psychologist, 41,* 765-782.

Brown, L. (1990). What's addiction got to do with it: A feminist critique of codependence. *Psychology of Women, Newsletter of APA Division 35, 17,* 1-4.

Cawthra, E., Borrego, N., & Emrick, C. (1991). Involving family members in the prevention of relapse: An innovative approach. *Alcoholism Treatment Quarterly, 8,* 101-112.

Cermak, T. (1986a). Diagnostic criteria for codependency. *Journal of Psychoactive Drugs, 18,* 15-20.

Cermak, T. (1986b). *Diagnosing and Treating codependence.* Minneapolis, MN: Johnson Institute.

Cermak, T. (1991). Co-addiction as a disease. *Psychiatric Annals, 21,* 268-272.

Chodorow, N. (1978). *The reproduction of mothering.* Berkeley: University of California Press.

Cronkite, R. C., Finney, J. W., Nekich, J., & Moos, R. H. (1990). Remission among alcoholic patients and family adaptation to alcoholism: A stress and coping perspective. In R. L. Collins, K. E. Leonard, & J. S. Searles (Eds.), *Alcohol and the family: Research and clinical perspectives* (pp. 309-337). New York: Guilford.

Dunn, N. J., Jacob, T., Hummon, N., & Seilhamer, R. A. (1987). Marital stability in alcoholic spouse relations as a function of drinking pattern and location. *Journal of Abnormal Psychology, 96,* 99-107.

Ehrenreich, B. (1989). *Fear of falling.* New York: Harper-Collins.

Ewart, C. (1991). Social action theory for a public health psychology. *American Psychologist, 46,* 931-942.

Fingarette, H. (1988). *Heavy drinking: The myth of alcoholism as a disease.* Berkeley: University of California Press.

Gilligan, C. (1982). *In a different voice.* Cambridge, MA: Harvard University Press.

Gilligan, C., & Wiggins, G. (1987). The origins of morality in early childhood relationships. In J. Kagan & S. Lamb (Eds.), *The emergence of morality in young children* (pp. 277-305). Chicago: University of Chicago Press.

Gomberg, E. L. (1989). On terms used and abused: The concept of "codependency." *Drugs and Society, 3,* 113-132.

Gordon, J. R., & Barrett, K. (1991). *Codependence: Empowerment or regression.* Paper presented at the conference, Addictive Behaviors Across the Lifespan, Banff, Alberta, Canada (March), and at the annual meeting of the American Psychological Association, San Francisco (August).

Haaken, J. (1990). A critical analysis of the co-dependence construct. *Psychiatry, 53,* 396-406.

Hahn, T. N. (1987). *Being peace.* Berkeley, CA: Parallax.

Haley, J. (1976). *Problem solving therapy.* San Francisco: Jossey-Bass.

Harper, J., & Capdevila, C. (1990). Codependency: A critique. *Journal of Psychoactive Drugs, 22,* 285-292.

Horn, M. (1991, October). *Drawing diagnostic lines: Historical parallels in the medicalization of deviance.* Paper presented at the National Consensus Symposium on Children of Alcoholics and Co-dependence.

Horney, K. (1942). *Self-analysis.* New York: W. W. Norton.

Jackson, D. (1957). The question of family homeostasis. *Psychiatric Quarterly Supplement, 31,* 79-90.

Jacob, T., Dunn, N. J., & Leonard, K. (1983). Patterns of alcohol use and family stability. *Alcoholism: Clinical and Experimental Research, 7,* 382-385.

Jacob, T., Dunn, N. J., Leonard, K., & Davis, P. (1985). Alcohol-related impairments in male alcoholics and the psychiatric symptoms of their spouses: An attempt to replicate. *American Journal of Drug and Alcohol Abuse, 11,* 55-67.

Jacob, T., Ritchey, D., Cvitkovic, J. F., & Blane, H. T. (1981). Communication styles of alcoholic and non-alcoholic families when drinking and not drinking. *Journal of Studies on Alcohol, 42,* 466-482.

Jordan, J. V., Kaplan, A. G., Miller, J. B., Stiver, I. P., & Surrey, J. L. (1991). *Women's growth in connection.* New York: Guilford.

Kaminer, W. (1990, February 11). Chances are you're codependent too. *New York Times Book Review*, pp. 26-27.

Kaminer, W. (1992). *I'm dysfunctional, you're dysfunctional*. Reading, MA: Addison-Wesley.

Katz, S. J., & Liu, A. (1991). *The codependency conspiracy*. New York: Warner.

Kaufman, E., & Kaufmann, P. (1979). *Family therapy of drug and alcohol abuse*. New York: Gardner.

Kerr, M. E., & Bowen, M. (1988). *Family evaluation*. New York: W. W. Norton.

Leonard, K. E. (1990). Family processes and alcoholism. In R. L. Collins, K. E. Leonard, & J. S. Searles (Eds.), *Alcohol and the family: Research and clinical perspectives* (pp. 272-281). New York: Guilford.

Lerner, H. G. (1989). *The dance of intimacy*. New York: Harper & Row.

Littrell, J. (1991). *Understanding and treating alcoholism* (Vol. 1). Hillsdale, NJ: Lawrence Erlbaum.

Luff, E. (1990). The codependency movement: The challenge to feminists. *Psychology of Women, Newsletter of APA Division 35, 17*, 1-5.

Lyon, D., & Greenberg, J. (1991). Evidence of codependency in women with an alcoholic parent: Helping out Mr. Wrong. *Journal of Personality and Social Psychology, 61*, 435-439.

Madanes, C. (1981). *Strategic family therapy*. San Francisco: Jossey-Bass.

Marlatt, G. A. (1992). Substance abuse: Implications of a biopsychosocial model for prevention, treatment, and relapse prevention. In J. Grabowski & G. R. VandenBos (Eds.), *Psychopharmacology: Basic mechanisms and applied intervention* (pp. 127-162). Washington, DC: American Psychological Association.

Marlatt, G. A., & Barrett, K. (in press). Relapse prevention in the treatment of substance abuse. In M. Galanter & H. D. Kleber (Eds.), *The treatment of substance abuse*. New York: American Psychiatric Press.

Marlatt, G. A., & Gordon, J. R. (Eds.). (1985). *Relapse prevention: Maintenance strategies in the treatment of addictive behaviors*. New York: Guilford.

McCrady, B. (1989). Extending relapse models to couples. *Addictive Behaviors, 14*, 69-74.

Mellody, P. (1989). *Facing codependence*. New York: Harper & Row.

Miller, J. B. (1986). *Toward a new psychology of women*. Boston: Beacon.

Moos, R. H., & Finney, J. W. (1983). The expanding scope of alcoholism treatment and evaluation. *American Psychologist, 38*, 1036-1045.

Moos, R. H., Finney, J. W., & Cronkite, R. C. (1990). *Alcoholism treatment: Process and outcome*. New York: Oxford University Press.

Murphy, R. T., O'Farrell, T. J., Floyd, F. J., & Connors, G. J. (1991). School adjustment of children of alcoholic fathers: Comparisons to normal controls. *Addictive Behaviors, 16*, 275-287.

O'Farrell, T. J., & Cowles, K. S. (1989). Marital and family therapy. In R. K. Hester & W. R. Miller (Eds.), *Handbook of alcoholism treatment approaches* (pp. 183-205). New York: Pergamon.

Orford, J. (1990). Alcohol and the family: An international review of the literature with implications for research and practice. In L. T. Kozlowski, H. M. Annis, H. D. Cappell, B. Glaser, M. S. Goodstadt, Y. Israel, H. Kalant, E. M. Sellers, & E. Vingilis (Eds.), *Research advances in alcohol and drug problems* (Vol. 10, pp. 81-140). New York: Plenum.

Peele, S. (1989). *Diseasing of America: Addiction treatment out of control.* Lexington, MA: Lexington.

Peele, S., & Brodsky, A. (1991). *The truth about addiction and recovery.* New York: Simon & Schuster.

Potter-Efron, R. T., & Potter-Efron, P. S. (1989a). Assessment of co-dependency with individuals from alcoholic and chemically dependent families. *Alcoholism Treatment Quarterly, 6,* 37-57.

Potter-Efrom, R. T., & Potter-Efron, P. S. (1989b). Outpatient codenpendency treatment. *Alcoholism Treatment Quarterly, 6,* 151-167.

Rapping, E. (1990, March 5). Hooked on a feeling. *The Nation,* pp. 316-319.

Rieff, D. (1991, October). Victims all? Recovery, co-dependency, and the art of blaming somebody else. *Harper's Magazine,* pp. 49-56.

Schaef, A. W. (1986). *Co-dependence: Misunderstood, mistreated.* Minneapolis: Winston.

Schnarch, D. M. (1991). *Constructing the family crucible.* New York: W. W. Norton.

Sontag, S. (1978). *Illness as metaphor.* New York: Farrar, Straus & Giroux.

Stanton, M. D., & Todd, T. C. (1982). *The family therapy of drug abuse and addiction.* New York: Guilford.

Stein, H. F. (1985). Alcoholism as metaphor in American culture. *Ethos, 13*(3), 195-235.

Steinglass, P. (1981). The impact of alcoholism on the family: Relationship between degree of alcoholism and psychiatric symptomatology. *Journal of Studies on Alcohol, 42,* 288-303.

Steinglass, P., Bennett, L. A., Wolin, S. J., & Reiss, D. (1987). *The alcoholic family.* New York: Basic Books.

Surrey, J. L. (1991). The "self-in-relation": A theory of women's development. In J. V. Jordan, A. G. Kaplan, J. B. Miller, I. P. Stiver, & J. L. Surrey, *Women's growth in connection.* New York: Guilford.

Szasz, T. S. (1971). The ethics of addiction. *American Journal of Psychiatry, 128,* 541-546.

Tallen, B. S. (1990, January). Co-dependency: A feminist critique. *Sojourner: The Women's Forum,* pp. 19-21.

Tavris, C. (1990, January-February). The politics of codependency. *Family Therapy Networker,* p. 43.

Treadway, D. (1990, January-February). Codependency: Disease, metaphor, or fad? *Family Therapy Networker,* pp. 39-42.

Van Wormer, K. (1989). Co-dependency: Implications for women and therapy. *Women & Therapy, 8*(4), 51-63.

Walters, M. (1990, July-August). The codependent Cinderella who loves too much . . . fights back. *Family Therapy Networker,* pp. 53-57.

Watson, L. (1991). Paradigms of recovery: Theoretical implications for relapse prevention in alcoholics. *Journal of Drug Issues, 24,* 839-858.

Wegscheider-Cruse, S. (1985). *Choice-making for co-dependents, adult children, and spirituality seekers.* Pompano Beach, FL: Health Communications.

Whitfield, C. L. (1992, Winter). Finding our true self: Recovering from co-dependency and reclaiming our life. *Lotus, 1*(2), 28-32.

Wills, T. A. (1985). Stress coping and tobacco and alcohol use in early adolescence. In S. Shiffman & T. A. Wills (Eds.), *Coping and substance use* (pp. 67-92). San Diego, CA: Academic Press.

Wilson, C. (1983). *Interactions in families with alcohol problems.* Unpublished doctoral dissertation, University of Washington.

Index

About the Authors

John S. Baer received his Ph.D. in clinical psychology from the University of Oregon in 1986 after a clinical internship at the University of Washington Department of Psychiatry and Behavioral Sciences. Since that time he has been a Postdoctoral Research Associate and Research Associate, and currently is Research Assistant Professor in the Department of Psychology at the University of Washington. He is also the Associate Director of the Addictive Behaviors Research Center within the Department of Psychology. His research interests center on etiology, recidivism, and early intervention in addictive behaviors. He is currently supported by two grants from the National Institute for Alcohol Abuse and Alcoholism; both projects address treatment and etiology of young people's drinking problems. He has also conducted training workshops on relapse prevention and early intervention for alcohol problems both in the United States and abroad. He has served as a reviewer for numerous scientific journals, and has recently contributed a chapter summarizing psychological, social, and developmental research issues in alcohol abuse to the NIAAA's *Eighth Report to the U.S. Congress on Alcohol and Health.*

Kimberly Barrett, Ed.D., obtained her doctorate in counseling psychology from the University of San Francisco in 1989, followed by a postdoctoral fellowship in addictive behaviors at the University of Washington in 1990. She joined the faculty in the Department of Psychology at the University of Washington as a Research Assistant Professor in 1992; she teaches courses in child development, family therapy, and race relations. She has spent the past several years as a researcher in the area of adolescent substance abuse, and developed a multiple-family therapy program for the treatment of adolescent substance abusers and their families, as part of the NIDA-sponsored treatment outcome study through the University of California, San Francisco. She has also worked extensively as a family therapist and consultant to several public school districts in California and Washington, and is the author of a forthcoming book, *Stress Strategies for Parents* (Berkeley-Putnam). Her current research is focused on cultural factors relating to the family dynamics of substance abuse.

Leonard M. Blumenthal received his bachelor of education degree from the University of Alberta and his diploma in management studies from the University of Manitoba. He is also a graduate of the Banff School of Advanced Management. He was a teacher with the County of Leduc School Board and with the Edmonton Public School Board until joining the staff of the Alberta Alcohol and Drug Abuse Commission (AADAC) as a counselor in 1966. In 1968, he was appointed Director of the newly opened Henwood Rehabilitation Centre. From 1973 to 1982 he served as Assistant Executive Director of AADAC, and was responsible for all program delivery in Alberta, including the extension of services to all parts of the province by establishing area offices and by funding local community societies and agencies to deliver programs. In 1982, he was appointed Assistant Executive Director, Support Services, for AADAC. He has also represented AADAC at a variety of provincial, national, and international committees, events, and activities, both as a speaker and as a resource person. He was appointed Chief Executive Officer of AADAC in 1988.

Sandra A. Brown obtained her Ph.D. in clinical psychology from Wayne State University in 1981. She joined the faculty of the Department of Psychology at Northern Illinois University and in 1983 became the recipient of the New Investigator Research Award from the National Institute of Alcohol Abuse and Alcoholism. In 1984 she moved to the Department of Psychiatry at the University of California, San Diego, where she is currently an Associate Professor. She directs the Psychological Services for the Alcohol and Drug Treatment Program at the Department of Veterans Affairs Medical Center, San Diego, and is Director of the Post-Traumatic Stress Disorder Clinical Team at the Medical Center. For 10 years she has studied reinforcement characteristics of various drugs and the role of anticipated drug effects in the development and progression of addiction. Her research into adolescent alcohol and drug abuse highlights important diagnostic issues of comorbidity and generational differences between adolescent and adult substance abusers. She has published widely in the area of the addictions, and she conducts training workshops throughout the United States and abroad. Her research is funded by the National Institute of Alcohol Abuse and Alcoholism and the Department of Veterans Affairs.

R. Lorraine Collins, Ph.D., is currently a Senior Research Scientist at the Research Institute on Addictions in Buffalo, New York. She received her doctorate in psychology (clinical) from Rutgers, the State University of New Jersey. She completed a postdoctoral position as a Research Associate in the Department of Psychology, University of Washington, and was a member of the faculty of the Department of Psychology, State University of New York at Stony Brook. She has conducted research on various topics within the areas of alcohol use and smoking. Her current research projects on substance use/abuse among female nurses and on drinking restraint as a risk factor for problem drinking are funded by the National Institute on Drug Abuse and the National Institute on Alcohol Abuse and Alcoholism, respectively. She serves as a member of the Drug Abuse Epidemiology and Prevention Research Initial Review Group for the National Institute on Drug Abuse, and is active in various professional organizations, including the Association for Advancement of Behavior Therapy and the American Psychological Association. She has published numerous journal articles and is coeditor of *Alcohol and the Family: Research and Clinical Perspectives.*

John A. Cunningham received his M.A. in psychology from the University of Toronto, Canada, in 1991. He is currently enrolled in the Ph.D. program in psychology at the University of Toronto. His current research interests include motivation for change in substance abusers, barriers to the utilization of health care services, and societal attitudes toward substance abusers.

Judith R. Gordon received her Ph.D. in counseling psychology from the University of Washington in 1978. A licensed psychologist, she conducts a private practice in Seattle, Washington. In addition to her clinical work, she is a Clinical Associate Professor at the University of

Washington. She has conducted research in the field of addictive behaviors since completion of her doctoral dissertation. Together with G. Alan Marlatt, she has participated in a number of research studies on smoking cessation, including a 4-year project (funded by the National Institute on Drug Abuse) investigating both self-quitting and treatment-aided quitting in smokers. Some of her articles on smoking cessation have appeared in recent issues of *Health Psychology* and the *Journal of Consulting and Clinical Psychology*. She has conducted numerous workshops and coauthored a number of publications on the topic of relapse prevention with G. Alan Marlatt, including their seminal 1980 article, "Determinants of Relapse: Implications for the Maintenance of Behavior Change" (in Davidson & Davidson's *Behavioral Medicine,* Brunner/Mazel), and their recent book, *Relapse Prevention* (Guilford, 1985). She was clinical director for 5 years of an NIMH-funded research project at the University of Washington to develop and evaluate an AIDS prevention program.

J. Robert Hunter has worked in the addictions field for the past 17 years as a counselor, trainer, and program manager of a residential treatment center. He is currently employed as a treatment consultant with the Alberta Alcohol and Drug Abuse Commission. He received his master's of education in counseling psychology in 1988 from the University of Alberta. His master's thesis, *Assessing Alcohol/Drug Troubled People: A Proposed Battery,* served as the basis for the implementation of an assessment package in the Alberta Alcohol and Drug Abuse Commission treatment units. He has recently completed an evaluation of the package's usability and is now completing revisions based on the evaluation results.

Lynn O. Lightfoot received her Masters of Applied Science and her Ph.D. in Psychology at the University of Waterloo. She was the Research Director of the Treatment Program Research Development Project, Queens's University, for three years, and then served as Centre Director, then Eastern Ontario Regional Director with the Addiction Research Foundation of Ontario for 10 years. Since 1983, she has been an Adjunct Assistant Professor of Psychology at Queen's University, Kinsgston, Ontario, where she is also the Principal Investigator on a National Health & Welfare Project that is assessing the effects of computerized lifestyle assessment as a tool in the prevention and brief treatment of substance abuse problems. She has authored over 50 scientific articles, book chapters, conference proceedings, and government reports in the field of substance abse. Dr. Lightfoot has specialized in the development and evaluation of substance abuse treatment programs for forensic populations since 1985. She has written and co-authored two treatment manuals and a staff training manual for Correctional Services Canada, and has conducted many training workshops and seminars. She has worked as a consultant to the Correctional Service of Canada and the U. S. National Institute of Mental Health, and was recently appointed to Ontario's Criminal Code Review Board.

G. Alan Marlatt is currently Professor of Psychology and Director of the Addictive Behaviors Research Center at the University of Washington. He received his Ph.D. in clinical psychology from Indiana University in 1968. After serving on the faculties of the University of British Columbia (1968-1969) and the University of Wisconsin (1969-1972), he joined the University of Washington faculty in fall 1972. His major focus in both research and clinical work is the field of addictive behaviors. He has conducted basic research on cognitive-behavioral factors in addiction. His applied research has focused on the effectiveness of relapse prevention and other self-management strategies in the prevention and treatment of addictive behavior problems. His most recent work has investigated the "harm-reduction" approach to reducing the risk of alcohol problems in young adults (including high-risk college students and Native American youth). He has published extensively in the addictions field, and his books include *Alcoholism: New Directions in Behavioral Research and Treatment* (Plenum, 1978), *Relapse Prevention* (Guilford, 1985), *Assessment of Addictive Behaviors* (Guilford, 1988), and *Addictive Behaviors: Prevention and Early Intervention* (Swets & Zeitlinger, 1989).

Robert J. McMahon obtained his Ph.D. in clinical psychology from the University of Georgia in 1979. He is currently an Associate Professor in the Department of Psychology at the University of Washington in Seattle and the Director of the Child Clinical Psychology Program. His primary research and clinical interests concern the assessment, treatment, and prevention of child conduct disorders. Much of his research has focused on the development, evaluation, and application of social learning-based family interventions for dealing with young children's conduct problems. He is coauthor (with Rex Forehand) of *Helping the Noncompliant Child: A Clinician's Guide to Parent Training* (Guilford,

1981) and of more than 40 scientific articles, chapters, and reviews. He is currently coinvestigator on a large, multisite collaborative study on the prevention of conduct disorders in school-age children.

Mary Ann Pentz obtained her Ph.D. in clinical and school psychology from Syracuse University in 1978. Her dissertation on the effects of social skills training with assertive, aggressive, and passive adolescents was awarded the Gilda Gold Award and a university letter of distinction for doctoral work. In 1979, she became an Assistant Professor in the Department of Psychology at the University of Tennessee, where she developed courses for a new doctoral program in community psychology and expanded her research to evaluate the potential effectiveness of social skills training for preventing adolescent drug use. Her NIDA-funded grant in this area represented the first experimental study of drug prevention in the state of Tennessee. She is currently an Associate Professor in the Department of Preventive Medicine and the Institute of Health Promotion and Disease Prevention Research at the University of Southern California, and serves as Associate Director of Community Prevention Research at the Institute. She is internationally known for her research in the areas of community- and school-based drug abuse prevention, and has authored more than 150 publications and scientific papers on the design and evaluation of interventions for prevention of adolescent drug use, stress, and chronic disease. For the last 8 years she has evaluated the effects of school, media, parent, community organization, and, most recently, local policy changes as interventions for prevention of drug use in adolescents and their parents.

Roger A. Roffman, an Associate Professor of Social Work at the University of Washington, has served on that faculty since 1973. He chairs the School's Chemical Dependencies Specialization and also serves as Director of its Innovative Programs Research Group, an applied research center that emphasizes studies designed to overcome barriers to reaching and effectively intervening with difficult-to-serve populations. He completed the B.A. in psychology at Boston University in 1963. He later studied at the University of Michigan, where he earned the M.S.W. degree in 1965, and at the University of California at Berkeley, where he received the D.S.W. degree in 1983. With funding from the National Institute on Drug Abuse, he and his colleague Dr. Robert Stephens have been studying models of marijuana-dependence treatment since 1986. He is also principal investigator of several AIDS-prevention studies designed to facilitate risk reduction in men who have sex with other men. Currently in process is an NIMH-funded study in which the intervention (cognitive-behavioral group counseling) is delivered entirely by telephone. This research is intended to assess the efficacy of this approach in overcoming geographical and psychological barriers to reaching and facilitating behavior change in individuals who would be unlikely to seek or accept assistance in an in-person setting.

Edward Sawka received his M.A. in sociology from the University of Alberta, in Edmonton, Canada. He is currently Acting Director of Policy and Program Analysis at the Alberta Alcohol and Drug Abuse Commission in Edmonton, Alberta, Canada. He has coauthored articles in *Contemporary Drug Problems* and *Medicine North America*. His current research interests include addiction issues in health care and workplace settings, applications of prevention models, policy research, and international context of substance use and abuse.

Kenneth J. Sher obtained his Ph.D. in clinical psychology from Indiana University in 1981 following an internship at Brown University. Since 1981, he has been a faculty member in the Department of Psychology, University of Missouri, where he currently holds the rank of Professor. He is Associate Editor of the *Journal of Abnormal Psychology* and has served on the editorial boards of several journals, including *Alcohol Health and Research World, Behavioral Therapy, Contemporary Psychology,* and the *Journal of Abnormal Psychology,* and has served as a reviewer for many scholarly journals and for federal research agencies, including the National Institute on Alcohol Abuse and Alcoholism, the National Institute of Mental Health, and the Veterans Administration. He has been the recipient of a New Investigator Research Award from the NIAAA (1984), the Young Investigator Award from the Research Society on Alcoholism (1988), and the Chancellor's Award for Outstanding Faculty Research and Creative Activity in the Behavioral and Social Sciences from the University of Missouri (1992). His primary research areas include individual differences in the psychological effects of alcohol, the etiology of alcoholism, and cognitive aspects of obsessive-compulsive behavior, and he has authored more than 50 scholarly publications in these areas. He is the author of the recent book *Children of Alcoholics: A Critical Appraisal of Theory and Research* (University of Chicago Press). His research is funded by NIAAA.

Harvey A. Skinner is Professor and Chairman of the Department of Behavioral Science, Faculty of Medicine, University of Toronto, and a Senior Scientist at the Addiction Research Foundation, Toronto. He received his Ph.D. in psychology in 1975 from the University of Western Ontario, and is a registered psychologist in the province of Ontario. He was a member of the Task Force on Curriculum Renewal in Undergraduate Medical Education, and has a broad interest in educational innovations at both the undergraduate and graduate levels. During 1987-1990 he was a member of a study for the U.S. Congress on the treatment of alcohol problems, conducted by the U.S. National Academy of Sciences. He has served as a Consulting Editor for both the *Journal of Abnormal Psychology* and the *Journal of Consulting and Clinical Psychology*. He was a member of the Board of Trustees, Toronto General Hospital, from 1982 to 1986. He was an adviser to a World Health Organization collaborating project on early intervention for alcohol problems, and is an expert adviser to the U.S. National Institute on Alcohol Abuse and Alcoholism. He has published numerous articles on diagnosis, assessment, and early intervention for alcohol/drug problems, and two of his assessment instruments are widely used for the assessment of alcohol dependence (Alcohol Dependence Scale) and the detection of drug problems (Drug Abuse Screening Test). Another instrument, the Alcohol Clinical Index, provides a list of clinical criteria for use by health professionals in identifying alcohol problems among patients. He is a pioneer in the use of microcomputer technology, and has conducted studies on how computer assessment compares with interview and questionnaire approaches.

Linda C. Sobell received her Ph.D. in psychology from the University of California at Irvine in 1976. She is currently a Senior Scientist, Chief, Guided Self-Change Unit, and Assistant Director for Research and Clinical Training at the Clinical Research and Treatment Institute of the Addiction Research Foundation in Toronto, Canada. She is also Professor in the Departments of Psychology and Behavioral Science at the University of Toronto. She has coauthored or coedited five books: *Emerging Concepts of Alcohol Dependence* (with E. M. Pattison and M. B. Sobell; Springer, 1977), *Behavioral Treatment of Alcohol Problems: Individualized Therapy and Controlled Drinking* (with M. B. Sobell; Plenum, 1978), *Evaluating Alcohol and Drug Abuse Treatment Effectiveness: Recent Advances* (with M. B. Sobell and E. Ward; Pergamon, 1980), *Moderation as a Goal or Outcome of Treatment of Alcohol*

Problems: A Dialogue (with M. B. Sobell; Haworth, 1987), and *Problem Drinkers: Guided Self-Charge Treatment* (with M. B. Sobell, Guilford, in press). She has also written more than 90 articles and 35 book chapters and given more than 100 invited presentations in the United States, Canada, Australia, and Europe. Her current research interests include natural recovery (self-change) processes, guided self-change treatments for low-dependence alcohol abusers, and combined pharmacological and psychological interventions as treatments for addictive behaviors. She has served on the Board of Directors of the Association for Advancement of Behavior Therapy for more than a decade and is currently President-Elect of that organization.

Mark B. Sobell received his Ph.D. in psychology from the University of California at Riverside in 1970. He is currently a Senior Scientist and Associate Director for Treatment Research and Development at the Clinical Research and Treatment Institute of the Addiction Research Foundation in Toronto, and Professor in the Departments of Psychology and Behavioral Science at the University of Toronto. He has coauthored or coedited five books: *Emerging Concepts of Alcohol Dependence* (with E. M. Pattison and L. C. Sobell; Springer, 1977), *Behavioral Treatment of Alcohol Problems: Individualized Therapy and Controlled Drinking* (with L. C. Sobell; Plenum, 1978), *Evaluating Alcohol and Drug Abuse Treatment Effectiveness: Recent Advances* (with L. C. Sobell and E. Ward; Pergamon, 1980), *Moderation as a Goal or Outcome of Treatment of Alcohol Problems: A Dialogue* (with L. C. Sobell; Haworth, 1987), and *Problem Drinkers: Guided Self-Charge Treatment* (with L. C. Sobell, Guilford, in press). He has also written more than 100 journal articles and 35 book chapters and has given more than 100 invited presentations in the United States, Canada, Australia, and Europe. His current research interests include natural recovery (self-change) processes, guided self-change treatments for low-dependence alcohol abusers, and combined pharmacological and psychological interventions as treatments for addictive behaviors.

Robert S. Stephens received his Ph.D. in clinical psychology from Florida State University in 1985 after completing an internship at the University of Washington School of Medicine in Seattle. He was subsequently awarded a Postdoctoral Fellowship from the National Institute on Alcohol Abuse and Alcoholism and trained in the area of alcohol and addiction research with Dr. Alan Marlatt. From 1986 until 1989, he held the position of Research Assistant Professor in the School of Social Work at the University of Washington and collaborated with Dr. Roger Roffman on federally funded applications of the relapse prevention treatment model to marijuana dependence and risky sexual behavior. In 1989 he became an Assistant Professor of Psychology at Virginia Polytechnic Institute and State University in Blacksburg, Virginia, where he teaches at both the graduate and undergraduate levels and is involved in the clinical and research training of doctoral students in clinical psychology. In addition to the ongoing study of the treatment of marijuana dependence funded by the National Institute on Drug Abuse, he conducts research on predictors of treatment outcome in outpatient drug counseling and explores the social-cognitive determinants of college student drinking.

Susan F. Tapert received her bachelor of arts degree in psychology from the University of Washington in 1990. Since that time, she has been working at the Addictive Behaviors Research Center in the Department of Psychology at the University of Washington as Program Assistant. She also volunteers at the Seattle-King County Health Department Needle Exchange. Her research interests include substance abuse, AIDS prevention, and risk reduction.

Tony Toneatto received his Ph.D. in clinical psychology from McGill University, Montreal, Canada, in 1987. He is currently a Scientist, Comorbidity and Behavioural Risk Factors Unit, at the Clinical Research and Treatment Institute of the Addiction Research Foundation in Toronto, Canada. He is also Assistant Professor in the Department of Behavioral Science at the University of Toronto. He has published in the areas of treatment for alcohol abuse, interaction of alcohol abuse and nicotine dependence, and natural recovery from alcohol abuse. His current research interests include the cognitive treatment of psychoactive substance abuse, the interaction of psychiatric disorders and psychoactive substance abuse, and the process of natural recovery from substance abuse.